CONSTITUTIVE CRIMINOLOGY

CONSTITUTIVE CRIMINOLOGY

Beyond Postmodernism

Stuart Henry and Dragan Milovanovic

SAGE Publications
London • Thousand Oaks • New Delhi

First published 1996

SAGE Publications Ltd
6 Bonhill Street
London EC2A 4PU

SAGE Publications Inc
2455 Teller Road
Thousand Oaks, California 91320

SAGE Publications India Pvt Ltd
32, M-Block Market
Greater Kailash – I
New Delhi 110 048

British Library Cataloguing in Publication data

A catalogue record for this book is available
from the British Library

ISBN 0 8039 7584 8
ISBN 0 8039 7585 6 (pbk)

Library of Congress catalog card number 95-072172

Typeset by Mayhew Typesetting, Rhayader, Powys
Printed in Great Britain by The Cromwell Press Ltd,
Broughton Gifford, Melksham, Wiltshire

*To the resurrection of subjugated knowledges
and the reclamation of impoverished souls*

Contents

Preface

In this book we develop a postmodernist 'constitutive' theory of crime. Unlike the skeptical versions of postmodernism that pervade social science and the humanities, *Constitutive Criminology* offers an affirmative approach. While it accepts much of the postmodernist critique of modernism, and particularly the critique of positivist empiricism in social science, it does not collapse into nihilism, subjectivism and defeatism. We disagree with postmodernists whose anarchy of knowledge denies them both projects and prospects. Rejecting an obsession with deconstructionism – the postmodernist analytical technique which seeks to endlessly 'undo' and reveal the contradictions and assumptions contained within our socially constructed world – constitutive criminology is concerned with reconstruction and redirection. For us, deconstruction and reconstruction are essential co-components for developing a less harmful world: a contingent, revisable world, ever open to change, accommodating of emerging and emerged social forms, but having shape and substance. Constitutive criminology might thus be described as a version of Borgmann's (1992) 'postmodern realism' (although we find these extremes no less incongruously linked together than hanging separately). Thus we prefer the concept 'constitutive' which simultaneously reflects our dual concerns of being built while building, of being made while making, of parts making the wholes of which they are constituents.

Constitutive criminology, then, is a theory proposing that humans are responsible for actively creating their world with others. They do this by transforming their surroundings through interaction with others, not least via discourse. Through language and symbolic representation they identify differences, construct categories, and share a belief in the reality of that which is constructed that orders otherwise chaotic states. It is towards these social constructions of reality that humans act.

In the process of investing energy in their socially constructed, discursively organized categories of order and reality, human subjects not only shape the world, but are themselves shaped by it. They are co-producers and co-productions of their own and others' agency. They are channeled and changed, enabled and constrained, but all the time, building.

Constitutive criminology is about how some of this socially constructed order, as well as some of the human subjects constituted within it, can be harmed, impaired and destroyed by the process, and by what is built: ultimately by each other as fellow subjects. Constitutive criminology attempts to provide sufficient insight into the discursive construction process to enable us to minimize these harms. Unlike many postmodernist influenced statements, it lays out a social policy whereby human energy can be redirected toward producing less, rather than more harm.

The implication of our theoretical position, in contrast to prevailing modernist analyses, is that the behaviors of human subjects who offend and victimize others cannot be understood in isolation from the society of which they are a part. Nor are they understandable as determined products of cultures and structures. Instead of setting out to identify factors that 'cause' offending, constitutive criminology seeks to examine the co-production of crime by human subjects, and by the social and organizational structures that humans develop.

We argue that co-production occurs through society's structure and culture, as these are energized by active human subjects – not only as offenders, but also as the social categories of victims, criminal justice practitioners, academics, commentators, media reporters and producers of film and TV crime shows, and most generally, as investors, producers and consumers in the crime business. We look at what it is about the psycho-socio-cultural matrix (the cloth of crime) that provides the discursive medium through which human agents construct 'meaningful' harms to others. The approach we take, therefore, shifts the criminological focus from narrow dichotomized issues focusing either on the individual offender or on the social environment, without losing sight of human agency *qua* human subject, and without reducing social agency, albeit seen as a virtual society. Thus constitutive criminology takes a holistic conception of the relationship between the 'individual' and 'society' which prioritizes neither one nor the other, but examines their mutuality and interrelationship.

Crime is defined as an expression of energy to make a difference over others, to the exclusion of those others who, in the instant, are rendered powerless to make their own difference. Crime is the power to deny others. It is a recursive production (i.e. a repeated, self-referential activity) born of historically, and culturally specific discourses which have attained a relative degree of stability. Materialistically rooted, these discourses become coordinates for social action whereby 'criminals' are no less than 'excessive investors' in the accumulation and expression of power and control.

Consciously striving to reconstruct the discourse of the excessive investor at both a societal and a systemic level, crime feeds off itself, expanding and consuming the energies intended to control it. The result is that conventional crime control efforts, whether in the form of growing criminal justice institutions – police and prisons – or as political rhetoric rehearsed in the media, fuel the engine of crime. Such control interventions take criminal activity to new levels of investment and to self-enclosed innovation. Here the contradictory emotions of brutalized insensitivity, 'compassion fatigue' (Cohen, 1993: 113), public horror, and outrage, call for more investment in control measures that further feed the cycle. In short, crime is an 'autopoietic' (self-referential) system that is 'self-sustaining' through its absorption of others' reactions to it.[1]

The implications of constitutive theory are, first that crime must be deconstructed as a recurrent discursive process, and second, that conscious attempts must be made at reconstruction with a view to preventing recurrence. In our analysis this can be achieved through the development of alternative, 'replacement discourses' that fuel positive social constructions. These constructions are designed to displace crime as moments in the exercise of power and as control. They offer an alternative medium by which social constructions of reality can take place. This is not a unitary medium but, as Smart (1990: 82) has argued, refers instead to 'subjugated knowledges, which tell different stories and have different specificities' and which aim at 'the deconstruction of truth' and the power effects of claims to truth. Instead of replacing one truth with another, replacement discourse invokes a 'multiplicity of resistances' to the ubiquity of power (1990: 82). Beyond resistances, the concept of replacement discourse offers a celebration of unofficial, informal, discounted and ignored knowledges through its discursive diversity.

The book is organized around six familiar themes that compare our affirmative postmodernist assumptions with those of existing modernist theories and builds a new criminological theory. These themes are: (1) human nature, (2) society and social order, (3) the role of law, (4) definitions of crime, (5) crime causation, and (6) justice policy and practices. We have chosen to organize our analysis and theoretical position around this framework because it has been recognized by several criminologists to be a helpful way of presenting and comparing the foundational assumptions of different theoretical positions.[2] Chapters 2–5 each begin with an analytical summary of modernist criminological theory on one of these themes which is followed by a consideration of postmodernist critiques. Drawing from postmodernism, semiotics, social constructionism, structuration and chaos theory we then examine transitional positions that have informed the development of our constitutive position. This does not completely abandon modernism, or completely embrace postmodernism, but transcends the limits of each toward a new synthesis. Chapter 6 is entirely devoted to modernist theories of cause, while Chapter 7 reviews and builds on postmodernist positions on causality and our constitutive variation. In Chapter 8 we return to the modernist/postmodernist positions on policy before developing our constitutive policy of replacement discourse. We conclude in Chapter 9 by focusing on the implied practice strategies necessary to implement our constitutive policy of replacement discourse.

The primary significance of this work is that it offers an approach to understanding and explaining crime that goes beyond the fragmentation of criminology into multi-disciplinary theoretical factions, while drawing together disparate perspectives toward a genuinely interdisciplinary integration.

Constitutive criminology extends our preliminary first published statements to present a new and balanced synthesis of previous theories of crime. We have been developing this position separately and in collaboration for the past six years. The constitutive approach first emerged in Stuart Henry's 1980s' studies on crime and social control in the workplace (Henry, 1983; 1985; 1989a) which were considerably influenced by Fitzpatrick's (1984) theory of 'integral plurality' and Giddens' (1984) *The Constitution of Society*. Drawing on the philosophical strands of symbolic interactionism, phenomenology, structural Marxism, structuration theory and postmodernist deconstructionism, Henry outlined a socio-legal theory concerning the relationship between social forms and social action, initially defined as 'integrated theory' (Henry, 1983). The term 'constitutive theory' came from a suggestion by Christine Harrington (1988) in her constructive critique of Henry's (1983) work, and it became the motif for subsequent renditions (Henry, 1987a; 1987b; 1989b), as well as being incorporated into other work in Brigham and Harrington's edited series 'After the Law' (e.g. Hunt, 1993). During a chance meeting at the 25th anniversary meeting of the Law and Society Association in Wisconsin, Madison, in June 1989, Dragan Milovanovic shared similar insights, based on his studies of theories in the sociology of law, particularly Lacanian postmodernism and psychoanalytic semiotic approaches (Milovanovic, 1988; 1992a; 1993a; 1993b; 1994a; 1994b; 1994c), and his studies on law and the prison (1988; Milovanovic and Thomas, 1989). Thus began our collaboration. In 1990 we wrote two preliminary position papers (Henry and Milovanovic, 1991; Milovanovic and Henry, 1991). In 1992 we wrote a third paper (Henry and Milovanovic, 1994) which laid out the framework for this book. In 1993 we published a short paper dealing with the definition of crime (Henry and Milovanovic, 1993). Most recently, Henry (1994) wrote on another key aspect of the theory, 'replacement discourse'. Milovanovic has also dealt with this topic in several recent publications (1993a; 1993b; 1994b; 1994c), and he devoted a chapter to it in his *Sociology of Law* (1994a: Chapter 6).

Clearly, over such a period, inspiration, insight and support have come from many sources. In particular we would like to thank: Gregg Barak for turning our theoretical idea of constitutive criminology into practice; Werner Einstadter for his indulgence and (postmodernism not withstanding) for his insistence that clarity should be prioritized over obscurity in writing any book; Marty Schwartz and Brian MacLean for being difficult about the concrete nature of constructed realities; T.R. Young, David Friedrichs, David Nelken, Christine Harrington, Bruce Arrigo, Susan Silbey and Mike Lynch for taking up the postmodernist challenge; Carol Smart whose resilience in resisting negativity showed us another way; Kathy Daly whose generous suggestions about how to proceed with an area she doesn't much care for proved very valuable; Piers Beirne, Alan Hunt and Don Gibbons for noticing we were on to something; Peter Manning and Stephen Pfohl for raising the level of our discourse; Trent Kane, Christine Garza and Kerry Horton for their inspirational graduate papers on our work. In addition, Stuart Henry would like to thank Eastern Michigan University for the Faculty Research Fellowship that made it possible for us to write this work in a timely fashion.

Finally, in writing this book we have been consciously aware that the reader will encounter words, concepts and sentence construction that encourage a suspension of taken for granted assumptions while venturing into the unknown. This is a challenging invitation. The journey will not always be smooth or comforting. We hope at its end you will join us in new beginnings.

Notes

1 See Maturana and Varela (1980), Teubner (1988; 1993), Milovanovic (1994a: Chapter 5).

2 See especially, Young (1981), Empey (1982), Vold and Bernard (1986), and Einstadter and Henry (1995).

Acknowledgements

The authors are grateful to the following authors and publishers for permission to reprint copyrighted material used in this book.

American Society of Criminology for excerpts from Delbert S. Elliott, 'Serious Violent Offenders: Onset, Developmental Course, and Termination – The American Society of Criminology 1993 Presidential Address', *Criminology*, 32(1): 17, © 1994. Reprinted with permission of The American Society of Criminology.

Cambridge University Press for excerpts from John Braithwaite, *Crime, Shame and Reintegration*, p. 99, © 1989. Cambridge University Press. Reprinted with permission of the publisher.

Harcourt Brace & Company for excerpts from *Criminological Theory: an Analysis of its Underlying Assumptions*, by Werner Einstadter and Stuart Henry, p. 22, © 1995 by Harcourt Brace & Company. Reprinted with permission of the publisher.

Michael King for adaption from Michael King, *The Framework of Criminal Justice*, London: Croom Helm, p. 13, © 1981 Michael King. Reprinted with permission of the author.

Nelson-Hall for adaption from Frank E. Hagan, *Introduction to Criminology*, Chicago, Nelson-Hall, p. 106, © 1986 Frank E. Hagan. Reprinted with permission of the publisher.

Plenum Publishing Corporation for excerpts from Hal Gregersen and Lee Sailer, 'Chaos Theory and its Implications for Social Science Research', *Human Relations*, 46(7): 780, 786, © 1993 Plenum Press. Reprinted with permission of the publisher.

Richard Quinney for excerpts from Richard Quinney, *Class, State and Crime*, 2nd edn, published by Longman, p. 42, © Richard Quinney 1980. Reprinted with permission of the author.

Sage Publications Inc for excerpts from Delbert S. Elliott, David Huizinga and Susan S. Ageton, *Explaining Delinquency and Drug Use*, p. 66, © 1985 Sage Publications Inc. Reprinted with permission of the publisher.

Tavistock for excerpts from Steven Box, *Power, Crime and Mystification*, Tavistock Publications, p. 64, © 1983, Steven Box. Reprinted with permission of the publisher.

The cover design was based on an image of the Mandlebrot set created and provided by Neal Kettler.

1

Introduction: 'Here There Be Dragons'

We borrow the sub-title of this introductory chapter from Trent Kane's (1990) graduate paper on constitutive criminology, a title he took from its appearance on maps in the 1500s used to denote unexplored terrain about which little or nothing was known. Our book explores such semi-charted territory in criminology. On the voyage we introduce the basic ideas of postmodernism in contrast to modernist criminological theory. We distinguish between two kinds of postmodernism, skeptical and affirmative, and we introduce the ideas of those writers who have had a significant influence on the development of our theoretical position. We drop anchor at constitutive theory and identify the central ideas of the approach before beginning the detailed charting that comprises the rest of the book. Let us first take stock with a brief overview of modernist theory in criminology.

The familiar coastline: modernist criminological theories

Criminological theory is a multi-disciplinary enterprise suffering an 'embarrassment of riches' which some would say is in need of integration (Gibbons, 1994: 183).[1] It comprises several competing theoretical frameworks, each rooted in a different discipline (Einstadter and Henry, 1995: 25–6). Theories influenced by economics, such as 'classical criminology' (Bentham, 1765; Beccaria, 1764), 'situational or rational choice theory' (Clarke, 1983; Cornish and Clarke, 1986; 1987) and 'routine activities or opportunity theory' (Cohen and Felson, 1979), assume a self-interested rational criminal who will only stop offending when the costs are too high, the crime targets are too difficult or, as in the 'control theory' variation (Hirschi, 1969; Gottfredson and Hirschi, 1990), sufficient childhood bonding to convention produces the 'self-controlled' citizen. From this perspective punishment, deterrence and situational manipulation are favored policies.

Bio-psychological theories, in contrast, subordinate free choice to the determination of genes, hormones, diet and a host of other internal bio-chemical processes that affect behavior and/or impede learning ability in a given environment (Lombroso, 1876; Eysenck, 1979; Eysenck and Gudjonsson, 1989; Jeffery, 1978). Here policy favors treatment or rehabilitation.

Psychologically rooted personality theories see humans as subject to the dictates of personality traits and criminogenic predispositions (Yochelson and Samenow, 1976; 1977), whereas psychoanalytic approaches argue that

humans are at the mercy of unconscious forces. These theories argue that
different societal pressures (i.e. structural, interpersonal) produce tensions
within the individual which are relieved by various 'adaptive', tension-
reduction mechanisms (Halleck, 1971; Salecl, 1993). Thus, theorists note
the 'adaptive value of crime' (Halleck, 1971), crime 'as a mode of
subjectivization' (Salecl, 1993), or the 'seductive value of crime' (Katz,
1988).[2] Few policy suggestions go beyond the focus on individual therapeutic change through analysis, family therapy, encounter groups,
counseling, and drug treatment.

Drawing on social psychology, others believe that social learning is
influenced by the 'wrong persons' (Sutherland and Cressey, 1966), 'poor
role models' (Bandura, 1977; 1979), or 'inappropriate rewards' (Akers,
1985; Jeffery, 1971). The result is criminal socialization. From such
learning experiences, people are readily able to neutralize the moral import
of law, a process which 'justifies' their commission of offenses (Matza,
1964; Cressey, 1970). Resocialization is deemed the appropriate policy and
attention is given to limiting exposure to, and production of, negative
learning experiences, not the least of which include those presented in the
media.

Social psychology also influences theories that focus on self-identity
which is said to be transformed through interaction with significant others
(Blumer, 1969), especially where these others are reactive social control
agents such as the police, courts and prisons (Becker, 1963; Lemert, 1951;
1967; Schur, 1971; 1973). As a result, some inadvertent or situational
deviants become labeled criminals and, in turn, proceed to a criminal career
(secondary deviants). Non-intervention, diversion and restitution are called
for in the policies of this approach.

Theories influenced by sociology and human geography shift the causal
force from the individual or social interaction at a group level to the
human organizational level. They assume that the social environment
places some people in disorganized or structurally strained settings. Here
normal adaptation for survival demands law-breaking and/or the formation
of peer-gang subcultures.[3] Policy includes the expansion of legitimate
opportunities and, by implication, the infusion of conventional institutions
and activities into affected neighborhoods.

Political theory, philosophy and history shape theories that give major
emphasis to power and interests as the active forces in generating crime.
Conflict, critical or radical approaches focus on the inequitable construction of laws that criminalize and criminally process the powerless but
exclude the powerful who commit equally, or more harmful crimes.[4] The
preferred policy is societal reorganization, redistribution of wealth and
development of a justice system aimed at limiting harm rather than being
responsive to class power.

Without question each of these differing theoretical orientations adds
insight to our knowledge about crime. Simultaneously, each also takes us in
different and conflicting policy directions. Empirical research can be cited

in support of each position, but to a limited extent (Empey, 1982). Several syntheses and resolutions of the assumptions underlying the central dimensions of these approaches have been attempted (Elliott et al., 1985; Akers, 1993), but these tend to favor some theories over others. New meta-paradigms are emerging, which themselves are now competing with each other for dominance (Einstadter and Henry, 1995: 301–10; Milovanovic, 1992a; 1995). A major problem that has not been resolved is the relative contribution of each of these theoretical positions to the overall production of the crime event.

Instead of setting out to identify the central causes of offending, post-modernist criminology takes a different approach. It is based *'on a different set of assumptions about reality, inquiry and criminality than those that guide mainstream criminology'* (Gibbons, 1994: 152, emphasis in original). Let us look at some of these different assumptions by delving into its recent history.

Uncharted waters: postmodernism

Although postmodernism is a relatively new and undeveloped approach to social science, and to criminology in particular, already its influence has been profound, pervasive and nothing if not corrosive, especially to the hierarchy of knowledges that form its academic disciplines. In the process '"postmodernism" has become a household word . . . a resounding cliché' about which 'everybody has an opinion' and in which 'everybody is already an expert' (Lash, 1990: 1–2). Interestingly, this is a fitting development since one theme of postmodernism is that there are no privileged knowledges: everyone or anyone is an expert.

Postmodernism is fundamentally opposed to many of the key modernist assumptions, and especially so in criminology which is seen as one of several instrumentalist knowledges (Foucault, 1977). Beyond this, any notion that postmodernism is somehow a unitary perspective, simply because it shares commonalities in its critique, is mistaken. As in modernism, there are 'many postmodernisms' constituting 'an almost infinite number of postmodern perspectives' (Schwartz and Friedrichs, 1994: 221–2). Again, this is con-sistent with its own methodological assumptions that celebrate diversity, plurality, and the subjugated, all of which have a birth in its kaleidoscope of perspectives. Thus postmodernists include not just the various authors informed by a postmodernist stance, but even those opposed and others, such as Baudrillard, classified as postmodernist who deny that is what they are (Gane, 1991: 46).

Postmodernist analysis had its roots in poststructuralist French thought of the late 1960s and the 1970s, although some who can be considered part of the postmodernist movement, such as Lacan, began writing in the 1930s. However, since the 1960s there has been a continuous disillusionment with conventional modernist and critical thought rooted in Hegel and Marx.

This disillusionment, together with the 1968 student protests in France and the breakup of Eastern European 'communist' governments, led to a paralysis of political economic structures and saw a transition from Marxist to Nietzschean thought. Indeed, Lyotard, Baudrillard, Foucault, Kristeva, Laclau and Mouffe, and many others who embrace a post-Marxist if not always postmodernist thinking, have indicated that major segments of Marxist analysis, which is said to be rooted in a modernist framework, are obsolete or need to be revised substantially in a postmodernist society.

Out of the debris of planned structures and controlled knowledges, an active critique of modernism was to unfold. Postmodernists, perhaps under the banner of Lyotard's 'Let us wage a war on totality', were to question the optimistic assumptions of modernist thinkers. They were to challenge their theory, their knowledge, and especially their claims to truth. The target of attack was especially profound with regard to modernism's structures: monopolies, manipulative advertisement industries, entrenched bureaucracies, dominant and totalizing discourses, and the ideology of the legal apparatus.

While not wishing to create distinctions (a pernicious modernist methodological and discursive practice!), it might be helpful at the outset to distinguish between postmodern society or the postmodern era, and post-modernism or postmodernist theory. The postmodern era is depicted as a historical period (to some, the one we are currently in; to others, the one that we are rapidly approaching), where industrial society is characterized by materialism and informational communications rather than social relationships. Here a shift of production has occurred from manufacturing of goods and services for their usefulness toward the production of goods and services valuable only for their image. This shift has been variously described as a movement from a manufacturing society to a 'consumer society', a 'service society' and/or an 'informational society', and most recently a 'risk society'. Whatever the terms, the shift is seen to have taken industrial society from a 'real' society to a 'virtual' society, one containing 'contingent human subjects' rather than individuals, humans or human agents (as in modernism). In so far as an actual state of reality is depicted, accounts of the existence of a postmodernist era are inconsistent with postmodern analysis/theory, since this, in its most extreme forms, denies the possibility of reality as anything other than the description. Thus, as a theoretical stance:

> In the social sciences, postmodernism is an attempt to reconceptualize the way we experience relationships and social structure, and a method to work through how the world around us appears real, thereby questioning that it is real in truth or fact, or that there is any way of making such judgments. Indeed, postmodernism challenges the whole idea of how reality is conceived. It questions the superiority of 'science' as a mode of analysis and explanation (just as it questioned high art). It questions all attempts to reduce life to essences or causes. It questions any attempt by communities or individuals as 'experts' to prioritize their knowledge over the knowledge of others, and it asserts that no one can claim their knowl-edge is privileged. (Einstadter and Henry, 1995: 278)

The attack on modernism's claim to superior knowledge is accomplished in many ways but particularly by 'deconstruction' of what are referred to as 'texts'. Postmodernists consider all narrative accounts to be texts, including books, stories, descriptions, reports, accounts, even non-verbal communication such as demeanor and gestures. Thus all discourse of any kind is a text, as are all phenomena and events (Rosenau, 1992: xiv). In this context the much used term 'discourse' refers to that which is communicated, whether written, spoken or depicted as images, such as in film or television (i.e. cinematic text). Dreams, too, as Freud (1965) had discovered, represent a text: they have their own structure and meaning. Lacan, in the same direction, was to see the unconscious as producing texts – 'the unconscious structured like a language'. In this more radical approach, the subject can be seen as a *parlêtre* or *l'être parlant*, a 'speaking' or the 'speaking being'.

Particular discourses develop around certain themes, within certain contexts and especially within academic disciplines. So, deconstruction, as Cohen (1990: 11–12) has clearly stated, involves: (1) the breaking up of something that has been built as in 'demolition', and (2) exposing the way in which it is built. Deconstruction, then, is an analytical technique which seeks to 'undo' all constructions: 'Deconstruction tears a text apart, reveals its contradictions and assumptions' (Rosenau, 1992: xi; Balkin, 1987). Deconstructionism displaces established truths, disrupts their smooth passage and undermines their regime, which is the meaning of critique as opposed to criticism (Smart, 1983). Postmodernists who develop and practice various techniques for deconstructive critique, and do that alone, have been defined as 'skeptical postmodernists' (Cohen, 1990; Rosenau, 1992). Those who retain revised elements of modernism, particularly the idea that deconstruction also implies reconstruction, and who use deconstructionist epistemology as the basis toward reconstructing a replacement text/discourse that goes beyond the nihilistic limits of the skeptical position, have been described as 'affirmative postmodernists'. As we have already indicated, our constitutive criminology is closer to this position than to skeptical postmodernism.

Winds of controversy and challenge: postmodernist influences

Several writers have contributed to the development of postmodernism in the social sciences. In this introductory section we focus on those whose ideas have significantly influenced our thinking in formulating constitutive criminology. As we shall see, French philosophy and social theory have been particularly influential here (Dews, 1987). The emerging field of chaos theory has also offered novel conceptualizations.

Most first generation postmodernist thinkers can be directly traced to Jacques Lacan (1901–81), a French psychoanalyst, who reinterpreted the early works of Freud in terms of Saussure's and Jakobson's structural linguistics.[5] Lacan's series of seminars in France during the 1950s, 1960s, and 1970s were attended by some of the most noted scholars of the time. Most of his work has yet to be translated into English. It is noted for its density in prose.[6] A number of key contributors to present-day post-modernism are associated with a Lacanian approach: Deleuze, Guattari, Derrida, Lyotard, Baudrillard, Foucault, and Kristeva. Lacan's seminar attendees are to be found applying his rather difficult material in a variety of disciplines and to a variety of topics.[7] Arguably, the most insightful theoretical analysis of Lacan's work has been done in polemic fashion by feminist postmodernists.[8] The question of seduction, cooptation, rejection, and a 'strategic' incorporation with the recognition of potential pitfalls has been well argued (Grosz, 1990).

One of the key insights of feminist analysis has been the nature of the phallic Symbolic Order from a Lacanian perspective. Feminist post-modernists following Lacan (1985: 149–55) have indicated that a woman is 'not-all' (*pas-toute*) in this order, without a voice. This idea has led to much analysis of other disenfranchised peoples, as well as the beginning point of the development of an alternative discourse. Early feminist analysis had argued for an *écriture féminine*, a women's writing. This was later rejected by many as being too essentialist and having the potential for simply reversing hierarchies and reinstituting forms of domination. Later versions argued for 'standpoint epistemology', whereby the various sites of sub-jectivity production should be privileged and in the process more liberating discourses would follow. This, too, was attacked by African-American feminists for overlooking the nature of differences.[9] A contemporary approach sees a plurality of sites of discourse production, hence 'stand-point(s) epistemology(ies)'.

In our formulation for a change in criminology's direction, we make the case for 'replacement discourses'. It is only through a new discursive form with alternative imaginary constructions that the human subject can better embody desire. But this is connected with materialistic changes. We shall refer to replacement discourse in the singular, but it should be seen as incorporating the various discourses of the oppressed seeking expression. A number of works – especially Freire's (1972; 1973; 1985) on critical dia-logical pedagogy and those inspired by him (Giroux, 1992; JanMohamed, 1994; McLaren, 1994), and Lacan's (1991) on the four discourses and imaginary play and those inspired by him (Cornell, 1991; 1993; Milovanovic, 1992a; 1993a; 1995) – we shall see, can be integrated in developing the beginnings of replacement discourses.

In doing postmodernist analysis and especially what we refer to as a constitutive criminology, an approach that is a post-postmodern inspired analysis, we need to confront and refute three false dualities that have arisen in the literature: (1) the question of accepting either modernist or postmodernist thought; (2) the issue of clarity versus complexity in discourse use; and (3) the notion of action as privileged over theory. In our view, all of these are counterproductive debates (see also Giroux, 1992: 23–5). As to the first, although throughout this book we often present the modernist and postmodernist positions as dualities, we do so for didactic purposes. These should, however, be seen as a continuum. Although some positions do tend toward continuous polarization, such as the differences between the centered and decentered subject, the privileging of order versus disorder, the emphasis on Logos rather than Pathos, the assumption of linear over non-linear developments (see also Milovanovic, 1995), it is clear that others do not. For example, some versions of biological theory and ecological theory (those that stress interactive and symbiotic relationships) have greater affinities to postmodernism than others. Similarly, who could argue that some renditions of social interactionism, social constructionism, and dialectical structural Marxism do not capture at least some of what is made manifest in postmodernism? Indeed, some positions, such as Mead's conception of the self and his dialectical interplay between the 'I' and the 'me', as well as Matza's theory of neutralization and drift, anticipated some postmodern analysis.

As to the second dualism, clarity versus complexity, some have argued that postmodernist prose is obscure and inaccessible and that the goal should be simplicity in narrative constructions.[10] However, Giroux has summarized the inadequacy of this dualist position, in that

> it often subscribes to a universal referent for clarity and linguistic unity that is elitist as well as anti-intellectual; it tends to simplify the politics of representation, reducing it to an unproblematic issue of clarity that is never deconstructed as perhaps complicitous with the construction of domination; and it reproduces a troublesome politics of erasure by claiming to represent a universal standard of literacy while failing to consider a plurality of audiences and constituencies. Hence, it eliminates the complexity and specificity of a readership that occupies multiple, diverse public cultures. (1992: 24)

In other words, this dualism overlooks important epistemological questions such as the assumption of a consensus as to what constitutes simplicity versus complexity, an understanding of the value-laden nature of discursive forms (e.g. their non-transparency), and the potential for developing new language forms that aim to 'reclaim new spaces of resistance, to establish new identities, or to construct new knowledge/power relations' (Giroux, 1992: 25; Aronowitz and Giroux, 1991: 90–2).

Third, as to privileging practice over theory, this dualism overlooks the important interrelationship between both, as Freire's inspirational work attests. As he has indicated, a word has two components: reflection and action. One without the other empties humans' activities and struggles. 'Speaking true words', as he calls it, is also engaging in change because 'there is no true word that is not at the same time a praxis. Thus, to speak a true word is to transform the world', and this can only take place in dialogical encounters (Freire, 1972: 77; 1973; 1985: 50–1, 167–72; Peters and Lankshear, 1994). History has shown us that some of the worst excesses can take place when a privileging of reflection over action or vice versa occurs, as in the case of simply reversing hierarchies, forms of political correctness, schmarxism (i.e. vulgar forms of Marxism), 'exorcism',

and the 'politics of revenge'.[11] An informed humanistic postmodern
analysis rejects these dualisms as exercises of exclusion and reductionism
(Giroux, 1992: 37).

Whereas the notion of praxis, a philosophy and practice rooted in Hegel,
has been the rallying cry for revolutionaries the world over, postmodernist
approaches look more to Nietzsche's notion of a transpraxis. If praxis is
taken to be purposive social activity born of human agents' consciousness
of their world, mediated through the social groups to which they belong,
then this must be supplanted by the richer notion of transpraxis. Transpraxis assumes that critical opposition must be aware of the reconstitutive
effects – the reproductions of exploitative relations of production – in the
very attempts to neutralize or challenge them. The dialectic of control is
such that praxis assumes dualistic forms – negation/affirmation, denial/
expression. In the process of negation, hierarchical relations of production
are often reconstituted along with the human subjects that are their
supports. But often neglected is that with affirmation, relations of production are also deconstructed along with those same human subjects.
Modernist theorists, even critical theorists, have been particularly myopic
as to the potential for change afforded by this insight, which suggests an
affirmative and active position rooted in 'contingent universalities' directed
toward change, as in, for example, Irigaray's notion of 'mimesis' (Cornell,
1991: 147–52).

Treacherous waters: Lacan and discourse analysis

Earlier we referred to the shift in postmodernism from the concept of
people as individuals to people as human subjects, or, from centered to
decentered subjects. This fundamental shift for understanding postmodernism derives from discourse analysis. Put very simply, discourse analysis sees
people as formed by and through their use of language and by the inherent
meaning that language use creates and invokes. Those who make use of
discourse analysis conceptualize human agents as occupying 'discursive
subject positions', rather than the more familiar but limiting notion of them
occupying roles.[12] This means humans are envisaged as located in assumed
structures formed by space and time coordinates (spatio-temporal), defined
and specified by discourse (Whorf, 1956).[13] Human subjects comprise a
coming together of several background and taken for granted relevancies –
in the context of whatever particular discourse is being used (the pragmatic
level). Social reality for the human subject, like the subject itself, is
constructed within such linguistic frameworks. The subject and social
reality are made to 'make sense' (are narratively coherent) only in the
context of the discourse in which one is situated (Jackson, 1988; Janikowski
and Milovanovic, 1995).

These various discourses are alternatively described as language games,
regimes of signs, discursive formations, rhetorics, linguistic coordinate
systems, etc. They can be viewed as bounded spheres within which words

'float' (Lacan, 1977; Laclau and Mouffe, 1985; Manning, 1988: 193–230). In postmodern discourse analysis, signifiers or acoustic images are represented in the most formal sense by words. These are connected to signifieds. A signified is the concept as it is used or as it appears in particular contexts. Otherwise signifieds are continuously in movement. They may convey various meanings and only periodic anchoring gives them the appearance of contingent stability. Perhaps the poet has the greatest license to show the variability of signifieds.

Signifiers are value-laden. They are accented with a particular nuanced meaning. Take, for example, the Fourteenth Amendment to the US Constitution where it is said that 'no person . . . shall be deprived of life, liberty or property without due process of law.' Each of these words, 'person', 'life', 'liberty', 'property', 'due process', and 'law', are signifiers that have attained a particular meaning in the legal sphere. A particular circumscribed signified has been connected to them that is specific to their use together, to the context of their use and so on (see also Milovanovic, 1987). Thus it is imperative to look toward a political economy at different historical moments to understand why a signifier is connected to a particular signified. In this view of semiotics, three levels are described. At the most rudimentary and unconscious level, 1, are the 'condensation–displacement' axes, first identified by Freud (1965) in his analysis of 'dream work'. Here psychic material, desire, first takes form in images (e.g. a dream is a picture puzzle to be deconstructed for its meaning). Here, 'condensation' stands for how numerous desires are given a compressed form in some image; 'displacement' refers to how desire has the ability to be attached, detached and reattached to different elements of a dream. The next level, 2, the 'metaphor–metonymy' axes, identified by Jakobson and later by Lacan, is the sphere where further embodiment of various desires unique to the person takes form: a signifier begins to materialize, even as various versions seek expression (e.g. consider the abortion debate and the evolution of the concept of fetus from an organic entity to a person and the differing images of at what precise moment the organism becomes a person). These are the 'metaphor–metonymy' semiotic axes. Here signifiers are seen to be connected in a signifying chain, where the specific sequencing of signifiers produces meaning. Jakobson showed that speech disorders were characterized as the inability to operate on either the metonymic axis (in word-association tests, the subject was not able to string words together in a linear sequence) or the metaphoric axis (the subject was not able to locate appropriate similar words). Lacan concluded that the unconscious operates by metaphor and metonymy in semiotic production.

In a more complex form, Lacan has provided two algorithms for metaphor and metonymy (1977; Milovanovic, 1992a: 64–72) which indicate the movement of desire. Metaphor stands for how one signifier comes to be replaced by another, and how the original signifier is pushed back into the unconscious where it remains connected to a long chain of signifiers. This becomes apparent in puns, 'Freudian slips', dreams, and constructions by film directors (Metz, 1981). When one says 'she is a dynamo' or 'he is a tiger' there is metaphor at play; as there is when one fixes in ideological constructions the notion of a juridic subject, the so-called reasonable man/woman in law. Metonymy, on the other hand, stands for how desire is displaced along a signifying chain; desire is in continuous movement. It has everything to do with 'word-to-word connections' (Lacan, 1977: 164). Consider the use of 'drinking a bottle' (of soda), or 'having a slice' (of cake), or 'a cup' (of tea). In each case, signifiers are only fully understood in their linear connectedness and in how desire is 'spread out' in an utterance, nevertheless each produces meaning. Consider also the utterance: 'families need protection from drugs and crime.' Here, then, desire shifts from one signifier to another, with a different nuanced meaning being created with each word connected in the sequence. For example, the first part of the statement almost always and generically invokes agreement; by adding 'drugs and crime' the self-evidence of the first part carries over to promote opposition to the words in the second part.

At the last level, 3, the 'paradigm–syntagm' axes, the most conscious, a signifier is expressed in a particular discourse. One of these, the vertical axis (the paradigmatic axis), stands for the available signifiers (or dictionary of word choices) that each human subject carries with her/him and from which particular words may be selected in the construction of an utterance. Consider the more specialized repository of signifiers drawn on by those practicing law (or in scientific, medical, oppositional discourses). The other axis, the horizontal (or syntagmatic axis), stands for the precise manner (syntactically, grammatically) in which signifiers can be positioned in the sequence of an utterance to produce meaning. In other words, a code governs the correct placement of signifiers in a sequence of words.[14] For example, Jackson (1988) has developed a 'narrative coherence' model in criminal justice which indicates that 'truth' is discourse specific and courtroom practices have everything to do with how narratives are constructed and how audiences (e.g. jurors) receive them. Jackson's work is an example of applying semiotic analysis to criminology using the paradigm–syntagm semiotic axes (see also the work of Greimas, 1990).

It is desire, a desire unique to the person, that animates the process (Milovanovic, 1994b: 156–66); 'at the root of all our speech there is a non-semiotic flow of desire' (Lecercle, 1985: 170–1; see also Sarup, 1989: 20–33; Archard, 1984: 79–80). Desire has a more conservative basis in Hegel's master–slave (Marx's bourgeoisie–proletariat) dialectics, one based on reaction-negation dynamics (see also Lichtman, 1982), or in a more progressive usage, as in Nietzsche's affirmative form. Whereas the former tends toward a homeostasis – that is, its end-state tends toward equilibrium dynamics – the latter is 'a forward movement, a flight towards an object which always eludes our grasp; the attempt, never successful but never frustrating, to reach the unattainable by exploring the paths of the possible' (Lecercle, 1985: 196).

Some theorists have indicated that the three sets of axes are interconnected (Metz, 1981; Silverman, 1983; Milovanovic, 1993a; 1994a: 162–3). Desire, initially in an amorphous state, is given form (embodied) by the interplay of the three sets of axes. Be that as it may, only with a punctuation, some pause, does an intuitive, retroactive 'grasping' of the whole spoken discursive chain produce meaning in particular contexts (Lacan, 1977: 303–4; Zizek, 1989: 100–5; Milovanovic, 1994a: 163–5). We will build on these basic concepts of semiotic analysis and how it becomes relevant to a postmodernist criminology in the subsequent chapters of this book.

Turbulent waters: orderly disorder

Postmodernist analysis has also focused on a number of novel conceptualizations beyond discourse analysis. For example, Godel's (1962) incompleteness theorem is valuable for it directly undermines any development of an over-encompassing gapless system from which truth can be deduced (see, for example, Weber's notion of the possibility of some gapless system in law: Milovanovic, 1994a). The insights of quantum mechanics and the (Heisenberg) indeterminacy principle (Heisenberg, 1958; Capra, 1988) are important since they stipulate the impossibility of simultaneously specifying the precise location and velocity of social phenomena, including the subject-in-process. Snapshots, for example, capture the moment but give little of the context or the meaning that led to the moment or the meaning that followed; they overlook the process of continuous change. Catastrophe theory (Thom, 1975; Poston and Stewart, 1978; Zeeman, 1976)[15] shows how non-linear change can take place. Topology theory, the 'rubber math', is important in showing how this qualitative mathematics can better conceptualize complex dynamics in movement.[16] Chaos theory is enlightening for its novel view of how transformations take place.[17] All these alternatives to the mainstream of conventional scientific thought fundamentally question doing science from a Newtonian framework, which has been the preferred paradigm of order since the Enlightenment.

Indeed, chaos theory, perhaps more than any other, has been a central thrust in much postmodernist analysis. It has been particularly helpful in offering novel conceptions that may be usefully incorporated in a constitutive criminology.[18] Although it is easy to create dualisms, with natural sciences being pitted against the social sciences, much evidence indicates researchers have moved both ways.[19] In our view constitutive criminology can be furthered by the conceptual tools offered by 'chaologists', as those subscribing to chaos theory are called.

Islands of familiarity: contributions from phenomenology to structuration

On the voyage out it behooves us to look back on several significant modernist contributions in social theory that stand out from the rest as islands of possibility. Not surprisingly, these have all been influenced by the hermeneutic turn, yet also embody an analysis of constituted structure. Significant examples that have been influential in our passing include Schutz's (1967) phenomenological sociology, Berger and Luckmann's (1966) social constructionism, Blumer's (1969) symbolic interactionism, and particularly Giddens' (1984) structuration theory. The latter, with its analysis of the interrelationship between human agency and social structure as continuous emergent outcomes, is consistent with our own stance, and as we develop our position we will continually receive sustenance from it. Thus the central thesis of our constitutive approach can find a basis of support in the thesis of co-production of social reality, in subjectivity and in the prospects for possible directions for humanistically oriented social change. Questions, for example, will remain as to the extent to which the subject is constituted by the use of language. Questions also remain as to whether it is beneficial to focus on the level of consciousness as is predominantly the case with Schutz, Berger and Luckmann, Blumer, and Giddens, with the danger of reverting to some conception of the transcendental subject, or to entertain the posited interactive effects of the unconscious as developed by Freud, revised along semiotic directions by Lacan, incorporated in a synthesis by the Frankfurt School with Marx, and further developed in the synthesis attempted by Deleuze, Guattari, Kristeva, and Cornell of Nietzsche and Hegel/Marx, with the danger here of reverting to a loss of integrity and to outright contradictions. Constitutive theory, in short, may yet diverge with further refinement as to its underlying base.

Charting new waters: toward an 'empowered democracy'

By way of providing an indication of what is to come, we conclude this introduction with a brief summary of where the subsequent chapters will lead. In the next chapter we examine ideas about human nature and conclude that a constitutive criminological vision of the human subject must be open to both human diversity and specificity, as well as being contingently formed so as to adjust to emerging renditions of subjectivity. For this reason, we use the term 'recovering subject', arguing that the human subject can never be 'recovered' because this limit is only reachable under the delusion that allows some contingent constitutive elements to slip away. We argue that such a vision is an important first step in developing a framework that captures the emergent, contingent and revisable notion of human subjectivity, and allows for the richness of human potentiality.

In Chapter 3 we show that neither the visions of social structure contained in modernist criminological literature, nor the critical position of skeptical postmodernism, are adequate to address the expansive possibility engendered by our recovering human subject. Affirmative postmodernism, however, provides several critical insights on the contingent nature of social agency and on the subject–society interrelationship. When joined with modernist and postmodernist ideas, our constitutive approach provides a dynamic and contingent conception of social structure as a virtual and infinitely revisable society.

In Chapter 4 we discuss modernist images of law, arguing that we need to transcend the view that law is the product of cultural consensus, structural forces, structural conflicts, interactive relations or system processes, since these presume law as an autonomous entity and thereby distract from addressing the complexities involved in the law–society relationship. In contrast, we develop a position in which law is seen as mutually constituted through social relations and discursive misreading. The discursive processes of non-state normative orders with which state law is interrelated and interwoven provide a formative context for the production of new legal and social forms. Here we begin to see how social control is not so much an alternative form of law but a necessary part of the ideological process whereby object-like qualities of law are created and sustained.

After reviewing earlier attempts to define crime, Chapter 5 offers a provisional and non-essentialist postmodern definition of crime as the harm resulting from any attempt to reduce or suppress another's position or potential standing through the use of power that limits the other's ability to make a difference. This definition accommodates multiple and often covert forms of harm and the present sites of race, class, and gender domination.

Chapter 6 reviews the variety of modernist analyses of causes and models of causality that seek to explain the various agencies of harm infliction. Each is said to contribute directly or indirectly to harms of repression and reduction.

In Chapter 7 we turn to an alternative postmodernist position on causality in which offender categories have been extended and deconstructed to include discourse and constitutive interrelational sets which we term COREL sets. Here we indicate an alternative mapping of 'causal' chains where the very notion of 'cause' becomes problematic. The notion of a revised structural coupling and autopoiesis thesis provides the basis of our constitutive dialectic approach which shows how harms of reduction and repression are often the outcomes of some of such semi-autonomous developments.

In Chapter 8 we turn to the question of how harm constitutes a basis of justice policy and practice techniques, and to the ultimate question of 'what is to be done?' about crime as we have redefined it. Existing criminal justice policy is reviewed and found deficient in its conception of the problem of crime and co-constitutive of crime's ongoing vitality. Instead of a criminal justice policy we suggest a justice policy of replacement discourse. This shows how the liberating forces of COREL sets can be harnessed, albeit contingently. We outline the theoretical foundation for our policy of replacement discourse, one grounded in historical struggles.

In the concluding chapter we discuss practical examples of how replacement discourses can develop with the power to transform those who frame the social realities of crime. We show that it is within far-from-equilibrium conditions of superliberalism that alternative replacement discourses are able to more freely develop, and provide illustrations of how this can be achieved through radical refraction, social judo and radical pluralism. In our final section we develop possible directions for an empowered democracy.

Our overall position, therefore, presents an affirmative postmodernism that seeks avenues toward liberating the spirit while at the same time not planting the seeds of new harm. It is rooted in material conditions, but is free itself from any inevitable linear unfolding of historical processes. Ours is a call for a transpraxis, a movement toward the never completed. We see the development of a multiplicity of sites of discursive production, dispersions that give expression to a plurality of voices otherwise denied a form. Here the recovering subject will co-produce recovering replacement discourses which offer to better embody diverse desires. Let's now begin the journey, with an analysis of the modernist, postmodernist and constitutive approaches to humans that moves us toward an open future.

Notes

1 See especially, Johnson (1979), Braithwaite (1989), Gibbons and Krohn (1991), Messner et al. (1989), and Barak (forthcoming).

2 Katz, no doubt, would not include himself as psychoanalytically persuaded. Indeed, O'Malley and Mugford (1994) see his ideas as more consistent with those of postmodernism, as we shall see in later chapters.

3 Shaw and McKay (1942), Merton (1938; 1968), Cohen (1955), Cloward and Ohlin (1960), Bursik (1988), and Bursik and Grasmick (1993).

4 Chambliss and Seidman (1971), Taylor et al. (1973), Quinney (1973; 1977), Reiman (1979), Schwendinger and Schwendinger (1970), and Greenberg (1981).

5 Secondary sources are a must in coming to terms with Lacan. See, for example, Mueller and Richardson (1982), Feldstein et al. (1995), Lee (1990), Ragland-Sullivan (1986), Borch-Jacobsen (1991), Zizek (1989), Sarup (1992), Marini (1992), Clement (1983), MacCannell (1986), Milovanovic (1992a), and Samuels (1993). See also feminist works by Grosz (1990) and Sellers (1991).

6 Reading and interpreting Lacan's work, for example, is a difficult exercise. Many who have taken on the challenge have spent several years before they make any dent in his work. Some react critically. Eagleton, for example, said, 'Lacan's deliberately obscure, hermetic, "high French" style makes any simple account of his theories almost impossible' (1983: 418). Yet others have found it inspiring and full of possibility.

7 In law, the main students are Cornell (1991; 1992; 1993), Goodrich (1990), Brennan (1993), Caudill (1991; 1992; 1993), Caudill and Gold (1995), Milovanovic (1992a; 1993a; 1994a; 1995). In criminology, we find Salacl (1993), Arrigo (1992; 1993; 1995), and Milovanovic (1989b; 1991b). In cinema theory, the work of Silverman (1983) and Williamson (1987) best represents Lacan. In literary criticism, Zizek (1989) is a must. Finally, in cultural change, see Bracher (1993).

8 Irigaray (1985; 1993), Kristeva (1986), Moi (1985; 1987), and Cixous (1986; 1990).

9 See Kerruish (1991), Butler (1993), Collins (1990; 1993), Smith (1992), and hooks (1989).

10 Some aligning themselves as modernists have said that postmodernism has made so much use of indulging language that it not only makes obscure the meaning of the familiar, but also has a tendency 'to invoke specialized jargon, to invent and discard terms, and to

"play" with words' (Schwartz and Friedrichs, 1994: 227). Add to this a proclivity for postmodernism's words to have both the grace of a butterfly and the density of a brick, for single phrases to congeal 100 sentences, and for any clarity to be shrouded by 1000 veils, and it is easy to see why dismissive evaluations of the movement as 'inaccessible', 'impenetrable' and 'opaque' appeal to all but the most dedicated or masochistic (Schwartz and Friedrichs, 1994: 228). Many sympathetic to postmodernists would reply that these criticisms are too rigidly rooted in dualisms of simplicity versus complexity.

11 Exorcism, here, refers to forms of practice whereby the evil is seen everywhere, and, where it does not exist, the would-be overzealous reformer attributes it where it is not and attacks her/his own construction. See Milovanovic (1991a), and also Cornell's (1991: 11, 139, 185) rejection of a 'politics of revenge' which she attributes to MacKinnon's and others' writing.

12 See, for example, Lacan (1977), Foucault (1973), Laclau and Mouffe (1985), Manning (1988; 1990), Milovanovic (1988; 1992b), Pecheux (1982), and Silverman (1983).

13 See also Benveniste's (1971) influential work on the nature of personal pronouns, and how the pronoun 'I' is a 'shifter', only filled in when a subject takes up a position as a speaker within a particular discourse with its variously offered subject positions (e.g. prosecutor, defense counselor, police, social worker, etc.).

14 See Milovanovic (1994a), Jackson (1988), Landowski (1988), Greimas (1990), and Bennet and Feldman (1981).

15 For more recent contributions see McRobie and Thompson (1994), Baack and Cullen (1994).

16 For a lucid discussion of topology theory see Weeks (1985), Firby and Gardiner (1982), and also Milovanovic (1993a; 1993b; 1994c).

17 For an introduction, see Briggs and Peat (1989).

18 See Lyotard (1984), Deleuze and Guattari (1987), Hayles (1990). The founding figures include Henri Poincaré, Edward Lorenz, Mitchell Feigenbaum, Benoit Mandelbrot, Ilya Prigogine. See accessible summaries by Briggs and Peat (1989), Gleick (1987), and Stewart (1989). Chaos theory has found beginning application to criminology in Young (1991a; 1991b) and Pepinsky (1991), and to law in Brion (1991) and Milovanovic (1992a; 1993a).

19 See Capra (1988), Kaplan and Kaplan (1991), Peat (1989), and Whorf (1956).

2

Human Subjects and Human Behavior: on the Problem of Similarity and Difference

In this chapter we address some dominant contemporary criminological assumptions about the human subject. Ideas about human 'nature' range from seeing humans as a cluster of essential needs required for survival and procreation, to identifying characteristics that differentiate us from other animal organisms (Bartol, 1991). Questions are raised as to whether humans can exist as separate individuals, or whether we are social beings representing the wider social formation, be this a group, culture or society. And if we have a unique human identity, is this predetermined by genetic codes or does it emerge from a process of communicative discourse and social interaction?

In this chapter we move beyond the simple dichotomy between freedom and determinacy to explore individual, social and cultural constructions of the human subject as these appear in criminological and socio-legal literature. First we examine some of the assumptions about the human subject made by modernist criminological theorists. We are especially interested in their notions concerning freedom of choice and in the counter-claim that choice is both channeled and limited by internal or external forces. Second, we examine postmodernist assumptions about the human subject. Skeptical postmodernists have offered an alternative to modernist paradigms, replete with its own unique domain assumptions (see Sarup, 1989; Milovanovic, 1995). Our main concern will be with the postmodernist notion that humans do not have central essences or core features but consist of multiple identities, layers of consciousness, etc. (i.e. decentered subject) and are constituted through discourse as emergent identities. We then present some shortcomings of skeptical postmodernism.

In the final section of the chapter we go beyond modernism and skeptical postmodernism to develop an affirmative postmodernist approach to the human subject based on our constitutive analysis. This situates the human subject as a creative, reflexive, but decentered social agent, making the world that recursively constitutes shared social reality, while simultaneously being made by that world through the inextricably intertwined relations humans have with fellow subjects.

Modernist assumptions about human subjects

Criminology makes use of the domain assumptions of a variety of conceptions of the human subject as these appear in different theoretical paradigms (Young, 1981; Empey, 1982; Einstadter and Henry, 1995; Michalowski, 1985). They often remain unexplored yet become the implicit basis of particular theories. We can conceptualize two dimensions on the subject within modernist criminological thought. In one, humans range from active agents creating and shaping their world to passive agents controlled by their world. In the other, humans range from being individual subjects to being social subjects.[1] Combining these analytical dimensions produces four ideal-typical positions on the human subject (see Figure 2.1). *Active-individual* positions include those that essentialize humans as capable of exercising free choice, reason and rational calculation limited only by the extent to which situational and contextual constraints are acknowledged. *Passive-individual* positions assume humans are determined by a variety of internal forces, be they biological, psychological (personality traits), or a combination of both. These indicate behavioral 'predispositions' whose force is limited only to the extent that theorists acknowledge environmental contexts. *Passive-social* positions assume external forces, be they environmental, cultural, or structural, that have a high degree of determinism. Finally, *active-social* positions see humans as agents involved in a social process of constructing their social identities, social reality, and the social forms and structures of their world. Active involvement is limited to the degree that humans are denied having a reflexive awareness of their involvement in social processes (reification) and to the extent that structure is acknowledged to have active agency.

As with any analytical scheme, actual theories vary in position along these dimensions. For example, while both social constructionist and Marxist dialectical[2] theories would be classified as active-social, their spatial position would be different, representing different strengths of active-passive and individual-social forces. Further, pure forms at the end of these analytical dimensions are not found in modernist theory. Rather, the various positions on the continuum are approximated by different authors as indicated in Figure 2.1. Let us examine the human subject assumptions of specific theories in relation to this broad analytical framework.

Active-individual assumptions about human subjects

Rational choice theories assume humans to be independent, aware, reflective, self-interested, in control, rational and reasoning decision-makers, capable of exercising 'free choice'. The idea of free choice assumes that: (1) humans are capable of acting as individual units, separate from internal or external forces; (2) at any point, a range of possible actions can be taken; (3) humans can discriminate between actions and alternatives; (4)

	Individual	Social
Active	× Classical × Rational choice × Situational choice × Control theory × Liberal feminist	Social constructionist × Interactionist × × Labeling × Structural Marxist
Passive	× Social learning × Differential association × Personality × Biological	× Subcultural × Socialist feminist × Conflict × Cultural × Ecological × Marxist feminist × Strain × Radical feminist × Instrumental Marxist

(These perspectives are located in indicative positions, which should not be read too strictly.)

Figure 2.1 *Analysis of modernist criminological theory*

humans are aware of these options; (5) humans are able to control their actions; (6) they can reason, by which process they select one or more preferred actions; (7) their selection is based upon rational principles, designed to optimize achievement of a preconceived goal or expectations; (8) humans can project sufficiently ahead to build separate actions toward a broader objective; and (9) they are able to adjust their behavior in light of expected and unexpected events.

In criminological thought these ideas have been expressed most directly by the Enlightenment classical criminology school, neo-classical theorists, economists of crime, rational choice and routine activity theorists, and by some versions of control theory.[3] For rational choice assumptions about the human subject, human differences are a central problematic. Any differences between humans are seen to affect the nature and extent of any action necessary to produce an outcome. So to have conceptual vitality, let alone explanatory utility, free rational choice theorists have to assume that humans are more similar than they are different. Thus humans are all individuals, all social atoms, all broadly identical in their orientation toward the underlying sensations of pleasure and pain. The idea of human difference is not vanquished but corralled into the outcome of a cost/benefit decision process. Rather than being a reflection of human diversity, difference is a measure of ubiquitous agency. It is not a quality of humanity but humanity's product.[4]

Rational choice theory promises and expects too much. It dissolves human difference along with social destiny. It substitutes for difference the ideal of formal equality and the potential of substantive social difference; it promises that although humans start out equal they can imagine, and by making the right choices and investing their time and energies wisely, they can work to become different. But this vision comes without instructions on the place of forces that emasculate choice, while simultaneously convincing its players of their supreme individual potency. Worse yet, its denial of the social holds humans accountable for failings that could not be of their individual making and ultimately bludgeons them with guilt for failing the impossible.[5] Redemption comes with the certainty of science.

Passive-individual assumptions about human subjects

Theorists adopting an individual positivist stance focus on internal forces as the basis of human behavior.[6] Rational choice gives way to biological and personality difference. Here human subjects are conceived as having only a limited similarity, one that ultimately submits to the differences between them. Biologically and psychologically oriented criminologists reduce the similarity in biological form and cognitive development and magnify the differences. Behavior is now the outcome not of choice alone, or even of choice at all, but of biologically and psychologically predisposed 'choices'. Here differences of behavior reflect differences in constitution, chemical balance, genetic codes, and personality traits.

Ultimately, it was to be claimed that the assumed difference in behavior can be explained by the differing physical and social environments in which humans were found. From this perspective human behavior is thus seen as an outcome of the interaction between biology and environment, mediated by brain function and intelligence. Thus Jeffery, for example, argues that 'the environment interacts with the individual by means of the brain, and the brain in turn controls behavior. This is an Environment→ Brain→ Behavior model of behavior, sometimes referred to as an Environment→ Organism→ Behavior approach' (1994: 21).

Thus, in their attempts to correct an overly deterministic image of the human subject, biologically oriented criminologists counter with the qualifying conception that human action is not wholly determined by genes: 'It is not Genes OR Environment, but Genes in INTERACTION with Environment. It is not heredity or environment, but heredity and environment'; and further, 'genes do not cause behavior . . . Genes in interaction with the environment create a brain and nervous system' (Jeffery, 1993: 6).

Once again in this construction of human subjects, active agency is vanquished. Human difference is the mechanistic outcome of different permutations of fixed entities. Rather than classical theory's pain and pleasure, diversity is governed by two new masters, biology and environment, that are co-conspirators of our behavioral fate, a fate that we falsely believe we freely chose. In the bio-criminological reality these forces are mediated by electro-chemical processes of the brain, which can themselves be affected by the very behaviors that emerge, in a self-regulating system of functional equilibrium.

What both biological and personality theories contribute to the constitutive criminological enterprise is an awareness that a *part* of being human is beyond individual choice. Human action builds on the shape created biologically and influenced by interrelations throughout the developmental process. However, how far the original shape is retained in the building processes, relative to how far it is changed, raises the critical issue of *relative contribution* that individual positivists fail to adequately address.

Nevertheless, a consequence of the cultural permeation of arguments about inner causes over individual choices is that passive human subjects are absolved from personal responsibility for action.[7] Under such scientific explanations of causality, responsibility for human action is no longer readily controlled by the human subject, but is a function of the conspiracy of cause and conditions. Humans are at once freed from their guilt and moral culpability, while simultaneously being denied their humanity. They are not active individuals who made bad choices, but passive carriers of genetic codes or personality traits confronted by environmental conditions that make manifest their hidden defects. Liberation from the treacherous minefield of passive individuality is indicated by a theoretical shift to defective social environment.

Passive-social assumptions about human subjects

Some theorists move away from privileging internal forces only to make external forces paramount. Thus we have social ecology theories, strain and subcultural theories, social learning theory and even some versions of Marxist and feminist criminology, that locate agency in the products of social activity.[8]

Criminological theorists taking a broadly sociological approach toward the human subject start out by suggesting that human subjectivity is a potentially creative, imaginative agency that can act in diverse ways, but that it is quickly limited to broad conformity with the prevailing social, cultural or structural environment through socialization and various structural constraints. In so far as there are seen to be significant differences in the social environment, there are likely to be significant variations in the ways people act. In other words, people are shaped by their environment.

Environmental constraint, in part, stems from people's interdependence and from their tendency to form social organizations with specialized role functions, which demand certain expected behaviors of their incumbents. Environmental constraint also comes from the structure of societal organization which, when based on hierarchical systems of domination, whether class, race or gender, with differential allocations of resources, precludes some people having the same range of behavioral choices had by others situated in different structural positions. Some, such as Agnew (1985; 1992a), have meshed this idea with the behaviorist pain–pleasure principle, suggesting that structural constraints can frustrate human pain avoidance, producing psychological stress.

An important contribution to the concept of human subjectivity brought by environmental and sociological approaches is an expanded conception of human learning. This is no longer tethered to the simplistic pain–pleasure/punishment–reward system but, through a process of socialization, includes learning about the social world, accruing knowledge about the appropriate behavior to accomplish tasks, and about how to successfully both perform and distance oneself from established social roles. Human appetites to act can therefore be structurally and culturally enhanced by the overall organizational system of society, manifest through socialization and social reproduction, as shown by various strain theorists' arguments (Durkheim, 1893; Merton, 1938; 1968). It can also lead humans to limited expectations of their own possibilities based on learned images of their capability or, conversely, to reject these as restrictive and unjust (Agnew, 1992a). Thus notions of justice and equity are seen as structurally contingent elements in human motivation to action (or inaction).

For differential association theorists (Sutherland and Cressey, 1966), it is the very process of human learning that provides all of what is human. This occurs as a person develops from a biological blank to a social being with beliefs, preferences and the capacity to think rationally and to choose reasonably. These theorists posit a universal process of social learning, involving interaction with intimate groups. The outcome of the learning process varies because of differences in the content of learning, rather than differences between human individuals. Thus variations in learning stem from differences in substructural classes and subcultural groups. So, from this perspective, different human types emerge as an outcome of the transmission of certain kinds of values, standards, skills, knowledge, techniques, motives, rationalizations and attitudes of socializers. Such learned knowledge is not simply imitated but taught so that the socialized human can use cognitive skills to determine the appropriate behavior for a typical context. Because of the variability and ambiguity of what is learned and the multiple affiliations that humans have with different sources of knowledge, the application of learned knowledge to social life can result in conflict and clashes of behavior between groups in different cultures or subcultures, which can include a transgression of societal laws (Sellin, 1938). It can also result in innovative use of language and thought processes that serve to resolve conflicts as non-problematic – at least in the eyes of the actor, and sometimes in the eyes of those whose rules have been violated (Matza, 1964).

Perhaps most extreme in this regard are the arguments of instrumental Marxists and radical feminists.[9] The former regard the human subject as an ideological product, the demoralized spirit and the false consciousness of the structures of class domination in a capitalist society (Bonger, 1916; Quinney, 1974; 1975). For Marxist feminists, men are socialized to dominant relations in the class structure of capitalism which are used as a basis of inheritance to perpetuate male class power. Finally, for radical feminists, humans are both biologically determined and repressed by gender power relations of patriarchal structures (MacKinnon, 1989). From these more extreme structural perspectives humans are shown not only to have their action limited by inner forces but, more significantly, to have it limited by determining social ones. This occurs to the extent that any residual human agency is channeled into, at best, a limited rational choice between socially learned sets of options facilitated by a class and/or patriarchal structure.

The value of theories holding passive-social assumptions about the human subject is that structural environment is given character and causal social agency: e.g. the 'identity' of the neighborhood, the 'culture' of the organization, the 'lure' of the gang, the 'pressure' of the peer group, the 'seductiveness' of subcultures, the 'order' of society, the 'exploitation' of the class system and the 'power and domination' of patriarchy. All are shown not only to actively influence human action but to write a particularly submissive subject, that excludes individual traits or choices.

As with biological and personality theory, the passive-social perspective certainly liberates human responsibility from the morality of action since, with so much causal agency, how can mere human subjects be accountable for their own folly? But it also liberates them from invasive individual treatment interventions. The conclusion is that whatever action is taken by humans it is as normal for them as it would be for any other human in their social environment: action is the result of the exercise of limited rational selection from a limited range of socially structured choices by humans who have little control over their capabilities, knowledge or circumstances, and virtually no insight into their part in these processes.

Again, what these approaches fail to explain adequately is the issue of difference. If the process of socialization is so total that any human placed in a similar learning context would conform to the group, culture or structure, from where does all the in-group difference and diversity come? Are biological and psychological differences between individuals enough to explain the diversity within groups, classes, races and genders? Deviancy theorists and others taking a more active-social view of human agency do not think that the passive, reactive, conforming human subject wrote the whole book, or even its most important story.

Active-social assumptions about human subjects

Social process theories move away from dichotomous arguments about freedom and constraint and develop more social-relational-oriented ideas on the human subject. Thus, some who give active and creative agency to human subjects focus on moral neutralization, bonding and social control, social interaction, labeling and social reaction, and social constructionism.[10] Others, who give a greater contribution to social structures while retaining the active (if unwitting) agency of individuals, include Weberian derived 'conflict' approaches, predominantly structural Marxists, anarchists, left realists, and socialist feminists.[11]

Human difference, from this perspective, is neither the outcome of choice, nor the product of forces; rather, it is the ongoing and changing property of human subjects in social interaction. The concept of meaning is central to explaining both human agency and human difference for several of the interactionist, labeling and social constructionist positions. The concept of meaning implies that humans and the social and physical world they inhabit have particular significance. It implies that this significance might coincide with that held by others in the past, present and future, and that, by changing how one acts individually or collectively, what is meaningful can be changed as it is being generated.

The idea that people act not only in response to stimuli, but based on what is meaningful, implies a sense of self-identity. Self-identity is drawn from how others acted toward the person in the past, and on how they act towards different others with whom one can identify or from whom one can dissociate. In other words, self-identity implies meaningful social experiences. Some theorists draw on Mead's (1934) distinctions between the 'I' and the 'me' in which the 'I' expresses a sense of the raw self, uncluttered by others, and where the 'me' represents an internalized sense of what others are expected to think and feel expressed as 'the generalized other'. Other theorists prefer Freud's similar distinctions between 'id' and 'super-ego'. In either of these constructions humans can actively make a difference in relation to others. At issue is Weber's insight that humans act by taking account of the actions of others. They do so in relation to their own sense of self, built up as a result of past interactions of the same kind and in an ongoing process of construction in the present. Thus, these theorists see humans as actively creating the meaningful nature of their world through a social process of interaction with others over time and simultaneously creating themselves in that process.

The medium for the process of meaning construction is communication through symbols and language. Symbols are conferred with meaning such that there is a tendency for humans to objectify their own contribution to human action. Thus they see meaning as societally pre-set and react to the words, gestures and cues of others as though all those interacting shared the same interpretation of actions and events. Unfortunately, this assumption, along with attempts to categorize social life, results in a confirmatory myth that meaning exists as an objective reality, rather than something created anew in each situation as human actors give new energy to acts and events they classify as 'the same'. Such is the power of human agency that it can lose its own authorship of social life to the meaningful constructs it ongoingly creates and recreates, a process referred to as 'reification' (Berger and Pullberg, 1966).

In this view of human subjects as active authors of their social world, human difference is not something pre-existing but is the outcome of the identification, definition and signification of features of others' existence or action. Differences are a human creation, and as such are subject to sustenance or change with regard to not only their significance, but even their recognition.

Not surprisingly, this vision of humans has been subject to considerable criticism from those who believe that the social world is a more permanent reality and that human behaviors are more subject to constraint than the interactionist and social constructionist versions would have us believe. Critics argue that even if the world is socially constructed, its repeated construction as substantially the same means we can assume it has a concrete reality. To ignore this is to attribute too much to human abilities to make a difference. For others, however, the conception of active human agency does not need to be abandoned in order to incorporate structure, but is tied to it such that human cultures, structures and discourse have a dynamic and changeable quality. This was the insight of the structural Marxist, Marxist feminist and socialist feminist positions.

Marxist informed criminological thought that emerged in the 1970s, and its 1980s eclectic form in the development of 'critical criminology', generally sees crime as an outcome of class conflict and economic exploitation. It assumes that dominant economic classes impose their ideological views on relatively powerless, disenfranchised, disempowered, and marginalized groups. Many subscribe to a vision of human subjects as active agents who transform the world in their use of it and accept that this exercise of agency simultaneously transforms those same humans in the process. Moreover, in so far as they collaborate with others in their use of the world, humans create a set of social arrangements unique for a particular historical period whose productive activity gives rise to changes in that world (and to themselves) which lead to new forms of collaboration and a new social world. At each period characterized by a similar set of collaborative relations of productive transformation, social institutions are formed and sustained that themselves exercise a force on their present creators and on those who work together in the future. For Marx, for example, on whose work radical and critical criminologists draw heavily for their ideas about the human subject, humans are primarily social beings who create the world in which they live, but not under conditions they have chosen for themselves, 'rather on terms immediately existing, given and handed down to them' (Marx, 1852: 115). Thus, 'Humans are both the producers and products of history; they create institutions and meaning within a particular historical period, which is in the last instance, determined by the mode of production of the time' (Young, 1981: 295).

At the same time humans are themselves made by the changes they make to the material world: 'As new needs emerge, people develop new means of satisfying the needs; the new products, in turn, give rise to still further needs, until the original human nature is completely transformed' (Jaggar, 1983: 54).

For Marxist influenced criminologists, the kind of social structure existing in the nineteenth and twentieth centuries, a capitalist society, had a particular effect on developing human agency, distorting its true potential. Whereas other theorists have argued that structures shape the opportunities for rational action or reflect the clash of groups having the different interests of their members, Marxists see capitalist social structure as actively amplifying some features of the human condition at the expense of others. For them, human identities are formed in cultural and structural arrangements that are divisive and fear generating. Rather than celebrate human cooperation, capitalist social structures generate self-images that are isolated and separate from each other. Thus, under capitalism humans see themselves less as social agents in a collective enterprise to transform the world through cooperative efforts, and more as individuals competing with each other to maximize their self-interests and individual material wealth.

In the capitalist celebration of individuality over sociability humans are claimed to be able to make a difference to their world for themselves, while simultaneously they are shown to be powerless. They are constructed as potentially able to succeed while being shown to be dependent upon those who own and control capital. They are encouraged to maximize their labor to enrich their lives while being shown that through this process their lives become more impoverished. As a result of these contradictions, humans are transformed from the potentially good and cooperative beings they would be under different social arrangements, into competitive, self-interested individualists, whose cooperation is instrumental – for defeating others and protecting themselves against others' invasions.

The structural-cultural matrix of capitalist society thus conceals and represses humanity's true potential and mutual dependence. It severs human interconnectedness, supplanting it with interdependence based on utility functions wherein humans 'conceive of themselves as isolated individuals, rather than as beings who are necessarily social' (Jaggar, 1983: 58).

Given this tendency to prioritize the power of capitalist social organization over the human subject's ability to see through it, it is perhaps not surprising that Marxist criminologists see the only possibility for a change in human condition to result from change in the structural conditions that generate its subjectivity. Unfortunately, the question never satisfactorily answered in the Marxist vision of the human subject (short of some grand revelation rooted in class interests, i.e. class consciousness) is that, if humans are so formed by the active social structure of capitalism, which in turn is energized by their daily interaction, how are they to free themselves from their own making? Moreover, if they are so susceptible to the capitalist structural form and its manufacturing of difference, what reason is there to expect that under an alternative structural form (e.g. socialism, communism, etc.) another difference, albeit no longer based upon property ownership and wealth, would not constitute a new basis of power relations? Further, in so far as difference would be celebrated, how would a new order prevent some specializing in the differences that they prefer rather than the differences they do not? And if such valuation is to be denied, what value has difference?

From our constitutive perspective the Marxist vision of the human subject is valuable in that it demonstrates how social organization is active in the making of human subjectivity, while acknowledging that social structures are themselves dynamically in a process of being produced and reproduced by active human agency. Marxism thus provides us with the constitutive dialectical interconnection between human subjects and their forms of social organization, recognizing that neither exists without the other and that in their existence each is a part of the other. As Marx said: 'the human essence is no abstraction inherent in each single individual. In its reality it is the ensemble of social relations' (1968: 29). Dialectically, then, human subjects and their social structures are co-producing.

Postmodernist visions: death and resurrection of the human subject

Postmodernism, especially in its skeptical form, is particularly opposed to the modernist construction of human subjectivity and its relationship to discourse, desire, and potential emergent identities.[12] The call is for an abandonment of centers or essences, whether these be of a subject or the subject's text, or framed from privileged or fixed reference points, and regardless of whether claims to truth embrace foundational first principles or origin (Sarup, 1989: 59). Most importantly, the notion of the human subject as a discrete 'individual' is seen as an ideological construct consistent with the overall logic of capitalist forms of social organization (just as the concept of 'socialist man' was an ideological construction of the logic of state socialist societies). As a result, for skeptical postmodernists the focus on establishing a centered subject is 'nonessential to their own analysis that concentrates on language, free-floating signs, symbols, readings and interpretations, all of which escape the concrete definitions and reference points required by the subject' (Rosenau, 1992: 43).

Those critical of skeptical postmodernism's vision of the subject argue that their anti-subject stance is unnecessarily extreme, rooted in its anti-modernity, anti-humanist position, and in its incorporation of the power to control others: 'Without a subject to announce logocentric meta-narratives, and without other humans with subject or object status to register recognition or approval, such devices are deprived of any voice, and theory cannot endure. This is consistent with post-modern skepticism about the possibility of theory altogether' (Rosenau, 1992: 50). The skeptical position has also been criticized for its assumptions that the subject is seen cast adrift in the floating sea of signifiers with little control of events, imprisoned within dominant discourse. However, one of the difficulties with the skeptical postmodernist position is that it caricatures the subject of modernism as but one type (the type we described above as active-individual), disregarding the modernist production of several human subjects, as demonstrated by our analysis of modernist criminological theory. As a result several affirmative postmodernists have called for a partial restoration, reinstallation or return of the subject and for a recognition that 'the death penalty may be too extreme a punishment for the subject' (Rosenau, 1992: 57). They argue that this repositioned human subject is necessary for reconstruction after deconstruction.

These affirmative postmodernists offer the notion of a *decentered subject*. This indicates that the human subject is not a unified entity or even a coherent social whole but is one or more ideological constructions, mere illusion (Derrida, 1978; Edelman, 1988). However, as constructions these illusions are inseparably connected to all that is written, spoken and gestured (i.e. discourse). Here they are constituted as positions in language (Flax, 1990). Moreover, because of the transience of discourse, this vision of subject can be better viewed as a subject-in-process or as an emergent subject (Kristeva, 1980; 1986; Moi, 1985; JanMohamed, 1994: 111; Young, 1992). Consequently, the subject in this special sense is decentered, never really being what it seems, always tending to be something else, an effect of discourse that changes as discourse changes. Indeed, as we have seen in analyzing criminologists' constructions of the human subject, these images are very different depending upon whose criminology is being written/read. The passive-individual human subject of biological theory is different from the active-individual human subject of rational choice theory and different again from the human subject of active-social agency. The issue from the affirmative postmodernist perspective is not which version of the human subject is true or correct, but what these accounts tell us about the power of thought through discourse to create a convincing truth claim about the reality of any subject. According to the postmodernist analysis, this construction process occurs via the power of discourse to evoke images through what words signify. Signifiers are acoustic images, psychic imprints. Different discourses construct different images of human subjects.

There are several postmodernist contributions that develop this idea of the human subject.[13] However, one of the key theorists whose work has been drawn on by affirmative postmodernists especially interested in discourse analysis is Jacques Lacan. Another dominant direction draws from chaos theory. To illustrate postmodernist analysis of the human subject we shall consider both, as well as some of their potentialities and limitations.

Lacan's construction of the human subject

Lacan has offered several views of the decentered subject. The schema in Figure 2.2 is his most rudimentary; he also develops more dynamic forms (Milovanovic, 1992a; Milovanovic, 1994a; Lacan, 1977).[14] In the figure (which Lacan refers to as his schema L) the subject can be depicted as simultaneously spread along two diagonal axes: an *intra*subjective axis on which a person communicates with their own unconscious self and an *inter*subjective axis on which a person speaks with another. These axes interplay. In this model *je* represents the 'I', the actual speaking or writing subject who assumes a position within a particular discourse (e.g. a defense counsel in trial proceedings). The *moi* is the imaginary construction of self seen through the other's eyes (e.g. the view a defense counsel has of herself as she believes the jury may see her).[15] It is the ego. The 'Other' is the domain of the unconscious, 'structured like a language' (e.g. a defense attorney's internalization and use of legal discourse, a discourse composed of value-laden signifiers, i.e. 'voluntary', 'malicious', or 'unintentional' behavior.[16] Lacan sees this 'Other' as a repository of floating signifiers charged with psychic energy seeking expression. The other 'other' is the person or persons with whom one shares discourse (interlocutes) (e.g. a member or the members of a jury). It is also an illusory idealization, an ideal ego.

The combined axis, *je*–Other, is the unconscious axis. The *moi*–other axis is imaginary. Both axes are at play, all at once, in discursive productions. The Lacanian subject is spread out along both axes to all four corners all at once. The human subject is therefore not only 'decentered', but also inter- and intrasubjectively constituted: that is, the subject is discursively constituted both via her/his internal conversation with self and through an external exchange with others. This subject is also implicated in three orders: (1) the Symbolic Order is the sphere of language and culture; (2) the Imaginary Order is the sphere of accumulated imaginary

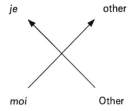

Figure 2.2   *Lacan's construction of the decentered subject*

constructions of self and others; and (3) the Real Order is the sphere of lived experience, beyond any accurate symbolization.

In Lacan's formulation, a desiring subject, the speaking subject (*l'être parlant*, or *parlêtre*), is embedded in a discourse. There is no separation between discourse and subjectivity (viewed here as the condition of individuality and self-awareness). Lacan portrays this as the 'fading subject' who disappears in its 'objects of desire'. In this portrayal, Lacan is suggesting that every word expressed embodies a person's unique being in the world, a combination of their biology, identity, circumstances, etc. The fading subject results from discursive production wherein the human subject is substituted by the 'thing' that is produced; the subject thereby disappears into the meaning of their words (e.g. gang members whose objects, paraphernalia, graffiti become the embodiment of idiosyncratic desire). Objects of desire are not necessarily literal objects but words describing entities or experiences that promise to overcome gaps between the lived experience and the human subject's place in the discursive system (consider a lover whose feelings of emotional love dissolve into symbolic gifts and adornments, even words and messages conferred upon the loved). These objects in turn come to stand for or represent the subject for other signifiers in discursive productions. They call out and invoke meaning in others all by themselves.[17]

A particular emerging signifier undergoes various stages of development from more unconscious to conscious. For example, consider the word 'them' uttered by an inmate to unconsciously refer to several forms of oppressive authority: cops, prison guards, school teachers, the system, 'the Man', etc. This discursive production not only expresses unconscious alienation and anger but can emerge to a more conscious form of anger as it is framed by and through different discourses such as the language of a court, or the language of a Farakan Muslim or an ethnic prison gang (e.g. Jack Henry Abbott's 1982 framing of anger via a version of Marxist sociology). This process of development takes place by way of what Milovanovic (1994a: 160–5) has referred to as three sets of semiotic axes: condensation–displacement, metaphor–metonymy, and paradigm–syntagm (see Chapter 1).

Lacan states in his 'elementary cell of speech production' that the subject is engaged in a two-stage process in the construction of meaningful

(i) The four positions

agent   other

truth   production

(ii) The discourse of the master

S1 (agent as sender signifies) ⟶ S2 (other as receiver produces signified
                                        image from learned knowledge)
$ (reinforces the sender's truth ⟵ a (image displaces other possibilities,
                                        excludes that on which it is silent)

(iii) The discourse of the university

S2 ⟶ a
S1 ⟵ $

(iv) The discourse of the hysteric

$ ⟶ S1
a ⟵ S2

(v) The discourse of the analyst

a ⟶ $
S2 ⟵ S1

Figure 2.3   *Lacan's discursive production of subjectivity and his four discourses (Lacan, 1991: 31)*

sentences. First, in an anticipatory way, the subject draws from the storehouse of signifiers (paradigm of word choices) and places them in correct linear form (syntagm). Next is a retroactive stage, whereby at any punctuation point or pause the subject goes back to the beginning of the developing word placements and grasps the whole meaning of what is being said, all at once.

Lacan maintains that four structured discourses shape subjectivity (Bracher, 1988; Milovanovic, 1993a). These discourses include four positions and four terms (see (i) in Figure 2.3). In the upper left-hand corner the term 'agent' represents the sender of some message. The 'other' in the upper right-hand corner is the receiver and enactor of some message. 'Production' in the bottom right-hand corner represents the effects in the unconscious. 'Truth' in the lower left-hand corner represents the unique truth for each person who sends the message. In parts (ii) to (v) of the figure, the symbol S1 represents master signifiers, which are key signifiers learned early through childhood socialization and reinforced or modified by the dominant political economic order (e.g. truth claims, core assumptions, ideologically charged symbols, etc.). Symbol S2 represents knowledge embedded in a discourse. Symbol $ represents the fading subject. Symbol a represents what is left out, the unspoken, in various discourses. Lacan offers many possible interpretations of a and has instructed his readers to understand it in context.

Four discourses, referred to as the discourses of 'the master', 'the university', 'the hysteric', and 'the analyst', are said to shape desire in particular ways. The discourse of the master is represented by the formula (ii) in Figure 2.3. This indicates that a sender of some message (S1) leads to an enactment of this material by the receiver (S2). In other words, s/he produces knowledge out of the material that is being sent to him/her. At the same time, this produces a certain 'left out' (a) in unconscious production (i.e. expression is denied to certain voices), which in turn reinforces the sender's truth, the basis of her/his message.[18] For example, consider a manager, say of a restaurant, who decides that traditional employee perks or payments in kind, such as food, that were allowed to be consumed on company premises, should be cut back. The manager decides to select a particular employee to 'set an example'. The manager, as agent, signifies that the employee should not be 'stealing' company property and if it happens again she will be fired. The employee produces an image of stealing based on the internalized collective or common-sense meaning this has, the implications of dishonesty, of publicity and future job loss, all of which squeeze out or deny the taken for granted meaning that payments in kind held for waiters, i.e. their shared and symbolic social understanding of working together, 'beating the boss', symbolic and social status, and so on. The signified recasting of these perks as 'stealing' half-completes the job of confirming the truth of the manager's message for the employee.

In the discipline of criminology we can see the effects of a master discourse at play in the explanation of various types of crime. Consider how Ditton's (1977) analysis of employee pilfering constructs a classical rationally calculating, materially focused, Machiavellian image of the human subject as pilferer who embodies 'the spirit of capitalism' in 'doing it for the money'. Contrast this with Henry's (1978) construction of a socially oriented subject as pilferer who embodies the 'spirit of community', 'doing favors' and 'helping people out'; in short, one who 'does it for love'. Each of these ethnographic accounts of pilfering leaves out the voice of the other's subject. Further examples of the master discourse in criminological accounts demonstrate that the subject is, to various degrees, imprisoned within discourses which facilitate the commission of a crime, and not least by the discourses of the criminologist as author.[19] The subject, in short, is discursively produced. Law can also be considered a version of the master discourse, though disguised in Lacan's second discourse, that of the university, illustrated by formula (iii) in Figure 2.3.

In the discourse of the university knowledge (S2), such as scientific knowledge, Christianity, or in our example, law as a body of knowledge, is offered to the 'other' (e.g. a defendant) as a framework for constructing 'what happened' in a particular event. This produces an alienated subject whose 'left out' (a) is that voice of the lived experience as it had been constructed during the discursive production of the referenced interaction which confirms the ideology of knowledge of the sender (here, law). What is most important in the discourse of the university is that something is left out, something remains unspoken, certain voices are not allowed expressive form in dominant discourses. The meaning of being a restaurant employee in our previous example is denied and narrowly framed in terms of an economic loss to the company, which the defense lawyer will likely represent in terms of the employer not treating like cases of dishonesty equally, or as has been done in the past or in industry generally. Hence the subject is not-all, *pas-tout(e)*, according to Lacan.

Various theorists have been influenced by Lacan's (1991) discourse of the master and university (Bracher, 1988; 1993; Milovanovic, 1993a). Lacan's notion of not-all as analyzed by feminist postmodernist analysis is perhaps the model form of how certain voices are left out of dominant symbolic understandings. Some feminist postmodernists, for example, have indicated how gender roles are created in discourse itself, one which is phallocentric in its very constitution (Irigaray, 1985).[20] A good illustration is provided by Smart's (1992) socio-legal analysis of law as a 'gendering strategy' in the human subject's construction. Smart (1992: 40), while seeing the subject as resistant and active in the construction of gender, also sees the power of law as a technology of gender as 'productive of gender difference and identity'. She distinguishes between the discursive construction of a type of woman and Woman. In defining certain behaviors as illegal, a type of woman is created as criminal, e.g. prostitute, female criminal, the un-married mother, the 'bad mother', etc. This definition sets women apart both as criminal and as being a Woman. Unlike men who may be criminal or not, in law the category of Woman is constructed twice. This 'double move' first constructs Woman as 'criminal woman' and second simul-taneously constructs 'Woman in contradistinction to Man'. As Smart says, 'the very foundation of the discursive construct of modern Woman is mired in this double strategy' (1992: 36).

Similarly, Althusser has offered the idea of the 'interpellated' subject, a person who has been constructed in a linear way by prevalent power arrangements. Metz (1981) and Silverman (1983) have offered the notion of the 'spoken subject' in cinema theory; Barthes (1974) has shown how, in a 'readerly text', subjects are constituted and reconstituted, whereas in the 'writerly text' they actively discover hidden voices and literary production devices.[21] Pecheux (1982) has shown the dynamics in the development of the 'good subject'. Foucault tells us how the subject is constituted by various 'disciplining mechanisms', the most noteworthy being the 'episteme' – historically sedimented discursive formations. Deleuze and Guattari (1987) have indicated how 'regimes of signs' (akin to Foucault's discursive formations) constitute subjects by 'territorializing' desire on the body.[22] Finally, Freire (1985) has indicated how colonizers force a mode of discourse on indigenous populations.[23]

Another suggestive line of postmodern inquiry, one that puts the 'false consciousness' thesis of much Marxist analysis in a different light, is to be found in Lacan's third discourse, that of the hysteric. In this formulation the alienated, disgruntled, brutalized, and despairing subject ($) attempts to communicate her/his plight to the 'other' but is offered only conventional categories and stereotypes (master signifiers) (S1) as explanations (e.g. clinically based diagnosis of disorders, stereotypical explanations of why such a person would do such a thing, dogma, etc.). This sustains a dominant ideology (S2) and leaves the hysteric not-all, with little support for a more satisfying construction of the situation.

Lacan's discourse of the hysteric, applied in a more general way toward the disenfranchised and disempowered, would reinforce a 'blaming the victim' ideology rather than provide the basis of linguistic empowerment. Indeed, the 'blaming the victim' ideology finds the psychic mechanism here for its continuance. Offenders, therefore, are often provided a narrative that 'explains' their evil or despairing ways, and hence offenders continue to have a relatively inarticulate explanation for their actions, often further used as evidence by modernist criminologists for the offender's irrational behavior (see, for example, Milovanovic and Thomas, 1989).[24]

The notion of discursive formation and constituted identities (subjects) influenced by Lacan suggests a transition to our constitutive position. As we have seen, the subject in this view is constituted by the assumption of various 'subject positions' existing within a discursive formation – 'every subject position is a discursive position' (Laclau and Mouffe, 1985: 109, 114–22). Meaning, too, is not a fixed entity. Transcendental signifiers do not exist; rather, the flow of differences is arrested by 'nodal points' (1985: 112), a term borrowed from Lacan in his idea of *point de capiton* whereby signifiers are temporarily attached to signifieds and given a provisional stability. A similar argument has been developed by Milovanovic (1993b) using Lacan's ideas concerning 'the Borromean knot', and how certain relations are fixed by a political economy and thereby produce a subject of desire who is in accord with socio-economic and political needs.[25] We might similarly consider criminology's many human subjects: classical and rational choice theory's 'economic subject', biology's 'genetic subject', personality theory's 'driven subject', ecology theory's 'disorganized subject', strain theory's 'maladapted subject', labeling and constructionism's 'creative subject', conflict theory's 'fighting subject', Marxist criminology's 'exploited subject', anarchist criminology's 'romantic subject', feminist criminology's 'gendered subject' and so on.

By applying Lacan's discourse of the master, for example, we can indicate how subjects are interpellated in their assumption of discursive subject positions intricately interconnected with other discursive subject positions within a particular criminology's discursive formation (linguistic coordinate system).[26] But the linear logic of each of these positions can be offset by comprehending the totality of their interrelations without losing sight of their specific subject positions, particularly in so much as in each of these constructions something, indeed very much, is 'left out'.[27] Moreover, following Irigaray's polemic on Lacan, a 'mimesis', a 'disruptive excess', of modernist criminology's human subjects can be the basis of an alternatively constructed discursive formation where different 'nodal points' might be established. In the negative and isolated presentation of these as competing discourses, pathways lead to essentialism and the reconstitution of previous forms of domination by way of a new self-justifying discourse of the master or university. An example of this is occurring with the establishment of the meta-narrative of 'integrated theorizing' in which tired but selected human subject positions are being melted together to form new authoritative multi-paradigms whose truth claim is that they lead to a more comprehensive understanding of the crime problem.

What is required instead of 'the alchemist's stone of integration' (Cohen, 1990) is a framework for analyzing discursive formations which renders the human subject polycentered and polyvocal, where subjects find an abundance of discursive subject formations within which to embody desire and to construct self, others, and society. Such a framework must not only recognize existing subject positions, all together, but be open to the incorporation of emergent forms. It must, therefore, be a contingent framework, one which is open to the ever-emerging subject, even to the 'recovering subject'. A possibly helpful direction in arriving at this position comes from chaos theory.

Chaos theory's construction of the human subject

Chaos theory has also offered a number of ideas on subjectivity that transcend modernist thought. While for several modernist positions the subject is centered, reflective, in control, self-directing, and whole, for the postmodernist chaos theorist the subject is decentered, unpredictable, spontaneous, and less in control. In chaos theory behavior occurring over time and space is plotted graphically which produces a visual pattern known as an 'attractor'. An attractor state refers to the regions in space toward which some complex phenomenon congregates. It is the area or region toward which a dynamic system is attracted. The term 'limit attractor' has been used by chaos theorists to indicate a tendency of system development or process to move toward some central point, or alternatively toward some outside limit. This is often diagrammatically portrayed as a circle implying closure (e.g. delinquents who undergo maturational reform, or the moral career of an alcohol abuser who tries to escape their addiction, repeatedly switching from detox and short-term sobriety to drunken binges until reaching 'rock-bottom'). Here there is little space for active human agency: the human subject is carried along a linear path to some limited position. For chaos theorists, however, the subject is a subject-in-process. This is better described as a 'strange attractor':

> a strange attractor is simply the pattern, in visual form, produced by graphing the behavior of a system in phase-space. Since the attractor tends to have a more or less stable geometric shape the system is said to be attracted to that shape. Since

the attractor does not fit the linear dynamics of Newtonian physics, it is said to be strange. Strange attractors are messy, fuzzy and fragmented, they have fractal geometry rather than Euclidean. (Young, 1991a: 3)[28]

An illustration of the strange attractor is found in Matza's (1964) neutralization theory of delinquency in his discussion of the delinquent human subject as one in 'drift', who moves along in time between convention and delinquency but who is uncommitted, who 'flirts now with one, now with the other' but who 'postpones commitment' and 'evades decision'. The strange attractor is often portrayed diagrammatically as what appears like butterfly wings, where movement takes place between at least two possibilities, termed 'attractor states' or 'butterfly attractors' (see Figure 2.4). A recent modernist reinterpretation of Matza's ideas shows a clipped version of the strange attractor (see Agnew, 1995: 85). Overall, one can be somewhat predictable, but at any instance indeterminacy prevails. Or in Agnew's modernist terms:

> behavior becomes more variable and less predictable as freedom of action and choice increases . . . Since the behavior of the individual in drift is no longer constrained by major social forces, it becomes more subject to the influence of minor events and temptations . . . The result is an increase in the variation and unpredictability of behavior. (1995: 90–1)

Agnew's concern is to specify more of the variables for the purpose of explaining differences in the level of and variation in crime between individuals or groups, ultimately for the purpose of prediction and control. However, the chaos theory version may equally allow us the imagery to 'provide space for human agency in ways not possible in those dynamics privileged by Newtonian physics, Aristotelian logic, Euclidean geometry and the linear causality they presume' (Young, 1992: 447). Here, as Young suggests, it is more a question of role-making than role-taking. For example, in the strange attractor, a person's outcome may be anti-social, pro-social, or something in between (where maximal indeterminacy prevails).

In short then, both Lacan and chaos theory provide useful starting points for our development. While Lacan makes a valuable move forward in showing the human subject is embedded in discursive formation, he also 'fragments' the subject into a series of analytical relational discourses, without showing how these may occur simultaneously. Thus we need to consider not only the stuttering and switching from one discourse to another, but how these might be occurring together. The freedom of chaos theory directs us to contingent outcomes, global prediction with local chaos.

Earlier we noted the limitations in the handling of human subjectivity by modernist criminological theorists. We have just shown that some post-modernist thinkers are grappling with the limitations found in skeptical postmodernism. However, notwithstanding a critique by some that post-modernist analysis is logically incapable of coming up with any coherent explanatory theories, given its assumptions about the death or dispersal of the subject, we see a number of emerging threads that together produce and

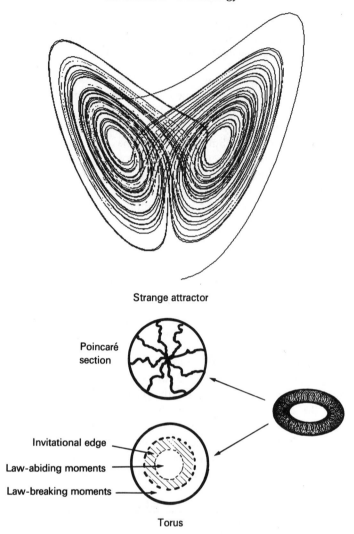

Figure 2.4 *Chaos theory's strange attractor and torus (software provided by Wegner and Tyler, 1993)*

build on the revised affirmative approach. This approach concerns the discursive co-production by subjects of social reality, which simultaneously constitutes those subjects. How we might build on these insights is the theme of our constitutive position.

Constitutive criminology and the 'recovering subject'

A constitutive view sees human subjects as active agents producing a dynamic social world which simultaneously produces them as both social and individual agents and as both active and passive identities. Both agents and structure are 'mutually constitutive', and their actions are both liberating and constraining. In addition to the ideas of Lacan and chaos theory, the structuration theory of Giddens (1984) in his seminal *The Constitution of Society*, Bourdieu's (1985; 1990; Bourdieu and Wacquant, 1992) notion of 'habitus' in his reflexive sociology, Freire's (1985) critical pedagogy, and Knorr-Cetina and Cicourel's (1981) social constructionism, have been particularly helpful here.

From Giddens we can see that production of both the constitutive human subject and the interrelated social order is continuous though it may appear continual. Moreover it is not necessarily fully reflexive:

> Human social activities . . . are not brought into being by social actors but are continually recreated by them via the very means whereby they express themselves *as* actors. In and through their activities agents reproduce the conditions that make these activities possible . . . Human action occurs as a *durée*, a continuous flow of conduct, as does cognition. Purposive action is not composed of an aggregate or series of separate intentions, reasons, or motives . . . 'Action' is not a combination of 'acts': 'acts' are constituted only by a discursive moment of attention to the *durée* of lived-through experience. Nor can 'action' be discussed in separation from the body, its mediations with the surrounding world and the coherence of an acting self. (1984: 2–3)

Indeed, Bourdieu argues that 'social agents are knowing agents who, even when they are subjected to determinisms, contribute to producing the efficacy of that which determines them in so far as they structure what determines them' (Bourdieu and Wacquant, 1992: 167–8; see also Freire, 1985). However, human subjects are not all-knowing agents. Social production may be continuous with regard to the ongoing production and reproduction of existing social order, but it is continual in that the world produced by human agency is only episodically perceived as the outcome of its own authorship: much of the time we are forgetful producers of our world. Most human subjects are then partially blind builders, intermittently aware that what they build is constructed by them, yet experientially subjected to the constructions they see in others. Typically, humans export their own agency to its product and to others with whom they interact (Lacan's 'fading subject'). They see themselves more acted on than acting. Because of what are encountered as overbearing conditions, human subjects submit to the dictates of their circumstances. This is a connivance in their subordination to the agency of others who are seen collectively as a greater reality, the power of the system, the government, the corporation, men, the Man.

From our perspective human agents can be envisioned as *both* unique, with a multiplicity of needs, drives, desires, and abilities, *and* inter-subjectively constituted: moreover these dimensions are constituted at both a conscious and an unconscious level. Any subsuming of such qualities to some 'equal' measure of their similarity, as in the concept of 'rational man', is an exaggeration of one constitutive dimension of their multifaceted socially and discursively constructed nature. Similarly, exaggeration of any one dimension of their difference, as in biological or personality traits, does injustice to their similarity. These are reductionist abstractions from aspects of the decentered human subject which, while able to be analyzed separately, are meaningless unless reconstituted in the totality of human biography as this is discursively constructed in particular culturally and historically specific societies. To imagine that, alone, such caricatures are enlightening is to submit to the folly of reductionism and holism. Instead, we might incorporate Bourdieu's (1984) notion of 'habitus':

> the cumulative, durable totality of cultural and personal experiences that each human being carries around as a result of life experiences (speech, mannerism, style of dress, table etiquette, posture, body shape). All these are found to have an impact on how one is perceived, on the patterns of interaction involving others, on the formation of the parameters that govern social outcomes. Habitus . . . is unique to each individual, it requires a specific, noncollective subject. (Rosenau, 1992: 59)

Human subjects then are also *both* individually self-interested *and* socially cooperative. Denial of either one of these apparently opposed dimensions is itself an actively sustained ideological construction with real and often negative consequences for self and others. Human subjects are interconnected agents rather than entirely free 'individuals'. Constructing the delusion of personal freedom can spur the action that sustains and symbolizes that claim through physical and momentary displays of difference, individuality, uniqueness, art, and style. Changing jobs and neighborhoods, leaving lovers and old lives to make new ones, taking a step beyond the invitational edge, often provides a sense of personal control, a perhaps delusional security from the precariousness of human existence that comforts restless souls. Regardless of its rationality and emotion, it is nothing if not discursive display.

The substance of being human must, therefore, entail what preceded us as biography, what looms ahead as prospect, caught in the contingent moment of the here and now, plowed by the discordant strands of unconscious processes. Human subjects, written as people, are process, moments of process, subjects-in-process. Human subjects are social projects in their own making. No amount of delusionary discursive display can sever the fundamental intrasubjectivity and intersubjectivity of the human subject in being. Without a discursive medium constructed with others through which people converse with themselves, without their unique turn of our cultural conglomerate of meaning, they and we would cease to exist. Connectivity to others is a partial life-blood that constitutes the constituted self, but it is as separate entities that the intersubjective discursive medium is invoked, through *it* that meaning is created and interpreted, and in terms of it that social structures are reproduced. Without the active individual human agent there would be no intersubjectivity, no society. In short, freedom and constraint, agency and subject, individual and social, are mutually implying, co-present themes in the constitution of human beings.

Human agency is connected to the structures that it makes, as are human agents to each other in making those structures.

Just as agents make structure so the structure makes agents through discourse. A central issue in constitutive criminology's vision of the human subject is the role of human subjects' discursive practices. This is not to reify human subjects by giving priority to their discourse, as though this somehow operated independently of those using it. We do not 'slide into the reverse notion of a language which itself produces' (Lauretis, 1989: 240). Rather, we stress the interwovenness of both agency–discourse–structure and individual–action–social.

This does not mean that humans are unable to create new meaning while recreating the old, though when they do, it is also done in interaction with others in an active, discursively constituted, structural context. Here humans are considered social projects in the process of continually creating themselves through the wider social context. In doing so, they recreate that context which channels and shapes their own human identity and its potential.

Consider, for example, Freire's dialogical pedagogy and his analysis of 'speaking true words' (1972: 57–67).[29] For him, a word has two elements: action and reflection. These are in a dialectical relationship. A 'true' word is constituted by both elements (1972: 75; 1985: 50) such that 'There is no true word that is not at the same time a praxis. Thus to speak a true word is to transform the world' (1972: 75). In his conceptualization, if either action or reflection is absent when subjects 'speak' to the world, they fall short of transformative activities in their very act of 'speaking'. This is a component sustaining the 'culture of silence' (1985: 50). In other words, the word is work. The word, absent either action or reflection, is, respectively, verbalism or activism (Peters and Lankshear, 1994: 178). Here, the word is unauthentic. It results 'when dichotomy is imposed upon its constitutive elements' (Freire, 1972: 75). In speaking 'true words', however, persons change the world: they become active agents in the process of becoming (1972: 76, 167; Peters and Lankshear, 1994: 178; McLaren, 1994: 200). The recovering subject, then, is one who is recovering the dialectical play of the word. And for Freire,

> To exist, humanly, is to *name* the world, to change it. Once named the world, in its turn, reappears to the namers as a problem and requires of them a new *naming*. Men [women] are not built in silence, but in word, in work, in action-reflection. (1972: 76)

Moreover, 'no one can say a true word alone'; rather, humans find themselves in dialogical encounters where the two speakers (interlocutors) are jointly engaged in 'an act of creation' (1972: 77, 167–8; 1973: 43–58).

Knorr-Cetina and Cicourel (1981) have shown us further how this process operates to produce social structures and social forms. They say that human agents transform events that they see or experience as micro-events into 'summary representations', or mind patterns, by relying on routine practices through which they convince themselves of having achieved the appropriate representation of those events; these are then objectified in coherent narrative constructions. Narrative constructions are essentially composed of words (as well as non-verbal cues and gestures and which collectively can be described as signifiers of meaning) that are routinely invested with value. These words are coordinated by the store of socially available words (signifiers) with delineated meanings and by the codes governing the correct placement of the words in utterances or sentences in order to make sense (syntagm). At the macro, societal level, in Western industrial society, capital logic and the integrally related processes of rationalization provide the medium through which people constitute categories that capture essential relations. Not the least are rhetorical structures, figurative expressions, metaphors, clichés, and verbal manner-isms that are used as primary signifiers of meaning. At the levels of intersubjective communication, organizational processing, and capital logic, discursive practices are anchored to meaningful contexts (Lacan, 1977; Manning, 1988; Milovanovic, 1989b; 1992a). Humans use discursive prac-tices to produce texts (narrative constructions) – imaginary constructions that anchor words to particular meanings, producing a particular image claiming to be the reality. These texts become the semiotic coordinates of action, which agents recursively use and, in so doing, provide a recon-struction of the original form.

Once social structures are constituted as summary representations, their ongoing existence depends upon their continued and often unwitting reconstruction in everyday discourse, a discourse replete with tacit under-standings whose basis lies outside the realm of intrinsic intersubjective communication and intersubjectively established meaning. Core meaning constructs are typically pre-constructed elsewhere as part of our common 'stock of knowledge' (Manning, 1988; Schutz, 1967). Agents in organiz-ational settings, for example, tend to reduce feedback which represents contaminating and disruptive 'noise' and in the process infuse existent explanatory discursive categories and texts with energy and sustenance.

In order to sustain abstractly constructed distinctions, these are made applicable to events, in spite of the contradictory evidence that comes from renewed micro-interaction. Contradictory evidence and potential disrup-tions are engendered by the internal transfer of messages, a basis of instability that is best negotiated by framing it into already understood narrative constructs that 'beg' us to make old reaffirming sense of the new nonsense (Goffman, 1974; 1981; Manning, 1988; Thomas, 1988).

Organizing action to defend representations – framed and objectified in narrative texts – is one of the principal means of both defending and conferring object-like reality upon them, providing life, form, energy, sustenance and a high degree of permanence.

Capital logic is a ubiquitous rationalizing social form: the more investment that is made in it, the more difficult it is to sustain that which it is not. This is not to imply conspiracy but to specify formal function, for while defending the wider totality, agents and agencies also compete to defend their own integrity within the framework of capital logic (Jessop, 1982).

As a result of the power of human investment in the social reproduction of existing structures, only rarely is the world perceived as open to transformation and change by those who experience it. Even then it is where subjects confront the 'invitational edge' that identities seem to fundamentally change. From this viewpoint, the human subject's qualities are envisioned not as fixed but as open to change through their relations with others. Such change is possible because of the potentials inhering in reflexivity about oneself and sensitivity to others to whom we relate and with whom we can empathize (Freire, 1972; 1985). Garza (1992) illustrates the duality of control and freedom inherent in structural forms, showing how the dynamic of oppression contained in the discourse of the dominant culture excludes, denies and subordinates the Chicana (and other persons of color), imposing an identity, a value, or attributes of its own. Unless they use the dominant discourse, she says, they are illegitimate and marginal to the dominant culture, but when they do use it they deny themselves, fracture themselves, lose themselves. Echoing postmodernism and drawing on chaos theory, she says that to speak in the existing discourse merely reproduces and remakes the very structures that oppress. Thus, she urges Chicana women to embrace and exalt the difference that they represent 'as a tool of creativity and to question the multiple forms of repression and dominance' to which they are subjected, for herein lies their source of power, emerging out of the 'instances of disequilibrium' (1992: 11, 12). She says, 'Chicanas must separate from the dominant discourse and continue to formulate their own space and language, always conscious of multiple differences' (1992: 13).[30] Thus Garza (1992: 1) glimpses the possibility that humans can develop a 'replacement discourse' (Henry, 1987a; 1994; Henry and Milovanovic, 1991; 1994) which shows us how to be self-reflectively aware and how human agency can be active in its own subordination and liberation.

Summary and conclusion

To summarize, we suggest that a constitutive criminological vision of the human subject must be open to its diversity and specificity, as well as contingently formed so as to adjust to emerging renditions of subjectivity. For this reason, we might use the term 'recovering subject'. Such a view allows the theorist, like the recovering alcoholic, to be continuously aware that there are forces over which the subject has little control and there are others over which it can exercise great control. The human subject can never be 'recovered' because this limit is only reachable under the delusion that allows some contingent constitutive elements to slip away. Instead the recovering subject must, one day at a time, confront the 'reality' of a decentered self by reclaiming the spaces between multiple subjectivities in order to forge new ones, all the time aware of attractions to the old. With this contingent recovering subject in mind we can now gaze through the other side of the constitutive lens at how social structure is constituted.

Notes

1 We have elected not to use the micro–macro continuum here since it does not discriminate between isolated or unitary individuals at the micro-end of our continuum and it excludes small-group relations from the macro-end. We prefer the continuum individual–social which accommodates the full range of possibilities of degrees of subjectivity. Consider Agnew's (1995: 90) assumption about the theory of determinism and indeterminism: (1) 'behavior may range from fully determined (no freedom of action or choice) to largely free (much freedom of action and choice)'; (2) 'the extent to which behavior is determined is a function of individual and social factors.' Further, we prefer active–passive agency instead of freedom–determinism, since this allows the possibility of humans' complicity in their own determinism.

2 This would also include other critical approaches which assume a historically situated active-social subject who often inadvertently co-produces reified and hegemonic structures of domination.

3 For classical criminology, see Beccaria (1764) and Bentham (1765); for neo-classical theorists, see American Friends Service Committee (1971), Fogel (1975), Von Hirsch (1976), Roshier (1989); for economists of crime, see Becker (1968), Ehrlich (1973; 1982), Sullivan (1973), Heineke (1978; 1988); for rational choice theory, see Clarke (1983; Cornish and Clarke, 1986; 1987); for routine activity theorists, see Cohen and Felson (1979) and Felson (1986; 1987); and for control theory, see Hirschi (1969; Gottfredson and Hirschi, 1990).

4 For the control theory version, the freedom to act can be limited depending upon the extent of bonding that occurs between significant primary or intimate group socializers and those subjected to the learning process (Hirschi, 1969; Gottfredson and Hirschi, 1990). This qualification moves the active-individual model of the human subject toward both the passive and social ends of the scale, but within those limits, individuals are still held accountable as active agents.

5 Although the neo-classical and post-classical rational-choice-based theories are careful to qualify the freedom of agency, they nonetheless still prioritize individual agency by holding humans responsible for their actions.

6 For biological focused theories see, for example, Lombroso (1876), Ferri (1896), Garafalo (1814), Goring (1913), Hooton (1939), Sheldon et al. (1949), Glueck and Glueck (1950), Mednick (1974), Mednick et al. (1987), Jeffery (1993; 1994), Ellis (1988), Wilson and Herrnstein (1985). For psychological/psychiatric theories, see Freud (1927; 1950), Healy and Bronner (1936), Aichhorn (1935), Eysenck (1977; Eysenck and Gudjonsson, 1989), Halleck (1971), Yochelson and Samenow (1976; Samenow, 1984), Salecl (1991).

7 On the way the media and geneticists discursively construct extreme versions of biological determinism in the popular culture, by using 'overblown rhetoric and misleading metaphors' that in turn help establish an importance for their research, see Nelkin (1993).

8 On traditional social ecology theories, see Park and Burgess (1925), Thrasher (1927), Shaw and McKay (1942), Suttles (1968). On more recent geographic spatial and community-based social disorganization theory, see Brantingham and Brantingham (1981; 1984), Sampson (1987), and Bursik and Grasmick (1993). On traditional anomie and strain theory, see Durkheim (1893; 1951), Merton (1938); and for subcultural strain, see Cohen (1955), Cloward and Ohlin (1960). For recent revised approaches to strain, see Agnew (1985; 1992a). On differential learning theory, see Sutherland (1939), Cressey (1960), Jeffery (1965), Burgess and Akers (1966), Akers (1985); and on social learning theory, see Bandura (1973; 1977; 1979). On the distinction between instrumental and structural Marxism, see Beirne (1979): examples of

instrumental Marxism include Bonger (1916), Quinney (1974; 1975). Consider also the radical feminism of MacKinnon (1989).

9 On the distinction between instrumental and structural Marxism, see Beirne (1979); on the distinction between liberal, Marxist, socialist and radical feminist positions, see Daly and Chesney-Lind (1988), Simpson (1989), and Muraskin and Alleman (1993).

10 On moral neutralization theory see, for example, Cressey (1953), Sykes and Matza (1957; Matza and Sykes, 1961; Matza, 1964), and Scott and Lyman (1970). For classic social control theory, see Reiss (1951), Reckless (1973), Nye (1958), Toby (1957), Hirschi (1969; 1983); and for more recent developments, see Gottfredson and Hirschi (1990) and Krohn (1991). For a sampling of the literature on symbolic interactionism, see Cooley (1902; 1909), Mead (1934), Goffman (1959), Blumer (1969); and for labeling and social reaction applications, see Lemert (1951; 1967), Becker (1963), Kitsuse (1964), Lofland (1969), Matza (1969), Mankoff (1971), Young (1971), Schur (1971), Cohen (1979). For social constructionism, see Sudnow (1965), Cicourel (1968), Quinney (1970), Douglas (1972), Pfhul and Henry (1993).

11 On classic and contemporary conflict theory see, for example, Simmel (1955), Sellin (1938), Vold (1958), Turk (1966; 1969), Quinney (1970), Chambliss and Seidman (1971), Box (1971; 1983), Hills (1971), Krisberg (1975), Pepinsky (1976), Reiman (1979). On structural Marxism, see Gordon (1973), Taylor et al. (1973), Quinney (1977), Platt (1974), Chambliss and Seidman (1982), Spitzer (1975), Greenberg (1981), Schwendinger and Schwendinger (1983), Michalowski (1985), Box (1987). On anarchist criminology, see Pepinsky (1978), Tifft and Sullivan (1980), Ferrell (1993; 1994), DiCristina (1995). On left realism, see Young (1979; 1986; 1987; Lea and Young, 1984; Matthews and Young, 1986; 1992; Young and Matthews, 1992), MacLean (1991; Lowman and MacLean, 1992). On socialist feminism see, for example, Klein (1980), Smart (1984), Carlen and Worrall (1987), Naffine (1987), Cain (1990), Daly and Chesney-Lind (1988), and Currie (1992).

12 See, for example, Huyssen (1986), Sarup (1989), Borgmann (1992), Best and Kellner (1991), Dews (1987), Rosenau (1992), and Milovanovic (1992a; 1995).

13 For example, Foucault (1973), Derrida (1978), Baudrillard (1983a), Edelman (1988), and Flax (1990).

14 These include his 'graphs of desire' and his notion of the 'Borromean knots' (Lacan, 1977; Milovanovic, 1993b; 1994a: 165–6). Lacan's ideas here have some similarities to the works of both Mead and Freud.

15 There are some similarities here to Mead's (1934) concept of the 'self' as an object emerging from role-taking, whereby people place themselves in the position of others and look back on themselves as they believe others do and become objects to themselves. Mead pointed out that when persons place themselves in the position of the collective view they can see themselves as a social status which he calls the 'generalized other'.

16 Lacan's 'Other' is also similar to Freud's concept of super-ego.

17 Lacan symbolized this relationship as '$\cancel{S}$<>a', where $\cancel{S}$ is the fading subject and a its objects of desire.

18 In various scholarly works, this effect has been called interpellation (Althusser, 1971), the 'good subject' (Pecheux, 1982), and the 'spoken subject' (Silverman, 1983; see also Deleuze and Guattari, 1987). It suggests a strong version of linguistic determinism.

19 Illustrations on juvenile delinquency, violence against women and 'white collar' crime can be found in the works of Schwendinger and Schwendinger (1985), Cressey (1953), Sykes and Matza (1957), Katz (1988), Salacl (1993), and Schwartz and Friedrichs (1994). Consider the examples of colonial powers making use of the master discourse to subjugate the indigenous population, and the imposition of a male-centered discourse in society.

20 For a good overview see Grosz (1990), Sellers (1991).

21 See also Deleuze and Guattari's (1986) analysis of 'major literature', akin to the readerly text, and 'minor literature', akin to the writerly text.

22 See also Howe's (1994) postmodernist feminist critique of Foucault's penality in which she describes his work as 'profoundly masculinist' and states that his valorizations of male inmates and the punishment of men 'overlook the question of gender, or better still, the deeply

sexed nature of punishment regimes and, by extension, their own analytical frameworks' (1994: 2).

23 See also Giroux (1992), Aronowitz and Giroux (1991), and Lecercle (1991).

24 Figure 2.3 also shows Lacan's fourth logical possibility, the discourse of the analyst. We do not need to go into this relatively unstable form here, but see Milovanovic (1993a), and see also Chapter 8.

25 For example, consider again Foucault's (1977) subject of docility and utility; Deleuze and Guattari's (1987) subject with constituted 'territorialized desire'; Althusser's (1971) 'interpellated subject'; cinema theory's 'spoken subject' (Silverman, 1983); and Pecheux's (1982) 'good subject'.

26 For an elaboration of this framework see Milovanovic (1993a; 1993b; 1994b; 1994c) and Arrigo (1994b; 1995).

27 Cornell (1991: 146, 171), following Lacan, refers to the 'left out' as 'slippage' and 'excess'.

28 Rather than integers of space (i.e. whole numbers 1, 2, 3, . . .), the fractal nature of space (derived from fractal geometry) indicates that fractions of dimensional spaces can exist. For example, close scrutiny of a coastline shows that, depending on the decreasing scale of observation, the length of the coastline increases infinitely. Thus a coastline may have a dimension between one and two (Mandelbrot, 1983). A cloud has more than two dimensions but less than three; and so on. Rather than having Boolean logic (yes/no, on/off, input/output) in law to determine truth or lie, there exist truth values that may vary between 0.0 and 0.99 (Young, 1991a), hence illuminating the gray scale of the honesty–dishonesty continuum.

29 See also Freire (1973; 1985: 50–4) and Peters and Lankshear (1994: 177–8).

30 See also Freire (1985), McLaren (1994), and Giroux (1992).

3

Society and Social Structure: Criminology's Visions of the House of Social (Dis)order

Just as they construct the human subject so, in thinking and writing about crime, criminologists and social theorists envision certain images or representations of society's structure which shape their explanations. Structure here includes a society's form and organizational arrangement, the nature, extent and basis of any government, and the specific practices embodied in its culture and subcultures as these are constituted in institutional arrangements and human consciousness.

In both functionalist and conflict versions of society structure is understood to be a patterning of social relations, 'often naively conceived of in terms of visual imagery, akin to the skeleton or morphology of an organism or to the girders of a building' (Giddens, 1984: 16). First, at its simplest, social structure has been defined as the total pattern of social organization produced by a culture's social practices. In the Spencerian (Spencer, 1858) and Durkheimian (Durkheim, 1893) derived functionalist versions, structure is described through the organic analogy wherein constitutive groups and institutions each have roles and status positions that are interconnected through a network of relationships (Fletcher, 1977: 584).

Second, the conflict version of social structure appeared in the sociological writings of Simmel, Weber and Dahrendorf and in the criminological works by Vold (1958), Turk (1969), and Quinney (1970). Later positions were Marxist oriented: in their various ways they saw the fundamental conflict in society between those capitalists who owned the means of production and those exploited wage-workers who only owned their labor. In the conflict-Marxist version then, architecture supplants organism in metaphoric imagery as people enter 'relations of production' whose 'totality ... constitutes the economic structure of society ... the real basis on which is erected a legal and political superstructure and to which correspond the forms of the determined social conscience' (Marx, 1859: 425).

In contrast, a third version of social structure, described in the anthropological works of Morgan (1877) and in Weber's (1978) sociology of human action, introduces the dynamic flow of structure as a system of actions and a process of interaction between actors oriented toward each other (Parsons and Shils, 1951; Parsons, 1951). Such a view allows ongoing transformations in the form of ordered change but, unlike the conflict view and more recent postmodernist approaches, does not account for disorderly change.

A fourth version of social structure, or perhaps more accurately 'unstructure', has been suggested by postmodernists who draw from chaos theory. Whereas the three versions of structure sketched above were predicated on privileging order, chaos theorists privilege disorder; order is but the deviant case. In chaos theory's description of social structure, far-from-equilibrium conditions and non-linear dynamics exist where chance, spontaneity, and a degree of indeterminacy prevail. In chaos theory, non-linearity means that disproportional outcomes can arise such that small inputs can produce large effects.[1] Within these environments 'dissipative structures' simultaneously imply a falling apart and a building up. These structures exist or 'live' in far-from-equilibrium conditions. 'Far-from-equilibrium conditions' refers to conditions where the smallest of fluctuations can produce radically new behavior.[2] Dissipative structures tend toward spontaneous self-organization and represent 'structures' of disorder (dissipative) and of order (structure). Dissipative structures are in continuous transformational states. They are able to overcome the conservative tendencies toward equilibrium by their continuous exchange with the immediate environment (Prigogine and Stengers, 1984; Briggs and Peat, 1989). This is understood in Nietzsche's philosophy, developed by Foucault in his idea of 'genealogical analysis', and in Unger's (1987) work on the call for a 'superliberalism', replete with criticizable institutions that are acutely responsive to the changing conditions of the socio-economic environment. It is explicit in Deleuze and Guattari's (1987) analysis of the 'rhizome', an indeterminate journey of desire seeking embodiment in signifiers and discourse (a conceptualization which indicates a non-linear flow).[3]

In this chapter it is not our purpose to exhaustively analyze criminological thought on the variety of forms of social structure, as this has been done elsewhere (Young, 1981; Empey, 1982; Einstadter and Henry, 1995). Rather, we intend to briefly review the range of images of society contained in the criminological and related literature with a view to seeing how each may inform our emergent constitutive criminology whose vision of social structure is more consistent with that contained in chaos theory and with Giddens' (1984: 17) notion of structure as a '"virtual order" of transformative relations'. Indeed, Giddens' analysis suggests that, in conceiving of social structure, we need to 'acknowledge both a syntagmatic dimension, the patterning of social relations in time–space involving the reproduction of situated practices, and a paradigmatic dimension, involving a virtual order of "modes of structuring" recursively implicated in such reproduction' (1984: 17). Our discussion will again be divided into modernist, postmodernist and constitutive approaches. Let us begin with a brief survey of modernist visions of society and social order.

Modernist visions of social structure and social order

For the most part, criminological ideas about social structure remain implicit. Exceptions are found in theories that have structure as a central feature of their causal analysis, such as strain theory, some varieties of feminist theory, conflict theory, Marxism, and recent critical/radical criminology.

In surveying these images of structure it is possible to identify several recurrent themes. These include: (1) whether the society is viewed as having a central government; (2) the assumed nature of its constitutive units; (3) the basis on which division or difference between constitutive units of the society is constructed; and (4) whether the whole society is seen to maintain order via a consensus on core values, norms and ideas, or whether it is viewed as primarily in conflict such that social order is an emergent and unstable outcome of continual struggle between its constituent elements.

Based on various combinations of these themes it is possible to further identify six basic images of social structure. These have been termed 'consensus acephalous', 'pluralistic', 'consensus power hierarchy', 'class hierarchy', 'power class hierarchy' and 'dual power class hierarchy' (Einstadter and Henry, 1995: 7–10).

The 'consensus acephalous' model depicts society as having a simple, non-hierarchical social structure and a relatively equal distribution of power between constitutive units, envisioned as families, households or cooperative work units.[4] A variation has the society structured by patriarchy through a simple division of labor based on gender distinctions. In either case, consensus is based upon allegiance to a common set of values and norms. Conflict is seen to be minimal as a result of mutual cooperation between units or (in the variant case) because of patriarchal dominance, dependence and persuasive practices within units (Kropotkin, 1912).[5]

A 'pluralistic' model is identified in the writings of interactionists, labeling theorists and conflict theorists. In this representation, alliances are seen to form between individuals, families, occupational specialties and/or other constitutive units around shared interests and beliefs. However, these social formations are separate from the shared interests and beliefs of others with whom they conflict, implying a weakness in societal consensus and multiple competing social orders. Criminologists embracing the pluralist model see a struggle for control, not only over economics but also over different interpretations of moral, religious, legal and social ideologies. They believe conflict serves as the driving force of society, continually threatened with instability and fragmentation. For example, Quinney (1970) posits a diversity of powerful 'segments' in conflict. A similar image is painted by social ecologists and the early Chicago School criminology (Park and Burgess, 1924; Shaw and McKay, 1942) and culture conflict theory (Sellin, 1938). Here pluralism occurs in the struggle for space among newly arrived ethnic immigrant groups in the cities of industrial nations. But structural differentiation is translated into cultural diversity and a consensual mainstream culture is hypothesized as a dominant and absorbing force.[6]

Of the varieties of hierarchical social structure in criminological theorizing, the multiple-strata 'consensus power hierarchy' is depicted as a hierarchically ranked class structure with upper, middle and lower class differentiations based on occupational structure and/or status and prestige rankings of social position. Although this model portends less consensus than is conjured up by the decentralized model discussed above, it displays relative stability; and its adherence to common societal values, expressed through such concepts as the 'dominant or mainstream culture', the 'prevailing ideology', the 'silent majority' and the 'American dream', consumes but does not digest a diversity of individual differences and a multiplicity of subordinate subcultures and ethnic groups.

The consensus hierarchy is also found as the contractual society of classical and neo-classical criminology, where 'free' individuals realize their own potential under the security and protection of a *laissez-faire* state (Beccaria, 1764; Bentham, 1765; Roshier, 1989). It emerges again as the residual outcome of individual decision-making in economic theories of crime including wealth maximization theory and time allocation theory, and in rational/situational choice and routine activities theory.[7]

This same stratified model is also to be found in biological theory where it is encountered as a reflection of the natural human differentiation in a given environment. Similarly in personality theory, control theory, and social learning theory, the stratified model appears as a measure of adequate socialization patterns, the strength of the family institution, and/ or an indicator of who is protected from personal trauma and crises.[8]

Indeed, even where individuals are assumed to start out as social blanks, as in social learning theory, a pre-existing hierarchical structure of differential opportunity is held as the framework wherein culturally imbued individuals and groups compete to succeed, by whatever means, at goal achievement. This takes place within a system of regulated order and rarely offers a direct challenge to the overall order, regardless of prevailing perceptions of its injustice. This is evident most clearly in anomie, strain and subcultural strain theory.[9] Absent in these essentially consensus functionalist views of the differentiated hierarchical model of society is anything other than a 'shadow' integrative role for constructions of the state. This contrasts markedly with the strong rendering of the state in critical conflict criminologies.

The single consensus power hierarchy comprises a dominant economic elite and a subordinate mass, which derives from Simmel's, Weber's and Dahrendorf's sociology and is perhaps the simplest of the conflict models. Turk (1969) and Vold (1958), for example, argue that some groups emerge from the plurality of conflict to command an authority relationship over others who have to learn to be subordinate. In the consensus power hierarchy model the process becomes less coercive, tending toward consensus as new generations are born into existing structural arrangements, including established rules, laws and ideology, through which they are socialized into giving consensual assent to the structure of power.

A sedimented version of this model is found in Quinney's (1974; 1975) 'instrumental Marxist' criminology.[10] Quinney presents society as economically divided between a dominant elite of powerful monopoly capitalists and a mass of proletarian wage-laborers. Here monopoly capitalists own powerful corporations, banks and insurance companies, and through trustees give money to influence elite foundations, elite associations, elite universities and research institutes. As a result the corporate rich are said to totally orchestrate the political economy of the state, and through it to control state law. With the assistance of lieutenant capitalists and criminal justice practitioners they coercively repress the subordinated masses.

A similar instrumental power hierarchy model is found in radical feminist criminological theory. However, in contrast to conflict theorists and instrumental Marxist approaches, the major structural differentiation is gender inequality in a patriarchal society. Here men form the dominant elite in all areas of public and private life, and maintain this position via the aggressive violent control and exploitation of women's sexuality. The socio-legal work of MacKinnon (1987; 1989) is illustrative. As with the basic instrumental model, MacKinnon's analysis presents a male state and legal system, coalescent with the economically powerful, regulating women as male property.

In contrast, in anarchist criminology (Tifft and Sullivan, 1980; Ferrell, 1994) power is envisioned as any authority over others, especially by a centralized elite fomenting and feeding off divisions between class, gender and race.

A more sophisticated analytical version of the class-conflict model is the 'dual power class hierarchy'. Here, although society is hierarchically ordered, conflict between economic classes is artificially minimized by a semi-autonomous state that mediates relations with the powerful economic elite (Poulantzas, 1978). There exists a mutuality of interests between these dual power holders, mediated by such organizations as political lobbyists, Political Action Committees (PACs) and the mass media. Moreover, in each of the dominant groups, a plurality of constitutive units are in conflict as well as cooperating with each other (Jessop, 1982). Thus, in a capitalist society, the dominant economic elite is said to comprise competing corporate, business, financial and professional interests while the political elite is composed of powerful competing political groups, bureaucratic agencies, think tanks, foundations and associations, any of which may ally themselves with the powerful groups that cross-cut differentiated subordinate classes. In this imagery, structural arrangements, along with various manipulative strategies operative through mass media, legitimate the existing order, gaining assent for its organizational arrangements from subordinated classes.

Two good illustrations of this model are found in the structural Marxist version of critical/radical theory and in socialist-feminist theory. Structural

Marxist analysis sees the state as having a degree of real power and autonomy to curb some of the excesses of exploitation by the economic elite of subordinated classes.[11] Together with the real but limited freedom generated by the capitalist system, and the state's claim to be a universal protector of humankind, this is enough to earn legitimacy and thereby preserve assent for the existing structural arrangements, albeit at the cost of fragmentation (Spitzer, 1980; Jessop, 1982).

The dual power model in socialist-feminist criminology sees patriarchy bound up with capitalism and other forms of repression.[12] Its advocates describe a semi-autonomous patriarchal state operating to reproduce the patriarchal class power structure. The state makes small concessions to women's interests while continuing to control them through the welfare system and by supporting a deceptive liberation agenda that imposes a double burden of control on women as wage-laborers and managers of the domestic economy. A less global but more precisely defined version can be found in the integrated criminology of Hagan's power control theory which explores the dual forces of patriarchy in the household and a command–obey class structure similar to that found in Turk's earlier conflict theory.[13] Here, however, any theory of the state is noticeably absent.

One of the most developed modernist analyses is found in the critical legal theory of Unger (1976; Collins, 1987). Instead of relying on one model to represent the reality of social structure, Unger integrates the ideas of Durkheim, Weber, and Marx through a historical analysis that depicts a recurrent cycle of development in which the various different models (discussed above) appear in successive historical eras. Decentralized consensus models are succeeded first by instrumental power hierarchies, then by structural dual power hierarchies. Each social order is marked by a transitional return to a fragmented state of conflict pluralism, during a stage of legitimacy crises that marks the demise of each prevailing social order. According to Unger, each emergent model of society has its corresponding system of law and form of legitimation whose structural appearance is an attempt to resolve the contradictions of the earlier failed order. More clearly than most, Unger's analysis suggests the integral role of law in the constitution of a society's structure, a point we shall return to in the next chapter.

In spite of their differences, modernist ideas about social structure share the assumption that descriptions of society are a reflection of an underlying reality whose truth is available through scientific empirical investigation. A central concern is to close the gap between representation and reality, between the description and the concrete. In this pursuit they share 'a belief that people can control objects, nature, and each other' (Schwartz and Friedrichs, 1994: 223) for the betterment of the whole. Modernists also rest their assumptions on the privileging of order. This includes the notion of linear development of society over time, the implied desirability of reaching a state of ultimate equilibrium/homeostasis, determinacy in the assumption of social forces on human action, and whole number dimensional spaces which obscure the importance of margins.[14] Very different assumptions about social structure are made by those taking a postmodernist stance.

Postmodernist visions of social structure and social order

Postmodernists recognize the socially constructed nature of images of structure, seeing these as representations of that which they purport to represent, devoid of any underlying reality or anchored referents. From a postmodern stance differences in interpretation are no more than alternative claims to truth, absent of any reality save that which is the outcome of human subjects acting as though such a reality existed. Following our earlier discussion (see Chapter 2), we will consider the images of social structure found in skeptical postmodernism and contrast these with the images in affirmative postmodernism, before turning to social structure as developed in our constitutive criminology.

Imagining social structure

Four elements bear on the image of structure presented in postmodern accounts. First is the idea that structure is unreal except for the images discursively produced by human subjects. While 'All post-modernists deny any view of reality that assumes the independence of individual mental processes and intersubjective communication . . . skeptical post-modernists doubt that a conception of reality need exist at all', whereas 'affirmative postmodernists . . . agree with a constructivist theory of reality' which holds among other views that 'there is no reality to any event apart from the meanings attributed by those who perceive them' (Rosenau, 1992: 110).

Second is the idea that among those images or representations of collective social forms and entities, especially prominent is a dissolution of older ideas of structure and the emergence of ones that point to cross-cutting ties based on fleeting, temporary cultural commodities of consumption rather than grounded in materialist relationships to production.

Third is postmodernism's goal of challenging the dominant power relations through Foucault's call to 'interrupt the smooth passage of "regimes of truth", to disrupt those forms of knowledge which have assumed a self-evident quality, and to engender a state of uncertainty in those responsible for servicing the network of power–knowledge relations' (Smart, 1983: 135). Implied here is a radical pluralism focused on local decentered sites, personal lifestyle change, self-transformation and idealism: 'Its goal is a radical plural democracy' emphasizing 'plural struggles from diverse standpoints' (Cloud, 1994: 224). Moreover, its politics combines a relativism, idealism and 'humanism' reflecting a celebration of the sovereignty of human agents through 'textualism . . . the assumption that the revolution will happen at the level of discourse and consciousness rather than economics' (Cloud, 1994: 225; Callinicos, 1990).

Fourth, and not unrelated, are the ideas that are currently infusing a number of affirmative postmodernist thinkers, the search for interdisciplinary instabilities: chaos theory, quantum mechanics, Godel's theorem, and catastrophe theory. These will be developed below in an attempt to show that the notion of structure undergoes a radical reformulation in the affirmative postmodern critique as it opens the criminological eye to novel conceptions of space, time, causation, and historical development. Let us look first at postmodernist denials of the reality of social structure.

Unreality and domination

As much a key focus in considering social structure as it was when assessing the human subject is the postmodernists' interest in discourse. Thus for Baudrillard (1975; see Poster, 1988), Foucault (1980), Lyotard (1984), Deleuze and Guattari (1987), the symbolic representation of social relationships and, through these, of social structures is the privileged in a world without privilege. There is some commonality here with social constructionist, phenomenological and ethnomethodological positions on the relationship between social structure and social forms, in spite of their differing visions of the human subject. Much of the skeptical and affirmative postmodernists' commonality with some conceptions of social constructionism and phenomenology can be traced to Lacan's unique synthesis of phenomenology and structuralism (Sarup, 1989).[15] The call, therefore, was for a critical postmodern phenomenology (Young, 1992).

In this hermeneutically informed vision, social structures are based, not on real materially grounded social forms, but on the categories of classification of the events that they allegedly represent (Knorr-Cetina, 1981; Schutz, 1967). As such they are 'strengthened', in the sense of seeming real, by routine construction in everyday life and by activity organized in relation to them, as though they actually existed as concrete entities. Social structures are constituted through the use of discursive practices that make distinctions and invoke differences to be perceived in the minds of those using them. This process produces texts (narrative constructions), imaginary constructions, that in turn paint a particular image claiming to be the reality (Derrida, 1973b; 1981; Lacan, 1977). Once social structures are constituted as images, their ongoing existence depends upon their continued and often unwitting reconstruction in everyday discourse, a discourse replete with tacit understandings and preconstructed meanings that form part of our common 'stock of knowledge' of floating signifiers.[16] Recurrent construction, through reference to allegedly real entities, provides these images of structure with a sense of stability. It is this that subordinates its unwitting users to the powerful effects of domination by orchestrated categories of reality, as well as by the logic of the discursive practices that they use.

At the same time, this perspective allows constructed reality to be vulnerable to transformation and dissolution, not least by the deconstruction and exposure of the way it is being built through discursive practices

(Laclau and Mouffe, 1985; Milovanovic, 1993a). As we have seen, discourse is an important factor in the transmission of certain realities and in the constitution of subjectivity. It is important in rendering other voices and emergent subjectivities silenced. But because there is no intrinsic logic that maintains discursive formations in their given form (rather there is a tendency toward fragmentation), then alternative, more humanistic forms of discourse are possible. How the social order is seen to move from one in which people relate to one another in terms of the materially based social 'subject–object' forms such as capitalist, boss, worker, family, household, etc., to one in which they relate in terms of images of style and moments of culture, has been a feature of several postmodernists' thought.

Fragmentation and (re)formation

Several postmodernist authors have suggested how fragmentation of the existing social order and its reformation can take place.[17] In the previous chapter we saw that Lacan provided much initial inspiration in his work concerning the wherewithal of the dominant phallocentric symbolic order where he tells us that the male voice populates all signifiers; the female voice finds a secondary status, in fact, 'does not exist', is not-all (*pas-toute*). But, Lacan (1985) tells us, she has access to other bases of desire and fulfillment (*jouissance*) which find little room for expression in the male dominated order. Some feminist postmodernist theorists find, in this analysis, the potential beginning for a critique of what is, and a possible prescription of what could be. They call for a female-based discourse (an *écriture féminine*). Cornell's (1991; 1993) Lacanian inspired work, for example, building on Irigaray's process of disruption and transformation into an affirmative (mimesis), and on Cixous' idea of redoing myth, shows how utopian thinking 'demands the continual exploration and re-exploration of the possible and yet also the unrepresentable' (Cornell, 1991: 169; see also Arrigo, 1992; Milovanovic, 1994a: 169–72). The Imaginary Order of Lacan, in other words, constituted by metaphor and metonymy (see Chapter 1), always implies a 'slippage', an excess (what Lacan calls *le plus de jouir*), especially apparent in myths, that can be the basis of reformation. Here myth can be reformulated and in the process repressed voices can be excavated. Because of the play of the indeterminate effects of the imaginary, then, this could be the basis of utopian thinking of the possible, particularly for a female discourse (see Cornell, 1993).

Baudrillard (1981; 1983a; 1985) is perhaps one of the key postmodernist contributors to the thesis of fragmentation and reformation. In his gaze Western industrial society is capitalist in character but he sees its core feature as relations of consumption which subordinate all subjects to the logic of their discourse. His central thesis is that today's capitalist society is a consumer society in which meaningful social relations have been expunged.[18] This occurred through a process that culminated in control and domination via the ideology of consumption. The products of capitalist society, originally demanded, produced and sold because they were useful to its members (they had use-value) were, in the growing modernist era, sold for their value relative to other products (they had exchange-value). As a result, products could be traded or exchanged to accumulate value or wealth, regardless of any intrinsic utility they possessed. The rise in importance of exchange-value was initially masked by the image of products as actually useful. In this stage of society there is at least some reference to the object or reality. However, says Baudrillard, in conjunction with the industrial order there has been a growth in communications technology and the media, especially television (the technological order), which have become semi-autonomous, serving the ideology of corporatism. This mediated order promotes the commodity form, i.e. the image itself (e.g. the brand name, the style, the color, the shape, together with the meaning that is signified by those signs or signifiers, i.e. 'its social standing'), as useful rather than the intrinsic use-value of the commodity itself, i.e. its concrete structure.

For Baudrillard, it is the images of objects as a series of signs and statements simulating an end in themselves that impose logic and order on social life: 'Advertising codes products through symbols that differentiate them from other products, thereby fitting the object into a series' (Poster, 1988: 2). Thus, says Baudrillard, 'The system of needs has become less integrated than the system of objects; the latter imposes its own coherence and thus acquires the capacity to fashion the entire society' (Poster, 1988: 15). Consumers do not simply buy chocolate or perfume, but sensation, a drug experience: 'Sweet dreams you can't resist' (Nestlé ad). Working through social relationships is rendered unappealing by a drug-fix culture promoting quick-fix solutions for those who 'haven't got time for the pain' (Bufferin ad).

For Baudrillard, 'The object has its effect when it is consumed, by transferring its symbolic meaning to the individual consumer' (Poster, 1988). Consumers buy a ticket into a package of meaning that is the collection of objects as a totality. Consumption of a product is consumption of the image to receive its illusion, irrespective of the material function, as in perfume for sex appeal, toothpaste for self-confidence, cars for eroticism, soft drinks for popularity, drugs for time. Thus, consumer objects 'constitute a system of signs, a network of floating signifiers, inexhaustible in their ability to incite desire'. It is the image that imposes its own logic, 'ordering society while providing the individual with an illusory sense of freedom and self-determination'. Baudrillard argues that in this capitalist system signs become completely separated from their referents. As the 'emancipated signs', signifiers are extracted from their social context and float, emitting meanings that require no response, forcing a silence on the masses, signaling rather than symbolizing.

Baudrillard (1981; 1983a; 1985) further suggests that this process extends to the construction of hyperreality. Here we make models of the images, images of images, which implies that the original images are a reality, which claims American society is real because Williamsburg and Disney-land are images. But, says Baudrillard, these images are images of images and the everyday life in which we play is a fantasy, masked by the hyperreality. It is a simulation, only real by reference to the hyperreal, a 'simulacrum' for which there is no original. As a result, any possibility of real social relations and meaning constructed to symbolize them is removed. Postmodern culture, says Baudrillard, involves social relations without content, fixed meaning or substance.

In short, then, for Baudrillard the existing social structure comprises industrial technological production serving the mass of society whose coalitions are formed around their transitory subscriptions to various orders of objects, which we might call 'clubs of identity'. Membership to these 'clubs' is momentarily conferred by consuming the appropriate style or model of an object from the group of objects. Unlike in the relatively rigid views of class structure, in this postmodern vision anyone, regardless of their economic standing, can buy a membership card to one or more clusters of signaled meaning. Distinctions of wealth or class no longer distinguish who can join, only how many times and how often membership can be renewed.

Visions of radical pluralism

This third element in the postmodernist vision of structure stems as much from its own vision of the future and prospects for social change as it does from its analysis of the past.[19] The shift away from economics and production, and from the state and the political, in deference to the discursive construction of consumption on many and dispersed sites, indicates a pluralism that becomes more robust when the radical pluralistic nature of the postmodern political agenda is understood. For Laclau and Mouffe (1985) and Mouffe (1992) the agenda of transformative politics cannot lie in the old class-interested order, since this has been displaced by the postmodern clusters of its consumer order. Like the class formations before it, these discursively produced categories now generate an antagonism to the system on a myriad of fronts. Here we have posited a kind of guerrilla consumerism in which the identity interests of varieties of differently bound interests-in-image congeal to resist their subordination to the discursively constituted order of objects that is the capitalist system.

Laclau and Mouffe's seminal work replaces social formation as the focal point of analysis with the notion of discursive formation. Here, no longer socio-economic relations but discursive relations become central (Bergesen, 1993: 14). Baudrillard, Lyotard, Foucault, Laclau and Mouffe and others have indicated that Marxism is unable to adequately explain developments in the emergent postmodern society (Bergesen, 1993; Ashley, 1990; Dickens, 1990). Others, however, continue to rely on a Marxist analysis (Jessop, 1990; Hunt, 1993).

For Laclau and Mouffe (1985) society is purely discursive. As Cloud

(1994: 7–8) points out, in this view 'culture becomes theoretically detached from material reality' and 'the state is a constellation of discursive nodal points, around which subjects are positioned in the process of articulating and re-articulating social identities and relations.' In such a vision, the state is seen as autonomous from the economic base of society, and the human subject is as one with agency (rather than class as an entity having social agency). Thus their discourse analysis indicates the 'ultimate non-fixity of anything existing in society' (Laclau, 1988: 254). In other words, no fixed relations exist. All is in flux. No essentialist Logos is ubiquitous. No unified totalities can be posited. Neither Althusser nor Poulantzas can save us, for 'the base cannot determine the superstructure because the superstructure is part of the constitution of the base' (Bergesen, 1993: 17; Laclau and Mouffe, 1985: 76–7, 97–105).

It is Laclau and Mouffe's position that what accounts for the structuration/constitution of nodal points (suturing) is the dialectical play of the 'logic of equivalence' and the 'logic of difference' (Laclau and Mouffe, 1985: 130). The logic of equivalence is rooted in capital logic and the commodification process. The logic of difference is rooted in the continued differentiation of society.[20] A 'hegemonic formation', for them, takes place when nodal points are provisionally established: 'In a given social formation, there can be a variety of hegemonic nodal points. Evidently, some of them may be highly overdetermined: they may constitute points of condensation of a number of social relations and thus, become the focal point of a multiplicity of totalizing effects' (1985: 139). Hegemony has its basis in the generation of a 'surplus of meaning' (1985: 141).

No unilateral cause can be attributed to a historically situated hegemonic formation, but the play of 'regularity' and 'dispersion': regularity as in the logic of equivalence, but dispersion as in the proliferation of differences (1985: 142). With nodal points constructed, some voices are denied expression. Here subjects are not-all. But 'no causal theory about the efficacy of one element over another is necessary' (Laclau and Mouffe, 1987: 90–1). The hegemonic formation remains in an inherently 'unstable equilibrium' (Laclau and Mouffe, 1985: 189; Hunt, 1993: 297). There remains, then, a focus on the search for 'nuclei of ambiguity' (Laclau and Mouffe, 1985: 113, 179–81). Moreover, Marxist analysis rooted in modernist assumptions can no longer convincingly account for new antagonisms in postmodern society (1985: 159–71). Here, no 'unique privileged positions [exist] from which a uniform continuity of effects will follow, concluding with the transformation of society as a whole' (1985: 169). The challenge, then, is to develop a strategy for reconstruction (1985: 189).

In this strategy, struggle is against any form of subordination but, at the same time, is a counter-hegemonic struggle unified through 'chainings of equivalents' as a resistance to the hegemony of the dominant order. As Cloud (1994) points out, it is resistance as discursively articulated antagonism and revolution in terms of displacing existing hegemonic discourse by establishing a more anarchistic anti-hegemony within the democratic imagery.

Perhaps predictably, modernists such as Cloud (1994) criticize Mouffe's (1988) dissolution of class politics into a myriad of fragmented movements as a relativistic collusion with the system that overstates the ability of individual consciousness to make a difference. Cloud argues that this fails to articulate the interests of the subordinated class (a point made more generally by Hunt, 1990). The irony of the post-Marxist position from the Marxist perspective (Geras, 1987; Callinicos, 1990; Eagleton, 1991) is that in seeking to present an empowered notion of the person as an agent of change against the discursively constituted capitalist system, the class formation of domination and political order is conceptually reconstructed as a static theory of class relations of exploitation and oppression.

In short, then, post-Marxism and postmodernism contain both images of a capitalist dominated class hierarchy and prospects for radical pluralism based on individual revelation and the multitude of 'fragmented discourses' generated by 'a patchwork of minorities . . . dispersed ethnic, religious, and cultural groups' and 'informal networks where [postmodernists] find the ingredients of postmodernity: the local, the plural, the subversive' (Teubner, 1992: 1443; see also Smith, 1987; 1992).

Further insight on the postmodernist vision of social structure as both an order of power and a chaos of plurality can be found in the work of Bourdieu (1987). In his analysis of the symbolic violence of modern society Bourdieu sees a society that proceeds from autonomous cultural fields. It is within the structures of these autonomous fields, what he calls the 'habitus', that culturally produced symbolic objects exercise domination over both their producers and consumers. Bourdieu's notion of structure includes the relations between human agents as an inseparable component that, Lash (1990: 256) says, 'structure the structures'. Interaction between cultural producers occurs within their fields of production whose outcome is a symbolic object that itself exercises symbolic power over the field: 'Bourdieu's notion of structure . . . in modernity . . . constitutes the supply side and individuals in the social field comprise the demand side . . . modern power stems from a relationship between fields (whose symbolic economy imparts to them their structure) and the "consumer" who is subject to this power' (Lash, 1990: 256–7).

Traditional classes in the hierarchy of power are, in Bourdieu's vision, transformed or even dissolved into an overall field of power imbued with a discourse of legitimation, subsuming a number of semi-autonomous fields striving to be free from its domination. Within these fields individuals compete in strategic battles for accumulation of symbolic capital. For Bourdieu, postmodernity is envisioned as 'a process of de-differentiation of fields or structures and of agency, or habitus' and 'a reversal of autonomization' comprising 'a partial breakdown or de-centering of the grid of classificatory rules which structure habitus' (Lash, 1990: 256–7).

The notion of radical plurality also appears in the theory of autopoiesis of Luhmann (1985; 1988; 1992) and Teubner (1992; 1993) and particularly their and others' notion of 'structural coupling' (Hunt, 1993; Jessop, 1990; Cornell, 1992; Milovanovic, 1994a). Although themselves severely critical of postmodernism, autopoietic theorists envision a social structure not as a class hierarchy but as a plurality of structurally coupled but relatively autonomous organizational systems, each focused around its own main-tenance. Autopoietic systems are said to maintain an equilibrium state by maintaining their own organization. Each system's own organization stays constant. This is achieved by continuously generating and specifying themselves (they are self-referential), and by specifying their own boundaries and their own components; and they do this endlessly. As Zeleny (1980) defines them, autopoietic systems are relatively autonomous. The components, through their internal interaction, repeatedly generate, maintain and recover *the same* complex of processes which produced them. They subordinate all changes to maintaining their existence, irrespective of whether they are transformed in the process. An interesting analogy here is the HIV virus and how it changes appearance, hides, nestles in the human immune system, growing with it rather than being destroyed by it and all the time transforming the mask of its identity in order to expand. According to autopoietic theory, institutions of society operate in the same manner. In this vision of society, it is not individuals, or classes, or groups that show active agency but the autopoietic systems themselves. Such organizational systems have individuality and identity and this is independent of their interactions with other systems.

Importantly, these systems are closed to their environment in that they parasitically consume it rather than being changed by it. In this process, Luhmann (1992: 1432), drawing on Maturana and Varela, suggests autopoietic systems are cognitively open through what are called 'struc-tural couplings' which 'provide a continuous influx of disorder against which the system maintains or changes its structure'. They have 'self-organization' (Teubner et al., 1994) and their 'self-referential closure' changes their relationship with their economic and political environment from exchange to 'structural coupling' (Teubner, 1994: 25; see also Maturana and Varela, 1987; Smith and Gemmill, 1991; Smith and Comer, 1994). This means that the ideas, formulations, conceptualizations and other data from outside the system will undergo a translation within the processes of the autopoietic system. The translated material will have an effect on the outside environment, but not a direct causal effect (Milovanovic, 1994a: 130). Rather, the effect is one of a mutuality of simultaneous shadow moves.

Clearly, one of the implications of this for the images of social structure is that of a plurality of systems in an environmental sea of other more or less organized systems. These relations are mediated through a common discourse of communication, while each develops its own autonomously generated system discourse that is specialized and comprehensible only by system members. In this vision 'society is seen as fragmented into a multiplicity of closed communicative networks' (Teubner, 1989: 741) and the subject is decentered according to the particular autopoietic system within which s/he takes residence.

The search for instabilities: 'waging war on totalities'

Recently, several ideas have infused a number of affirmative postmodernist thinkers in their attempt to visualize structure as a contingency of instabilities. Particularly informative have been chaos theory, quantum mechanics, Godel's theorem, and catastrophe theory, each of which offers novel conceptions of space, time, causation, and historical development.

Elements of chaos theory have been incorporated either explicitly or implicitly into some postmodernists' views of social structure (Lyotard, 1984; Weinstein and Weinstein, 1993; Baker, 1993; Young, 1992). For these theorists, order is the exception. The prevailing image is that of a universe in disorder (Serres, 1982a), 'messy, fuzzy and fragmented' (Young, 1991a: 3). In Nietzsche as well as Foucault is found the argument that order is something that is imposed, discursively, on a more chaotic world (Dews, 1987: 186; Love, 1986: 2, 53). Order gives the illusion of understanding and control. It provides manageable horizons within which predictability exists, and the illusory assurance – 'semiotic fictions' or other ideologies according to Nietzsche – that the subject is in control (Love, 1986: 53). Contrary to the inevitability theses that exist in modernist assumptions of order,[21] postmodernists who draw on chaos theory see the more normal state of the world to be a proliferation of far-from-equilibrium conditions replete with a plurality of logics, within which 'dissipative structures' abound (Prigogine, 1977; 1978; see also Leifer, 1989). Dissipative structures are those which simultaneously tend toward dissipation and order, an orderly disorder (Briggs and Peat, 1989). They are unstable and sensitive to their environment, and in such conditions, 'small changes produce large differences' (as shown by non-linear dynamics and chaos theory: Young, 1991a: 3). Thus chance, spontaneity, uncertainty prevail (Gleick, 1987). In this model, social structures are not permanent states; rather, 'It points to the constructed nature of all totalities and their aesthetic mediations' (Weinstein and Weinstein, 1993: 227). Hence, dissipative structures present very different images from those of bureaucracies, with their tendencies toward closure and stasis. Accordingly, in contrast to Weber's inevitability thesis concerning the continued rationalization of society in the form of the bureaucracy, chaos's alternative 'structure' tends toward openness and responsiveness.

Certain aspects of the notion of dissipative structures have similarities with both Luhmann and Teubner's notion of autopoiesis and Bourdieu's notion of habitus that we discussed above. Our constitutive approach will argue that the outside 'environment' to such 'self-organizations' already includes components of the organization's dissipative structure, and vice versa; each has parts of the other and therefore cannot be neatly conceptualized as an inside/outside dichotomy. In addition, since 'inputs' can never be precisely coded – they appear with 'noise' – with iteration, as chaos theorists inform us, these otherwise supposedly inconsequential variances, and hence the undecidability status of the initial 'inputs', can have disproportional and unintended effects.[22] At best, contrary to the modernist versions of autopoietic structures, they exist in states of tension and inextricable interrelatedness with their world.

Some integration is beginning to take place between chaos theory and other postmodern ideas. Consider, for example, Hayles' (1990: 176) analysis of Derrida's work and her conclusion that there is an 'ecology of ideas' between that work and chaos theory. That is, topology theory – the 'rubber math' – may indicate that both deconstruction and chaos theory's non-linear dynamics were possible forms that evolved with postmodern culture: 'they are similar because they share in the constraints that define the overall topology' (Hayles, 1990: 185; see also Lem, 1981). The work of Derrida and chaos, in other words, are coupled, indicative of non-linear dynamics.[23] For example, Derrida's notion of the 'trace' indicates an effect is always already present, producing indeterminacies as iteration proceeds. Initial uncertainties are then compounded, tending toward textual chaos.

Similarly with Nietzsche and Foucault and their genealogical methodology where the researcher searches for de-privileged terms in historical development and raises these 'insignificances' to the level of visibility in indicating their disproportional effects. Deleuze and Guattari (1987) have shown that even though normal science proceeds within the coordinates of two-dimensional Euclidian x–y grids and Newton's calculus (linear dynamics), which underlies positivism and order in criminology, an alternative chaos conceptualization has it that a fractal geometry exists (i.e. fractional numbered dimensional spaces: see Mandelbrot, 1983).[24]

Thus, rather than a logic of yes/no (Boolean) or a binary code of input/ output, such as at play in courtroom proceedings or in an empiricist's research operationalizations of variables, gray areas abound (Cornell, 1992: 77). Truth is fractal (Young, 1991a; 1992). And in fractal geometry there is always more in existence than is mapped by conventional Euclidian geometry with its reliance on regular geometric figures such as the cube, sphere, triangle. The 'web of life' is always richer than words or holistic images can describe. Narrow discourses such as in legalese are therefore doubly restrictive. Consider the work of Katz, in *Seductions of Crime* (1988), where he reorients our understanding to take into consideration the unexamined spaces in criminological theory.[25]

In the Newtonian paradigm, the 'point' is privileged. The individual particle, the entity 'person', can be followed through time. Actions, with the correct amount of scientific knowledge, are potentially predictable. For example in positivist criminology consider how causation is depicted in path analysis diagrams. (We develop this illustration more fully in Chapter 7.) In contrast, for quantum mechanics, only probabilities exist. For some, only the 'moment' should be considered, a probability event that finds no precise coordinates in time and space (Bohm, 1980). For others, 'what does matter are recursive symmetries between different levels of the system' (Hayles, 1990: 170). As Hayles suggests:

> The regularities of the system emerge not from knowing about individual units but from understanding correspondences across scales of different lengths. It is a systemic approach, emphasizing overall symmetries and the complex interactions between microscale and macroscale levels. From this perspective, a proper explanation is one that is able to model large scale changes through the incremental evolution of a few iterative equations. (1990: 170)

Deleuze and Guattari have also integrated this material and stated that in their postmodern approach 'there are no points or positions in a rhizome [a non-linear flow of desire, a 'semiotic flow'] . . . There are only lines' (1987: 8). The important idea to extrapolate from chaos theory is that spaces have more dimensions (are infinitely complex) than are assumed in the three-dimensional paradigm of order. Spaces often hide important factors that do, or can, even in supposedly insignificant quanta, make a difference in social development. Perhaps, one day, rather than a predominant use of regular Euclidian constructed geometric figures, social sciences will portray social phenomena in the complex and infinitely intricate figures offered by chaos theorists. We see, for example, that the 'Mandelbrot' set portrays global symmetry and at any local level, however finely detailed, we find recursive symmetries, either self-similar (linear fractals) or statistically self-similar (non-linear fractals) (Hayles, 1990: 13; Garcia, 1991: 61–4).[26]

According to Hayles (1990: 13) recursive symmetries or self-similar structures (such as recurring logics) are characterized by 'coupling points': 'at any one of these coupling points, minute fluctuations can cause the flow [e.g. laminar flow, turbulent flow] to evolve differently, so that it is impossible to predict how the system will behave' (1990: 13, see also 155, 157). Indeed, Hayles' (1990: 218) example of Foucault's work on discursive structures indicates that within a historical period one can locate, at times, the same organizing language turns and figures of speech (tropes) in biology, political theory, grammar, and psychology: in other words, a self-similarity.

The search for instabilities in social structure can also be furthered, postmodernists tell us, by the assumption of the indeterminacy or uncertainty principle of quantum mechanics. This developed to explain the wave–particle duality of systems so small that they were unexplainable by Newtonian mechanics. Contrary to modernist assumptions that social structures rest on orderly processes and can be situated with precision,[27] postmodernists drawing on the uncertainty principle argue that it is impossible to specify location and momentum (velocity) at the same time. Measuring one with precision leaves the other in an indeterminate state and vice versa. Thus, an otherwise seemingly adequate description of a social structure or system captured in time is deficient, for the inclusion of momentum, of the velocity variable (i.e. movement through time, historicity), nullifies any static conceptualization. For example, in modernist positivist empiricism, holding constant such factors as class, religion, etc., and then indicating the independent effects of some other variable(s), is an orderly imposition on the ebb and flow of social events. With the uncertainty principle complete determinism is lost, replaced by probabilities for position, momentum, etc. Indeed, in spite of attempts by some to factor in the 'hidden variables', and in spite of Einstein's assertion that 'God does not play dice', 'quantum mechanics is supported by a great mass of experimental evidence . . . and must be regarded as one of the greatest intellectual triumphs in all physics' (Berry, 1977: 517–18).

Some postmodernist analysis also embraces Godel's theorem. Godel offered a mathematical demonstration that it is impossible to prove or disprove the consistency of a formal system from within the system. Thus an implication of Godel is a rejection of the theoretical possibility of encompassing all within an axiomatizable system, as in Weber's 'gapless' system in law. Godel's is an incompleteness and undecidability thesis that denies the possibility of ever creating a deductive explanation in which truths can be deduced from a few foundational axioms. Indeed, it is consistent with postmodernism's denial of foundationalism (see Penrose, 1989: 102, 105–8; Hayles, 1990: 35). The ideal of an overall, all-embracing, self-consistent global theory of social structure, in this view is impossible. Nor is the claim that such an analysis is merely an ideal-typical heuristic device helpful. Gaps will always exist. Any device that ignores the gaps for the sake of order is ignoring important defining qualities that can be described. Perhaps the operating metaphor here is the Penrose triangle, a figure sketched in three-dimensional space which became the basis of Escher's *Ascending and Descending*, that cannot exist in our real world. At any corner (the local) of the triangle a self-consistency prevails. Overall, however, the figure has no global consistency (Peat, 1989: 165–6). It cannot 'fit' into a consistent axiomatizable structure.

There are ramifications here, then, for the description of social structures that must be historically situated. For postmodernists, if initial states are always uncertain and undecidable because of the implications of quantum mechanics and of Godel, and if iteration over time produces disproportional effects, then the outcome of any structural or system development must be unpredictable. In this view, cracks and slippage always exist. And these provide the basis for strategic intervention (a point we shall develop in Chapters 8 and 9).

Thus, in the postmodern view, it is senseless to search for universalities as in Habermas' ideal speech situation, or to posit any form of essentialism as was the case for some feminist postmodernists. This is a return to a celebration of post-Enlightenment's preoccupation with order. Genealogical analysis of social structure, as inspired by Nietzsche in the works of Foucault, would instead celebrate (but as we shall indicate in our constitutive approach, not necessarily prioritize) chance, indeterminacy, spontaneity, irony, and the unexpected. We shall return to these issues and their implication for causation in Chapters 6 and 7.

The search for instabilities by postmodernists has also found some resonance in catastrophe theory (Lyotard, 1984: 58–60).[28] This theory, drawing from the French mathematician René Thom (1975), posits that even in determinate systems discontinuities may prevail.[29] Unexpected forms can still be generated. Lyotard provides the example with aggressiveness. A dog may at times undergo a linear state, and at other times an abrupt, non-linear, undefinable state, even as the initial variables are constant and measurable. With an increase in the dog's anger, aggressiveness is predicted. At a certain threshold, attack may be an outcome. However, if we look at fear, we shall see that when it reaches a certain threshold, flight will be produced. In the absence of anger or fear, stable behavior is predicted. If, however, both variables (anger, fear) increase and the two thresholds are reached simultaneously, the behavior of the dog becomes unpredictable: it can switch back and forth from flight to attack. Here the system is unstable even as anger and fear are continuous (determinate). Catastrophe theory thus illustrates the different ways a dynamic system can pass through points of instability.

The implication of catastrophe theory for postmodernists is not only for alternative notions of causation (see Chapter 7), but for notions of social structure and how various institutions or subsystems are predicted to interact, producing stability or instability. It might be, in other words, that even if we could specify with a great degree of exactness the nature of two or more particular social structures (or autopoietic systems), we would still be in a position not to know precisely how they would interact. On some occasions stability would be produced; on others, instabilities.

This unstable outcome has certain affinities with chaos theorists' notions of the strange attractor, where two possible outcome states may exist and indeterminacy prevails. In this view, social structure is inherently unstable. Structural functionalist analysis or the inevitability thesis approaches of modernist thinkers cannot adequately explain inherent instabilities in an apparently stable system. In catastrophe theory's view, deviation is not an aberration; it is a normal outcome of social structural interactions and developments.

Postmodernism's shortcomings

A number of criticisms of postmodernist ideas about structure have been made. We saw that Bourdieu's legal habitus, and Teubner's autopoiesis thesis, while presenting the idea that language and communication are important ingredients in the analysis of social structure, are not able to provide an adequate depiction of: (1) the constitution of the subject in relation to structure; (2) how the legal discursive formation is itself a provisionally constituted structure, having effects in its very indeterminacy; and (3) how non-linear changes can be accounted for. The idea of a discursive formation replacing that of social formation is seen to beg the question of how opposition materializes (Bergesen, 1993). Laclau and Mouffe's thesis has overcome some of these deficiencies. Recent critical psychoanalytic semiotic and chaos theorizing has also provided some suggestive directions. It has been claimed that the autopoiesis and habitus theses begin the analysis of operationalizing dissipative structures, but leave little room for socio-political change. In short, they are, ironically, ultimately deterministic. Still lacking is a statement concerning not only how co-production takes place and how an alternative order (orderly disorder) can be envisioned, but how to progress from here to there. Indeed, postmodernist analysis of social structure has been accused of being the reactive-negative form, describing and critiquing the modernist forms, then positing the postmodernist forms, but without an analysis of the transition between the two. Related, it has also been argued that no overall systematic theory is available connecting the disparate threads offered by different postmodernist analyses on social structure. That skeptical postmodernists would deny the usefulness of such an exercise is considered an evasion of critical scholarship.

Another problem is that no ethical principle guides a chaotic process of change. It is argued that given a particular contingently based revolutionary coalition, some underlying ethical principle guiding their transpraxis needs to be specified, even though it too is contingent.[30]

Finally, instabilities are predicted to be the norm in social structures, and the question of whether these are desirable (be they contingent and provisional structures) is said not to be answerable as an outcome. As a result it is suggested that the position of postmodernists borders on abdication, resignation, and fatalism. In short, skeptical postmodern analysis is too preoccupied with reaction-negation dynamics without a vision of what could be.

Some of these criticisms imply important revisions that might be necessary to an emerging affirmative postmodernism. Affirmative postmodern analysis is a movement to what could be, tempered by the realities of modernism. Our constitutive approach suggests several answers are possible. In drawing from the strengths of postmodern positions as well as modernist contributions, particularly from the three discussed above, we believe that our constitutive position moves the discussion beyond point and counterpoint.

Constitutive constructions of social structure

Constitutive theory is both a critical commentary on our (postmodern) times, and a statement of what could be. It is a statement of negation of the past and a utopian affirmation of future possibilities. Constitutive theorizing is a contingently and provisionally based humanistic vision of what could be, a radical superliberalism. It offers a critical postmodern phenomenology that links structure with agency.

Our times

Our constitutive position suggests that at any historical point, social structure is a cluster of ideas and images about order and its maintenance, a collection of humans oriented to uphold their version of these images, the reality of the outcomes that follow from actions they take to bring this about, and the potential to transform these images, actions and outcomes. In this regard we tend to agree with Cloud's (1994: 246) conclusion that 'The ordering of society into relations of domination and subordination is no less real for being the product of discursive articulations.' However, we translate Cloud's (1994: 242) interpretation of postmodernism that 'There is a reality to oppression outside its discursive construction, a reality on which we can base political analysis and strategy' to there being a reality to oppression brought about through its discursive construction, and therein lies the key to transformation.

Indeed, constitutive theory's view of structure asserts that it is necessary to analyze precisely how those constructions of reality become real enough to harm, and strategizes the ways to interrupt this process and to substitute for it less harmful constructions. To do this it is crucial to ground any theory of society and social order in both a reality-oriented view of the power of structural and cultural forms to both constrain and enable, and a constructionist-oriented view of the relationship of human agency to the ongoing creation of those forms, without prioritizing one or the other.

Our analysis of social structure begins with the strengths and limitations of recent Marxian theorizing concerning the discursive formation posited as a replacement to conceptions of the social formation and with affirmative postmodernism's insights about instability and plurality.[31] This is the transcendent position which we identify as a constitutive theory. In this theory a central concept is the *co-production of reality*. This is a thesis which situates constructions of social reality in historically changing conditions. In the constitutive framework, truths are contingently and provisionally based. Our critical postmodern phenomenology sees a simultaneously vertical and horizontal mutual interactive model whereby structure (the individual–social) and agency (active–passive) are mutually implicated in any production of knowledge. This starting point of constitutive criminology can find a useful synopsis of Marxian movements in the work by Bergesen (1993).

It is Bergesen's contention that Marxist analysis has undergone four stages of development. The first stage, an inversion of the usual base–superstructure metaphor, we find identified with Gramsci's work of the 1930s where three distinctive spheres – ideological, political and economic – exist and where the primacy is on the ideological sphere as the dominant determinant. The second stage has been identified with the work of Althusser in the 1960s where the inherent logic of the ideological sphere absorbs the political and together they have a decided effect on the economic through the emergent, omnipotent and ubiquitous 'ideological state apparatus'. In the third stage associated with Poulantzas of the 1970s, all three spheres are unified into a superstructure. Here causal relations among the three spheres begin to be eliminated. Finally, in stage four, associated with the work of Laclau and Mouffe of the 1980s, causal relations among the three spheres are eliminated (Bergesen, 1993; Laclau and Mouffe, 1987: 90–1). Here the logic of 'base' and 'superstructure' converge. Previously Marxian notions of social formations are replaced by the idea of an over-encompassing discursive formation understood as 'semiotic Marxist' (Bergesen, 1993).

A return to Saussurian linguistics with a political economic analysis indicates that this discursive formation loses its embeddedness in material conditions. Signifiers become self-referential as in autopoiesis. They are the constitutive elements of the newly emerging hyperreality. As Laclau (1988: 254) informs us, we now have a structure where 'there is a constant movement from the elements to the system but no ultimate systems or elements . . . a structure in which meaning is constantly negotiated and constructed, is what I call "discourse". The concept of discourse describes the ultimate non-fixity of anything existing in society.' Here all political, economic and ideological elements float in a sea of signifiers; implicitly, too, the subject. According to Bergesen:

> Now, any fixed relation, not an interaction between base and superstructure, but within either, is so intertwined with conscious willed action – 'contingency' – that there can be no such thing as a fixed relation of any kind. The extension of this is the argument that there can be no determinate logic at all, only contingencies, resolved in struggle, alliances, bonding, agreement, consensus and articulations, between different and infinitely plural social subjects. (1993: 17)

Drawing also on Giddens' (1984) structuration theory and Knorr-Cetina's (1981) theory of summary representations, our constitutive criminological vision suggests that social structures are the categories of classification of the events that they allegedly represent. As such they are strengthened by routine construction in everyday life and by activity organized in relation to them, as though they were concrete entities (Knorr-Cetina, 1981: 36–7). But these structures are, intrinsically, provisional and contingent, and instabilities are maintained within any logics at play, both at the structural and at the subjective level. Thus we accept Giddens' theory of the 'duality of structure' in which he argues:

> The constitution of agents and structures are not two independently given sets of phenomena, a dualism, but represent a duality. According to the notion of duality of structure, the structural properties of social systems are both medium and outcome of the practices they recursively organize. Structure is not 'external' to individuals: as memory traces, and as instantiated in social practices, it is in a certain sense more 'internal' than exterior to their activities . . . Structure is not to be equated with constraint but is always both constraining and enabling. (1984: 25)

We also accept a qualified notion of autopoietic structure and 'structural coupling' developed by Luhmann and Teubner, tempered with political economic qualifications specified by critical theorists such as Jessop (1990), Hunt (1993), and Cornell (1992) and infused with postmodernist insights. Our vision has autopoietic structures being more approximate to dissipative structures, and they reach stasis only in equilibrium or homeostatic conditions. A constitutive autopoiesis argues that within the various pluralities of autopoietic structures in existence in society, each exists with its own logic, but nevertheless carries with it the logic of the other. Each exists in tension, in conflict, with perhaps one polarity (logic) being dominant. Poulantzas had posited the notion of overdetermination of structures, that spheres (economic, political, ideological, juridical) exist in relatively autonomous states and that only in a historically situated 'articulation of instances' can we identify the dominant configuration at play. However, he overlooks the fact that within each 'instance' or 'sphere' there is already, in articulated form, the other instances or spheres. There is no clear separation; they exist in dynamic and dialectical flux. This becomes an internal basis of instability. Consider, too, how because inputs cannot be precisely defined (they are indeterminate according to chaos theorists: 'noise' is always a remainder with effects), iteration will produce disproportional effects.

Foucault's genealogical analysis argues how different discursive autopoietic structures temporarily stabilize over time but yet remain unstable and convert to other forms. Certain logics may gain ascendancy. Consider this in the cases of: forces of rationalization (Weber); disciplinary mechanisms and epistemes where duplicity of the dominant logic is found in various disciplines (Foucault); new steering mechanisms rooted in power and money (Habermas); the shift from production to consumption as a dominant force (Baudrillard); the autonomization of a hyperreality (Baudrillard); and the stabilization of the modernist-order paradigm.

In criminology we see the same processes with the development of the positivist paradigm and its medical ideal, and in its transformation to one that shifts to neo-classical principles of utility, hedonism and responsibility. But these logics defy axiomatizability into an overall system that is 'gapless', and that attains global stability. With the insights of Godel's theorem, quantum mechanics, and chaos theory we can posit that constitutive autopoietic structures remain unstable and tend toward transformations, sometimes in unexpected ways. The subject, too, in this model both co-produces her/his 'reality' and has the seeds of its deconstruction embedded within.

It should be clear by now that we believe the principal means through which social structures are constituted are language use and the discursive practice of making conceptual distinctions through the play of difference (Derrida, 1973b; 1981; 1978). At the broadest social level, in Western industrial society, capital logic, the integrally related processes of rationalization, and other autopoietic structures vying for dominance provide the medium through which people constitute categories that capture essential relations. Not the least are rhetorical structures, figurative expressions, metaphors, clichés, and verbal mannerisms that are used as primary signifiers of meaning.

At the level of intersubjective communication, organizational processing, and capital logic, discursive practices are given anchorings, a 'pinning down', a 'nodal point' according to Laclau and Mouffe (1985).[32] In other words, humans use discursive practices to produce texts (narrative constructions), imaginary constructions, that anchor signifiers to particular signifieds, producing a particular image claiming to be the reality. These texts become the semiotic coordinates of action, which agents recursively use, and in so doing, provide a reconstruction of the original form.[33]

Once social structures are constituted as summary representations, their ongoing existence depends upon their continued and often unwitting reconstruction in everyday discourse, a discourse replete with tacit understandings whose basis lies outside the realm of intrinsic intersubjective communication and intersubjectivily established meaning. Core meaning constructs are typically pre-constructed elsewhere as part of our common 'stock of knowledge' (Pecheux, 1982; Lacan, 1977; Schutz, 1967; Manning, 1988). Agents in organizational settings, for example, as both the autopoiesis thesis and the habitus thesis suggest, tend to reduce feedback which represents contaminating and disruptive 'noise'.[34] In the process, they infuse existent explanatory discursive categories and texts with energy and sustenance.

Of course, missing in this is Serres' (1982b: 66–7) vision that any communicative exchange (interlocution) will inevitably attempt to deal with 'noise', that implicitly 'to hold a dialogue is to suppose a third man [woman] and seek to exclude him [her].' This third, the excluded one, the parasite, represents the nonverbalized, the unsaid. It is the possible that remains excluded, but which nevertheless exerts a force. It is this third person that is excluded, the site of local knowledge. As we have seen, feminist postmodernist analysis has indicated that in Lacan's discourse of the hysteric, where the disempowered, disenfranchised, and marginalized despairing subjects find no adequate discourse within which to embody their desire, they revert to what is available: the discourses of the master and the university. In the process, certain voices are left out (Milovanovic, 1993a). It is here also that such theorists as Clifford Geertz (1973) argue for the superiority of local knowledges because these knowledges and logics reflect 'culture as complex semiotic systems organized around local sites' (Hayles, 1990: 212; Geertz, 1973: 3–32). 'Meaning', therefore, is site-specific, and 'local knowledge is superior to global theory because, far from reinscribing differences that have marked oppressed people as inferior, it reveals fissure lines marking the interests of the oppressed as different from those of the people in power' (Hayles, 1990: 212–13). It is for this reason that Habermas' call for universality, for consensus in his 'ideal speech situation', is so much modernist talk. Rather, justice must not be linked to a desire for consensus or to universally posited agreement on language games transcending local sites and unique grammars and pragmatic rules found there (Lyotard, 1984: 66–7). We shall return to the question of policy implications in Chapters 8 and 9.

In order to sustain abstractly constructed distinctions, discursive constructions are made applicable to events, in spite of the contradictory evidence that comes from renewed micro-interaction. Contradictory evidence and potential disruptions are engendered by the internal transfer of messages, a basis of instability that is best negotiated by framing it into already understood narrative constructs that 'beg' us to make old reaffirming sense of the new nonsense (Manning, 1988; Thomas, 1988).

Organizing action to defend representations – framed and objectified in narrative texts – is one of the principal means of both defending and conferring object-like reality upon them, providing life, form, energy, sustenance and a high degree of permanence. As we shall see in a subsequent chapter, this is precisely what criminal justice presently does (though not what we think it should do) through prevailing current constructions.

Capital logic and other more dominant, global rationalizing forms are ubiquitous. As autopoietic structures they tend toward stability with the more investment that is made. As a stable structure, the more difficult it is to sustain that which it is not. This is not to imply conspiracy but to specify formal function, for while defending the wider totality, the global, agents and agencies also compete to defend their own integrity within the framework of capital logic. Criminal justice practitioners, then, are defenders of prevalent constructions as well as of their own current identities tied to and fed by the agencies that they staff.

In summary then our constitutive approach, perhaps situated as stage five of Bergesen's typology, begins with the strengths and limitations inherent in: the insights of Laclau and Mouffe; the notion of hyperreality developed by Baudrillard; the semiotics of Saussure and Lacan; the auto-poiesis/dissipative structure theses; the paralogism of Lyotard; the structuration theory of Giddens; the dialogical pedagogy of Freire; the summary representation hypothesis of Knorr-Cetina; the calls for deconstruction or 'reversal of hierarchies' of Derrida. Recognized in stages one through four is that Marxism as it was traditionally interpreted is a theory of modernity still situated in the Enlightenment (see especially Lyotard, 1984), and that a movement away from the analysis of production to consumption in postmodernist theorizing is emerging where the sign bears no relation to any extrinsic reality, it is self-referential, it is its own simulacrum (Baudrillard, 1981; 1983a). In stage four, structure and subject are dissolved: each is merely a reflection of the other. The constitutive approach, however, indicates the relative autonomy of structures and subjects as well as their dependence in the co-production of social reality.

Utopian visions: the new house of radical superliberalism

A constitutive approach links deconstruction with reconstruction as an inseparable whole, a transpraxis rather than a praxis. The notion of a transpraxis, the politically mobilized movement from here to there, will be dealt with in Chapters 8 and 9. Here we would like to offer visions of social structure, an alternative (dis)order, a radical superliberalism.

A constitutive approach prioritizes conceptualizations of social structure that liberate human potentialities, without in turn undergoing stasis. We have already indicated that the model that comes to mind is a social formation where far-from-equilibrium conditions prevail, within which dissipative structures, as modified autopoietic forms, provide contingent and provisional stabilities necessary for assuring (as Nietzsche would tell us) 'horizons' for intersubjective interaction. Here we would have the subject-in-process, a role-maker rather than a role-taker, a subject looking very much like a strange attractor in terms of its patterned overall behavior, but yet indeterminate in any specific act. This is our 'recovering subject' who can simultaneously de-identify with a social position, the possibilities of which are often restricted within equilibrium forms of dynamic, and engage in re-identification with others, a strategy of 'defining equivalences and constructing alliances' (JanMohamed, 1994).[35] The 'recovering subject' crosses borders, identifies with the other, and engages in the co-production of 'contingent universalities' (Butler, 1992; Giroux, 1992) that provide provisional bases for social action. It is in the direction posited by Mouffe, in her movement toward 'a common political identity that would create the conditions for the establishment of a new hegemony articulated through new egalitarian social relations, practices, and institutions' (1992: 380).

This constitutive approach integrates Freire's work on the pedagogy of the oppressed by indicating how new discursive structures, such as liberation theology, can develop with consequential effects. These dynamics oppose the privileging of order and its derivatives – homeostasis, equilibrium, tension reduction, etc. It rejects conceptualizations of social structure that are in tune with it, and notions of the subject that are in sync with it. The model being offered by constitutive theory has within it structures that tend toward a provisional and contingent status, that tend toward dissipation and toward 'contingent universalities'. In other words, what constitutive theory advocates is not a new Logos that would resist change, but only provisional logics which tend toward fragmentation and change. We need not resign ourselves to the status of inconsequential beings. If anything, chaos theory has indicated that the 'small' person's engagement can make major differences in social change; the recovering subject can recover the social world.

A model that has recently appeared that moves somewhat in this direction is Unger's (1987) call for an 'empowered democracy' that he unflinchingly calls 'superliberalism'. Although eclectic in his approach, and although a number of reservations can be levied against it, superliberalism nevertheless offers conceptualizations that are consistent with our constitutive vision. Hence we advocate a strategic incorporation toward developing an alternative, more humanistic social structure. Of course, the danger of such advocacy is that integrating mutually incompatible conceptualizations may undermine symmetry in the model. Let us take a few exploratory steps here.

Unger's work is predicated on the idea that in equilibrium conditions social structures tend to stasis, such as the bureaucratic apparatus, or consider the criminal justice system. They ossify and become insensitive to change, become institutions, guided by their own internal logic: according to Weber, rationalization; for Foucault, the disciplinary technologies; and for Giddens, those practices which have the greatest time–space extension. Unger offers a number of mechanisms that perpetually challenge the inertia of bureaucracy. In short, Unger advocates the mechanism by which far-from-equilibrium conditions can be produced and sustained. Unger's possibility for a more humanistic social structure integrates many emerging concepts of affirmative postmodernism and is in accord with the image provided by constitutive theorizing. In this sense, co-production of social reality is not a reifying process in which subordination prevails; rather, it is a process where an open future is negotiated with acknowledgement of conflict and the possibilities of transcendence. (We will explore how this is possible in Chapters 8 and 9.)

Summary and conclusions

In this chapter we have shown how alone the visions of social structure contained in the modernist criminological literature are inadequate to address the expansive possibility engendered by our recovering human subject. Similarly, the more extreme postmodernism affords considerable critical tools for unpacking the modern, but little delivery in terms of presence and future. Affirmative postmodernism provided several critical insights on the contingent nature of the social and on the subject–society interrelationship, and, when rejoined with modernist and postmodernist ideas, delivered a dynamic and contingent conception of social structure. While it is tempting to want to describe this new house for our recovering subject and especially how to build it, we first need to inspect more closely the security problems of the old house. Thus we defer our enthusiasm to an examination of law.

Notes

1 This contrasts with Newtonian physics which posits that, given some incremental increase in some independent variable, a proportional effect results.

2 Contrast these with conditions explained by Newton and conventional thermodynamic theory, where stability is the state to which the system is said to move because of entropy production (e.g. homeostasis, or structural functionalism).

3 See also Young (1992), Lyotard (1984), Weinstein (1993), and Baker (1993).

4 Kropotkin (1912), Barkum (1968), and Michalowski (1985).

5 Examples of consensus acephalous society appear in the accounts of those who have

theorized about: social control in non-industrial society (Black, 1976) and stateless societies (Roberts, 1979); pre-industrial Western society and life in post-revolutionary communist society (Lenin, 1949; Quinney, 1975); matriarchy after patriarchy; and anarchist, communist or decentralized socialist utopias (Tifft and Sullivan, 1980; Abel, 1982b; Pepinsky, 1991).

6 Matza's (Matza and Sykes, 1961; Matza, 1964) neutralization theory, with its emphasis on subterranean values, differs in that it recognizes the plurality of subcultural values to be a permanent nether side of any assumed dominant cultural order.

7 For economic theory generally see Becker (1968), Sullivan (1973), Ehrlich (1973; 1982). On time allocation theory see Heineke (1978); on wealth maximization see Schmidt and Witte (1984). Rational choice and routine activities theory are represented by Clarke and Cornish (1983; Cornish and Clarke, 1987) and by Cohen and Felson (1979; Felson, 1986), respectively.

8 On social control theory see Nye (1958), Hirschi (1969; 1983; Gottfredson and Hirschi, 1990); and for differential learning theories see Sutherland (1939), Cressey (1960), Akers (1967), and Reckless (1973).

9 See Merton (1938; 1968), Cohen (1955), Cloward and Ohlin (1960), and Agnew (1985; 1992a).

10 See Beirne (1979) and Milovanovic (1983; 1989a) on the distinction between instrumental and structural Marxism.

11 See Hirst (1975), Spitzer (1975; 1980), Greenberg (1981), and Chambliss and Seidman (1982).

12 See Eisenstein (1979), Messerschmidt (1986), Ursel (1986), and Currie (1989).

13 See Hagan (1989; 1990; Hagan et al., 1985; 1987).

14 Much of this is a derivative of Newtonian mechanics, Aristotelian logic, and Euclidian geometry with its x–y coordinating grids.

15 The influence of Hegel and Heidegger is also apparent in his work. An indirect effect of Nietzsche through the works of Freud also could be ascertained. However, Lacan and those who followed in the postmodernist tradition of analysis would elevate the importance of discourse and discount much of the phenomenologist's embracing of some transcendental subject (the centered subject). See particularly the Lacanian inspired works of Laclau and Mouffe (1985; Mouffe, 1979; 1992; Laclau, 1987; 1988).

16 Schutz (1967), Knorr-Cetina (1981), Pecheux (1982), Giddens (1984), and Manning (1988). See also Lacan's (1985) description of the phallocentric Symbolic Order.

17 Lacan (1985), Cornell (1991; 1993), Milovanovic (1994a; 1994b), Arrigo (1993), and Baudrillard (1981; 1983a; 1985).

18 Note here Baudrillard's lingering modernism, consistent with his denial that he is postmodernist, suggestive that more substantive and satisfying social relations have occurred and are possible.

19 Representative work here is the post-Marxism of Laclau and Mouffe (1985) and Mouffe (1992), and feminist postmodernist analysis, particularly concerning multiple forms of consciousness and a potentially new Symbolic Order. See, for example, Harris (1991), Crenshaw (1988), Matsuda (1987), Cook (1990), Goldfarb (1992), Smith (1992). See also contributions from chaos theory and neo-systems theory such as Young (1991a; 1992), Unger (1987), Milovanovic (1992a), and pedagogically oriented theories focused on the Freire-Giroux-Aronowitz work that highlight multiple sites for the production of knowledge, languages of possibilities (Aronowitz and Giroux, 1991; McLaren, 1994).

20 In our constitutive approach, below, we envision these as two autopoietic structures, loci of logics, vying for dominance – where one among many others may find ascendancy.

21 This ubiquitous Logos assumes the development of certain logical structures tending toward equilibrium or homeostasis, such as in Durkheim's spontaneous division of labor, Weber's forces of rationalization, Hegel and Marx's working out of the Absolute Spirit, Parsons' structural functionalism, Freud's tension-reduction (homeostatic) model, and some of Lacan's more conservative views of desire as a response to lack.

22 'Iteration' refers to any process by which some result of some calculation is fed back into the algorithm for recomputation. It is a continuous loop and it has been found that even very minor 'rounding' can produce vastly unexpected results with continuous iteration. This is

referred to as a 'sensitive dependence on initial conditions' (Gregersen and Sailer, 1993). Words, for example, have slightly different meanings in new contexts (Derrida, 1973b; Balkin, 1987).

23 For an application in law see Balkin (1987), Brion (1991; 1995), and Milovanovic (1993a; 1995).

24 For an accessible presentation see Garcia (1991); for an application to the social sciences, see Hayles (1990: 164–5), and Lyotard (1984: 58).

25 See O'Malley and Mugford's (1994) suggestion that Katz's work is in the tradition of postmodern analysis.

26 By this, chaologists mean that symmetries within some dynamic systems are replicated at ever-increasing fine points of examination. For example, Foucault (1977) showed how disciplining mechanisms are duplicated in various sites of production.

27 As found in Euclidian geometry aided by a Newtonian calculus.

28 Lyotard refers to this as part of his 'paralogy'.

29 See also Baack and Cullen (1992; 1994).

30 Consider Reiman's redistributive principle (1990), Schwendinger and Schwendinger's 'good society' (1970), and Lacan's 'avowal of desire' (1991).

31 On the former see Laclau and Mouffe (1985; 1987; Laclau, 1988; Mouffe, 1979; 1988).

32 See also Lacan (1977), Manning (1988), Milovanovic (1992a; 1992b).

33 Elsewhere, Milovanovic (1993b) has indicated how these dynamics can also be explained by Lacan's mechanism of the Borromean knots, where knot-breaking, the disentanglement of three orders (the Imaginary, Real, Symbolic), may lead to new configurations, a new knotting, a basis of alternative knowledge production.

34 See Luhmann (1985), and also Manning's (1988) application to the processing of emergency 911 calls coded by the police.

35 Similarly, Unger (1987: 564) has advocated practices of 'role defiance' and 'role jumbling'.

4

The Structuring of Law: a Constitutive Socio-Legal Analysis

Sutherland (1939: 11) observed that 'an understanding of the nature of law is necessary in order to secure an understanding of the nature of crime.' But, ideas about society's 'political and especially legal institutions are based on particular assumptions about society. Indeed, it has long been recognized that no answer to the question "What is law?" is possible without a theory of society' (Einstadter and Henry, 1995: 6–7). In the previous chapter we established that modernist and postmodernist thinking had very different assumptions about how society is constituted. As a result we would expect their ideas about law to reflect different visions of law and its relationship to social order. Here we trace the variety of modernist views of law as these relate to and are derived from the different modernist criminological views of society. Seven modernist approaches to law are discussed ranging from consensus to a variety of conflict approaches. After sketching out each direction we focus on postmodernist ideas about law. We explore the skeptical postmodernist view that law is at best a myth and at worst, 'dead'. Then we develop our constitutive approach, arguing for the reassessment of law as integrally related to other social forms.

Modernist ideas of law

Modernist ideas about law mark a break from earlier theological and supernatural ideas that present law as a god-given reality. Modernism rejects the hierarchy of levels such as proposed in Aquinas' thirteenth century theology. In this premodern 'descendant' foundational view, 'God was considered the supreme lawgiver. Law had to conform ultimately to this mythic origin for its being or validity . . . God remained the necessary and unavoidable source of law's being' (Fitzpatrick, 1992: 51).

The traditional theological view of law was replaced by a modernist vision centered on rationality, objective analysis and innovation directed toward progress. Here human law was separate, distinct and independent of other forms of law, human customs and convention. The challenge began with an elevation of natural law as the universal and uniform law, as 'Enlightenment replaces God with nature' (1992: 51). Then positive law philosophers, such as Austin and Kelsen, further distilled human law from natural law, assuming that law contained essential, irreducible, logical elements rooted in the political fabric of a society that were commanded by a sovereign on its subjects. Fitzpatrick comments on this modernist break: 'The sovereign is no longer God's earthly representative and is now the autonomous and self-sufficient source of law. Law . . . is no longer tied to any extraneous order, now deriving its force and origin purely from its intrinsic being' (1992: 55).

But by the middle to late nineteenth century even this early modernism was under attack, most notably from the founding sociologists Marx, Weber and Durkheim who, through the application of realism and scientific method, believed in law's essential connection to structural conditions and social processes (for an overview of these sociological classics, see Milovanovic, 1994a). It was believed that only social forces explained the role law played in society: 'The gist of these social accounts is . . . that law, rather than dominating society, is itself wholly a product of society. It changes as society changes and it can even disappear when the social conditions that created it disappear or when they change into conditions antithetical to it' (Fitzpatrick, 1992: 6). Social theorists also relieved natural law theorists of their embarrassing inability to explain how the natural was articulated. They enabled us to peer behind the discursive mask to see who decides what counts as 'natural', 'essential', 'moral' and 'universal'. They expose the processes through which law is legitimated by reference to gods, common-sense notions of right and wrong or the 'general will'.

In subsequent modernist theory, law appears in several guises. All have to do with demonstrating the connection between law and social forms. Galliher (1989: 142–3) has identified five intellectual traditions on law that relate to the different views held about society and social order. We have divided his fifth view into two versions and added an additional systems perspective. We will briefly review the first five positions before giving extended discussion to the last two.

The consensus-functionalist view

This view argues that law is 'a product of widespread consensus in society'. This includes visions of liberal legal order said to reflect an agreement over societal values and norms. For example, classical Enlightenment theorists such as Beccaria (1764) and Bentham (1765) saw human law expressing a rational agreement contained in the idea of a 'social compact', an agreement drafted by assemblies of representative legislators, declaring cooperation among humans over a desire for mutual defense of 'the public', 'the society', 'the nation', or 'the collective human rights of the community'. To be defended was a utilitarian idea: that of maximizing useful activity, well-being, happiness and pleasure for the greatest number of persons, based on assumed 'natural rights' and 'freedom of choice' of individuals. In individual positivist theories of crime, law is a reflection of normal patterns of behavior produced by biologically normal humans or by normal minds or personalities in a given environment; law prohibits what is defined as abnormal or deviant (see Garafalo, 1914).

The same notion appears again in sociological positivist thought. In Durkheim's anomie theory, law expresses the common consciousness (*conscience collective*). In Mertonian strain theory, it protects the society's cultural values, norms and goals, and helps maintain order, through integrating its members and providing them with a mechanism to resolve conflicts that threaten to create social friction and disrupt harmony (Merton, 1938).[1] In short, consensus theorists see law as both reflecting and shaping the moral and behavioral consensus of whole societies.

The symbolic-pluralist view

This view sees law serving 'a symbolic or public relations function, as opposed to actually controlling behavior'. It assumes a liberal legal order of organized interest groups. For social ecological theorists such as Shaw and McKay (1931), and culture conflict theorists (Sellin, 1938), inclusion or passage of some of their subcultural norms as law can be a symbolic marker of their acceptance into the mainstream, just as resistance to such incorporation can be a symbolic affirmation of their subordination. Thus law can be tied to the status politics of constituent groups (Edelman, 1964; Gusfield, 1967).

The conflict-pluralist view

This view sees law as 'a product of a democratic compromise among competing interest groups', as a site for meshing the diversity of interests. Each struggles to define their social reality as *the* reality and mobilizes support for banning behaviors that clash with their own (Becker, 1963; Schur, 1980). What emerges is law as the outcome of compromise rather than outright victory (Carson, 1971). Legal pluralism extends this view, recognizing that interest groups create their own 'normative orders' (Weber, 1954) or 'living law' (Ehrlich, 1913) which have as much coercive power as law. What may mesh or clash are these multiple normative systems.[2]

The elite-domination view

This view sees law as 'a product of political domination by some type of elite interest group'. Here conflict theorists (Vold, 1958; Quinney, 1970) see law as an outcome of the exercise of power by *particular* interest groups who maintain a dominant position. Regardless of whether interest is rooted in status, morality, religion, ideology, culture, or social issues, the outcome is that 'certain groups – variously and vaguely termed "the powerful", "the bureaucracy", "the moral entrepreneur" . . . enforce their values upon the less powerful, labeling those who infringe their rules with stereotypical tags' (Young, 1981: 288). Law thus becomes a weapon in the battle between groups vying for dominance and creates conflict by being a resource to be won, whose control is crucial for maintaining supremacy over competing groups (Turk, 1976). The battle is won when the state is 'captured', and major law enforcement agencies are empowered to act, in the name of the whole society, on behalf of the dominant group.

A variation sees domination structured by gendered male concerns as in radical feminism[3] or by the concerns of one racial or ethnic group (e.g. critical race theory). Law is an instrument for domination, and for the perpetuation of division. Under radical feminism, domination is attributed to men who subordinate and exploit women in a patriarchal society whose state and legal system reflect the interests, experiences and viewpoints of men. Control and the subordination of women by the state are achieved through the legal control of women's sexuality, their capacities for reproduction, and through their legal regulation as male property (Edwards, 1990: 149; see also DeKeseredy and Hinch, 1991). Radical feminists (e.g. MacKinnon, 1982; 1983; 1987) see both law and the state as instruments to power, to be taken over and used in the interests of women (e.g. a form of the call for the 'reversal of hierarchies'). Similar assumptions are found in critical race theory by those who argue that law reflects the racial interests of dominant white society.[4]

The instrumental coercive-power view

This view sees law as 'a product of a dominant economic class'. Domination is by economic class in a capitalist system of exploitation, rather than by race or gender or some other difference. These other divisions are seen as mere epiphenomena of the underlying class-based conflict. Law is an instrument of economic class power, a repressive apparatus of government working on behalf of a monopoly capitalist elite class who provide the definitional content of law, thereby controlling lesser 'lieutenant capitalists', the political and administrative apparatus, and through them the whole society. The law is an instrument of the state, controlled by the dominant economic elite to repress subordinate classes for the purpose of maintaining and perpetuating the existing economic and social order (Quinney, 1974; 1975: 55). Similarly, Marxist feminists see the law perpetuating the inheritance system for the benefit of class-divided males and to the detriment of women who are bound to domestic labor. Also similar is the critical legal pluralist suggestion that state law and its institutions for administering justice are but one form of social control in a hierarchical system of capitalist state power (Diamond, 1973; Hooker, 1975; Fitzpatrick, 1983).

While each of these five views has some merit, they have been well reviewed in the established criminological (Einstadter and Henry, 1995) and socio-legal literature (Milovanovic, 1994a). We shall now elaborate on the remaining two views.

The structural ideological-power view

The sixth view of law sees it as a 'consequence of the economic conditions or institutions prevailing in society'. Consistent with the dual power model of society discussed in the previous chapter, the structural power view sees law as an ideologically coercive and yet semi-autonomous means of class domination, one which is influenced, rather than controlled, by semi-autonomous economic and political elites. In this version, law, as a legitimating and ideological institution of a semi-autonomous state, exercises power both on subordinate classes and against dominating classes in the interests of the more powerful and in the long-term interests of preserving the capitalist system.[5]

Thus laws, such as those on health and safety at work, on price fixing, or on environmental protection, reflect an ideological need to develop consent for and assent to the existing social order. In this model consensus reappears, but as an ideological construction legitimated through law. Indeed, as Young (1981: 300) points out, the contradictory role of capitalist law must embody some real protection against the powerless, and in the process it sustains the legitimacy of the very system of exploitation that gives rise to these crimes.[6]

In Unger (1976; see also Collins, 1987) we see a more fragmentary version of the structural power model in which late capitalist or post-industrial society is shown to divide into sectors of state welfarism, corporatism, and an anti-formalist, anti-state, anti-bureaucratic communitarianism. State welfarism, for Unger, arises because of the irony of the state's semi-autonomous role in protecting certain oppressed groups produced by the capitalist system. Thus the state, in the ideological role of protector of individuals rights and autonomous administrator of fair justice, becomes subject to pressures from people to actually protect their rights, rather than to pretend to do so. The state empowers law to act against dominant classes and to protect certain groups based on a substantive form of justice oriented to results. At the same time, economic elites are described as increasing their direct control over the lives of the unprotected through private justice, other non-state laws, and discipline. Here law, then, is both facilitative and an outcome of social transformation.

A similar version of law as ideological domination is found in the ideas of socialist feminists in their attempts to 'challenge the reconstitution of patriarchy through law' (Currie, 1991: 10; Smart, 1989) and to eliminate 'relations of domination and subordination' (Daly, 1990: 10). Combining a Marxist analysis of class with a radical feminist analysis of gender, they present law as the outcome of a male dominated capitalist state. They see a danger inherent in law genuinely being used by subordinated and oppressed women to episodically improve specific instances of their unequal situation, because doing so ideologically strengthens the very long-term stability of the male state that represses and exploits women in general. They argue it is the state's relative autonomy expressed through law that institutionalizes women's oppression (Eisenstein, 1979) since it operates to maintain the patriarchal class power structure. Moreover, for some socialist feminists, as the bastion of patriarchy, welfarism is seen as less a protection than a means of controlling women through 'public patriarchy' in an era when capitalism has abandoned patriarchy's cause (Ursel, 1986; Currie, 1989). In contrast to radical feminists, the idea of taking over the state is no more adequate than a postmodernist position that allows men to remain dominant through their control over the local, customary and parochial sites of resistance.[7]

Many critical theorists of advanced capitalism see the latest turn of the ideological screw in the celebration of informal law and justice.[8] They claim these are subordinate normative orders, whose semi-autonomy serves the ideological function of blurring state power so that it appears to be a benign part of the social fabric. They show how this is accomplished by the cooptation and exploitation of a 'communitarian' human desire for informal, localized, community justice. The episodic tendency toward an 'informal', decentralized state control serves a dual legitimating and net-widening function for the state, an observation that seems particularly applicable to the growth of state sponsored dispute settlement institutions (Harrington, 1985; Merry and Milner, 1993).

Elsewhere, a 'structural interpellation' variant of Marxism was developed indicating the primacy of superstructural practices (e.g. political, ideological and juridical) over economic. Here, a top-down linear causality was posited where subjects are narrowly constituted (interpellated) as juridic and economic subjects (Milovanovic, 1986; 1987; 1994a: 143–54). Although much material could be brought to bear in support of this thesis, the position must be tempered by an acknowledgement that it may lead to an excessive linearity and determinacy.[9] Without substantial qualifications, this position is subject to the challenge and scrutiny of affirmative post-modernist thought, particularly our constitutive approach (Milovanovic, 1994a: 80–1; Henry and Milovanovic, 1991).

The systems-power view

Finally, this seventh view sees law as a self-defining, self-regenerating semi-autonomous system that serves the interests of its own continuance (i.e. autopoietic).[10] Law, like other autopoietic systems, has a tendency to maintain equilibrium in face of changing conditions or unsuspected disturbances that may come from the state, the society or other systems (e.g. the perception of a 'living law').[11] This is possible because the constitutive components of law and the legal system are sufficiently functionally flexible that they can maintain the whole organization of law as a constant. The underlying structure here, as Weber poignantly indicated, was the ubiquitous forces of rationalization, best captured in the development and growth of bureaucracies, and stabilized, with the onset of the capitalist order, in formal-rational law (Weber, 1978; Milovanovic, 1994a: 36–60).

Luhmann (1985; 1988) argues that the legal system is *both* open and closed. It is closed in that it is self-referential and self-reproducing. Only the legal system can bestow legally normative quality on its elements, such that it reproduces its own elements by its elements. Milovanovic (1994a: 129) summarizes Luhmann's view that

> law attains a degree of relative autonomy. It takes on qualities of being objective and thus retains a resistance to direct manipulation. The immediate environment is but a factor which further fuels the relatively independent factors within the legal system itself. A form of self-justifying circularity thus reigns.

However, law is also cognitively open, oriented to its particular environment allowing it to be able to learn and internally adapt. It uses 'inputs' to change its programs to coordinate that which is produced by its self-reproduction and it uses the environment as a resource. In Teubner's (1989; 1993) autopoietic view of law, the legal system is self-referential in producing legal acts or court decisions and, through its own internal reordering and regulation, law reinterprets the world around it: 'The claim made is that law can regulate social life only by regulating its own elements (including its own images of society and of other disciplines)' (Nelken, 1994: 29). Teubner develops the concept of hypercycles, multiple feedback loops and the co-evolution of autopoietic subsystems which, as Fitzpatrick (1992: 9) critically observes, is a social account 'which would hermetically secure law by according it the self-creating power to absorb and order society in its own terms', a feat managed only because 'it incorporates . . . a myth of law's transcendence.'

Bourdieu (1987) has offered a similar idea to autopoiesis in his notion of the 'legal habitus', although he does attempt to separate himself from Luhmann. He identifies a juridic sphere as a social space which includes the symbolic structure, that 'does not contain within itself the principles of its own dynamic'. He distinguishes this from the notion of system which includes 'the order of objective relations between actors and institutions in competition with each other for control of the right to determine the law' (1987: 816). In Bourdieu's view, a legal habitus produces 'categories of perception and judgment that structure the perception and judgment of ordinary conflicts, and orient the work which converts them into juridical confrontations' (1987: 833). As Yngvesson's (1993) study on the role of the court clerk demonstrates, getting 'caught up in the law' entails a 'subjecting' process in the sense that humans must 'frame their wants and their needs in terms that tend to confine them to pre-existing relations, traditions, and institutions as they go to court, speak with a lawyer, appear before a zoning board, call the police, talk to a social worker, or fight with their neighbor' (1993: 120). Disputants and/or defendants before the court must necessarily abandon other efforts of resolution (i.e. self-help). They must resign themselves to the discursive subject position of 'client', seeking a professional (lawyer) who offers the correct skills in the construction of an appropriate case for litigation and resolution. Thus, 'the professionals create the need for their own services by redefining problems expressed in ordinary language as legal problems, translating them into the language of the law.' This circularity is not only apparent, it is the working of the law (Bourdieu, 1987: 834, 836).

Bourdieu's thesis of the juridical field and legal habitus, although going beyond some of the earlier more simplistic views as to the self-generating form of legal thought, is problematic since it harbors the metaphysics of order.[12] In contrast, consider the notion of autopoiesis which offers a degree of openness to 'inputs' from the environment, and the notion of 'dissipative structure' (discussed in Chapter 2) which suggests not only inherent centrifugal but also centripetal forces in tension or in a state of orderly disorder, with built-in possibilities of dissipation. Bourdieu's thesis also falls short of a fully developed theory of the relationship between agency and structure. As a result Bourdieu's conceptualization provides little guidance for transcendence.

Having said this it must be pointed out that there are several strengths to his position. First, he persuasively indicates that more formalistic legal theories (those which assume law as some kind of independent, concrete structure) or more instrumentalist legal theories (those which assume that understanding law is only connected with the inevitability of some power group assuming the reins of the legal system) have the limitation of simplistic analysis. Second, Bourdieu, like autopoietic theorists, has developed an account of how the discursive structure is the key concept in legally constituted 'realities'. Third, he advances the view that law may maintain a degree of independence within a social formation and that it can function to constitute 'realities' in its own language. This is the case, for example, in a trial where 'a struggle in which differing, indeed antagonistic world-views confront each other' and where 'what is at stake in this struggle is monopoly of the power to impose a universally recognized principle of knowledge of the social world' (1987: 837). But ultimately, law has final authority, indeed structural agency, in this view. As he tells it: 'It would not be excessive to say that it creates the social world, but only if we remember that it is this world which first creates the law' (1987: 839). Although our constitutive approach would agree with his conclusion, we would suggest a different interpretation as to the underlying dynamics, especially in regard to how both law and structure are energized by active human agency. But we are ahead of ourselves.

Let us summarize our position on modernist views of law. With the exception of possibly the structural ideological-power view, and the neo-systems theory that we have just examined, modernist social, socio-legal, and criminological depictions of law are narrowly conceived. They position law as an object, separate from, produced by, and subject to the actions of external social forces, whether these be society, classes, groups, agencies, or individuals (Griffiths, 1979). Moreover, they assume law to have a real power in itself, the power to legitimate social orders, the power to minimize conflict, the power to oppress and even the power to resist its own destruction. As we shall shortly see, for postmodernists all this is just so much myth.

The skeptical postmodernist view of law

The skeptical postmodernist view of law takes the position not only that law is a social construction, but that it is 'mythic' both in its origin and as a continuing social force, going so far as to claim that 'outside of myth, it has no existence' (Fitzpatrick, 1992: 210). Law is said to be produced and reproduced as part of the production of other constructed social forms as well as through the discourse of its own self-production. Law, for postmodernists, is neither legitimate nor legitimating but a source of texts (Balkin, 1987). Invoking the discourse of legal text is symbolically violent in that it represents differences as wholes and, in its desire to contribute to the meta-narratives of progress, it can 'empower some entities and cast others into subjugation' (Schwartz and Friedrichs, 1994: 224). As such it is subject to deconstruction.

Skeptical postmodernists have been indebted to Derrida's work on deconstruction. His philosophical position on the deconstruction of different hierarchies, forms of logic, and metaphysical underpinnings to various forms of texts led to a flurry of critical work in legal studies, particularly in the 1980s by members of the critical legal studies movement. Derrida's two major deconstructive strategies concern 'the reversal of hierarchies' and the 'liberation of the text from the author' (Balkin, 1987). As to the first, he identifies how hierarchies are ubiquitous but always found in diads where one term is privileged: for example, man/woman, law/custom, rule/norm, formal/informal, public/private. In such diads, each of the elements depends for its existence on the other even if one of the terms is more overt. For example, the term 'law-abiding citizens' may be stated but its comprehension depends upon the assumed existence of 'law-breaking citizens'. Similarly the concept of 'formal economy' implies an underlying and lesser 'informal economy'. This process Derrida refers to as the 'metaphysics of presence'. It is a play of presence and absence. The absent term, nevertheless, has a function: it acts as a 'supplement' for the privileged term. It provides the privileged term a basis of being.

By a philosophical reversal of hierarchies, it is argued, an investigator may understand this dynamic relationship in more profound ways, and why the privileged term is so elevated. Accounting for much of the privileging of one term over the other can be traced to the inherent logic of a phallocentric symbolic order (i.e. Logos) which acts as an anchor of sorts to the constant slippage of signifiers (i.e. displacements by metaphor as in the use of say the term 'crack' which selects out certain negative imagery over all the other associations it might have, or the word 'coke' whose image is much more positive). Much of the early forms of postmodernist analysis simply saw the reversal of hierarchies as a method to do away with sexism, racism, classism. Investigating further might have revealed that this, by itself, may re-establish the previous form of domination, or lead to rigid forms of essentialist arguments. A good example is found in Cornell's (1991: 11, 139, 185) concerns about the institutionalization of a 'politics of revenge', as is implied, she tells us, in MacKinnon's work.

The second contribution Derrida makes concerns the 'trace'. Each of the terms in a hierarchy lies in opposition where differences give them their respective coherence (e.g. man/woman, serious/non-serious, yes/no, speech/ writing). A social theory thereby privileges some human values over others. We saw examples of this in our analysis of modernist assumptions about the human such as free choice or determinism in classicism. Each term not only differs from but defers to the other. The de-privileged term must always wait for the privileged term. Derrida refers to this process as 'différance'. However, each of the terms carries within it a trace of the other; each leaves a mark in the other. Thus, embedded in the sign is always the trace of an absent other sign. For example, referring to a dictionary or a thesaurus shows one can always continue a search for the definition of a word until eventually one returns to the starting point. A dominant signifier, therefore, always hides an absent one. As Sarup tells it: 'each sign in the chain of meaning is somehow scored over or traced through with all the others, to form a complex tissue which is never exhaustible' (1989: 36).

Lacan (1977) made a similar argument to Derrida's 'trace' with his notion of 'metaphor' where the dominant signifier can become the signified, which in turn will be the signifier for the previous signified which has been now pushed back further into the unconscious realm but always remaining connected in a long chain, a chain of signifiers. For Lacan (1977), this very 'crossing of the bar' between signifier and signified produces meaning; it is the creative spark by which 'sense' is created from 'nonsense'. Consider such crossings that occur in the critical metaphors that have been used to describe both criminologists and postmodernists who 'in the evocative Texas phrase are "all hat and no cattle"' (Schwartz and Friedrichs, 1994: 233), or the creative filling-in necessary to make sense of the bumper sticker 'postmodernists do it in their heads.'

For Derrida, we can never go back to some original point of demarcation. Meaning, therefore, is inherently unstable. Moreover, since the subject is totally immersed in language, s/he too is inherently unstable (Derrida, 1973b),[13] a position we developed in Chapter 2.

Applying this argument to our present concern, a text, such as a legal text, once produced, is liberated from the author. This is so because words are reusable in different contexts, but as they are, they acquire different nuances of meaning. This is referred to as 'iteration'. Since an infinite number of contexts can appear, iteration will produce an indeterminate number of nuanced meanings: it produces undecidables (Derrida, 1973b: 157–62).[14]

If initial uncertainties pervade the text and no 'origin' can be specified, then iteration must produce indeterminacies. As a result, linguistic systems, discursive formations, are inherently unstable and tend toward the indeterminate. In this sense, Derrida anticipated some of the findings of chaos theory (see particularly Hayles, 1990). In law, as iteration proceeds, as the founding fathers' 'original intent' is interpreted in ever-new contexts, we see the dynamic of the free play of the text. Once said or written, the sign is now out of the control of the author's intent. Its meaning varies as to the interpretive community (Fish, 1980).

For the critical legal scholar, deconstruction as a methodology implies that relatively stabilized hierarchies can be momentarily reversed to discern the elements at play and to explain why one remains the privileged term. Some critical legal theorists embraced this methodology in their now famous 'trashing' approach to reading legal texts. Each text, they would argue, is ideologically constituted with a privileging of certain ideas and ideals over others and the purpose of trashing is to discover what these are (Kairys, 1982).

Skeptical postmodernists reject the mythical consensual view of law as a form of 'privileging', referring instead to 'subjugated knowledges', which 'tell different stories and have different specificities' and which aim at 'the deconstruction of truth' and deconstruction of the effects of claims to truth through a 'multiplicity of resistances' to the ubiquity of power (Smart, 1990: 82).

However, the skeptical postmodern analysis of law, like that found in some critical legal studies, does not address the variety of images of law in the different literatures. With few exceptions and with some irony, given its desire for the resistances told by others' claims to truth, it ignores the diversity of images of law shown in our review of modernism. Moreover, it discredits the challenge of the interpretive legal school (Dworkin, 1968; 1986) that law comprises the different images of its participants, arguing that this ultimately collapses diversity into unity (Fitzpatrick, 1992: 4–5). Instead, skeptical postmodernism takes a narrow cluster of modernist work, that of the ideology of traditional legal positivism and neo-positivism (legal formalism, or classicism), and trashes *its* image of law as though this were the only picture.[15] It examines *this* law's claims to be 'neutral, fair – an uncontroversial way to resolve disputes in an impersonal, predictable, noncontroversial manner', to be 'factual, analytical, free of bias, neutral, objective' with 'determined meaning', where 'legal statutes constituted a system of self-contained, codified rules' that are 'independent of arbitrary and compromising political, economic, and social factors', and 'turns these assumptions upside down' (Rosenau, 1992: 125). In contrast, for their part postmodernists take law to be so subjective that no truth claims can be made: a totalizing text where all meanings are imposed.

In constructing a 'counter-myth' (Fitzpatrick, 1992: xi), the claim is made that law's own mythology is sustained through 'a mixture of image, myth, oral memory and written text, custom and judicial legislation' (Goodrich,

1992: 8). Thus, for Fitzpatrick (1992), modern law is a form of anemic perfected mythology absent, indeed, cleansed of its contradictory existences, born in denial of the mythical other. For Goodrich (1987) law gains its power from these multiple extra-legal sources but then these beginnings are systematically denied by the rhetoric of law: 'the law is principally a discourse of power which conceals its conditions of production through a series of rhetorical techniques' (McCahery, 1993: 414, on Goodrich, 1987).

The skeptical postmodernist has faced the dilemma raised by Fish that no foundational positions can be established and hence arrives at the logic of nihilism or fatalism: why bother? Fish's work seriously undermined the American version of critical legal studies with this devastating and continuous critique (see Fish, 1980; 1984; 1989).

One recoil to this challenge came from some feminist critical legal theorists who advocated a standpoint epistemology. As Bartlett states: 'Feminist standpoint epistemology identifies woman's status as that of victim and then privileges that status by claiming that it gives access to understanding about oppression that others cannot have' (1991: 385). And Jaggar comments that the 'special social or class position of women . . . gives them a special epistemological standpoint which makes possible a view of the world that is more reliable and less distorted than that available either to capitalist or to working class men' (1983: 370). This logic could also be extended to other disenfranchised groups.

As appealing as standpoint epistemology may seem, however, it contains at least two serious problems. First, even the oppressed in constructing a text of their oppression must make use of the dominant discourse and its available discursive subject positions (e.g. client, defendant, complainant, service receiver, etc.). Hence the oppressed become subject to discourse's constitutive effects. Second, standpoint epistemology can slip into essentialist arguments privileging, now in a more sustained way, via grandiose statements concerning objectivity and universality, *its* particular view of the world thereafter sustained by a newly based discourse of the master (Lacan, 1991).[16]

Critical legal studies, thus, confronts a crises over 'how to proceed?' Some direction has been provided by affirmative feminist postmodernism in law, particularly the analysis developed by women of color. For example, Ahluwalia (1991: 12) has argued that 'the sexism of deducing the experience of all from the experience of men is rivaled only by the racism of asserting white middle class experience as normal, and designating black people's experience to the category of "other"'. She points out that, 'Understanding men as the bearers of power and the perpetrators of all evil denies the privilege that white women have over black men and neglects to implicate white women in perpetuating racism and using violence against black people' (1991: 12). As Einstadter and Henry comment, any contingent position 'would also need to overcome the simplistic black/white distinction within gender analysis. Different cultural experiences, such as Latina women, Asian women, American Indian women and women with disabilities, would also benefit from such a broadened feminist analysis' (1995: 275).[17] Our constitutive approach draws inspiration from this contemporary postmodernist feminist position as well as from developing conceptions of constitutive theorizing. Let us now turn to this affirmative form.

Affirmative postmodernism: a constitutive view of law

The constitutive perspective on law argues that recognition of the interpenetrating role of social forms with law requires a new and different conception of the role of law in society. Perspectives in law that stipulate either the autonomy or the dependence of law must give way to a more comprehensive account. Constitutive theory is based on the idea that law is, in part, social relations and social relations are, in part, law.[18] It is the movement and tension whereby these are socially constituted, 'the way "society" is produced within "law"' (Nelken, 1986: 325), and the way law is produced within society, rather than how they interact, that is crucial to understanding the law–society interface: 'law and society inextricably yet somehow distinctly constitute and inhabit each other' such that, unlike in modernist approaches, 'there can no longer be any inexorable mode or structure connecting law to society' (Fitzpatrick, 1992: 8). Moreover, we need to unpack the holistic vision of 'society' as a unitary entity and, as we established in Chapter 3, conceive of it as a dissipative structure, itself constituted both internally and externally.

A constitutive concept of law differs from the liberal-legal conception in that law is understood as having the power to frame politics and legal processes: doctrine and institutions shape political possibilities.[19] As Hunt (1993: 293) says, 'law constitutes or participates in the constitution of a terrain or field within which social relations are generated, reproduced, disputed and struggled over.' Law, then, is 'inextricably mixed in the totality of social relations and institutions' (1993: 147). Here, the key term is 'interrelation'.[20] Clearly, a new discourse is one of the agenda items for a constitutive methodology.

Glimpses

Brigham's (1987: 306) research on social movements demonstrates how these social relations are 'constituted in legal terms when they [activists] see the world in those terms and organize themselves accordingly . . . Legal forms are evident in the language, purposes, and strategies of movement activity as practice.' Therefore, instead of merely assuming that state law is the hub of social control whose spokes radiate as unidirectional pathways of influence to other social and normative orders, as in the instrumental coercive-power view, constitutive theory also directs our attention to the reverse process: forms and mechanisms whereby legal relations are interpenetrated by extra-legal social relations, and neither direction can be reducible to the other. We shall see below that we also need an alternative conceptualization of space than is offered by modernist thought. This is necessary in order to conceptualize the interrelational nature of phenomena. Fractal geometry is one possibility which offers the idea of infinite complexities existing in multiply interconnected planes. Space is not therefore, merely a two-way directional process, but a multi-directional form.

The interrelated process has also been spelled out by Salyers' studies .(1989; 1991) of various early struggles of women in gaining rights which in turn became new sources of empowerment for yet newly formulated liberation demands. Gordon's (1988) study of immigrant women during nineteenth century America showed how the 'right not to be beaten' was shaped by social workers' responses to existing cultural and class domination where they provided services and definitions of rights that the victim often did not entirely embrace. These rights nevertheless contributed to changes in power relationships.

Merry's (1985) ethnographic work on working class involvement with the courts showed that working class subjects involved in the criminal justice system do not just absorb the top-down dominant legal ideology, but also make it a basis for a situational ideology, reformulating their grievances in terms of a rights discourse. This 'bottom-up' ideology then becomes the basis of the subject's 'symbolic system by which social relationships with neighbors, friends and families are understood' (1985: 67). Similarly, Yngvesson's study (1993) of the function of the court clerk demonstrated that a clear separation between law and other social forms cannot be maintained. Rather, the production and reproduction of law and what constitutes 'trouble' recognized by the court entails 'agents who are both constituted by the law and who confront the law, editing its meanings by their very presence at the court' (1993: 12). Finally, Henry's (1983) study of private justice in the workplace showed that rather than being separate from the wider system of state law, workplace systems of disciplinary control were interrelated with state law and with their own internal subsystems of norms, rules and sanctions. Each of these 'legal' discourses reconstituted the other and the wider system as it constituted theirs, and yet each semi-autonomous part also had its own identity.[21]

In short, these studies indicate that setting up linear causal chains of relationship between the properties of societies and their effects on law, what Nelken (1986) calls 'the correspondence thesis', overlooks discontinuities, looping effects, reformulation processes, iterative effects, identity constructions, and their deconstructions and reconstructions. Crucially, what is missed is the constitutive work in process.

A constitutive approach examines both the presence and the source of other social forms, 'which are not simply variant forms of legal reasoning but derive their significance and their legitimating capacity from the forms of social relations from which they originate' (Hunt, 1987: 18). However, the nature of this relationship is mutually constitutive such that 'neither is reducible to or explainable in terms of the other' (Hunt, 1993: 179). The claim that this formulation undermines theoretical rigor (Douzinas et al., 1991: 120) can be seen more as a reflection of a commitment to a traditional understanding of causality. (We shall return to the question of causality in Chapters 6 and 7.)

It is not, therefore, just that law is created by classes or interest groups to maintain or increase their power. Rather, some of the relations of these groups, particularly their rules and procedures, are and indeed become the relations of law, just as some of the relations of law become the relations, rules and ordering of social forms. This suggests that 'any site of social relations is likely to be traversed by a variety of state and non-state legal networks' and that 'what constitutes "the law" in any specific site therefore will depend upon which legal agencies (or more precisely which parts of which networks) intersect in that context, how these orders are mobilized, and how they interact' (O'Malley, 1991: 172).

All this implies a representative geometry within which phenomena take place. As we saw in the last chapter, modernists offer a Newtonian framework expressible in Euclidian geometry, with typical path analysis diagrams showing 'causal connections'. Postmodernists are more likely to make use of alternative notions of space, such as fractal geometry (Lyotard, 1984; Deleuze and Guattari, 1987; Hayles, 1990) and topology theory (Milovanovic, 1993a; 1993b; 1994c; 1995). Thus, rather than the simplistic and narrowly conceived path analysis, we can make better use of Deleuze and Guattari's notion of 'lines of continuous variation' which depict, at any point in time, only probability moments that have a range of probable occurrence. If we also assume a number of these lines of continuous variation permeating various formations, some of which interact producing a source of perturbation at strategic coupling points, then we can see how small fluctuations, in combination with other fluctuations, iterated over time may have disproportional effects. We might rely on 'phase maps' (portraits of chaos) that chaos theorists use to depict dynamic, non-linear phenomena interacting over time (Hayles, 1990: 147–52). The advantage here is that multi-dimensional spaces could entertain an unlimited number of variables, each of which indicates a degree of freedom existing in some dynamic system.

This approach could also portray 'attractors' or relatively steady states that appear such as the 'strange attractor' discussed in the previous chapters. As changes are produced ('bifurcations') we can also keep track of the nature of the new attractors that appear. Bifurcations represent qualitative changes, or splitting, in some dynamic system, some abrupt non-linear change into a new attractor state. Increased agitations in some dynamic system also show that it will produce further splitting known as period doubling. After the eighth splitting, many complex systems exhibit full chaos: they become infinitely complex.[22]

Arrival at such a position leaves us at odds with concepts such as Poulantzas' notion of causation as 'overdetermination' (1973; 1978). He indicated that phenomena can be explained by specifying the 'articulation of instances' (i.e. ideological, economic, political, juridical) in existence at a particular historical juncture. Although overcoming simplistic notions of unicausality this assumes separateness, in contrast to our constitutive vision which suggests that each of the instances has embedded within it instances of the others: clear demarcation is considered a constructed fiction.

Thus, instead of treating law as an autonomous field of enquiry linked only by external relations to the rest of society, or assuming 'law' and 'society' are concrete entities that 'influence' or 'affect' each other, the constitutive approach takes law as its subject of inquiry but pursues it by exploring the interrelations 'between legal relations and other forms of social relations' (Hunt, 1987: 16; 1993: 15–16, 224–6; Nelken, 1986: 324). More accurately, then, we may speak of interpenetration rather than interaction or cause and effect.

One of the first to recognize the mutuality between state law and non-state forms was Moore (1973). She argued that law is not a fixed autonomous entity but a 'semi-autonomous field' which, while having rule-making and enforcement capacity, is also 'vulnerable to rules and decisions and other forces emanating from the larger world by which it is surrounded'. She argues that law is 'set in a larger social matrix which can and does affect and invade it' (1973: 720).

Considering this interrelationship, there is some relevance in Foucault's (1977) demonstration that the modern era has seen state control dispersed into the social fabric to become part of a hidden totality of surveillance. Important, too, is Foucault's (1979) 'rule of double conditioning' in which power is exercised not only from the top, but through distinct, localized machinery, which itself is only effective as part of a general overarching strategy of power (see also Hunt, 1993: 179). At the same time as the general strategy is distinct, it is also, in turn, dependent for its effectiveness on local strategies. Deleuze and Guattari (1987) have indicated that we can conceptualize power relations as beginning with political economy, following a path by which recipients make use of the essential relational terms, and ending by subjects interjecting the essential hierarchical forms as constitutive of psychic economy (see also Deleuze, 1988). Identifying any particular moment along this path would indicate, not simply a passive receiving subject, but agents who actively incorporate elements from 'above' within existing narrative constructions in producing coherent texts.

Given the affirmative postmodernist's recognition of the importance of constitutive social and legal orders it is not surprising that there is considerable recognition of the diversity of legal truths offered by legal pluralism. As Santos says:

Legal pluralism is the key concept in a post-modern view of law. Not legal pluralism . . . in which different legal orders are conceived as separate entities coexisting in the same political space, but rather the conception of different legal spaces superimposed, interpenetrated and mixed in our minds as much as our actions. (1985: 279; see also Santos, 1987)

We do not accept the distinction between the plurality of legal orders and state law, but argue that these spheres are mutually constituting and are encouraged by Fitzpatrick's (1984) idea of 'integral plurality'. He says that the reason state law is, in part, shaped by the plurality of other social forms, while these forms are simultaneously being shaped by it, is because 'elements of law are elements of other forms and vice versa' (1984: 122).

While law incorporates other forms, transforming them into its own image and likeness, the process is not unilateral but mutual, such that 'law in turn supports the other forms but becomes in the process, part of the other forms' (1984: 122). As such, 'state law is integrally constituted in relation to a plurality of other social forms' and 'depends on social forms that tend to undermine it' (1984: 118). His theory of integral plurality is a considerable advance, both over earlier legal pluralism, and over critical legal theory, for it demonstrates not so much that there is a unilinear relationship with other social forms but rather that 'law is the unsettled product of relations with a plurality of other social forms. As such, law's identity is constantly and inherently subject to challenge and change' (1984: 138).

Fitzpatrick's fundamental insight is to recognize that state law obtains some of its identity from its interrelationship with non-state forms and vice versa; that without this connection each would be constitutively different. He argues elsewhere that the interrelations between state law and non-state normative orders constitute new entities, as a common discourse and set of practices is worked out between participating arenas of power (Fitzpatrick, 1988). This is particularly evident in the context where law is being synthesized from other existing sets of rules and norms. Fitzpatrick says that in the process of synopsis of existing rules and practices the participating networks retain their own relative autonomy, but 'integrating homologies' (corresponding structures) are formed which merge selected elements of the component networks into an emergent whole that becomes new law.

O'Malley, similarly, describes such attempts at legal synthesis as 'synoptic projects' which

> are characterized by the emergence of a common and integrating discourse and set of practices worked out between interacting agencies. Such negotiation involves suppression of incompatible elements of the different participating agencies' knowledges and practices, translation of other elements into more compatible forms, and the integration of all into a workable whole, albeit often inconsistent, labile and conflicting. In this process emergent, synthetic or synoptic social practices and knowledges may appear. (1991: 172–3)

O'Malley claims that these 'synoptic projects' are most likely to occur where changing conditions, such as the emergence effectiveness of existing arrangements, make their continued operation problematic. In other words, agents more often imperceptibly confront bifurcation points, where the problematic nature is of such magnitude that existing and otherwise explanatory narrative constructions fail to provide convincing resolutions.

This does not mean, however, that the newly created narratives will necessarily become objectively more correct – only that they will now become discursive coordinates for further social action.

System-power theorists such as Teubner (1992: 1453–4) also contribute to this idea of constitutive interrelationship with their notion that law is the outcome of a process of 'interdiscursivity' where intraorganizational legal discourse 'productively misunderstands' and misreads (through rereading, reinterpreting, reconstructing and reobserving) 'organizational self-production as norm production and thus invents a new and rich "source" of law'. A similar misreading occurs, says Teubner, when the organization reincorporates legal rules developed and refined in disciplinary proceedings and makes use of them to restructure its organizational decision-making. Although constructively critical of this new legal pluralism, Teubner (1992: 1443) accurately observes that the position assumes that the relations between the legal and the social are characterized by 'discursive interwovenness', 'are highly ambiguous, almost paradoxical: separate but intertwined, closed but open'. He acknowledges that this postmodernist version of legal pluralism sees law 'no longer defined as a set of conflicting social norms in a given social field, but as a multiplicity of diverse communicative processes that observe social action under the binary code of legal/illegal' (1992: 1451). However, Teubner does not indicate the potentials for a possible replacement discourse or discourses out of which alternative narrative construction could take place. Thus, at best, a praxis not a transpraxis is partially explained.

Constitutive view of legal formations: engaging autopoiesis

Constitutive criminology can fruitfully draw from a number of these sometimes rather overlapping, at other times conflicting, approaches on the nature of 'interrelationship'. We have argued earlier that a modified thesis of autopoiesis is a useful conceptualization of how various semi-autonomous, self-referential, and intersecting localities maintain a degree of stability and in combination contribute to what subjects see, collectively, as structure and law.[23] This articulated state is co-produced as social reality by subjects in a discursively constituted social formation, a co-production which then has effects back on the subject. This apparent circularity is not metaphor: it is the real. The question then becomes one of interconnections, imbrication and interpenetration. We will return to a more complete explanation of this conception of 'cause' in Chapter 6.

Luhmann's position, rearticulated and applied to law by Teubner, has offered the thesis of structural coupling. A number of critical theorists on law have embraced aspects of this thesis to various degrees as a key explanatory concept for the maintenance of an interconnected totality with effects that retain a degree of historical specificity and stability (Cornell, 1992; Hunt, 1993; Jessop, 1990). This attempt to escape economic determinism, the prioritizing of the economic sphere, implicit or explicit in much theorizing on law, focuses on linkages, couplings throughout a socio-legal and political system that remain a contingent source of variation of the legal. This 'contingency' has been expressed in Laclau and Mouffe's (1985) notion of 'contingent variation', and in a more structured form in Jessop's (1990) 'contingent necessity'. The former privileges continuous variation and 'the ultimate nonfixity of anything existing in society' (Laclau, 1988: 254). Thus, it has been subject to some pronounced critiques (see Jessop, 1990: 288–305) as begging an explanation of historically appearing contingent fixities. For its part the 'contingent necessity thesis' begs questions concerning the specificity of relatively stabilized institutional structures such as law. In either view, it would seem that the subject, without more being said, is relegated to passivity, and is only able to 'grasp the moment' when 'slippage' or 'cracks' appear and are recognized as such. Thus discursive production, said to be inherently unstable, provides the open possibility for rearticulation.[24] Even though Jessop, Hunt, and Cornell have improved on the Luhmann-Teubner thesis, each still finds her/himself within the modernist order paradigm and thus does not escape its metaphysics. We can transcend this modernist lockdown by once again borrowing from chaos theory.

Chaos theory suggests the idea of dissipative structures which are the normal 'structures' within far-from-equilibrium conditions.[25] In this view, law is seen in a perpetual state of displaced, contingent equilibrium. Formal rationality (Weber), in other words, would be replaced by substantive rationality in various local sites.[26] We shall return to this in a later chapter.

This notwithstanding, a reasonable escape from this dilemma has been suggested by Hunt (1993) in his tentative analysis of 'relational sets' which he tells us is Marxist informed. This approach 'proposes an analysis that posits the existence of a number of different forms of legal relations that interact in varying ways with other forms of social relations' (1993: 224). Thus each historically appearing relational set can be examined by the relative dominance of any constituent relation and particularly any configuration where domination exists (1993: 252). It should be kept in mind that whereas Hunt appears perilously close to giving each sphere a status of relative independence, reminiscent of Poulantzas' thesis of the articulation of instances, we should temper this with acknowledging that each instance is already composed of aspects of each of the others in a particular complex, relatively stable structure. Hence, he offers the legal relation that could be coupled with various dimensions of social relations: power, institutional, ideological and discursive (1993: 254). Each relational set can be examined in terms of whether the constituent elements are supplemental or conflicting. We should add that subjects, too, find themselves at the intersections of various relational sets and abstract from these relational categories, classifications, and understandings with the help of the various discourses that pervade relational sets. While setting out in a helpful direction, Hunt's position on 'mapping relations' is rooted in the modernist order paradigm and thus cannot be developed further with the conceptual tools offered. A postmodern framework, however, nudges us toward a further refinement of his suggestive thesis.[27]

In order to develop this direction further, we must resituate Hunt's underlying assumed metaphysics of Newtonian and Euclidian geometry, which are the coordinates of his 'maps', into fractal geometry (recall Lyotard's 1984 search for instabilities). By doing so, we quickly realize that relational sets are infinitely complex, multi-layered and interacting configurations that are contingently situated in historical developments. What conventional Euclidian geometry misses, then, are the spaces which fractal geometry specifies: that is, their increased dimensionality (Deleuze and Guattari, 1987). Here, privileged is not the point, the individual event, the individual act, but *moments* constituted by intersecting lines we define as interpenetrating logics from other contiguous and intersecting relational sets. Consider here also the notion of coupling points existing between recursive symmetries (Hayles, 1990). Perhaps Bohm's offering of the hologram is a working metaphor here: when only a particular section of a photographic plate is illuminated by a laser light the whole structure appears, 'each region contains a total structure "enfolded" within it' (1990: 144–7, 149). He even suggests that 'the principal function of Cartesian coordinates [Euclidian geometry] is just to give a clear and precise description of explicate order' (1990: 150).

Deleuze and Guattari (1987), for example, have suggested the provocative thesis that within fractal spaces, logics may follow a zig-zag and indeterminate journey (the 'rhizome', a line of continuous variation) and, we add, through the articulated relational sets with effects. These are 'lines of flight', 'lines' along which desire flows with effects. Even the notion of a one-dimensional line has to be reconsidered. For Deleuze and Guattari, following fractal geometry, the line traces a fractional dimension between one and two (a line of continuous variation). It appears along several planes (relational sets). Different configurations will be negotiated differently by the rhizome, producing different effects. According to Deleuze and Guattari (1987), as well as Foucault (1977), Kristeva (1980) and others in the postmodern tradition, lines of flight are coordinated by configurations of power.[28] In this view, some emergent logic(s) may attain dominance in their reappearance in relational sets such as explained by Baudrillard in his notion of simulacra, a self-similarity that reappears in the various intersecting relational sets. These, then, may appear as 'contingent universalities' (Butler, 1992) and may be the dynamics that provide the knotting (nodal points) specified by Laclau and Mouffe (1985) who follow the Lacanian notion of *point de capiton* (1977). It is this process by which otherwise 'floating signifiers' in various discursive formations attain a degree of relative stability in law (fixity), thereby providing the medium by which reality is constructed by subjects, a reality which then comes to dominate social constructions by subjects.

However, other relational sets interpenetrate these dominant forms and provide other logics by which a signifier potentially is knotted (e.g. capital logic, the change from commodity logic to the logic of consumption as in Baudrillard, etc.). These 'traces' (Derrida) may be compounded, or iterated with disproportional and significant effects according to chaos theory (Hayles, 1990). Even what appears to be relatively insignificant relational sets may, under appropriate circumstances, be the basis of an iteration process which culminates in having effects on other intersecting relational sets. This then leads to a change in the overall configuration of relational sets in often unpredictable ways.

A useful depiction of the working of constitutive relational sets can be seen in Collins' (1993) study of the intersections of race, class, and gender.[29] Collins asks us to redirect our analysis away from 'additive' forms of analyses of repression (Spelman, 1982), for they are inherently constituted by two counterproductive elements: (1) dichotomous ways of thinking (dualities) such that the interconnected nature of differences and similarities are lost; and (2) hierarchical rankings where, for example, white is dominant, black is subordinate (Collins, 1993: 27–8). Thus, in the literature on oppression, we often find statements reflecting the 'additive' quality of oppression. For example, in considering the African-American woman, she is subject to the oppression of gender and class and race. Collins, however, points out that this overlooks the 'interlocking nature of oppression' (1993: 28). For her,

> Race, class and gender may all structure a situation but may not be equally visible and/or important in people's self-definition . . . This recognition that one category may have salience over another for a given time and place does not minimize the theoretical importance of assuming that race, class and gender as categories of analysis structure all relationships. (1993: 29)

Thus for Collins, the methodological task is one of 'reconceptualizing oppression by uncovering the connections among race, class and gender as categories of analysis' (1993: 29). She draws from Harding (1986) and indicates that oppression finds its roots in three contexts: social institutions (e.g. schools, hospitals, workplaces, etc.), the symbolic sphere (i.e. the discursive), and the sphere of the individual. These three are interpenetrated by race, gender and class. Although we do not subscribe to Collins' unitary construction of the human subject as an independent 'individual' (e.g. 'I as an individual always have the choice of accepting things as they are, or trying to change them', 1993: 35), she does convincingly argue that opportunity and oppression are structured by the intersections of race, gender and class.

Constitutive theory is at one with Collins' central question in investigating oppression: 'How do race, class and gender function as *parallel and interlocking systems* that shape this basic relationship of domination and subordination?' (1993: 29, our emphasis). We see her analysis of the 'interlocking' and 'parallel' nature of oppression as portraying the dynamics of constitutive relational sets whereby each 'element' – race, gender, class – is always already populated by the other. They appear in configurations, and attempts to separate them overlook the interpenetrating quality of their conjunction in producing oppression.

Cornell (1991) begins her argument with the always present slippage and metaphorical displacements inherent in the dominant symbolic order and offers a way out of the rigidity of the phallocentric symbolic order by way of a *mimesis* (a re-reading of myths toward establishing utopian possibilities). However, others root their view of relational sets in a Freirian inspired model where an alternative dialogical pedagogy leads to the creation of new nodal points in struggle.[30] Arguably, either position draws on some portion of Lacan's psychoanalytic semiotics to produce change in master signifiers and discursive formations. We, however, see greater benefit in developing a perspective in which theory and action are both constitutive forces for the development of legal structures; hence, Freirian derived positions must be integrated with others, such as Cornell's more imaginary focused vision, in developing a constitutive approach of law.

Several insights already appearing in criminology have been suggestive as to the existence of structural couplings. Consider, for example, Matza's (1964) position of 'drift' where the juvenile is said to episodically drift between conventionality and deviance, who suspends her/his commitment, most often chooses the conventional, but occasionally drifts into deviance.[31] Here, critical is how law – the juvenile court's principle of individualized justice and its rendering of some excusing conditions – is replicated (recursive symmetries) throughout juvenile subcultures and becomes the basis of movement toward deviance. In other words, 'rudimentary conceptions of tort pervade their mentality' (Matza, 1964: 174).

A somewhat similar situation is found in Katz's *Seductions of Crime* (1988). Here hyperreality (a logic which is connected with the increased alienation experienced in the work arena) permeates various relational sets. This may point to 'a transcendent route for the individual . . . in adopting pursuits that, by their excess and danger, stir powerful emotions that recreate and reassure oneself of oneself' (O'Malley and Mugford, 1994: 203).[32] Here the coupling is between law, consumption standards and alienation.

One could also look at Cressey's (1953) early study of embezzlers where it was noted that verbalizations (rationalizations) justifying embezzling that are found in the work arena in a predominant form can be the basis for the motivation for embezzlement.

Similar is Schwendinger and Schwendinger's (1985) study of how an 'instrumental rhetoric' derived from the logic of the marketplace (1985: 274–5, 280, 284, 287–8, 304) pervades the juvenile relational sets and how it attains dominance leading to delinquency. Even though not shared by all street corner youth, they tell us, youth who 'linguistically coordinate their behavior' are nevertheless affected by this rhetoric as well as others (1985: 148). Some juveniles now have available a rhetoric to justify violence on the basis of street situational exigencies (1985: 149). Not without importance the authors were struck by youth's 'absence of reflective awareness' about their violent activities (1985: 151).

In each of the above, we see relational sets interpenetrated by various discourses – tort, pleasure, lack, egotism – that may culminate in deviant acts. In each of the examples, couplings at different levels could be the starting point for investigation of deviations from the law.

Summary and conclusions

In summary, what we can draw from the constitutive perspective is that top-down discursive constructions of law, as stipulated by most modernists, especially in the instrumental and structural power theories discussed earlier, distract us from addressing the complexities involved. In contrast, recent developments in constitutive legal pluralism take an affirmative postmodernist stance and argue that law is mutually constituted through social relations and discursive misreading. The discursive processes of non-state normative orders with which state law is interrelated and interwoven provide a significant context of synoptic projects wherein old power is molded into new forms. With such an approach we begin to see the possibility of transcending the view that law is the product either of culture and consensus, or of structure and structural conflicts, or of interactive or system processes. We begin to see how social control is not so much an alternative form of law but a necessary part of the ideological process whereby the crystallized, formalized, object-like qualities of law are created and sustained in an ongoing manner, be it within a different arena. Thus constitutive criminology directs our attention to the way law, crime and criminal justice are conceptualized and implied as though they are objective realities having real consequences, consequences that we attribute to their claim, but that they do not possess in any intrinsic sense.

Notes

1 See also Parsons (1962: 57) 'law as an integrating mechanism', Pound's (1959) 'social engineering' view, and Hart's (1960) notion of 'the primary functions of law'.

2 On traditional legal pluralism see Ehrlich (1913), Gierke (1900), Gurvitch (1947), Ross (1901), and Pospisil (1971). For a critical overview see Merry (1988).

3 The term 'radical feminist' here is distinguished from other feminisms such as socialist feminist, Marxist feminist, postmodern feminist. For discussion of these differences see Jaggar (1983), Daly and Chesney-Lind (1988), Simpson (1989), and Muraskin and Alleman (1993).

4 See Curtis (1975), Petersilia (1983), Georges-Abeyie (1984; 1990), Freeman (1982); see generally Lynch and Patterson (1990). Some theorists suggest that we must look at the intersections of race and sex and race, class, and gender (Harris, 1991; Williams, 1991; Cornell, 1992: 91; Schwartz and Milovanovic, 1995), a position that is perhaps more consistent with that of socialist feminism discussed below.

5 Pashukanis (1978), Althusser (1971), Balbus (1977a; 1977b), Beirne and Sharlet (1980), Chambliss (1975), Chambliss and Seidman (1982), Hindess and Hirst (1975), and Milovanovic (1986; 1987).

6 See also Balbus on 'repression by formal rationality' (1977a; 1977b) and the notion of repressive formalism (Milovanovic, 1981; 1994a: 17–18); and Weber's analysis of the contract concerning its potentials for freedom and coercion (see Milovanovic, 1994a: 58–9).

7 In this regard, Lovibond (1989) has argued that feminism should persist in seeing itself as a modernist project, a daughter of the Enlightenment, moving toward global abolition of the sex–class system.

8 Abel (1981; 1982a), Brady (1981), Harrington (1985), Cohen (1985), Hofrichter (1987), and Matthews (1988).

9 In contrast, as we saw in the last chapter, a non-linear metaphysics, for example, would include such things as the dialectics of struggle where unintended outcomes prevail, including the inadvertent reversal of hierarchies re-establishing previous forms of domination.

10 This position has some similarities to the early modernist Enlightenment views, the consensus-functionalist views, and several of the pluralist views, but also some important differences. See Luhmann (1988; 1990; 1992) and Teubner (1989; 1992; 1993), and also Hunt (1993) and Cornell (1992).

11 See also Weinrib (1988) who argues for an 'imminent rationality', an 'inner coherence' to law.

12 Consider Hunt's critique that the very terminology 'field', for example, as a metaphor, implies such things as a magnetic attraction but also implies an area of open space bounded by fences. See our discussion of Moore (1973) later, for a more constitutively framed interpretation that shows field as a semi-autonomous arena interrelated with its surrounding environment.

13 See also Balkin (1987), Sarup (1989), and Hayles (1990: 178–86).

14 See especially Hayles (1990: 181–5), Cornell (1992: 85). For a chaos application to the law of tort, see Brion (1991; 1995).

15 See Kairys (1982). For a chaos view of legal formalism, see Brion (1991; 1995).

16 See also Kerruish (1991: 33–4, 167, 174, 177–93, 196–8), Grant (1993: 91–125), Cornell (1992: 11, 139, 185).

17 See also Mama (1989), Rice (1990), and especially Minow (1990).

18 Klare (1979), Fitzpatrick (1983; 1984); Harrington and Yngvesson (1990), Yngvesson (1993), Hunt (1987; 1993).

19 Brigham and Harrington, (1989), Yngvesson (1993). See also the critical semiotic analysis of jailhouse lawyers by Milovanovic (1988) and Milovanovic and Thomas (1989), as well as of activist lawyers before the court by Bannister and Milovanovic (1990).

20 The words 'imbricated' or 'interpenetrated' can also be used instead of 'interrelated' but there are some reservations with finding words that are not already value laden with Newtonian, or even phallocentric, assumptions and metaphysics. See Hunt (1993: 148, 346 n. 50, 348–9), Bohm (1980), and Whorf (1956).

21 See also Henry (1985; 1987a; 1987b; 1989a; 1989b), Nelken (1986), Itzkowitz (1988), and Harrington (1988).

22 We could also make use of 'trouser diagrams', rather than path analysis, which topologically depict interactions (see Milovanovic, 1992a). Each 'trouser' stands for a line of continuous variation with a radius of possible probability occurrences. We shall return to this in Chapter 7. Another description of chaoticians for this uncertain prediction is a 'torus' which portrays global patterning, yet local indeterminacy. Visually it has the shape of a doughnut showing a pattern of fluctuating variation and uncertainty. For elaboration on this and the strange attractor see, for example, Young (1991a; 1992), Butz (1992a), Milovanovic (1992a; 1993a; 1995).

23 Bourdieu's position merely establishes that the symbolic violence inhering in discourse, once stabilized, gives little guidance as to the potential for change.

24 See Cornell (1991; 1993), Laclau and Mouffe (1985), and Hunt (1993: 297).

25 See also Unger's (1987) suggestion for an empowered democracy that finds compatibility with this metaphysics. We shall return to this in Chapter 9.

26 See also Lyotard's suggestion for justice at local sites: 'we must thus arrive at an idea and practice of justice that is not linked to that of consensus' (1984: 66).

27 Chaos theorists offer, as an alternative, phase mapping. It is the mapping, modeling or portrayal of complex phenomena in movement, or how different variables interact and change over time, or alternatively, the region of space where they settle down or converge (Hayles, 1990). The totality of possible outcomes is known as the outcome or causal 'basin' or field.

28 See for example Foucault's 'diagrams', maps of changing structures of power (Deleuze, 1988: 34–44, 72–3), and also Santos' (1987) 'mapping' of law.

29 For further exploration on the 'intersections' of these three, see the essays in Schwartz and Milovanovic (1995).

30 See McLaren (1994), Zavarzadeh and Morton (1990), Ebert (1991), JanMohamed (1994).

31 We are again reminded of the strange attractor, with butterfly wings representing two possible outcome basins with indeterminacy prevailing in between.

32 See also Salecl's (1993) Lacanian inspired explanation of crime as 'modes of subjectivization'.

5

Definitions of Crime and Constructions of the Victim

In this chapter we analyze various definitions of crime in the criminological literature.[1] At the outset we must sympathize with those who have embarked on a similar journey and who might agree with McCabe (1983: 49) that: 'There is no word in the whole lexicon of legal and criminological terms which is so elusive of definition as the word "crime".' Part of the reason for this elusiveness stems from the difficulty of finding 'any definition of crime that does not have a large element of circularity' (Wilkins, 1968: 477). In addition, there is the varying content of what counts as crime. This reflects the cultural and historical relativity of definitions and the 'somewhat arbitrary', 'highly selective process of identifying particular behavior as being appropriate for official condemnation' (Barak, 1995: 38). Indeed, Barak says 'when it comes to defining crime there are no purely objective definitions; all definitions are value laden and biased to some degree' (1995: 38).

However, there is some logic to the difference and variability in the content of crime which we argue is related not least to the assumptions that are made about humans, society and law. For example, most criminology texts take a legal definition of crime as their starting point. At its simplest: 'crime is an act prohibited by law upon pain of punishment' (Hall-Williams, 1964: 147). Tappan's (1947: 100) classic statement goes further: 'crime is an intentional act or omission in violation of criminal law (statutory and case law), committed without defense or justification, and sanctioned by the state as a felony or misdemeanor.' This idea of intentionality shares an ecological space (Hayles, 1990; Jessop, 1990) with the classicist assumption that humans are rationally calculating individuals capable of acting with intent (*mens rea*). Roshier's neo-classical legal definition tells us as much:

> the legal definition of crime incorporates the assumption of its 'naturalness' to free and rational human beings. Indeed, if the actions are not deemed free and rational (in the sense that the offenders are capable of understanding their nature, moral meaning and consequences) then they will not usually be defined as crimes in legal terms. (1989: 76)

It should be clear, therefore, that if criminological assumptions about humans change, so does the content of their definition of crime. In other words, we should expect different premises about human subjects (identified in Chapter 2) to harbor differing ideas about what counts as crime.

Modernist assumptions about society (identified in chapter 3) also shape the content of definitions about crime. These range from the classical view that a consensus about state law provides the ultimate definition (whether this is justified by morality or nature, or is expressed through a political process) to the critical/conflict view that crime is a socially constructed category whose content depends on powerful interests. Thus, from the consensus perspective, Wilkins (1968: 477) argues: 'Crime is always defined in terms of the social institutions and their organization in a society. The crimes will be defined through some organized process as behavioral deviations from the values as institutionalized in the norms and rules.' Perhaps one of the most comprehensive in this regard is Hagan's definition of crime as 'a kind of deviance, which in turn consists of a variation from a social norm, that is proscribed by criminal law' and that 'the more serious acts of deviance, which are most likely to be called "criminal", are likely to involve (1) broad agreement about the wrongfulness of such acts, (2) a severe social response, and (3) an evaluation of being very harmful' (1985: 49–50).

But changing consensus to conflict assumptions constructs a different definition of crime. Consider, for example, Quinney's (1970: 15–16) conflict position: 'crime is a definition of human conduct created by authorized agents in a politically organized society . . . [that describes] behaviors that conflict with the interests of the segments of society that have the power to shape public policy', or Pavarini's (1994: 56) dialectical Marxist view that 'the definition of what counts as deviance and as social control is seen as decisively influenced both by those who have "the power to define" and also those who have the possibility to "resist these definitions".' Indeed, Pavarini (1994: 57) argues that 'the more resistance is offered and opposed to the activity of control the more "freedom" to define their own conduct is given to deviants, and vice versa.'

Our purpose here is not to provide an exhaustive review of the range of these definitions. Rather, by way of a probing analysis we aim to reveal the underlying constitutive elements in modernist and postmodernist criminological writing on the issue. It is our intention to show what such definitions include, what they exclude, and how they play a part in constituting the phenomena taken to be crime. To achieve this we will develop an analytical schema (see Figure 5.1) that exposes a variety of constitutive dimensions and shows the ways in which differing modernist definitions rely on different conceptions of subjects and objects within this schema. We will conclude this review of modernist definitions of crime with a brief illustrative discussion on modernist images of the criminal. Rather than drawing these out for each modernist criminology we shall concentrate on how they have been constructed in the specific case of white collar crime.

In our discussion of postmodernist approaches we shall argue that rather than merely deconstructing modernist definitions, a constitutive postmodernism demands a definition of crime as harm that takes account of the experienced reality of existing harms and yet is sufficiently flexible to accommodate harms in emerging social forms.

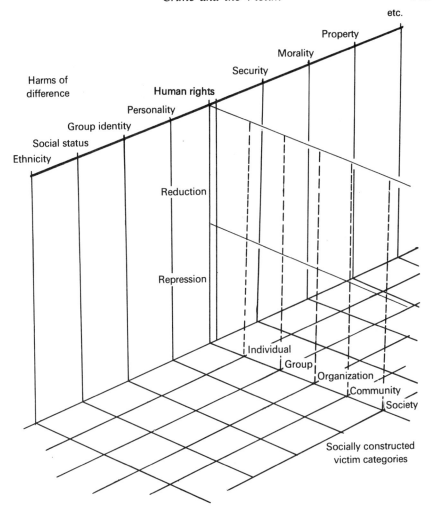

Figure 5.1   *Harms of repression and reduction*

Modernist definitions of crime

Perhaps it is appropriate to frame our exploration of modernist visions of crime by acknowledging that their initial formation was against certain historical developments. On one level, modernism rejected the premodern association of crime as sin, where crime, as an issue of morality, as a pact with the Devil, was defined as an act 'against God . . . also . . . against the whole order of nature itself, against the entire cosmos', against 'cosmic disruption' (Pfohl, 1985: 21).

On another level, modernist approaches to crime opposed the escalating arbitrary increase in the severity of penalties for offenses under English common law. This classification of crime began around 1100 as a division of crimes based on their alleged seriousness which resulted in a tripartite distinction among treason, felony and misdemeanor. The main distinction was between offenses deemed resolvable by compensation from offender to victim, and those which neither compensation nor fines could resolve.

Several features in modernist definitions of crime require consideration. Important is the issue of where definitions of crime are to be found. Since Michael and Adler (1933), most commentators agree that criminal law specifies the acts or omissions that constitute crime. Again, Roshier's post-classicist position is illustrative: 'Crimes are violations of legal rules; legal rules are those rules that are defined and enforced by agencies of the state that have, ultimately, the authority to use coercion' (1989: 76).

Modernists disagree, however, about whether the law contains all of the behavior that should be prohibited. Should crime be restricted only to the activity of those convicted of offenses (Tappan, 1947; Korn and McCorkle, 1959: 46), or should it include only illegal acts reported to the police (Reckless, 1950: 8), or, more broadly, should it include behavior that violates 'conduct norms' as in Sellin's (1938) culture conflict view? Might crime be harms for which sanctions are administered, regardless of whether they exist in the criminal statutes, as Sutherland's (1949: 511–15) view of crime as 'socially injurious' suggests? More recent critical contributions have suggested further that criminalized harms be expanded to include the socially injurious activities of powerful groups against the powerless, and behavior which violates or intrudes into others' human rights (Schwendinger and Schwendinger, 1970).[2] Indeed, Schwendinger and Schwendinger suggest that it is the social relationships and conditions such as imperialism, racism, sexism and poverty that should be criminalized, rather than actions of individuals: 'the social conditions themselves must become the object of social policy . . . it is not an individual or loose collection of atomistic individuals which is to be controlled, but rather the social relationships between individuals' (1970: 147).

Central to this debate, therefore, is the intrinsic content of the behavior which is designated offensive and/or harmful. Several modernist approaches to defining the content of crime try to establish that there is something harmful about the behavior contained in the definition that warrants its prohibition. Some, notably individual positivists, relate the quality of this behavior to its perpetrators, either to their deviant mental state or to genetic difference, but most relate it to the social definitions held by others. The concept of 'others' is one of two fundamental dimensions in analyzing social constructions of crime. The second has to do with the content of action that these others find objectionable. Let us examine each in creating a typology of harm offered by modernist theorists.

Mapping harm

Who are taken to be 'others' varies from broad inclusive generalized categories such as 'society', 'community', 'the public', the 'consumer', and 'humanity', to specific powerful groups such as 'the state', 'agencies', and 'organizations', down to the relatively powerless groups of 'audiences', 'victims', types of victim or social categories (employee, gender, sexual preference, etc.), to the ultimate universal category 'individual'. In short, the definition of crime addresses socially constructed subject categories that can be offended and/or that can find offense.[3]

A second related theme in the construction of definitions of crime concerns the quality of the behavior that is found offensive. While behavior that is statistically different from the normal, and thereby offensive, might have been enough to constitute crime in premodern definitions, it typically becomes deviance in modernist definitions. To qualify as crime the difference has to be deemed harmful or injurious to others. Of course, this varies depending on whether it is recognized as harm by those victimized (see, for example, Halleck, 1971; Quinney, 1977).[4] In criticism of modernist views, we argue that harm is something that undergoes discursive construction. While what is considered injurious varies, we believe it is helpful to consider harm in terms of the concepts of reduction and repression from a position or standing.

Harms of reduction occur when an offended party experiences a loss of some quality relative to their present standing; *harms of repression* occur when an offended party experiences a limit or restriction preventing them from achieving a desired position or standing. Considered along a continuum of deprivation, harms of reduction or repression may be based on any number of criteria. These criteria might include economic (property), political (power), morality, ethics ('avowal of desire'), human rights, social position (status/prestige, inequality), psychological state (security, well-being), self-realization/actualization, biological integrity, etc. Whatever the criteria, these are harms either because they move the offended away from a position or state they currently occupy, or because they prevent them from occupying a position or state that they desire.[5]

To develop this conceptual analytical schema further, we may combine these two dimensions. If we consider the socially constructed categories of offended others on a horizontal plane and the range of harms of reduction and repression on a vertical plane, then it is easy to see where the variety of definitions of crime in the modernist literature fall (see Figure 5.1). Let us look at some illustrations.

Consensus theories Consensus theories are essentially concerned with three categories of victim: the 'abstract individual', the broad collective 'society' and 'the state'. Classical theories such as Beccaria's (1764) notion of crime as the restriction on individuals' freedom to accumulate wealth address both economic reduction and economic repression (or more accurately here restriction), although only reduction is typically referred to in the familiar notion of 'crimes against property'. Clearly, the approach could include a loss of biological integrity in so far as this might limit the ability to accumulate wealth. For Bentham (1765), harm is considered as pain to one or more individuals and, as such, a crime to the community. This is far reaching since 'pain' can be experienced because of physical, psychological or social injury against the person, and results from reduction or repression. Bentham thought harms against community members' property and personal security important but also included harm against the collective category 'the state' which ultimately was seen to affect an individual's security. However, other abstract categories were not considered to suffer injury. So excluded from criminalization were harms against morality, and what Bentham called 'transactional crimes', those where consent had been given. In this vision drug transactions, consenting sexual activity and a variety of other crimes without victims would also be excluded from criminalization.

In contrast, individual positivists prefer the term 'deviance' to 'crime' because of their 'belief that there is a consensus of value in society that can be scientifically ascertained. Against this it can be judged whether an act is deviant or not' (Young, 1981: 269). Their problem with the term 'crime' is that it is limited to violations of legal codes which may not reflect consensual values, do not encompass all acts of deviance, and are 'based on legal concepts which are unscientific reflecting metaphysical concepts of free will and intent' (1981: 269).

Some, like Garafalo, recognize not only harms against individuals, but also those against the 'morality' of society, as does the sociological positivism of Durkheim with his crime as an offense against the common consciousness. This morality dimension, based upon the reaction of others, is also acknowledged in Roshier's (1989: 76) neo-classical definition of crime 'as only identifiable by the discouraging response it evokes'. Importantly, though, for Durkheim, action that 'offends certain collective feelings' is not merely based on an abstract construction but 'needs to be found in each individual consciousness without exception' (1982: 99).

For some interactionists and social ecologists, the absence of public perception of crime, regardless of what the law stipulates, should exclude some activities from being crimes. Thus, for Burgess (1950) 'a lack of public outrage, stigma, and official punishment attached to social action indicates that such action is not a violation of society's rules, independent of whether it is legally punishable' (Green, 1990: 9). The clear suggestion here is that definitions of crime should be based on socially constituted morality, rather than existing legality, otherwise they include too many harms that are not perceived as harmful and exclude too many 'acts or sets of conditions whose consequences are similar to those of illegal acts' (Michalowski, 1985: 317).

Critical and conflict theories The idea of crime being a morally constructed category is also found in critical and conflict approaches. Indeed, 'whether one is talking about crime as a violation of human rights, a social harm or a social injury, each of these definitions can be characterized as moral ones' (Barak, forthcoming: 44). However, rather than being representative of an existing moral order, the approach is suggesting a humanitarian view of change: 'The notion of crime as social injury, social harm, or a violation of human rights is, in effect, basic to those who strive to improve the human condition, for it provides the intellectual and practical tools for the reconstruction of society' (Quinney and Wildeman, 1991: 5).

An important difference, however, between consensus theorists and those holding a pluralist/conflict position is the different concern shown to expand the number of dimensions of inclusion. In terms of our analytical schema critical modernists move away from the extremes of generalized victim categories, individual, state and society, and instead dramatically expand the number and variety of particularistic categories that are subject to harm. These include the underclass, women, racial and ethnic groups, sexual preference, employees, professionals, people with disabilities, people with AIDS, etc. For example, Schwendinger and Schwendinger's (1970) notion of crime as a violation of human rights relates not just to human rights in general, but to crimes against specific groups including exploited classes, oppressed groups, and those dominated because of race or gender. Moreover, it raises new victim categories such as 'abused women' (DeKeseredy and Hinch, 1991),[6] 'the homeless' (Barak, 1991a), consumers (Goff and Reasons, 1986), and victims of various state crimes (Tifft and Sullivan, 1980; Barak, 1991b; Quinney, 1977).

The tendency toward creating new victim categories is particularly evident in realist criminology where, critics of realism, Young and Rush (1994: 157) point out, 'the victim is present to excess'. Indeed, these authors critically comment on what they call the discursive over-production of 'victimage':

> The identity of the victim is fragmented into a proliferation of archetypal categories. 'Victim' is now not only a unitary category, but also simultaneously contains, within its unity, various predicates of identity. These constitute sub-species or types of victim. Those favoured most by Realism include: ethnic groups subject to racist harassment; residents troubled by burglars . . . the working class exploited by corrupt employers and corrupt police officers; the inner-city dweller confronted by drug dealers; females victimized by violent men . . . Thus any particular event is understood in terms of a plethora of typical victims . . . the proliferation of types of crimes – and hence victimisation – is interminable . . . the more the experiences of the victim are taken into account, the more the identity of the victim is fractured into proliferating types. (1994: 157)

Yet another impetus to this fragmentation and proliferation of the victim is presented by those who see a shift to 'actuarial justice' and the discourse of insurance in the 'risk society'.[7] Here, as Ericson and Carriere (1994: 102) argue, 'discourses of risk penetrate a range of institutions'. Particularly pernicious is the discourse of insurance which:

> constitutes society and its various security institutions . . . It produces social configurations based on particular interests and memberships in risk categories, which in turn affect inclusion and exclusion, hierarchy, solidarity and justice . . . This sensibility is enhanced by the logic of insurance in particular, which offers

solidarity and justice through common interests in the distribution of risk. Risks cut across traditional categories and boundaries based on class, labour and property, blurring and even refiguring those bases of hierarchy and boundary maintenance. (1994: 103)

Pluralist, conflict, critical and realist modernists also draw attention to crimes of repression and expand the number of dimensions beyond the traditional property, person and state to include social/prestige and political standing, human rights, crimes against racism, patriarchal oppression, hate, invasions of privacy and autonomy, humiliation and harassment, etc. Crimes here are not only a reduction of a certain class or group standing, but also a restriction, limitation, repression or prevention of that group or its members changing their relative standing.

In spite of their differences, most modernist thinkers make the assumption that the word 'crime' both signifies and stands for some real human activity and much of the debate focuses on what criteria capture its content. For example, Reiman's (1979: 55) 'crime by any other name' argues that 'if the label "crime" is applied appropriately, this means that its content is dictated by objective facts – real harm, independent of our decisions', unlike Quinney (1970) where there exists merely a play of definitions. Similarly, and not surprisingly, radical realism 'systematically references the real' through its expanded notion of victimization (Young and Rush, 1994: 158). As such, modernist definitions of crime are extreme examples of hegemonic discourse, foundationless yet, as definitions *per se*, harboring a potential for symbolic violence by excluding the myriad of other voices and thereby empowering or privileging certain voices over others. Thus, although modernist conflict and critical theory has brought to our attention the specificity of certain victims whose experience of harm remains obscured in the highly generalized categories of classical privileging of the individual or the society, they have themselves privileged a selective few.

Modernist images of crime and the criminal: the case of white collar crime

Sutherland's ground-breaking definition of white collar crime, which has reoriented much investigation in the notion of crime (Poveda, 1994: 38), argued that this broad concept involved 'a crime committed by a person of respectability and high social status in the course of his [her] occupation' (1940: 5). This was to eventually induce a flurry of analyzes of different forms (typologies) of crime.[8] It also brought to the surface several ambiguities in the original definition that have been the subject of much subsequent debate (Braithwaite, 1985; Green, 1990). What, for example, constitutes 'high social status'? Are blue collar crimes also to be considered white collar crimes since they too are conducted in the course of an occupation? If so what is the relevance of respectability and high social status? And what about crimes committed against the government such as tax evasion that emerges because of an occupation but not typically in the course of it? Other crimes are committed against the government based on the absence of an official occupation, such as social security fraud. Are these white collar crimes also? What distinguishes crimes by professionals from crimes by corporations? Can collective organizations commit crimes or are they always only committed by individuals? What are the different types of white collar crime? So problematic has the concept become that some have argued for its elimination (Hirschi and Gottfredson, 1987; 1989), while others have sought to replace it with alternative concepts.[9]

Certain features distinguish individual white collar crime (occupational crime) from organizational crime. In the case of organizational crime, first, someone outside of the organization authority judges the act to be a norm violation. Second, the act finds support by the internal normative order of the organization (Ermann and Lundman, 1978). The latter is further operationalized as support from peers, and also elites, although this also applies to occupational crime.[10] Support can be active in the form of direct encouragement (Ditton, 1977) or passive involvement in the form of tolerance or 'turning a blind eye'. Third, the organization's goal(s) rather than the individual's is at question in any gains made (Edelhertz, 1970: 19–20; Coleman, 1994: 8–10), although this is a grey area since an individual benefits concurrently with the organization that in turn provides the cloak of legitimacy.

What distinguishes corporate organizational crime from organized crime (e.g. Cosa Nostra, Mafia, Columbian drug cartels, etc.) is that the former is engaged primarily in legitimate business activity, while the latter is engaged in primarily criminal activity. In the former, the criminal activity is a way of increasing legitimate profits; in organized crime the business is merely a front for criminal enterprise.

Some, investigating organizational/corporate crime, have combined the nature of the offense (economic, human rights, violent) with the type of victim (employee, consumer, public) to produce a three-by-three grid (Goff and Reasons, 1986), while others arrive at a similar typology by combining constructions of the offender with constructions of the victim resulting in numerous different types (Hagan, 1986).[11] A composite version of these various attempts with examples is shown in Table 5.1. Thus, included in organizational (corporate) crimes can be false advertising, fraud, tax evasion, controlling the uncertainties of the marketplace, violent crimes (e.g. unsafe production and products), bribery and corruption; while under state crimes we have such offenses as civil liberties violations (e.g. illegal government surveillance, FBI's COINTELPRO, Watergate, etc.), harassment, political repression, international violations (e.g. the CIA-Contra experience, and organized crime).[12]

Modernist theory construction is arguably advanced by these kinds of distinctions and the resulting typological constructions. However, the typological constructions clearly depend on the researcher's assumptions, purposes, and interests. For example, we may have a legalistic typology

Table 5.1 *Typology of white collar crime*

Victim (harmed by crime)	Offender (benefits from crime)			
	Individual	Employee	Corporation/ organization	State/ government
Individual (public or consumer)	Consumer bribes seller to gain market advantage	Retail clerks short-changing or overcharging	Price fixing Pollution Faulty products Deceptive ads	Human rights violations Medical/radiation Indian treaties
Employee (blue collar and white collar)	'Dine and dash' Race or sex baiting	Union sweetheart contracts	Unsafe production	Failure to protect
Corporation/ organization	Price tag sweeps Sabotage Espionage	'Dipping' till Embezzlement Time theft	Industrial espionage Patent violations Price fixing	Regulating small business State monopolies Subsidies
State/government	Tax evasion Fraud after disasters Social security fraud	Off-books employment Overestimating expenses	Bribery Off-books employers saving tax	Crimes against other states

Source: Adapted from Hagan, 1986: 106

focused on state defined crime, individualistic typologies focused on the characteristics of the offender, etc. (Poveda, 1994: 68; Clinard and Quinney, 1973: 1–14).

Following Box, Michalowski (1985) has developed the notion of crimes of the powerless and crimes of capital (or Box and Balkan et al.'s crimes of the powerful).[13] Reiman (1990), too, indicates a difference between one-on-one harm (the typical criminal),[14] and indirect harm (the absentee killer). These distinctions (akin to an earlier distinction between white collar and blue collar crime) allow us to concentrate on modernists' views of the substance of crimes of the powerful.

Other theorists have made a distinction between occupational crime (sometimes still referred to as white collar crime, i.e. embezzlement) and corporate/organizational crime.[15] Edelhertz (1970) distinguishes between personal crimes, business crimes, abuses of trust, and con games. Green (1990: 12–13), on the other hand, collapses all white collar crime into the single category of occupational crime, referring to activities against the law 'committed through opportunity created in the course of an occupation that is legal'. Under this category he sees four types: organizational, state authority, professional, and individual occupational crimes. Occupational crime has been defined generally as crimes committed for personal gain, whereas organizational or corporate crime is committed for the furtherance of the organizational goals (see Clinard and Quinney, 1973; Poveda, 1994: 68–71; Coleman, 1994: 8). Some stress, however, that although white collar crime can be subdivided it should retain an emphasis on the often neglected but consequential dimensions of crimes of the rich and powerful (Friedrichs, 1995a; 1995b; Braithwaite, 1985; Geis, 1992; Simon and Eitzen, 1993).

From our perspective, it seems that this kind of analysis of crimes, offenders and victims leaves something out. What is missing is the observation that crime is an act of the powerful, regardless of the form or organization power takes. Thus we are encouraged that Box (1983) includes the crimes of rape and sexual assault along with crimes by corporations and crimes by the police. All are crimes of the powerful. Indeed, the point made by Box is that distinctions between harms caused by one type of offender and another are part of the mystification that sustains crime and the distinction between it and convention. Drawing on Durkheim's (1898) insight that crime and deviance are 'merely the exaggerated form of common practices', Box argues:

> there is considerable overlap between deviance and convention, rather than the former being distinctly different and opposite to the latter . . . that good business practice merges imperceptibly into sharp business practice, effective policing merges imperceptibly into defective policing, and prison discipline merges imperceptibly into prison brutality; in each case the latter has an unbroken connection with the former . . . a similar lesson can be obtained from considering how 'normal' sexual encounters merge imperceptibly into sexual assaults of which rape is the most serious, and how the former provides just the ingredients out of which the latter can emerge. (1983: 121)

So the critical issue is not what is different about crimes of the powerful and crimes of the powerless, or what is different about the different types of offender, but what is similar about what they do. This similarity lies not in their legal definition of having broken the law but in their substantive practice of creating differences of position for those with power to exploit against those without power: and this is as true for the urban terrorist as for the corporate raider, for the date rapist as for the environmental polluter, for the armed robber as for the armchair swindler. All are investing their energy in creating and exploiting differences in power. All are excessive investors in power. Little wonder then that Durkheim was concerned to point out that personal freedom depends upon preventing some profiting from their physical, economic and other superiority to the detriment of others' personal liberty (see Box, 1983: 16). Again, we are in early anticipation of our constitutive position. Let us first examine the postmodernist assault on modernist criminology's contribution to the perpetuation of crime through *its* investment in typologies of difference.

Skeptical postmodernism

The postmodernist approach believes that while the castles of victimage must be torn down, replacing them with more identifiable manor houses does a grave disrespect to those in less visible social habitats. Thus, the language of modernism is seen as a contributor to victimization, for, by raising a few, it negates the many, denying them a voice for recourse.

Skeptical postmodernism has been accused of virtually elevating discourse and discursive practices to the level of agency responsible for creating the definitional category of crime and victim (Lauretis, 1989; Schwartz and Friedrichs, 1994: 225). For example, in Foucault's (1977) famous discussion of punishment, crime is not some real quality but the construction of a 'truth' about crime. Thus 'The nature and gravity of punishment defined the offense of which the condemned was guilty . . . the extent of the offense was defined for all to see by the pains the offender was forced to experience' (Katz, 1988: 35). Moreover, the pains that defined crime were not a reflection of any intrinsic quality of the act but, like the human body on which they were wrought, an occasion for the expression of relations of power. For Foucault, then, it is the discourse of punishment as a symbolic expression of power relations that constructs some behavior rather than others as crime. It is power relations through discourse that construct the subjects and objects of crime and ultimately constitute a part of the reality of crime. When these power relations change, or proliferate, so do their expression and the discourse of that expression, and thereby the content of what is crime. Foucault's (1977) argument is that the relations of power have become dispersed through society such that the whole society is now imbued with the discourse of power as numerous but disconnected power holders participate in a normalization of the total social body (see also Deleuze, 1988).

The deconstructive challenge of such postmodernism seeks to reverse this unifying hegemony, to de-differentiate crime and behavior, 'to explore how images and meanings pertaining to such violence are constituted' thereby 'giving privilege to the experience and perspective of the victimized over the victimizers, attending to the marginal rather than the representative cases' (Schwartz and Friedrichs, 1994: 225). Rather than privileging the empty protections of grand conception, or the exclusive domain of the signified victim, privileging is concerned with embracing the multiplicity of harms suffered by discursively produced subjects (i.e. the 'violence of language').

However, because of its often nihilistic and relativistic tendencies, insisting that all harms are constructions, many modernists have been critical of the skeptical postmodern position, especially with regard to the denial of concrete victims. Schwartz, for example, has serious questions about the value of deconstructing victim categories:

> when I think about theories which problematize and deny meaning to concepts of crime, I have flashbacks of survivors I have met in shelter houses. There are many types of 'crime', to be sure, but to someone who has just been beaten or raped and received 75 stitches, the idea that crime only exists because we affirm the reality of existence, sounds a lot like victim-blaming, or at least, as Hunt points out, an ethical relativism that can be very scary. The absence of presence, so to speak. (1991: 122)

Indeed, Baudrillard (1991) has come in for severe criticism from Cohen (1993) for his account that denies the reality of state violations of human rights, such as in the Gulf War. He says that not only is this an insult to the dead and the maimed but as an academic discourse it feeds the language of denial employed by those with the power to violate human rights.

Constitutive theorizing

Here we again interconnect modernism and skeptical postmodernism, arguing that while crime is unquestionably a socially constructed category, the outcome of humans acting toward its culturally mediated product as though it were a reality renders their action, in the words of W. I. Thomas (1923), 'real in its consequences'. Thus we argue for affirmatively reframing the definition of crime toward one that is sufficiently reflexive to allow humans to produce different realities, ones freeing them from the logic of their own constructions by allowing them to induce different behavior as real, behavior that is less harmful to themselves and others. But we heed Cohen's call that 'to travel the subways of New York, I need more help than a deconstructed map of the category of "mugging"' (1990: 24).

Transitions

Postmodern definitions of crime are in the process of development. However, before specifying our constitutive definition it is worth noting, as we did in the previous chapters, some glimpses offered in the literature. Lyotard, for example, though not directly providing a definition of crime, does indicate a direction. Arguing against any form of consensus metaphysics, such as those provided by progressive theorists such as Habermas,[16] Lyotard suggests a privileging of local sites in the production of justice. This is rooted in his alternative metaphysics which he refers to as paralogy, the undermining of the arbitrary character of existing truth. Here acknowledged is (1) that speakers (interlocutors) come to agreement in concrete situations with pragmatic rules at play, and (2) that consensus cannot be an end but only a moment in discussion: the end can only be instability and dissent (Lyotard, 1984: 65–6). Habermas' focus, Lyotard tells us, is a search for universalities. This direction is inherently non-liberating and does not contribute to justice. A definition of crime implied by Lyotard would seem to privilege the local character of dissent, conflict, and potential regulation. Our notion of 'harm by repression' or 'harm by reduction' could then be applied to this more micro-level, local site where various tensions and conflicts are produced. This gets us away from universalities and forms of essentialism, but does not suggest any valuative definition of 'harm', a critique that has been made of left realists (see especially Young and Rush, 1994).

A second direction can be teased out of Lacan's notion concerning the desiring subject and his proposed ethical principle which argues for maximal opportunities for the fulfillment (avowal) of desire (Lacan, 1992: 309, 319–21; 1977: 275).[17] Although posing a solution that revolves around the psychoanalytic encounter,[18] a reasonable direction in establishing a definition of crime could argue that various social forms (which we are calling constitutive interrelational sets) may contribute to harms of reduction or repression. This direction could specify the possibilities of desire finding more liberating forms of embodiment.[19]

For Lacan, within the human subject the sphere that provides an illusory source of identity and consistency in the psychic apparatus (the *moi*) is infinitely changeable in providing new sources of contingent stability. Thus psychoanalysis, for Lacan, is an *ethical* discipline whereby 'the analysand emerges as a responsible, ethical agent, that is, as a fully human being' (Lee, 1990: 97). Here the key is discourse: 'if it is only through discourse – through symbolically determined articulation – that the human subject stands out (and thus "ex-ists") in his essential humanity, then it is only in discourse that he [she] can finally come to terms with what is real and what is not' (1990: 169). Begging in Lacan's analysis is precisely how new social forms take shape in a political economy and how various levels interact having repressive or reductive effects. His analysis of gender formations has much merit; his non-prescriptive position, however, remains undeveloped.

Elsewhere, Milovanovic (1993b) has shown how Lacan's three main spheres, the Symbolic, Imaginary, and Real Orders, are implicated in the contingent stabilization of identification and discursive production ('Borromean knot'). He shows that these can be temporarily stabilized (but remain inherently unstable) by various identifiers offered by the political, economic and legal orders and the advertisement industry. These are objects of desire or *objets petit* (a). Thus Lacan's vacuous political position could be augmented by one that is rooted in historical developments and political, economic, and legal relationships. A definition of harm, then, could ask: to what extent has a particular stabilized set of relationships provided the basis for harms of repression or reduction? Therefore a constitutive perspective might provide the explanatory framework within which Lacanian dynamics may operate.

A third possibility might start with the new logic of 'risk management' and the potential for repression or reduction by actuarial justice.[20] This logic 'is concerned with techniques for identifying, classifying and managing groups assorted by levels of dangerousness' (Feeley and Simon, 1994: 173). It provides a new basis of a constituted order: 'risks cut across traditional categories and boundaries based on class, labour and property, blurring and even *refiguring* those bases of hierarchy and boundary maintenance' (Ericson and Carriere, 1994: 103, emphasis added). Conceivably, a definition of harm with an underlying 'social defense' (incapacitation) could develop with this logic as its cornerstone. Ericson and Carriere have argued that police, for example, have become the new 'knowledge brokers and expert advisers on risk to other institutions' (1994: 104). It is but a short step for the judicial branch in their 'interest balancing' formula to prioritize these criteria of risk management and actuarial justice.

These risk technologies, as forms of disciplinary mechanism (Foucault, 1977) or diagrams of power (Deleuze, 1988), tend to penetrate major institutions (Ericson and Carriere, 1994: 104; Feeley and Simon, 1994: 185–96). Those interested in developing a postmodern definition of crime would be concerned with these developments in so far as a new master logic, a universality, a global knowledge may emerge and stabilize. In this logic, harms of repression and reduction could occur, not only in producing 'false positives', but also because of the construction of overbearing centripetal societal forces which may lead to more crimes such as those stemming from 'edgework' (O'Malley and Mugford, 1994).[21] For example, studies of the hidden economy have shown that this deviant work is manifest in the spaces and cracks of the formal economy, not as a separate realm as expressed by the terms 'underground', 'shadow', 'subterranean' etc., but at the interstices of formal activity.[22] The more clearly and publicly the formal economy is distinguished from the informal or hidden, the more that activity finds expression (Henry, 1987b; 1988). Moreover, while the defining characteristics of the formal economy are publicly constructed as economically instrumental, those of the informal/hidden economy are significantly experienced as social, involving meaning construction that celebrates social rewards, social status and prestige, network connections, excitement and fun, competitive play and reconciliation (Henry, 1978). In this connection a question is raised of whether or not the harms of reduction or repression are manifest in the cultural construction and social organization of 'alienated economic man', rather than in the hidden economy, which itself might express a counter-tendency toward self-help justice.

In short, then, the flip side of chaos theory is a proliferation of differences that develop in social conditions that approximate far-from-equilibrium conditions; this necessitates new coordinating mechanisms, that deny stasis and homeostasis a prioritization. We shall return to this in Chapters 7 and 8 in offering some policy suggestions, including Unger's call for an 'empowered democracy' which we see rooted in such far-from-equilibrium dynamics.

A fourth direction worth pursing is found in Hunt's notion of relational sets and structural coupling and our integration of this into constitutive criminology (see Chapter 4). We argued that a modified autopoietic and structural coupling thesis could sensitize the postmodernist theorists to historically situated harms of reduction and repression. This position argues that various co-evolving constitutive relational sets are 'structurally coupled' (i.e. they maintain interrelational effects). This may begin with various logics (e.g. capital, actuarial, phallocentric, rationalization, etc.), but because of genealogical developments, one or several in combination may attain a more dominant position. This is illustrated by Feeley and Simon (1994: 185–93) in their analysis of the rise of actuarial logic due to developments in tort law (i.e. a focus on a discourse of social utility and management rather than on individual responsibility), systems analysis (i.e. operational research in manufacture and warfare), and the ascendancy of the law and economics movement (i.e. the privileging of a discourse based on utilitarian considerations rather than on moral ones, quantitative discourse over qualitative, etc.). An approach to harms of reduction and repression in this view would require us to specify the historically changing configurations of constitutive interrelational sets.

In this view, discourses, knotted signifiers,[23] and structurally constituted, discursive subject positions which are reflective of constitutive inter-relational sets must be examined for their capacity to generate harms of reduction or harms of repression with regard to their exclusion capacity. Consider, for example, Freire's (1972) idea of the 'culture of silence' imposed on human subjects. He states: 'If men [women], as historical beings necessarily engaged with other men [women] in a movement of inquiry, did not control that movement, it would be (and is) a violation of men's [women's] humanity. Any situation in which some men [women] prevent others from engaging in the process of inquiry is one of violence' (1972: 73). Consider, too, Collins' (1993) analysis of the interlocking nature of race, gender and class oppression, configurations that are shifting in terms of context but nevertheless lead to harms of reduction and repression. Indeed, these 'interlocking' logics affect everyone differently (1993: 33). For example, women of color and white women have different relationships with white male authority structures, the reactions to which might lead to rejection of certain images, as with African-American women, to such images as the mammy, the matriarch, etc., or to their seductions, as with white women, those that promise reward in exchange for the support of the dominant structure. As Collins tells us, 'Each of us lives with an allotted portion of institutional privilege and penalty, and with varying levels of rejection and seduction inherent in the symbolic images applied to us' (1993: 34). Accordingly, a constitutive approach would target these forms of harm.

Forms of harm, then, can be engaged. Alternative discursive forms leading to human liberation can similarly be embraced and given a 'contingent universality' (Butler, 1992) standing for the provisional articulation of concrete political agendas for social change. So much for getting there. Let us now be quite definitive.

Constitutive definition: the power of crime

We agree with sociologically informed modernists that a legalistically based definition misses what it means to define an act as a crime, that is as harm or injury. Crime is not just what is defined in the written laws or rules, nor is it merely arrests and convictions, nor judicial declarations accumulated as precedent. This is mere tautology. To say this is to say nothing of crime's content or meaning or how particular instances of behavior are interpreted. It is to say nothing of how instances of meaningful action are transformed from these constructed by the participants to those signified by legal functionaries who make their behavior stand for, exemplify, or be another case of this or that type of offense. It is to say little of which actors and agencies are involved in the definition of whatever took place to make it into crime. It is to ignore the dimensions that had to be exaggerated and those that had to be omitted or discounted for the instance to be compressed into the general case. Finally, it is silent on the work done by alleged perpetrators and apparent victims (themselves constructed categories in the making of crime) for them to declare a 'crime' had occurred. The legalistic definition of crime merely provides closure where robust debate must begin. So what is a constitutive definition of crime?

We agree with skeptical postmodernists that crime is a socially constructed and discursively constituted category. It is a violent categorization of the diversity of human conflicts and transgressions into a single category 'crime', as though these were somehow all the same. It is a melting of differences reflecting the multitude of variously motivated harms of reduction or repression into a single entity such as 'violent crime' or 'property crime'. As such it is the celebration of homogeneity, and the epitome of global theorizing.

But does this mean the behavior and experience of action that subsequently results in this classificatory and translation work are unreal, fictional, imagined? Of course not. Only some radical realists seem to imagine that postmodernist criminology adheres to this view (Matthews and Young, 1992). Let us be very clear about constitutive criminology's view of crime. What is taken to be crime involves pain and conflict and instances of harm and injury. People involved in those relations taken to be 'crimes' are, for that moment (but typically over longer time periods), in relations of inequality. They are, as discursively constituted human subjects, being disrespected; reduced from what they are (reduction), prevented from becoming what they might be (repression). Thus, as we define it here, *crime is the expression of some agency's energy to make a difference on others and it is the exclusion of those others who in the instant are rendered powerless to maintain or express their humanity.* Whether this agency is comprised and energized by people, social identities (men, women, etc.), groups, parties, institutions, the state or even constitutive interrelational sets, is less important than that it manifests a disrespecting power. Crimes then are nothing less than moments in the expression of power, such that those who are subjected to them are denied their own contribution to the encounter and often to future encounters, are denied their worth, are simultaneously reduced and repressed in one or several ways. Crime then is the power to deny others their ability to make a difference. It is the ultimate form of reification in which those subject to the power of another agency suffer the pain of being denied their own humanity, the power to make a difference, on any one or more of the scales of repression or reduction that we identified earlier. The victim of crime is thus rendered a non-person, a non-human, or a less complete being. The victim is *pas-toute*. The victim is nothing. That is the harm of crime. That is its pain. Crime is the expression of power, the master of difference and the handmaiden of pain.

So what of law and crime? Law does not include most of the behaviors that fit our definition of crime. Law is a very partial list of harms. An adequate listing of laws to capture the behavior that we define as crime would have to start from the contexts of pain resulting from such denials of others. It would thus have to include much of what currently stands for business practices, governmental policies, hierarchical social relations, historically contingent constitutive interrelational sets, and a lot of what occurs in family life, since these arenas of power are premised upon the inequality that liberates the expression of agency to the creation of pain. Law designed to uphold power differentials cannot protect against harm; it frames its construction (Young and Rush, 1994).

The significance of the interconnectedness of law with other social forms that we discussed in the previous chapter is that law will inevitably contain the self-same expressions of power (e.g. simulacra, diagrams, disciplinary mechanisms, logics, recursive symmetries, etc.) that create the 'formative contexts' (Unger, 1975) of crimes that are subsequently omitted from definition, sloughed off like used molds. Uncritically celebrating existing legal definitions of crime, and its accompanying rule-of-law ethic, constitutes and reconstitutes existing power relations. In this it recursively constitutes the suffering and pain in more insidious forms, such as when the more powerful benefit from otherwise perceived 'free' contractual relations. This is not the same, for example, as saying corporate interests shape the law in order to be immune from prosecution and are thereby free to create harm. Rather, it is saying that corporations, as excessive expressors of power, like the state, marriage or family, will inevitably attempt to constitute law to reflect the legitimacy of their power and the illegitimacy of the power of others. This is not because they objectify it as an external instrument (which they may also do) but because law affords them the theater whose props and backdrop are fine-tuned for the production of pestilence. Law is the playhouse of power; crime is its *Mousetrap*.

This is why, from our perspective, much of what counts as business, governmental policy, hierarchical social relations, marriage, family and the state is crime. It is why homelessness can be a crime, why neglect of health and safety considerations is a crime, why sexual harassment and violence against intimates (whether in emotional torment or physical beating from either spouse to the other or to dependants) are crimes. It is especially why child abuse is a crime. However, it is also why suicide may only sometimes be a crime, more often the emergent outcome of daily death decisions, each representing a search for release from the indignities of harms and injustices too potently present to survive, too obscurely absent to ignore. Indeed, it is why emotional terror by employers over employees through at-will employment is a crime. Finally, it is why several of the actions of agencies of government are also crimes. This is not in the sense of specific incidents like police brutality (as in the Rodney King case and countless similar beatings of those held in custody by government agencies on a global scale), but rather in the sense of the pervasive hidden crimes of domination that Bourdieu (1977: 192) describes as 'symbolic violence'. This is 'the violence which is exercised on a social agent with his or her complicity' (Bourdieu and Wacquant, 1992: 167). It is a form of domination which is exerted through the very medium in which it is disguised, wherein it is the 'gentle, invisible form of violence, which is never recognized as such, and is not so much undergone as chosen, the violence of credit, confidence, obligation, personal loyalty, hospitality, gifts, gratitude, piety' (Bourdieu, 1977: 192). But we have forgotten this dimension of domination and neglected to see how this power play can itself be crime.

Again, let us be very clear. The activities of many of those in the institutions in Western industrial society are premised on the exercise of power over others denying their humanity – the witting or unwitting denial of others' right to make a difference. This is the root of why capitalism is criminogenic, why ours is a violent society. It is also why party hierarchy state socialism is criminogenic.[24] The activity of those who construct occasions for the deliverance of power is crime. It is crime because it takes from people any present dignity and, further, represses their attempt to change their person.

We might also draw from chaos theory here to underscore how we are not saying all of what occurs in arenas traditionally conceived as legitimate is criminal. We are not making categorical distinctions. Instead we are throwing into relief the interrelatedness of harmful practices with legitimate ones and vice versa. Thus Young tells us that:

> In formal, rational models of crime, one expects a clear and sharp distinction between the criminal act and the prosocial act; between those who are 'criminal' and those who are 'law-abiding' citizens; between organized crime and legitimate business. Given some set of acts, persons, corporations or nations, chaos theory would tell us to expect that some fraction of their behavior would be criminal and some fraction, prosocial. Some societies are organized to keep that ratio low and stable; some high and unstable. (1991a: 4)

Of course, crime is a discursive construction and as such has various capabilities of being expressed within given discourses. It also undergoes translation/transformation between discourses as is the case of the lower class defendant or other marginalized, disempowered, and disenfranchised groups before the court, a translation often unreflective of the complexities of existence. This is the violence of language. It is its harm. The call for universality in discourse (as in Habermas' call for a search for consensus in 'ideal speech situations') is a form of harm: it makes common that which is irregular, it homogenizes the heterogeneous. As an alternative to the legalistic definition of crime, our postmodernist definition of crime focuses on harm inflicted *in all its guises* and would certainly include the 'violence of language' (Lecercle, 1990), particularly how the disenfranchised, disempowered, and marginalized have been denied expressive forms for their desires and yearnings, that is to say, how their voices are denied (Freire, 1985; McLaren, 1994; Aronowitz and Giroux, 1991; Giroux, 1992).

Crime, then, must be redefined in terms of the power to create harm (pain) in any context. But because law can only be reconstituted (because of its interrelations with other social orders) by reconstituting the relations of other social forms with which it is interrelated (discussed in Chapter 4), changing law's definition of crime to include more types of offended victim is futile. Rather, to change the social construction of harm it is necessary to change the social forms and their implied power relations so that harm is not carried under the guise of law, in the expression of power over others.

In short, premised upon our view of law and crime, law is not just a definer of crime, it is also the maker of crime, the manifestation of which provides sustenance to the classificatory schema. This is because it conceals some agent's (person, agency, institution, state, constitutive interrelational set) harms by institutionalizing and legitimizing the power relations whose continuance brings harm. To take the example of conjugal violence discussed by Young and Rush: '"conjugal violence" is a product of a crimino-legal practice which stands in as proxy for the violence of the marriage relation. There is then a legal culture of violence in which conjugal homicide takes place. Violence resides in the house of law, the house of marriage' (1994: 166). As they argue, it is necessary to abandon the 'smooth surface of the universal victim' for this sacrifices too much of its particular in silence. We need to define crime and its harm in terms of specific, but historically contingent, victim categories, but *to be aware of the changing nature of the emerging social constructions whose relations of power are relations of harm.* Our definition of crime as 'the exercise of the power to deny others their own humanity' needs to be anchored to the specificities of endless substitutable existent and emergent social constructions through which humanity is constituted and along whose discursive dimensions it takes shape. Only in such a way can we be continuously aware of the relations of crime and of the social space needed to replace these with less harmful forms.

Summary and conclusions: contingent universalities

We have taken heed of Cohen's (1990) 'triple loyalty' for doing critical criminology: (1) 'an overriding obligation to honest intellectual enquiry itself (however skeptical, provisional, irrelevant and unrealistic)', (2) 'a political commitment to social justice', and (3) 'short term humanitarian help' (1990: 28–9). We need not wallow in despair, in skeptical nihilism, incapable of establishing a provisional and contingently based political agenda for change. We can articulate 'contingent universalities' (Butler, 1992; McLaren, 1994: 211) in order to pave the way toward 'a new hegemony articulated through new egalitarian social relations, practices, and institutions' (Mouffe, 1992: 380). The sign, indeed, may be provisionally 'decidable' in the sphere of social struggle.[25]

Our provisional and non-essentialist constitutive definition of crime is necessarily subject to ongoing refinement, specificity, challenge, modification, and substitution; but it answers the call for immediate direction and action, and it answers the call for identification of multiple and often covert forms and present sites of race, class, and gender domination. It is consistent with the development of both a language of critique and a language of possibility (Giroux, 1992). Embedded in the latter is a call for social relations that move away from harms of reduction and repression. Nor should our provisional constitutive definition of crime be confused with global theorizing and support for enduring universalities. As McLaren has argued:

> Only when they are used unjustly and oppressively as all-encompassing and all-embracing global warrants for thought and action in order to secure an oppressive regime of truth, should totality and universality be rejected. We need to retain some kind of moral, ethical, and political ground – albeit a provisional one – from which to negotiate among multiple interests. (1994b: 207)

Unanswered questions, to be sure, persist within the postmodern definition we offer: accounting for various degrees of consciousness of harm (victimization), specifying degree of harm, response mechanisms to harms inflicted, valuative criteria, change, etc. But our approach is in the spirit of engaging the simplistic legalistic definition of crime.

Notes

1 The flip side of a definition of crime is some theoretical framework accounting for the 'causes' of crime, the question of the wherewithal of the agent perpetrating the harm. This we will investigate in the next chapter.

2 See also Reiman (1979), Michalowski (1985), Von Hirsch and Jareborg (1991), Cohen (1993: 98–101), Lea and Young (1984: 55).

3 An extension of this 'finding of offensive' is the construction of categories of abstract objects (i.e. those that are not categories of people) as though they are victims. In this treatment 'what is crime' is determined by whether acts are offensive to the constructed meaning of objects valued by human audiences: e.g. offensive to 'property', to 'public order', to 'security'. However, although these categories are often personified, here we take them as objects which can be changed, but which cannot themselves be harmed, and so we consider them as various dimensions of the harm scale.

4 Even though this may be the case, we do not subscribe to arguments that a linear progression is part of a dialectical materialism working towards a transformation into consciously aware, politically motivated revolutionary work (Quinney, 1977: 59–60), for this overlooks the dialectics of struggle.

5 Most definitions include more than one criterion, and the criteria are not wholly discrete. Also 'offended subject' here is not restricted to individuals but includes socially constructed groups, as discussed above.

6 See also Chesney-Lind (1989), Daly and Chesney-Lind (1988), Currie (1990).

7 See especially, Simon (1987; 1988), O'Malley (1991; 1992), Beck (1992), Feeley and Simon (1992; 1994).

8 See, for example, Schwendinger and Schwendinger (1970), Clinard and Quinney (1973), Edelhertz (1970), Clinard and Yeager (1980), Michalowski (1985), Reiman (1979), Quinney (1977), Braithwaite (1984), Goff and Reasons (1986), Green (1990), Frank and Lynch (1992), Ermann and Lundman (1992), Simon and Eitzen (1993), Coleman (1994), Friedrichs (1992; 1995a; 1995b).

9 Alternative definitions have included: 'occupational crime' and 'corporate crime' (Clinard and Quinney, 1973; Green, 1990), 'fiddling' (Ditton, 1977; Mars, 1982), 'workplace crime' (McCaghy and Cernkovich, 1987), 'blue collar crime' (Horning, 1970), 'business crime' (Conklin, 1977), 'organizational crime' (Schrager and Short, 1978; Gross, 1978; Vaughan, 1980), 'elite deviance' (Simon and Eitzen, 1982), 'corporate and government deviance' (Ermann and Lundman, 1978), 'crimes against bureaucracy' (Smigel and Ross, 1970), 'crimes of the powerful' (Box, 1983; Balkan et al., 1980; Michalowski, 1985; Coleman, 1994; Pearce and Snider, 1992; Simon and Eitzen, 1993), and 'state crime' (Barak, 1991b).

10 Ermann and Lundman (1978: 7–9), Horning (1970), Henry and Mars (1978), Mars (1974; 1982), Hawkins (1984).

11 See also Michalowski's (1985) typology on political crimes.

12 See Coleman (1994: 14–71); see also Reiman (1990), Frank and Lynch (1992), Barak (1991b), and Poveda (1994: 92–8).

13 See also Coleman (1994), Pearce and Snider (1992), Simon and Eitzen (1993). However, Hirschi and Gottfredson (1987; 1989) found that no significant differences existed between crimes of the powerless and powerful; in other words, the typological distinctions separated crime according to offense not offender. Their analysis has come under severe attack for using official definitions and unreliable Uniform Crime Report statistics and for ignoring the significance of a sizable and serious problem (Steffensmeier, 1989; Daly, 1989; Wheeler et al., 1988; Weisburd et al., 1991).

14 It should be pointed out that this excludes group crimes, gang crimes and especially crimes by criminal organizations.

15 For other typologies of white collar crime, see Poveda (1994: 68–70), Edelhertz (1970), and Green (1990).

16 See Habermas' notion of the 'ideal speech situation' guided by the search for universal consensus.

17 See Lee (1990: 95–9, 168–70) and Rajchman (1991: 42–3).

18 Thus 'desire is avowed only when the analysand assumes the full truth of his [her] being a subject, and this assumption of subjectivity entails a new relationship between the subject and desire' (Lee, 1990: 96).

19 See, for example, Lecercle's (1985) notion of délire and Kristeva's (1980) notion of the semiotic chora – each being more primordial forms of embodiment of desire.

20 On actuarial justice see Ericson and Carrier (1994), Reichman (1986), Simon (1987; 1988), O'Malley (1991), Feeley and Simon (1994).

21 See also Lyng (1990), Katz (1988).

22 See Henry (1978; 1987b; 1988), Mars (1982), Ferman et al. (1987; 1993), and Gabor (1994).

23 Consider Laclau and Mouffe's (1985) point concerning nodal points, and Lacan's idea of *point de capiton*.

24 This is not to deny that the same is not true in other systems based on domination, such as fascism, feudalism, etc.

25 See Zavarzadeh and Morton (1990), McLaren (1994), Freire (1985), Giroux (1992).

6
Modernist Theories of Crime Causation

Causality is the central concept of the modernist criminological enterprise. Criminologists and social theorists have hypothesized how the events they define as crime are produced by antecedent events. They are concerned with the 'relation between two events or states of affairs in which one brings about or produces the other' (Quinton, 1977: 92). With the exception of the dialectical causality of critical criminology, modernists model linear causal relationships among the variously identified variables. Much of the research done by criminologists and published in professional criminology journals strives to test these various theories of causation. It seeks evidence for whether antecedent 'factors' were present or absent prior to crime being committed, or it attempts to show that all other causal factors are absent apart from specific ones correlated with crime. Empirical researchers most typically operate from a positivist, quantitative perspective, and operationalize these relationships for research testing. They employ variants of 'path analysis', which is a technique for estimating the relative effects of a set of independent variables on a dependent variable, based upon the observed correlations among the hypothesized causal relations among variables. Interconnections are analyzed in order to establish a path coefficient for each of the indicated causal connections, building up a complete picture (i.e. variance explained, R^2) of the independent effects of each variable relative to the rest. However, as has been acknowledged, 'The major limitation of the technique is the assumption that the researcher knows in advance the correct causal ordering among his [her] variables' (Bohrnstedt, 1974: 205). However, it is not just that failure to know the correct causal ordering can result in serious error (1974: 205) but that, from our perspective, there is no correct causal ordering in the first place. This is merely a research construction that privileges one method of research over another.[1] As DiCristina says, 'there appears to be no logical grounds for privileging particular research methods in criminology . . . No method is demonstrably the most plausible means for discovering causes of crime, probabilities of association between crime and other phenomena, false theories of crime, truth about crime, or strategies for controlling crime' (1995: 58).[2]

In this chapter, we consider modernist criminological approaches to causation, and then go on to discuss different types of causality in modernism, before showing how these appear in particular criminological theories. We divide our consideration of modernist causality in criminology into three parts. First we consider theoretical explanations of crime that locate causality at the individual level, either within a person or within their immediate social relations. Such explanations can be termed micro-level. Second, in contrast to these, are explanations where causality is located at the level of broader structural units of a society such as institutions, organizations, the state and the system. These are designated macro-level. Third we shall consider the integrational approaches to theory, the more recent development, which seeks to combine various elements from micro- and macro-theorizing. After each discussion we shall illustrate how criminologists have applied these theories to explain crime. In this appli- cation, we have selected what is broadly known as 'white collar crime' or 'crimes of the powerful' as a corrective to modernist criminological theory's tendency to focus on 'crimes of the powerless' (conventional crime). Indeed, with the exception of some versions of Marxist theory and feminism, most modernist theories envisage crime as conventional property and violence offenses of 'street crime', to the exclusion of harms by corporate and white collar offenders or 'suite crime' (Simon and Eitzen, 1982). Nor is this surprising given the predominant acceptance of legal and, therefore, state definitions of criminality in modernist criminology (see Chapter 5). Thus for our illustration in this chapter we wish to show how these theories have been applied to corporate and white collar crime or 'crimes of the powerful'.[3]

Consideration of causality in criminological theory needs some qualifi- cation from its general discussion in philosophy and methods. Most, if not all, established theoretical perspectives in criminology imply general causal statements that locate the cause or causes of crime in some antecedent events. Few, however, specify precisely the strength of the causal connec- tion, such as whether cause is necessary for crime to occur, is sufficient for crime to occur, or is one of several greater or lesser contingents that result in crime. Second, few theoretical positions describe the type of causality implied in their theory. Is it linear? Is it direct or indirect? Is it multiple? Is it interactive? Is it dialectic or reciprocal? Third, proponents of crimino- logical theories only occasionally specify the precise ways in which their theory should be operationalized for empirical research testing. Indeed, it is rare to even debate such issues as inductive versus deductive reasoning, the value and credibility of probability statements or issues of falsification.

Several of these issues are discussed by researchers attempting to test theories developed by others and by philosophers of criminological method (see especially, Messner et al., 1989; DiCristina, 1995), but few original statements of theory even contain formal propositions derived from the theory (Sutherland and Cressey's differential association theory and Hirschi's control theory are exceptional in this respect). In analyzing modernist criminology, therefore, we shall restrict our concern to a dis- cussion of (1) what kinds of causal relationship are implied by the variety of criminological theories, and (2) what constitutes cause. Let us first examine the broad picture of causality in criminology before turning to the specifics.

General approaches to crime causation

The history of criminology has shown several shifts in its romance with the concept of causality. The premodern demonological perspective contained the essence of a dilemma whose manifestation was never expunged. At its core are the age-old issues of freedom and determinism. Both were present. Demonology held the view that human relationships were subject to supernatural forces and that harmful events were the outcome of malevolent interference by 'other-worldly' forces. In the West these forces were designated as demons or the Devil (Mair, 1969). Coercion was the result of being possessed or taken over by the Devil who directed his subjects to commit crime, regardless of will. But demonology also held that harm, particularly crime, could result from choice. Choice, in the form of a 'compact' with the Devil, came about through the concept of 'temptation' to worldly and especially carnal pleasures, in the face of a weakness of faith in God (Pfohl, 1985: 20–1; Einstadter and Henry, 1995: 29–42). So human subjects were both agents of their destiny and objects controlled by external forces.

With the Enlightenment's release to reason and rationality came the ascendancy of free will, and the theoretical liberation of humans from the shackles of other-worldly powers. People were not compelled to evil by supernatural forces, argued Enlightenment philosophers, they chose evil after rationally weighing its pleasures against its pain. So, from an ambivalent romance with the causal certainty of the supernatural, began an affair with free will that lasted until a new promise of certainty offered by a marriage to science.

Scientific criminology promised a search to deliver the causes of crime. However, as Reckless (1970) admits: 'The causes of crime have never been satisfactorily isolated.' With increased recognition of crime's complexity 'there has been a steady trend away from single, specific, explanations of behavior in the direction of multiple explanation' (Cole, 1949: 45). But as Reckless points out, to be useful, any explanation should limit the multiplicity of causes since 'the inclusion of almost any and all kinds of causes is almost as bad as the fixation on one cause. Everything under the sun cannot be included under multiple causes, unless we desire to discover some very remote and indirect connections with crime which are not at all causative' (1970: 74). Not surprisingly, therefore, 'when it began to be clear that for any given crime, let alone all crime, there may be thousands of "causes" (rather than a few) and a complex degree of interaction, the search for causes was abandoned and attention turned to the process of crime commission' (Walsh, 1983: 31).

The history of criminology has reflected this longing for certainty tempered by a flirtation with freedom and despair at the impossibility of its task. Causation in criminology, rather than being the result of a steady accumulation of knowledge, has instead been a litany of false starts and abandoned idols, raising more questions about causality than confirmation of its efficacy. However, consideration of causality is pivotal to under-standing the contributions and limitations of modernist criminology, since these are based upon its premises and affect the formulation of criminal justice policy. Let us first look at examples of the different types of causality that form the basis of modernist criminology, before focusing on specific theories.

Types of causality

The issue of causality can be addressed by considering different types of causal relationship. The basic notion of causality is expressed by the idea of independent cause in which an event A produces an event B, such that either B cannot occur without A (in which case A is a necessary cause) or B will be produced by A but can also occur without it (in which case A is a sufficient cause). Beyond this, Einstadter and Henry (1995: 12–18) have identified four broad types of causal relationship in criminological theory which they call linear, multiple, interactive and dialectical.[4]

Linear causality consists of a sequential chain in which each subsequent occurrence of an event produces the conditions for the next event, until the final criminal event occurs. Empey and Stafford (1991) describe such a model of causality as *interdependent*. They illustrate the argument with a version of Hirschi's control theory of delinquent behavior. Weak attach-ment to parents → weak attachment to school → weak commitment to conventional means → identification with delinquent peers → causes delinquent behavior. They say that this model 'implies that each variable in the causal chain is not only dependent on those preceding it, but also is linked to delinquency only through the variables following it . . . Unless each step is present a child will be unlikely to violate the law' (1991: 286–7). This type of causality is also an example of the 'collocation of causes' or 'conditional' causal relationship since no one event in the sequence can produce delinquency alone (DiCristina, 1995: 6). In short, each preceding event is necessary for each subsequent event and the whole sequence is necessary for the delinquency outcome.

The second type of causality is *multiple*. There are two versions of this: many causes and combined causes. In the 'many causes' version each of several events can independently produce crime. In other words, each is sufficient but not necessary for crime to occur. Thus, in the control theory example, delinquency might be the direct result of either a weak attachment to parents, or a weak attachment to school, or an identification with delinquent peers, and so on. Here each factor alone is sufficient to produce delinquency, but no single factor is necessary since the same event (delinquency) could be produced by any of a number of causes. Empey and Stafford (1991) point out that delinquent behavior may be the outcome of both independent multiple causality and interdependent linear causality.

However, where several causes of delinquency must occur together, then we have special interdependent versions of multiple causality. Unlike linear causality, this does not require a temporal order of events, just that they occur. Each of the different causes is necessary for the outcome but none alone is sufficient. Here it is the *combination* of multiple causes that together co-produce the delinquent outcome. We may describe this as another example of the collocation of causes since, as in the case of linear causality, no one cause can produce the event.

With the concept of *interactive causality*, the issue becomes much more complex because, not only are events produced by preceding events, but once produced these causal outcomes act back (feed back) on the original causes which themselves then become outcomes of the events they produced. Empey and Stafford (1991: 288–9) and DiCristina (1995: 6) describe this as a case of 'reciprocal causes', since cause and effect influence each other, are cyclical and move forward and backward. Again considering the control theory example:

> children whose attachments to their parents are already weak may further weaken those attachments by getting into trouble at school, failing to pass their courses, and running around with delinquent peers. The same might be true of children's relations to their teachers. The more new problems they cause, the greater their old ones become, creating a steadily worsening situation. (Empey and Stafford, 1991: 228–9)

Thus interactive causality implies a sequence of cyclical cause and effect events over time, that form a spiral process leading to ever-increasing rule violations.

The fourth type of causal relationship, *dialectical or co-determination* (Einstadter and Henry, 1995: 15–18), might be considered to be a special case of multiple interactive causation since it involves reciprocity between several causes and outcomes. However, there are certain crucial differences. First, the cause and outcome are not conceived as discrete entities but are interrelated and overlapping, such that some part of cause is constituted by some part of the event produced in part by it and vice versa; but all of the event is not all of the cause (and vice versa). Second, and related to this, neither 'cause' nor 'event' has causal priority since each has simultaneous transformative powers over the other, regardless of the extent. Third, changes in either the 'cause' or the 'event' are not temporarily separated because their interrelatedness means that as one changes, the other must change, and with it the first must change also. Reciprocity of influence then is instantaneous, although cumulative mutual transformation may extend over time.

As an illustration, consider a formal history lesson taught by a teacher who allows little interaction with students. The teacher asks what has been learned. The student knows that the teacher wants a repetition or recitation of the content of the lecture, its facts, its causal sequence, its morality, etc. The student also learns a series of informal messages such as obedience to authority, to accept rather than to question, to avoid criticism, to stigmatize difference, to accept prevailing knowledge as truth, to 'play the game'. The student knows/learns that, in spite of recognizing such messages, they are not to be spoken but to be concealed. So in responding in ways honored by the teacher, rather than raising questions, the student also learns a hidden lesson that deception and deviousness are necessary to succeed. This overt conformity and hidden deviance are constructed not by delinquent subcultures but in school, as part of the underbelly of the formal learning process, as its informal knowledge. Thus attachment to school values also involves attachment to delinquent values.[5] As we shall see in Chapter 7, the dialectical co-determinacy model of causality is the only one having affinities with our affirmative postmodern position.

Criminologists' notions of cause are considerably affected by their assumptions about humans, their models of society and the role that law is given in defining crime. Theories we have called individual positivist, that prioritize the individual over structure and which assume law as a consensual reflection of the social whole, seek the causes of crime at the level of individuals. Those that assume humans to be shaped by the socially constructed meaning emerging from their interactive relations, such as interactionists and ethnomethodologists, are less interested in causes than in a descriptive account of the social and interpretive processes of crime. Those theories we classify as sociological positivist, that prioritize the organization of society, such as strain theory, or the relation between society and the state, such as Marxist theory, seek the cause of crime in the totality of structures of society and its relations of power. In contrast, those who see humans as affiliated to interest groups in a conflicting society struggling over the definitions of crime, such as culture conflict, social ecology and conflict theory, seek the cause of crime in group interactions. Finally there are the attempts at integration that rely on a composite of elements from the other approaches.[6]

Micro-level constructions of causality

Micro-level causal explanations in modernist criminology range from those that see crime resulting from individual choice, to those locating it in predisposing traits, to others that see cause developing from a socialization or learning process with primary groups, and yet others focusing on the interactive construction of identity.

Causality in classical and rational choice theory

Classical theory purports to be non-causal. In its primary analysis it suggests that rational free choice by human agents explains crime. However, several writers imply that a degree of both internal and external force is inherent to the concept of will and in the limits placed on choice. Beirne (1991: 807) argues that classical theory draws on Locke's 'sensationalism', in its celebration of the desire for pleasure and the avoidance of pain. For example, Beccaria (1764) relates acts of will to 'the sense data from which it springs' (Beirne, 1991: 808). Bentham suggests that pain and pleasure are 'two sovereign masters' that 'govern us in all we do, in all we say, in all we think' and that 'the chain of causes and effects' is fastened to them (Bentham, 1765: 11). However, as Einstadter and Henry (1995: 49) argue, while the sensations may stem from human biology, freedom is restricted to the limited choice over which behaviors will deliver pleasure over pain. Classical free will, therefore, is a determined rather than a free will. It involves '"free" rational calculation and "determined" action' (Beirne, 1991: 812). Crime is, therefore, 'caused' under classicism when a combination of constitutive elements informs a decision to choose criminal behavior (over a range of less obvious or relevant behavioral possibilities) as an action likely to satisfy the desire for pleasure and/or to avoid pain. The aspect of determinism shaping the choice to violate law enters via different types of pleasure and pain, having different intensities, different durations, and different guarantees of outcome.

Recent economic theory, rational choice theory and routine activities theory also offer a reasoning, 'free choice' explanation of crime, tempered by varieties of internal and external forces. Cohen and Machalek's (1988) routine activities theory sees humans differently endowed with abilities to reason, to perform, and to be cognizant of their actions resulting in limited and different choices. Economic wealth maximization theory (Becker, 1968; Ehrlich, 1973; 1982; Sullivan, 1973) and time allocation theorists (Heineke, 1978; 1988) recognize the importance of perception in conceiving of the benefits of criminal action. Although differing over whether rewards are more monetary or psychological satisfactions, these variations of classical economics claim that whether individuals choose criminal activity depends upon their perception of the likelihood of apprehension, the probability and severity of punishment, and the ratio of gain from illegal behavior compared to gain from legal behavior where gain is a composite of satisfaction or rewards and where cost is the total composite cost. As Heineke (1988: 303–5) argues, people are purely rational but 'behave as if they were maximizing their own expected utility'.

Similarly, rational choice theory (Clarke and Cornish, 1983; Cornish and Clarke, 1987) employs the concept of 'limited rationality', one modified by variations in human motives that include issues of excitement, enjoyment, money, status, honor, prestige, lifestyle choices, freedom from controls, etc., as well as variations in analytical ability, level of skills, physical capability, and situational and opportunity structures in the environment.[7] A typical causal sequence of a composite rational choice model is shown in Figure 6.1.

Causality in biological theory

In biological theory the causal antecedent to crime is identified as some defective biological trait that is different from traits held by normal law-abiding members of the population. Under certain triggering environments,

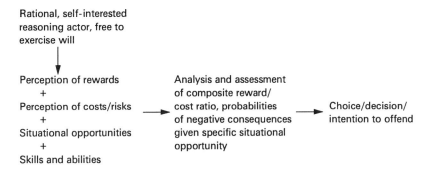

Figure 6.1   *Classical, rational choice, routine activities model*

this abnormality predisposes those afflicted to criminal acts. At various times, different theorists have conceived of one or many of these biological traits of predisposition. They range from general vague notions of physical defectiveness such as in Lombrosian 'atavism', 'heredity', 'constitution' or 'body type'[8] to specific 'causes' in the mind or brain such as 'feeblemindedness', 'mental defectiveness' (Goddard, 1912; Goring, 1913), brain disorder (Hare, 1970; Hare and Connolly, 1987; Moyer 1976), differential conditionability (Eysenck, 1977), and low IQ (Wilson and Herrnstein, 1985). For others, the defect was located within the physiological processes of the body such as in 'biochemical and hormonal imbalances' (Schlapp and Smith, 1928; Dalton, 1961), blood chemistry or vitamin or allergen or mineral deficiencies (Hippchen, 1978; Dorfman, 1984), or chromosomal abnormality, such as the XYY pattern (Jacobs et al., 1965; Telfer et al., 1968; Nielsen, 1968; 1971).

However, the universally popular biological defect held out by modernism to explain human predisposition toward crime is 'genetic constitution' (Jeffery, 1978; 1994; Mednick and Christiansen, 1977; Mednick et al., 1987). In spite of a distortion in media presentations that suggest 'genes cause crime' (Nelkin, 1993), the position of genetic theorists on crime is that genes alone do not cause criminal behavior. Rather, 'genes in interaction with the environment create a brain and nervous system' (Jeffery, 1993: 6) which is variously sensitive to generating pleasurable sensation, and this can be satisfied by manipulating one's behavior in the environment, which for some involves criminal behavior. The causal issue, therefore, is an interactive combination of genes and environment, the outcome of which can be affected by manipulations of behavior.[9] A typical composite of biological causal sequence is presented in Figure 6.2.

Causality in personality and psychological theory

In some versions of psychological theory, biology's discrete immutable constructs are transformed through the course of the process of human

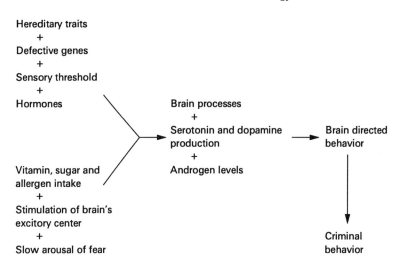

Figure 6.2 *Biological model*

development. Theories range from those in which biological attributes provide the basis for subsequent learning, to those where the learning process constitutes the whole personality.

Biologically oriented psychological theories see inherited or genetically determined attributes (such as sensitivity to pain, fear, excitation, anxiety) affecting how humans learn in primary group settings, and how they are able to be conditioned and perceive pain, such that socialization into norms is rendered ineffective or at least less effective than in unaffected individuals.[10] For Freudian psychoanalytical theory, biologically inherited drives and instincts fail to be curbed by patterns of parental socialization which can result from the failure to develop adequate ego and super-egos. Alternatively, egos and super-egos are, in some ways, weakened or damaged in the developmental process. This, then, produces an inability to control behavior, an inability to sublimate or otherwise discharge tensions in socially acceptable ways, a lack of awareness of the harmful consequences of behavior, and an unconscious pursuit of consequential behavior in order to satisfy uncompensated desires and/or to receive punishment.[11] In this sense the immutability shifts from biology to become fixed in a personality whose traits distinguish the offender from non-offenders.

For other personality theorists, however, it is not so much fixed personality traits that are defective, but thinking itself. Criminal patterns of thinking emphasizing an excessive search for immediate excitement and dominance over others are learned and once learned are ingrained and immune from other influences (Yochelson and Samenow (1976; 1977; Samenow, 1984). A composite of the typical psychoanalytic and personality model of causality is shown in Figure 6.3.

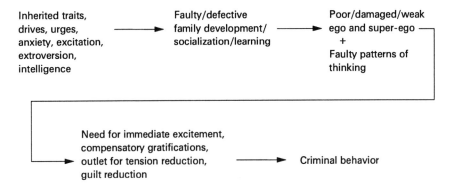

Figure 6.3   *Psychological and personality models*

Causality in social control and learning-based theories

Like psychological theories of personality, learning theorists emphasize how individuals are influenced by the socialization they receive in childhood and youth and how this affects their subsequent behavior. The difference from personality theory is that, rather than forming immutable personalities, humans are seen in a continuous process of being made through a building up of learned behaviors and experience from interacting with others. Variations in theories arise when theorists place different emphases on what is learned, how it is learned, and how it affects human action.

Control theory assumes that humans are born to behave in ways that disregard others (born selfish/evil) and that they will commit crime unless adequate socialization techniques bond them to conventional society in a manner that becomes self-sustaining. Thus, for Reiss (1951), the central issue is a failure of socialization to develop adequate internal and external controls. In Nye's (1958) version, adequate internal controls are built through family relationships toward the installation of an effective internal conscience. In Reckless's (1961; 1973) containment theory, self-control depends on positive reinforcement of self by others in order to resist the internal and external forces that push and pull a person to deviate. For Toby (1957), the bond to conventional society is induced by getting people invested in something they do not wish to lose, thereby establishing a 'stake in conformity'. Hirschi (1969; Gottfredson and Hirschi, 1990) identifies several kinds of bonds to conventional society that together establish a high level of self-control when developed through nurturance, discipline and training. Hirschi argues that it is necessary to forge bonds that attach children to conventional role models. Through these attachments they become highly involved in conventional behavior, and committed to carry this out. Without forming these bonds, and without forbidding their involvement in rule-breaking activity, youth will not develop adequate self-control and thus will be vulnerable to committing delinquent acts.

Social learning theorists do not assume humans to be anything other than what they learn and how they learn it. For example, Bandura (1979: 200) says 'People are not born with preformed repertoires of aggressive behavior. They must learn them.' Differential association theory (Sutherland, 1939; Sutherland and Cressey, 1966), differential reinforcement theory (Jeffery, 1965; Burgess and Akers, 1966; Akers, 1985) and differential anticipation theory (Glazer, 1978) take the view that humans start out as social blanks and through contact with others have some behaviors reinforced, not only by family, but by other groups such as peers and subcultures. In addition, new knowledge, skills, rationalizations and justifications are learned and, when learned early, often, and over long periods of time, from others who are held in high esteem, result in a definition of rule-breaking as acceptable behavior.

For some social learning theorists (Tarde, 1890) learning is by imitation rather than reinforcement. In Bandura's (1973; 1977) view, learning need not occur in small primary groups but can result from identification with media images. He argues that human emotions are aroused as a result of a variety of aversive stimulation experiences. These are then converted into different behaviors depending upon how they are cognitively appraised, the kinds of responses that have been observed and modeled, and how these have been responded to by both self and others. Again, it is self-regulation, not as a psychic agent to control behavior but as 'cognitive structures that provide referential standards against which behavior is judged, and a set of subfunctions for the perception, evaluation, and regulation of action' (Bandura, 1979: 225). Once begun, law-breaking behavior may be sustained depending upon the perceived consequences.

Neutralization theorists (Sykes and Matza, 1957; Matza and Sykes, 1961; Matza, 1964) believe that people are socialized into conventional behavior and bonded to conventional morality. But part of this process involves also learning rationalizations, in the form of words and phrases that will neutralize people's commitment to convention and excuse and/or justify their violation of conventional rules, under certain situations or circumstances, depending on how these are defined. Thus, for these theorists, humans are episodically released from the bonds of convention at which time they may choose to deviate. In this sense, language use becomes part of the motivation for rule-breaking activity.[12] A composite causal sequence of typical social learning theories is shown in Figure 6.4.

Causality in interactionist and labeling theory

As is the case with much social learning theory, interactionist/labeling theory assumes that humans are malleable and that their identities are formed through a process of interaction over time. But here people are significantly, even overwhelmingly affected by how others react to them, and particularly how others attempt to control their behavior by dramatizing it as evil (Tannenbaum, 1938). What is affected by the reaction

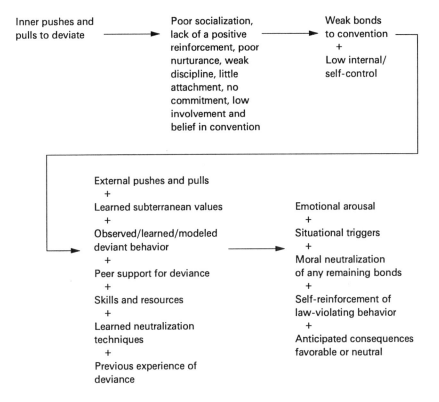

Figure 6.4 *Social learning models*

is not self-controls but self-identity. This undergoes progressive transformation as a result of numerous and powerful negative social reactions to
their minor rule-breaking behavior (Lemert, 1951; 1967; Becker, 1963;
Lofland, 1969; Schur, 1971).

In this model, crime and deviance start when rule-makers (moral
entrepreneurs) form powerful interests to influence the political process in
order to ban some kinds of behavior as illegal (Becker, 1963; Schur, 1980;
Matza, 1969). These rules/laws are then enforced on members of relatively
powerless groups by social control agents, such as law enforcement officers,
who act on their own socially constructed, self-reinforcing, stereotypical
categories, to impute 'ancillary qualities to rule violators' (Schur, 1971).
Those actors initially engaged in 'primary deviance' see no special significance in their behavior until it is reacted to by such enforcers (Lemert,
1951). But with increasing attempts at control, some conceal their behavior
only to find that its secrecy confers the meaning of something real, while
other conventional behavior, conducted in public, appears unreal, as a
'front' (Goffman, 1971). Thus the problem of transparency (Matza, 1969;
Box, 1971) leads some to suspect they have a real hidden identity, which is
confirmed by further deviancy conducted in order to conceal the original

rule-breaking, and by further reactions of audiences to their behavior and labeled identity.

As people are processed through society's formal control institutions, attempts to have their moral status degraded and negatively labeled (Garfinkel, 1956) are resisted and negotiated (Schur, 1971), until eventually they receive official confirmation of the reality of their deviant identity. The label acts as a 'master status' (Becker, 1963; Goffman, 1963), with the result that rule-breakers are now excluded by others from normal roles and activities. This exclusion further entrenches them in deviant patterns of behavior (Mankoff, 1971) and results in their signified behavior being amplified (Wilkins, 1964; Young, 1971). The result of the whole reaction process is a transformation of self-identity into a deviant stereotype. As such, subsequent acts of deviance (secondary deviance) are performed in conformity with the stereotype. Adjustments are made to accommodate to the social reaction which is then normalized by interaction with similarly classified deviants as the secondary deviant enters a deviant career (Lemert, 1951; 1967). In this process of becoming deviant (Matza, 1969), then, humans are transformed from creative individuals, free to construct a wide range of meaningful behavior, into narrowly defined, stigmatized social types whose range of behavior is restricted to that which is expected of them by the label imposed. A composite of the typical interactive causal model of this approach is shown in Figure 6.5.

Application: micro-level explanations of 'occupational crime'

Recalling the modernist distinction between occupational, corporate and state crime discussed in Chapter 5, we find that there are some interesting differences that occur in the application of criminological theory. Occupational crime, which is considered to be crimes committed by employees against their employer (Clinard and Quinney, 1973), has been explained by modernists by using traditional theories of the crimes of the powerless. Thus, prominent in the literature we find differential association theory (Sutherland and Cressey, 1966: 77–9); neutralization theory (Cressey, 1953; Clinard and Yeager, 1980); and control theory (Hirschi and Gottfredson, 1987; 1989).

More specifically, some biological and psychological theories argue that, because of IQ scores, a predisposition to commit crimes in a corporate setting exists (Frank and Lynch, 1992: 100–1; Jeffery, 1990; Reckless, 1973). Others have focused on rational choice (Hirschi and Gottfredson, 1987; Jeffery, 1990; Box, 1983: 37–43). Yet others assert that white collar offenders are distinguished by their reckless and egocentric behavior (Coleman, 1994: 195–8).[13]

Neutralization theory has also been included in a wide number of explanations. Thus, much of this theorizing is based on Sykes and Matza's

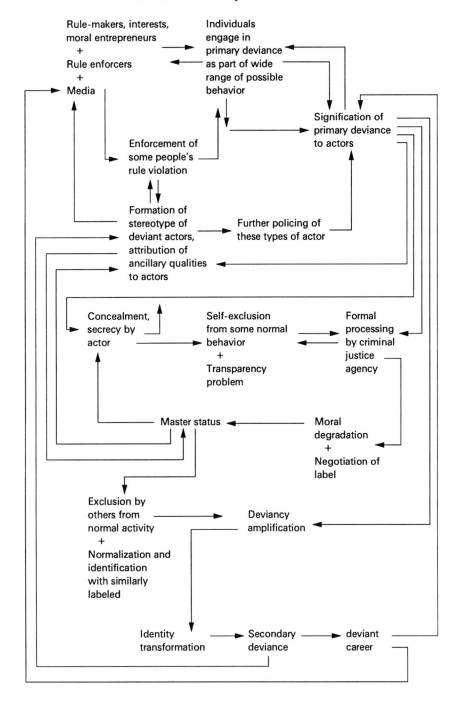

Figure 6.5   *Interactive and labeling models*

(1957) 'techniques of neutralization' discussed above.[14] Interestingly, we
find organizational crime being explained at the micro-level of analysis by
modernists by using much of the same theorizing applied to the conventional crimes of the powerless.[15]

Macro-level constructions of causality

With the possible exception of some aspects of social learning theory and
interactionist theory, the central causal focus of theoretical explanations of
crime has been on the individual. Even with the exceptions, the broadest
structural component of cause is the group. In contrast, in macro-causal
explanations the causal force is located at the wider level of societal
organization, such as culture, or the structure of capitalist or patriarchal
society. Thus priority is given to sociological forces rather than individual
ones in explaining criminal behavior. In the following discussion we
consider three versions of these sociological-type explanations.

Causality in social ecology and social disorganization theory

Here crime is seen to be generated by the 'socio-spatial environment' or,
put more simply, by kinds of places rather than kinds of people (Stark,
1987). Crime's cause is rooted in the 'pathological' conditions of particular
communities, areas or neighborhoods, and especially in places of greatest
social change, such as the city.

This geographically influenced perspective takes as a starting point the
uneven patterning of crime and attempts to explain why some areas are
consistently more crime-ridden than others, even though their populations
constantly change (Stark, 1987). Ironically, although opposed to the individualistic biological theory of positivism, ecological theory borrows a
biological analogy concerning the interrelationship between species and
their natural environment. Human ecology refers to the relationship of
human organization which forms a mosaic of different communities in
given environments (Faris, 1944; Hawley, 1950). These communities are
both competitive and cooperative within the same environmental space
(Warming, 1909; Walker, 1994).

Especially significant in the application of social or human ecology to
crime was the Chicago School sociologists' analysis of the city (Park and
Burgess, 1924; Burgess, 1925). This was seen as a series of concentric circles
of development spanning outward from the city center, in which each circle
contained its own distinct characteristics. Not the least important was
the area of a city immediately surrounding the central business district
which was thought to be between periods of social organization and with
deteriorating properties, transient populations and speculative landowners
awaiting expansion of the city to increase their property values (Shaw and
McKay, 1942; Walker, 1994). This 'zone of transition', as it was called, was
an area of social disorganization, instability and deterioration, and was

both predicted to, and found to, have the highest rates of crime (defined as officially reported street offenses).

In such areas, social disorganization produced little or no community feeling, a predominance of temporary relationships, and a lack of ties to either traditional families or the wider society. This resulted in a breakdown of the self-regulatory structure of informal and formal social control (Bursik, 1986). Community disorganization translated into personal disorganization and a lack of moral direction. This, in turn, led to crime and delinquency, not directly, but because of the contradictory and conflicting moralities which left crime and law-breaking as an available, environmentally structured choice (Walker, 1994). This choice was made especially attractive when an alienated youth joined with others in similar situations to form alternative primary groups (gangs) having powerfully competing values relative to the surrounding disorganization (Shaw and McKay, 1942). Thus it was only when conventional values were weakened by the surrounding environmental disorganization that the competing system took hold, and once established could itself be culturally transmitted over time.[18]

Recent contributions to this perspective have introduced the importance of social and geographical spaces as structuring forces that create different opportunities for crime or for its absence, and which lead to different ideas about intervention and manipulation of environmental spaces (Brantingham and Brantingham, 1981; Newman, 1972; 1973). For others, a central issue is the force of power and political decisions, such as the decision to construct new housing projects in already deteriorated neighborhoods. These decisions can further destabilize a community, increase its residential turnover, magnify existing inequalities, and further undermine its ability to self-regulate, thereby facilitating delinquency.[17] The political decision to concentrate low-income families into these stereotyped problem areas creates 'hierarchies of desirability' (Gill, 1977: 5) and a 'bad' public reputation can result, which, in turn, reinforces the existing process of disorganization (Armstrong and Wilson, 1973; Scraton, 1981), and can reconstruct the identity of residents resulting in 'a defeated neighborhood' (Suttles, 1968; 1972). The whole causal process is diagrammatically represented in Figure 6.6.

Causality in structural and subcultural strain theory

Strain theory takes for granted the cultural homogeneity of the society on certain core values, assumes that most of the population are socialized into these through families, schools and via the mass media, and not least advertising, and then seeks to explain why some rather than others choose to deviate from the rules. Strain theorists' answer to this is that those who break rules and laws do so because they are responding normally to their own abnormal or pathological societal circumstances, which are maladapted and incongruous with those of the wider society. Thus strain theorists locate causality in the social organization of society, rather than in

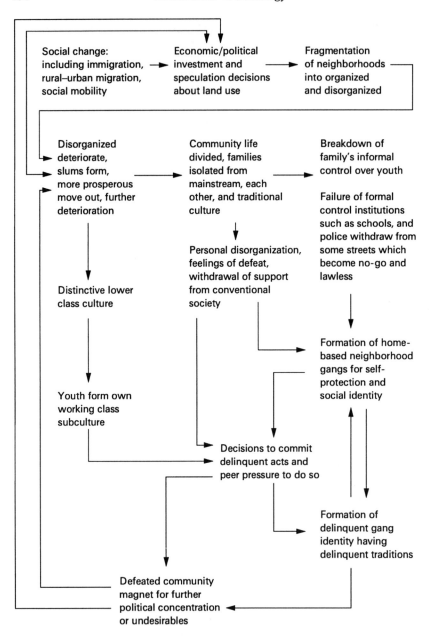

Figure 6.6 *Social ecology and social disorganization models*

its subcultural divisions, which they contend emerge in response and as adaptions to initial structural problems.

The failure of some members of society to achieve the society's overall values results from a differential access by those members to the means, resources and opportunities available to achieve legitimate success. In the Durkheimian version of anomie theory the failure is partly located in the culture's inability to define and limit individual aspirations, but in Merton's adaptation, the failure is a lack of access to institutional opportunities to achieve legitimate material success (Merton, 1938; 1968). The individual response to this structural misalignment, lack of societal equilibrium, or strain between goals and means, is an illegitimate choice, i.e. to rebel or to cheat.

Whether individuals rebel or cheat alone or in the company of others is the issue that distinguishes Merton's ideas from those of subcultural strain theorists, such as Cohen (1955) and Cloward and Ohlin (1960). These theorists see the adaptive response as a collective enterprise undertaken by similarly situated and like-minded youth, who form peer subcultures and gangs as their delinquent solution to the problems of strain.

Of the range of possible adaptations to strain, those who reject society's values and the means to achieve them are the most extreme and form various revolutionary groups or alternative societies. But not all escape. Others stay within the society. This mode of adaptation which Merton calls 'rebellion' has parallels with Cohen's 'delinquent subculture', whose translation of strain into status frustration is resolved collectively by reaction formation. Here the values of the middle class are inverted to form violent, destructive and hedonistic values of the delinquent subculture. Similar, too, are Cloward and Ohlin's (1960) 'conflict gangs' who are angry at, and feel humiliated by, the system for rejecting them as failures, and resolve their tensions through collective expressions of hostility, violence and symbolic terror of neighborhoods in preservation of their own honor, territory and reputation.

Less extreme are those of Merton's youth who adapt to structural strain by rejecting the means while continuing to pursue the goals of the wider society through 'innovation'. By the illegitimate means afforded by classic street crimes such as theft, burglary, shoplifting, fencing or, more recently, drug dealing, they achieve the visible signs of acquired wealth. Again, the subcultural collective response to this strain has parallels in Cloward and Ohlin's (1960) rationally motivated 'criminal gangs' who engage in theft, vice and other criminal rackets to achieve visible success.

Recent revisions of strain theory by Agnew (1991a; 1991b) include a relatively more sophisticated model of humans, that allows them to be seen as having a far wider range of goals than pure materialism, status or prestige. Instead of simply reacting to anger and the frustration of failure, Agnew's delinquents also react to the frustration of being unable to escape or avoid the aversive situations they are in. A composite representation of strain theory is presented in Figure 6.7.

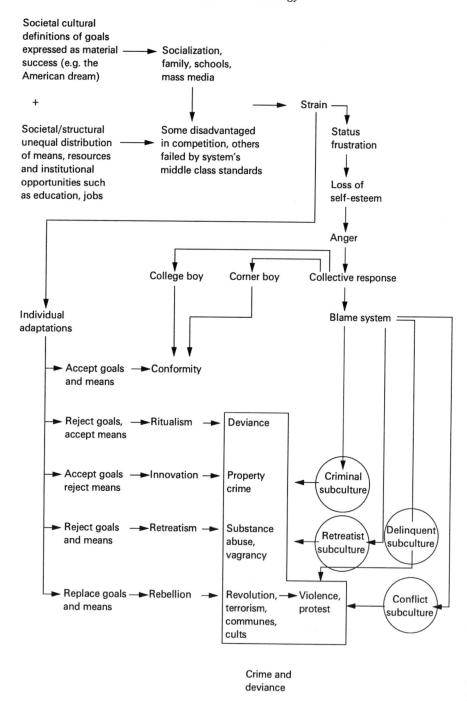

Figure 6.7 *Strain and subcultural models*

Causality in conflict, radical and critical theory

This group of modernist macro-theories is united in their view that the fundamental driving force toward crime comes from structural conflict and from the attempts by some groups, classes, or segments of society to maintain their position of power. From their perspective, industrial societies are not simply broken, and in need of repair; they are fundamentally flawed, and in need of replacement.

Depending upon which version is considered, there are differences in the alleged source of conflict. Conflict theorists of the late 1960s took a Weberian view in which society was divided into competing groups, each defining their own interests and struggling to win control over the whole society.[18] Conflict criminologists recognize that crime may stem from any one or more differences, and that these differences are not simply restricted to money or wealth. They may include conflicts over differences in culture, or social status, ideology, morality, religion, race and ethnicity. Groups that are able to capture the instruments of power in society are able to make and enforce laws that serve their own interests. In particular, they are able to criminalize those whose behavior is different from their own, especially where such behavior threatens their position of domination (Sellin, 1938; Vold, 1958; Quinney, 1970).

Marxist criminologists, however, were critical of this fragmentary conflict approach which they accused of distracting from the fundamental economic conflict in society (Taylor et al., 1973; Quinney, 1973; 1974). Drawing on the work of Marx (1868), Engels (1845), and Bonger (1916) they argued that in class-divided societies, where class is based on the private ownership of property, a small proportion of the population (the bourgeoisie) own a large proportion of the wealth, while the remainder (the proletariat) only own their labor. The competition and conflict between these classes create the conditions and relationships conducive to crime, and as a result the societal organization is said to be criminogenic. The way this occurs depends upon the particular model of society held by the theorists (see Chapter 3).

Marxist influenced criminologists writing in the 1970s, who took an instrumental view of the social order, saw the economically powerful as an elite class who dominated the mass of the population through the use of state law and the criminal justice apparatus to criminalize those who were a threat (Chambliss, 1975; Quinney, 1974; Krisberg, 1975). Here crime was caused, not only by economic exploitation, brutalization, immiseration and demoralization of the masses, which undermined their sense of self-worth, but also by encouraging egoism over altruism (Bonger, 1916) and by marshalling the state against those who would protest against their bosses. Here, the state acted only against law violations by working class offenders, allowing those with wealth and influence to escape its clutches.

By the 1980s a structural version of Marxism emerged in which the state was seen as a more neutral semi-autonomous political force that could control both capital and labor in the long-term interests of the capitalist system and itself (Beirne, 1979; Greenberg, 1981; Chambliss and Seidman, 1982). Under this view, the capitalist state was more responsive to the fear of crime than to acts of crime themselves (Box, 1987), and was also empowered to control individual corporations whose excessive exploitation was likely to threaten the legitimacy of the whole capitalist system. Thus Chambliss (1988) points to a cyclical struggle between capital and labor from which is born an impoverished underclass whose only solution to their situation is the resort to illegal, underground activity.

Critics of the structuralist position have included anarchists, left realists and socialist feminists, as well as critical race theorists. All have argued that exploitation not only is class specific, but has more to do with powerlessness based on a number of criteria, most notably gender, race and ethnicity. Among this group of critical theorists, left realists believe exploitation produces relative deprivation, inequality and injustice which are angrily responded to by crime, often confined to other members of the powerless. But critical (radical and socialist) feminists see the cause of crime in a patriarchal class structure. This perpetuates violence and intimidation against women, resulting in their oppression both at work and at home. Together with their sexual exploitation and reproductive control, acceptance by the state of women's violent subordination legitimates masculine violence and exploitation throughout the society (Daly and Chesney-Lind, 1988; Simpson, 1989; Messerschmidt, 1986; 1993). Indeed, for anarchists (Ferrell, 1993; 1994; Tifft and Sullivan, 1980) all authority structures are problematic and ultimately criminogenic, since they displace the ability of people to relate to one another directly and cooperatively. A composite diagram of the causal logic in these arguments is represented in Figure 6.8.

Application: macro-level explanations of 'crimes of the powerful'

While some theorists use macro-level functionalist strain and subcultural theory to explain occupational crimes,[19] macro-level explanations are more generally used to explain crimes of the powerful, such as corporations and the state. This is because the focus is more on organizational contexts and larger structural factors such as the economic system, which is said to provide the environment within which organizations function. In this sense, micro-level explanations are subsumed and collapsed into macro-level arguments that explain cause.

Some modernist criminologists argue that organizational crime should be refocused away from the individual toward the dynamics of the organization itself.[20] Coleman, for example, has provided analysis indicating that there has been a historical movement away from social relationships that focus on individuals towards those where the person finds her/himself

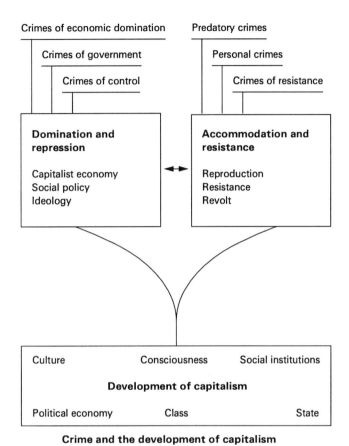

Figure 6.8 *Radical and critical models (Quinney, 1980: 42)*

increasingly in organizational roles, i.e. the notion of 'organizational man/ woman' (1978; 1982). Analysis in this area argues that the culture of the organization or corporation itself becomes dominant over the person.[21] Here, patterned behavior finds relative stability, and it is within this setting that individuals find settled roles and prescribed relationships that commit them to be loyal to the corporation, to be a 'team player' and to 'mind their own business' (Vandivier, 1971).

Other modernist theorists on organization/corporate crime have been more explicitly conflict or Marxist in orientation, indicating that the organization has to be situated in a broader political economy.[22] Simon and Eitzen have argued that 'perhaps the most basic cause of elite deviance is the structure and intra-workings of the contemporary political economy' (1993: 311). Quinney (1977: 50–2), for example, has identified four 'crimes of domination' in capitalism: crimes of control (i.e. law enforcement's violation of civil liberties), crimes of government (i.e. crimes of elected officials which repress internal dissent and undermine foreign governments), crimes of economic domination (i.e. those done to assure capital accumulation and survival in capitalism such as price fixing, environmental pollution), and crimes of social injuries (i.e. denial of human rights, not necessarily found in the legalist definition of crime, such as gender, class, and race discrimination and exploitation of the worker). In this view, capital accumulation becomes the overarching framework within which corporations/organizations operate. In the attempts to maximize profits and minimize costs, corporations violate regulatory laws protecting the environment, workplace, health and safety, advertising, etc. which places the person at risk of death, injury and illness.

For conflict Marxist approaches, the motivation and opportunity for commission of crime is greater for the powerful (Frank and Lynch, 1992).[23] Consider Friedrichs' point that: 'The advantaged, in this interpretation, have stronger deviant motivations, enjoy greater deviant opportunities, and are subject to weaker social control' (1995a; 1995b).

Integrated constructions of causality

Gibbons (1994: 176) has argued that as well as generating theoretical positions, some criminologists have recently been integrating those theories that already exist.[24] Elsewhere we have debated some of the problems of this approach (Einstadter and Henry, 1995: 301–18; see also Messner et al., 1989). Here we will simply point out that integration, synthesis or amalgamation which attempts to produce a 'comprehensive' explanation of crime is often a narrowly selective affair. Certain theories are over-represented, especially in explaining conventional street crime and delin-quency where 'learning and control theories are more often part of the integrative mix than any other of the theories', and where 'the component theories drawn on are individual-level (micro) theories rather than societal-level (macro) theories' (1995: 304). The result is that 'integrated theories may have a bias reflected in which theories they combine. In considering an integrated theory we must assess this bias and decide at least whether the overall integration is conservative, liberal or radical/critical' (1995: 308). The causal logic of integration tends to be a composite of causal relationships taken from the other theories. Figure 6.9 shows a diagrammatic representation of this approach taken from Elliott's integrated theory of delinquency which combines elements of social ecology theory, social learning theory, social control theory, and sub-cultural theory.

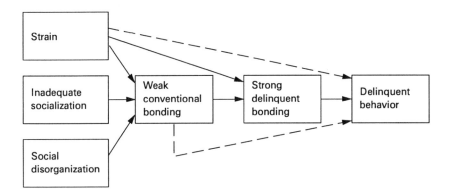

Figure 6.9   *Elliott's integrated model (Elliott, 1985: 66)*

Application: integrated explanations of 'crimes of the powerful'

With much growing critique and disillusionment with either just micro-level or just macro-level explanations, a movement within modernist literature on corporate crime has been toward integrative approaches (Frank and Lynch, 1992: 114–21; Poveda, 1994: 98–102). Accordingly, several approaches have been identified.[25] We will consider examples from Box, Braithwaite, Coleman and a general critical integrationist position.

Box's (1983) integrative approach seeks to understand corporate crime in terms of corporations attempting to achieve their particular goals in an otherwise uncertain environment. Uncertainties arise due to economic competition, the government, workers, the public, consumers, etc. The corporation attempts to overcome uncertainties by illegally eliminating or otherwise reducing them through fraud, bribery, manipulation, price fixing, and several other devious practices. To explain this further, Box makes use of several traditional modernist approaches: from anomie theory (Merton) he draws the notion of strain and the source of motivation; from control, neutralization, and subcultural theories he draws the mechanisms by which 'motivational strain' is translated into illegal acts. Unlike traditional strain (anomie) theory, however, where this theory is applied to the pre-dominantly lower classes, Box sees anomie as endemic among the higher elites. The corporate elite see themselves as 'above the law' and thus free to commit infractions. Here control mechanisms are not deterrents, since the risks of detection and punishment are low. Further, the higher circles have available neutralizations (verbalizations, rationalizations) which have stabilized in the forms of a corporate subculture that allow the corporate elites to neutralize any felt moral bonding to the law. Finally, Box's last element of an integrative approach consists of the existent opportunity structure: control agencies are relatively lenient; public response sees corporate violence as a matter for regulatory rather than criminal justice agencies; and corporations have the ability to maneuver to keep their activity beyond incrimination. All these provide opportunities: in other words, they facilitate corporate crime. Figure 6.10 illustrates Box's integrated theory.

Braithwaite's (1989) integrative theory of reintegrating shaming is an attempt to provide an explanation of the crimes of the powerless as well as powerful in terms of many traditional theories with the labeling perspective being dominant. The key concept is shaming, a dimension ranging from very serious forms to mild rebuke. Rather than using a shaming that relies on stigmatization where the offender undergoes further strain, even further involvement such as forming subcultures, Braithwaite advocates a reintegrative shaming based more on a 'family model', where the offender is both rebuked for her/his behavior but also reintegrated by being reaccepted back into society.

In his explanation of corporate crime, Braithwaite incorporates aspects of opportunity structure/anomie theory. Corporate crime is most likely to occur where strain exists, legitimate opportunities are blocked, and illegitimate avenues (opportunities) exist as alternatives. Blocked legitimate opportunities, much as in Cloward and Ohlin's analysis, provide the basis for the development of subcultures, or group responses that attain some stability. The key question becomes: at what point do the efforts at social control 'tip' the corporation's behavior in the direction of compliance versus infraction? His theory of 'tipping points' argues that two forms of responses, 'stigmatizing shaming' and 'reintegrating shaming', produce, respectively, deviance amplification and possible resistance subcultures, and law-abiding behavior where the law-breaker (or potential law-breaker) is given positive reasons for her/his maintenance of bonding to society and hence compliance. He goes on to show that where adversarial and punitive styles prevail, resistance subcultures tend to form; whereas styles relying on a 'family model' – firmness but reintegrative – produce an incentive for law-abiding behavior. Figure 6.11 illustrates Braithwaite's integrated theory.

A third integrative approach is provided by Coleman (1987; 1994). This claims to explain corporate as well as occupational crime. Two key elements in his theory are motivation and opportunity (1994: 194–228). Moving away from any psychological explanation of motive, Coleman argues that 'most white collar offenders are free from major psychiatric disorders' (1994: 195). Nevertheless, he tells us that these offenders are more likely to be 'reckless' and 'egocentric' (1994: 195–7).[26] More important for answering the question of the wherewithal of motivation is the existence of 'cultures of competition' (1994: 202–5). He tells us that the intense desire for success and profit embedded in this culture is only checked by ethical standards, generated from schools, religion, media, etc., as well as by the symbolic force of law (1994: 205–6). In other words, the

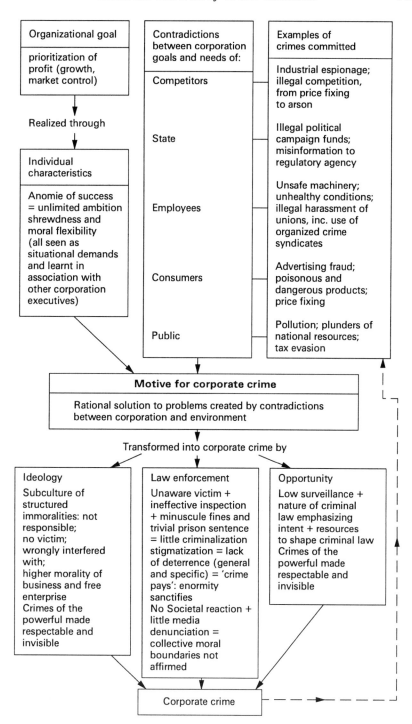

Figure 6.10 *Box's integrated model (Box, 1983: 64)*

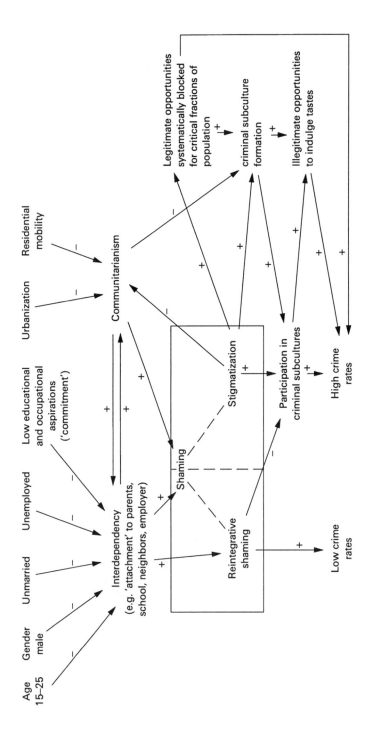

Figure 6.11 *Braithwaite's integrated model (Braithwaite, 1989: 99)*

stigmatizing label is acutely felt by business people, professionals, and politicians. Thus, in order to go beyond the binds of the law, what is necessary, says Coleman, is that these ethical standards be neutralized through various rationalizations (1994: 206–12), much as in Sykes and Matza's techniques of neutralizations.

Another factor in explaining 'motivation' for corporate crime is 'organizational conformity' (1994: 212–17). Here, the good organizational person is one who takes orders, the 'cheerful robot' of C. Wright Mills. As Coleman tells us: 'the efficient bureaucracy breeds moral conformity – or, perhaps more often, a kind of amoral pragmatism' (1994: 215).

The second element in Coleman's integrative approach is the structure of opportunities (1994: 217–28), where opportunity is read as both legitimate and illegitimate. Thus, the legal system offers a range of opportunities. However, opportunities are differentially distributed within corporate structures, for occupational as well as for corporate forms of crimes.[27] For occupational crimes, the availability of rationalizations and subcultures is significant in their motivation. For corporate crimes, Coleman argues that given the strong emphasis on the profit motive, those firms 'with declining profitability' are especially ripe for the commission of crime (1994: 223).

A fourth illustrative attempt at an integrative approach to explain corporate crime has been provided by more Marxist-oriented analysis.[28] Here the beginning point is political economy. According to Quinney, 'Ultimately . . . to understand crime we must understand the development of the political economy of capitalist society' (1977: 32). The development of capitalism, says Quinney, results both in crimes of domination and repression, and in crimes of accommodation and resistance (see Figure 6.8). We are here concerned with the former. As we earlier summarized (Chapter 5), Quinney identifies crimes of control, crimes of economic domination, crimes of government, and crimes of social injuries. All these are the result of the capitalist class's attempt to accumulate profit, assure survival, and subdue counter-forces. For Quinney, all these crimes result from the contradictions of capitalism. Although his anlaysis is not exhaustive as to the connecting links between capitalism and the onset of corporate and occupational crime, Quinney lays out a broad framework by which further Marxist analysis can be conducted. Consider, for example, Frank and Lynch's (1992) analysis that capitalism, as a profit-oriented system, produces differential life-chances (see also Groves and Frank, 1987). Thus 'class location . . . provides the opportunities to commit certain types of crime' (1992: 117). Therefore, differential opportunities and motivations are class specific. As to why some in similar situations of opportunity commit and some do not commit corporate crimes, they argue that, first, the total organizational context may either encourage or dissuade criminality and that, second, in some cases, particular types of persons may be vulnerable: 'People who are ruthless or daring . . . may be more likely to take risks and violate the law. If we place this person in an organizational structure in which violating the law is viewed as normal corporate behavior, the probability that a crime will occur is increased' (1992: 118). In a further variant of Marxist explanations of corporate crime, Messerschmidt (1983) points out how the FBI's repression of American Indian Movement leader Leonard Peltier had much to do with its desire of being a 'colonial police force' for assuring the expropriation of rich energy resources on the indigenous lands. This is but one example of a long history of the FBI's involvement in repression (e.g. the McCarthy era, COINTELPRO, etc.) for the corporate state (see especially, Poveda, 1994).

In sum, theories of causation applied to white collar crime and, more specifically, crimes by the powerful have more often utilized traditional modernist theories of the crimes of the powerless. Integrative approaches have attempted to combine micro- with macro-level analyses.

Summary and conclusions

In this chapter we have indicated that a variety of causes, relying on several models of causality, have been offered in the modernist literature. Constructed images of offender categories focus on individuals, social relations, organizations and the state.[29] Each is said to contribute directly or indirectly to harms of repression and reduction. In the next chapter we turn to an alternative postmodernist position on causality in which the offender categories have been extended and deconstructed to include discourse and constitutive interrelational sets. We will also indicate an alternative mapping of 'causal' chains where the very notion of 'cause' becomes problematic.

Notes

1 See also Gregersen and Sailer (1993: 793–9) and Smith (1995: 31).

2 As we shall see, postmodernists not only do not believe that variables can be desegregated, other than in a hypothetical construction, but they believe that doing so destroys the very interrelationship that constitutes the phenomenon.

3 For the extent of crimes of the powerful and comparison with crimes of the powerless see Box (1983), Reiman (1990), (Coleman, 1994).

4 These are not the only ways to classify causality. Aristotle identified four types: material, formal, efficient and final. DiCristina (1995: 6) describes nine, but includes strength of causal relationship along with the nature of the causal relationship.

5 Similarly, relations of the family and school are not exclusively conducted in the context of these institutions but are also constituted by delinquent peers through their delinquency and through their relations with each other. Values toward material success, consumerism, etc., are not simply the outcome of conventional institutions but are generated by adolescent peers as part of their constructions of delinquency.

6 Whatever the premises, criminologists' analysis of causality also has certain implications for crime control policy which we shall discuss in detail in Chapters 8 and 9. Here it is worth considering that each theory of causation implies different policies designed to manipulate the causal antecedents of crime for the purpose of controlling and/or reducing it.

7 In some sociological versions of this broader perspective on rational choice, crime is

chosen in an environment where a sense of self-identity and dignity has been stripped, reduced, or repressed as a seductive means to restore lost identity and self-worth, as an attempt to restore a 'mood of humanism' over 'fatalism' (Matza, 1964), and as a righteous resolution to such alienation (Katz, 1988).

8 See, for example, Lombroso (1876), Ferri (1886), Henderson (1893), Dugdale (1877), Garafalo (1914), Estabrook (1916), Hooton (1939), Kretschmer (1921), Sheldon et al. (1940; 1949), Glueck and Glueck (1950), and Cortes and Gatti (1972).

9 For a similar enlightened genetic theory of crime see Di Tullio (1969), Shah and Roth (1974), Hurwitz and Christiansen (1983), and Jeffery (1994).

10 See Trasler (1962), Eysenck (1977; 1983), Eysenck and Gudjonsson (1989).

11 For Freudian-based criminology see Freud (1950), Healy and Bronner (1926; 1936), Abrahamsen (1944; 1960), Friedlander (1947), Aichhorn (1935), Redl and Wineman (1951; 1952), and Halleck (1971).

12 For related theory on the role of language as a motive see also Mills (1940), Cressey (1953), and Scott and Lyman (1970).

13 See also Frank and Lynch (1992: 101), Bromberg (1965), and Blum (1972).

14 See, for example, Cressey (1970), Box (1983), Conklin (1977), Benson (1989), Coleman (1985: 206–12), and Hollinger (1991).

15 See generally, Frank and Lynch (1992: 97–121), Passas (1990), Box (1983: 34–6), Vaughan (1982), and Groves and Sampson (1987).

16 There are clear parallels here between control theory and neutralization theory, but the difference lies in the assumptions from control theory that people will commit crime if left to their own devices, whereas control theorists suggest they do so because they choose to do so out of a desire to conform to a subcultural group's norms (Empey and Stafford, 1991: 179).

17 Morris (1957), Bursik (1988), Bursik and Grasmick (1993), Sampson and Wilson (1993), and Wilson (1987).

18 See Simmel (1955), Coser (1956), Mills (1956; 1969), and Dahrendorf (1959).

19 Vaughan (1983), Clinard et al. (1979), Coleman (1985), Raab (1993), Clinard and Yeager (1980).

20 Ermann and Lundman (1978), Jackall (1988), Coleman (1978; 1982; 1994: 212–17), Clinard and Yeager (1980: 45).

21 Poveda (1994: 92–8), Ermann and Lundman (1978; 1992), Schrager and Short (1978), Gross (1978), Jackall (1988).

22 See Quinney (1977), Barnett (1981), Frank and Lynch (1992), Reiman (1979), Simon and Eitzen (1993), Messerschmidt (1986), Michalowski and Kramer (1987), Chambliss (1975), Gordon (1971), Pearce (1976).

23 See also Hagan (1989).

24 See especially, Elliott et al. (1979; 1985), Colvin and Pauly (1983), Hawkins and Weis (1985), Pearson and Weiner (1985), Messner et al. (1989), Akers (1993), and Barak (forthcoming).

25 Box (1983), Coleman (1987), Braithwaite (1989), Quinney (1977), Frank and Lynch (1992), Hirschi and Gottfredson (1987).

26 This is especially likely to be true if they have been organizationally selected for this purpose by the corporation in pursuit of the ruthless go-getter with dubious moral qualms (Box, 1983; Gross, 1978).

27 Just as Cloward (1959) showed they were in illegal street cultures.

28 Quinney (1977: 31–62), Frank and Lynch (1992), Groves and Frank (1987), Barnett (1981). See also Simon and Eitzen's (1993) notion of 'elite deviance'.

29 On the state in particular consider Schwendinger and Schwendinger (1970), Quinney (1977), Goff and Reasons (1986), Michalowski (1985), Barak (forthcoming).

7

Postmodernist Approaches to Causality and the Constitution of Crime

Here, we continue the analysis of causality begun in the previous chapter. We review the extreme postmodernist critique which, because of its denial of history, antecedents or even the possibility of accumulating knowledge, argues that 'causal statements in the usual sense are impossible to make' (Einstadter and Henry, 1995: 290). We then turn to our affirmative position which relies on dialectical assumptions about causality and presents crime as a co-produced outcome of constitutive interrelational (COREL) sets.

Skeptical postmodernism

Skeptical postmodernist thought denies both agency and causal relations. This stems in part from the notion of 'intertextuality' and its claim that the social world is 'so complex and interactive as to defy disentanglement' (Rosenau, 1992: 32–3). Indeed, for skeptical postmodernists it is 'impossible to establish any specific causal links' since 'everything is related to everything else' (1992: 32–3). Rejection of causality also comes from discarding the concept of linear time which is seen as an imposition of order on a disorderly, rhythmical and cyclical world. This is a world in which present and past merge, and where there is no difference between forward and backward directions (Derrida, 1973b; 1981).

Although skeptical postmodernist theories of crime have not been fully developed (but see Young, 1996), indications are that discourse replaces other factors as the primary 'cause'. In the extreme, a form of linguistic determinism is offered. Laclau and Mouffe's social theory (1985), for example, has been said to advocate the automation of discursive formations, much in the spirit of Baudrillard's (1983b) construction of a hyperreality. Within this hyperreality a relatively autonomous logic is at work. This is what Lacan (1977) meant when he defined a signifier as 'that which is the subject for another signifier'. Instead of the concept of 'overdetermination' as 'cause', Laclau and Mouffe (1985: 99) see 'contingent variation' as the major influence. And here lies a qualified determinism. They build on Foucault's (1972: 33–9) argument that relatively stabilized discursive formations, although offering stability and becoming the bases of effects, are nevertheless inherently unstable.

Embedded with them are 'strategic possibilities that permit the activation of incompatible themes' (1972: 37). Thus, for Laclau and Mouffe, all is contingent; all is articulated in discourse, and cause is discourse specific. Hence, they are liberated to make the extreme statement: 'no causal theory about the efficacy of one element over another is necessary' (1987: 90–1).

Similarly, Foucault's (1977) exploration of disciplining mechanisms, epistemes (stabilized logics), and historically stabilized discourses, would indicate the relative nature of what constitutes crime and how, ultimately, 'causes' are discursive constructions. Extreme versions of Derriderian analysis would suggest that since no stable, externally valid or universally 'correct' positions exist, no position can be established that identifies the determinants for the onset of crime. Any claims to have established such a position are illusory, at best.[1]

While we believe skeptical postmodernism has been a helpful polemic in unsettling the certainty of modernism's search for causes, and in encouraging us to look again at its established truths and logic, we find its position on causality in modernism too extreme. As shall be seen from our affirmative position, what Matza (1964) referred to as 'soft determinism' in causality has considerable merit over either 'hard determinism' (positivism), or the complete abandonment of any notions of influence, steering or effects.

Transitions: toward the notion of mutual influence

Constitutive criminology, like skeptical postmodernism, rejects those modernist approaches to criminological theory that reduce crime to an outcome of either micro-causes or macro-contexts. Our position calls for an abandoning of the futile search for 'the' causes of crime since this simply elaborates the distinctions that maintain crime as a separate reality, while failing to address how it is that crime is a part of human agency and society. Without acknowledging this integral interrelationship no analysis of cause can provide an adequate basis for effective justice policy. It is toward an understanding and more comprehensive account of this inter-relationship that constitutive concepts of causality are directed.

An affirmative postmodernist analysis of cause in criminology can begin by drawing from a number of provocative concepts and insights already established in both the modernist and postmodernist literature. These include: genealogy, drift, seductions, chaos, discourse, social construction, structuration, and structural coupling. We will briefly examine each for their contribution. We will then move on to a conceptualization of a constitutive dialectics that builds on these insights and on a critical materialistic analysis.

Genealogical analysis, rooted in Nietzschean philosophy, has been developed by Foucault (1972; 1980). It opposes modernist views in so much as it does not privilege points of origin, unitary knowledge or linear continuities. Instead it captures the singularity of phenomena, the multiplicity of factors at play, the instability of forms, the non-linearity of developments, the destabilizing influences of local variations, fragmentary knowledge, and the spontaneous development of resistances to power. In this perspective, causes of crime cannot be mapped in a linear manner, as they are in modernist theory and its empirical derivative, path analysis. Rather, effects of chance, indeterminacy, randomness, and the unexpected will be at play. At historical junctures, however, certain more stabilized logics (epistemes), with 'discursive regularities', may bring about influential effects (Foucault, 1972: 191–2). From this perspective, a number of provocative theories allow us to move toward a constitutive explanation of influence.

The notions of 'drift', 'seductions' and 'chaos' provide useful conceptualizations for our notion of influence in preference to that of cause, in developing a constitutive criminology. Matza's (1964; 1969) studies indicated that juveniles, like others, vacillate or 'drift' between constraint and choice, intermittently favoring one over the other, at times even acting as if committed to one rather than the other.[2] Capturing (arresting) this process at any point in time, as happens through the snapshots of empirical investigation, is to arbitrarily stabilize a dynamic and changing flow. Consider, for example, analysis which tries to operationalize variables to make use of standard empirical methodology in order to investigate the dialectical qualities that resist these impositions. More generally, consider the positivist empiricists' ordering of data in order to control for spurious effects. In these and several similar ways modernist criminology selectively shapes the outcome of its analysis by minimizing disorder in the ironic belief that it is actually rendering a more understandable account of the phenomena!

Contemplate, in contrast, Schwendinger and Schwendinger's (1985) investigation of delinquent youth which shows that, although juveniles respond to investigators' prodding in sometimes apparently traditional ways, put in the context of their peers they act out in an entirely different manner. In that context they reveal different rhetorics and knowledges justifying and explaining their law-breaking behavior. A further illustration of this indeterminacy of causal relations is found in Henry's (1978) study of the hidden economy. Here, the discourse of the economic marketplace facilitates the purchase of stolen goods, as 'cheap goods', 'bargains', 'discounts' and in other ways that legitimate the illegal activity. Discourse also provides the motivational answers to rhetorical questions about why participants take part, and these are used by both researchers and the courts: 'We do it for the money. Why else?' However, Henry revealed a wholly excluded body of discourse and motivation that took place between participants. As one of his subjects said, 'It's not important in money terms . . . They might say it is in order to justify the risk in terms that everyone can understand, but that's not it. When it comes right down to it, nobody *really* makes any money. The rewards are more social than monetary'

(1978: 93). Thus the socially constructed meaning involved in these illegal trading networks highlights different principles than those of classical rational economics. These include: reciprocity, credit without debt, community sharing, and mutual aid, none of which is afforded space in the accepted public discourse of the market economy (1978: 80–122; Henry and Mars, 1978).[3]

Similarly, in an organizational context, Jackall (1988) has shown various processes producing what he refers to as 'moral mazes'. Corporate managers find it necessary to develop 'dexterity with symbols'. Here their communication may allow them not to be pinned down, or may permit them to avoid taking responsibility for action. Their discourse is much more likely to be 'a kind of provisional discourse, a tentative way of communicating that reflects the peculiarly chancy and fluid character of their world' (1988: 134). Consistent with the Schwendingers' analysis of adolescents, and Henry's analysis of hidden economy traders, Jackall's subjects find themselves immersed within two dominant discourses or rhetorics. One discourse is used for a public audience – where corporate managers use training seminars, make policy statements and other displays as a time for 'the solemn public invocation . . . of conventional moralities and traditional shibboleths' (1988: 6; see also Schwendinger and Schwendinger, 1985: 133). The other discourse is a situationally constructed peer rhetoric: 'what matters on a day-to-day basis are the moral rules-in-use fashioned within the personal and structural constraints of one's organization' (Jackall, 1988: 6; Schwendinger and Schwendinger, 1985: 133, 151).[4]

Given these often overlooked and subjugated knowledges, positivistic empirical investigations of 'crime' typically sample the more public rhetoric and hence make reifying conclusions as to 'motivations' or causes. In the process some predefined hypothesis or conventional wisdom will be reaffirmed, adding another constitutive brick to the social construction of reality.[5] Indeed, gathering 'data' is often dependent on which region of 'phase space' is sampled (Young, 1991: 10; Gregersen and Sailer, 1993: 794–8). Phase space is a mapping of specific moments of occurrence of some phenomenon. It might, nevertheless, be that both rhetorics are operative at the same time (as in chaos's butterfly attractor depiction). In such a modality, which one is dominant is more a question of context and chance factors, with little consequence for understanding the overall constitutive process.

We might also take account of the indeterminacy principle of quantum mechanics that stipulates the impossibility of accurately specifying, simultaneously, the momentum (velocity) and location of an event. From the perspective of chaos theory, quantum mechanics' 'indeterminacy principle' means that different theories might have some marginal significance given their particular sampling; but each overlooks that the chosen points have their own bifurcation dynamics (see Chapters 3 and 4) and complex assumptions about causality (Young, 1991a: 10).

Ultimately, for Matza, indeterminacy is the predominating influence: a person is caught up in the vacillation between the mood of fatalism and the mood of humanism (again consider the strange attractor). At times the affinity to crime produced by circumstances is allowed expression when the subject is 'pacified': s/he becomes what circumstances dictate (1969: 93–4). During this movement, the subject engages the 'invitational edge' where s/he experiences an option. Only a 'leap' allows this 'edge' to be hurdled (1969: 117) – a leap that the mood of fatalism might suggest as the corrective action.

The notion of drift, a non-materialistic analysis of the causes of crime, has recently been resurrected by Katz, in his *Seductions of Crime* (1988), with the notion of subjective desires as 'causes' of crime. It has also appeared in psychoanalytic literature as the 'adaptive value of crime' (Halleck, 1971), or as a 'mode of subjectivization' (Salecl, 1993). Here the human subject attempts to resolve his/her inner conflicts by changing her/his environment through crime or activism. Ultimately, these approaches are tension-reduction models rooted in homeostasis and the modernist (order) paradigm. However, what postmodernist analysis in criminology might argue is that Matza, Katz, Halleck, and Salecl's insights bring to the foreground subjective factors, more Nietzschean in character. They each showcase the seductive character of crime.

The underlying argument, then, is that over time a political economy produces the loss of freedom and control as epitomized in the works of numerous social observers such as Weber (1978) on bureaucracy, Foucault (1977) on disciplining mechanisms, Deleuze and Guattari (1987) on territorialization of desire, Lacan (1977) on symptoms as a function of constituted Borromean knots (Milovanovic, 1993b), and Laclau and Mouffe (1985) with their notion of 'nodal points'. At some indeterminate point in this process 'edgework' (Lyng, 1990; O'Malley and Mugford, 1994) becomes the invitational edge, an object of desire (Lacan's *objet petit* (a)) within a hyperreality (Baudrillard, 1983b). For Lyng, 'edgework involves the extreme state . . . [of] "anxiety-producing chaos"' (1990: 863). It is a confrontation with the 'boundary between order and disorder, form and formlessness' (1990: 858). The edge produces a potential for extreme experiences of altered consciousness, a hyperreality that holds out the possibilities for resisting or escaping the mundane. It offers a person the opportunity to develop a unique skill: 'to maintain control over a situation that verges on complete chaos' (1990: 859). At the edge, it might manifest itself in a 'leap'. For Katz this is rage, a complete abandonment of self. For Lyng it is the opportunity to exercise great skill rather than submitting entirely to an abandonment to emotions.

Suggestive here is the insight from studies in white collar crime, that the attributed egocentric and reckless behavior of corporate executives who commit crime[6] may have some basis not only with the recruitment and selection process of manager types, but also with a propensity to situate oneself at the frontiers of an otherwise felt rigid bureaucratic world.

Illustrative is Jackall's (1988: 46–74) discussion of how bureaucracies not only attempt to rationalize work, but also order workers' public faces, their appropriate appearances, etc.

Here, then, in Nietzsche's, Derrida's, and Baudrillard's analyses of the emergence of images, replacing the real, the hyperreality, a world of simulacra, an invitational edge is presented (O'Malley and Mugford, 1994). At the edge danger and excess stir latent and repressed emotions that ultimately hold out the promise of reassuring identity, and the experience of self-actualization, realization or determination. It is at the edge that we are caught in Matza's (1964) mood of humanism. For Lyng (1990: 878), edgework is the antidote to reification and alienation. O'Malley and Mugford have indicated that Katz's study of crime suggests a 'phenomenology of pleasure [that] may be linked to social and historical theories of pleasure' (1994: 209). It is this component, the pleasures or seductions of crime, that demands a 'historically contextualized phenomenology' (1994: 210).

The negotiation of edgework has affinities with a created hyperreality (1994: 203). Baudrillard's work on the construction of hyperreality suggests that seductions are contrived, particularly transmitted through media. Along with the work of cinema theorists,[7] it suggests that the 'spoken subject' is constituted by way of discursive subject positions that provide the promise of overcoming schisms, gaps-in-being ('lack', in Lacan's formulation), alienation, disempowerment, etc.: 'Things go better with a Coke' as well as with an oozie. Here the gun is its image. The gun is the identity of power, rather than an instrument to purvey death. But the one begets the other in the tension of the edge. Indeed, Salecl's (1993) idea of 'modes of subjectivization' argues that some crimes can be explained by the identification conferring and status enhancing quality of doing crime, regardless of its negative form. And even in its more mundane form, little illegalities can invoke magical meanings. Listen to one of Henry's amateur traders talk about the attraction of her illegal hidden economy activity:

> Sure, I'd get more [money] by doing an hour's overtime, but I don't want to do that do I? I see enough of that all day long. It's repetitive. It's boring. I'm tired of doing my work all day. Do you think I'm going to stay here a minute longer than I have to? . . . But this isn't the same as work. It's money earned in your own time. You're your own master. No one's telling you what to do. It's the way you want to spend your time. (1978: 95–6)

Similarly, the reconstruction of material forms can confer new realities on objects of crime as well as on the subjects who construct them. Listen to one of Henry's subjects account for the attraction of stolen cigarettes: 'It's not just because you got them cheap. There's something special about them. Somewhere along the line they've become special cigarettes. They're no longer just the average pack . . . There's something different about them' (1978: 93).

Nor is this local reconstruction of the subjects and objects of crime separable from the wider material context of the class relations in which it occurs and through whose discursive and relational spaces it is created. Indeed, as Scraton and South have argued,

> workers' involvement in the hidden economy represents a dynamic form of opposition to the interests of capital by the daily enactment of processes which inhibit the exploitative relations of capital over labor . . . It constitutes an attack on the hegemony of class discipline from what 'autonomous space' is available, both mentally and material, to workers. (1984: 11)

Clearly, therefore, any explanation of influences needs to take account of both the local agency of human subjects, and the social agency of institutional and societal structures. We are in agreement with O'Malley and Mugford that:

> Katz bridges the gap between agency and structure, between a 1960s phenom-enology that got excited about meanings of actions, but did so in an historical and structural vacuum, and that of mainstream criminology, which compre-hended the structure of opportunity, but then slid, via a black box assumption, toward a premature closure of explanation. (1994: 210)

Although provocative, and on the way to the development of a notion of causality consistent with postmodern analysis, this vibrant criminology lacks a medium through which experiences are symbolized. We believe that the thematic connection between the otherwise disparate ideas of the authors considered here could be augmented by a constitutive theory of discourse. Fowler's (1985) analysis of power is helpful here, since it sees social forms as constituted by discursive practices. Fowler argues that 'language is a reality-creating social practice' whose use 'continuously constitutes the statuses and roles on which people base their claims to exercise power' (1985: 62). Invoking discursive construction preserves existing hierarchies of power, 'guarding the exploitative opportunities of the ruling classes and keeping the lower orders in voluntary or involuntary subservience' (1985: 64). The constitutive nature of discourse is as a co-producer of power. As such it is the medium for the production of power to deny others through harms of reduction and repression, which we defined as crime:

> possessing the terms crystallizes the relevant concepts for their users; using them in discourse keeps the ideas current in the community's consciousness, helps transmit them from group to group and generation to generation. In this way ideology is reproduced and disseminated within society – ideology in the neutral sense of a world view, a largely unconscious theory of the way the world works, accepted as common sense. (1985: 64–5)

Thus we have a constitutive theory of the production and maintenance of power through ideology, which implies a central role for discursive practices of constituted human subjects. But our constitutive theory of the generation of power needs to be supplemented by an explanation of how it is that subjects in different constructed relations of power inflict harm on each other. Support here can be found in the social constructionist's notion of how discursively produced social forms write out (and write off) their producers in the course of their own construction: put simply, reification.

As Berger and Pullberg (1966) formulated the concept, reification is the outcome of a process whereby human subjects forget that they are producers of their surrounding social world. Similarly, Giddens has stated that 'reification is a discursive notion' which 'refers to the "facticity" with which social phenomena confront individual actors in such a way as to ignore how they are produced and reproduced through human agency' (1984: 180). In Giddens' structuration theory, human subjects and the socially constructed structures they produce are not separable, but 'social practices ordered across time and space' (1984: 2). Knorr-Cetina (1981) and Cicourel (1968; 1981) have shown us how the relationship of humans to their discursive product becomes one of subject-to-object rather than of dialectical interconnection. They argue that discursive practices produce 'representations':

> which thrive upon the alleged correspondence to that which they represent, but at the same time can be seen as highly situated constructions which involve several layers of interpretation and selection . . . agents routinely transform situated micro-events into summary representations by relying on practices through which they convince themselves of having achieved appropriate representation . . . Not only are summary representations actively constructed and pursued in everyday social interaction, the equivalence between these constructions and that which they represent must also be seen as actively negotiated, interpreted and constructed. (Knorr-Cetina, 1981: 33–4)

As Henry (1987a: 95) argues, the constitutively produced social form therefore 'is a set of relations . . . in terms of summary representations recursively generated through discourse and routine construction practices'. Human subjects invest energy not into their relations with each other but into the summary representations of social forms seen as objects and object positions. The amplification of discursive distinction, through summary representations that become social forms, simultaneously and progressively separates us from each other and from ourselves. As we invest more energy in the fictions of what we produce, and in attempting to resolve the artificial differences between these social forms and our human subject positions, we cease to invest in direct relations with each other: hence Baudrillard's simulacrum. This is not to imply pure fiction since human subjects act toward their representations as though they are real. As Knorr-Cetina says, 'representations as understood here are not imaginary pictures of the world which belong to the realm of free floating ideas', rather 'they are also routinely invested with faith and interest, they are fought over and manipulated' (1981: 36). It is, therefore, as subject/object positions established within socially constructed social forms and through the interrelated representations that human subjects relate to one another. They relate not as interconnected humans, but as fellow investors in their respective representations (constructions of reality). As we saw in Chapter 5, it is as excessive investors that human subjects destroy other's contribution to this process. Social relations and their discursive constructions (which take on various contingent configurations) can be the basis of harms of reductions and repression. In order to understand how the human subject, as investor in representations, becomes the excessive investor producing these harms, we have to delve deeper into the nature not only of micro-level inter-relationships, but also what become macro-level interrelationships. Helpful here is an approach which delineates the effects of constitutive inter-relational sets and the related notion of structural coupling. For ease of terminology we refer to constitutive interrelational sets as COREL sets.[8] Let's explore these in some detail.

Deleuze and Guattari (1987) have advanced a provocative thesis concerning how a new form of a discursive formation, the 'post-signifying regime', has found some stabilization in late history. This is always interpenetrated by other formations, and is characterized by the mechanism of 'subjectification' (1987: 119). Here, at some point 'a discourse emerges which constitutes a "line of flight" along which desire flows and along which the subject is constituted' (1987: 125–48).[9] Our constitutive approach envisions various relatively stabilized and interpenetrating relational sets being productive of different logics which may or may not be given accurate 'idealized expression', but which nonetheless produce harms of reduction or repression. Unlike Deleuze and Guattari, however, at each moment along the 'line of flight', or the 'line of continuous variation', we perceive other intersecting 'lines of flight' constructed by yet other configurations of relational sets which may have an influence on the outcome. Consider, for example, Collins' (1993) notion of the nature of oppression having race, gender, and class bases, not additive in form, but intersecting – 'parallel and interlocking systems' (1993: 29) – where one may, at times, be more salient. This subterranean flow of desire, in a modified form of the chaotic (expressed as the rhizome in Deleuze and Guattari), indicates that various logics are, at some moments, coincidental, at odds, antagonistic, complementary, etc., and that these combinations have their own influences.

A further beginning for the constitutive dialectics we develop below comes from several critical lines of examination, each of which seemed to have much original promise. Althusser's (1971) and Poulantzas' (1978) thesis of 'overdetermination' alerted us to the possibility that rather than attributing cause to some specific autonomous sphere (economic, legal, political, ideological), the critical social theorists must search for how relatively autonomous instances combine to form specific articulations which then have effects. In other words, the Hegelian notion of totality as a configuration of differential moments in movement, a self-unfolding of an Absolute Spirit, an essential Logic, is countered by the idea of over-determination, by which all social relations are multiply constituted. But this position suffered a substantial critique by Hindess and Hirst (1975) in which the notion of 'structural causality' became suspect, partly because of the specification that 'the economy was determining in the last instance'. This reintroduced a universalizing and monocausal analysis. More recently, in attempting to overcome these shortcomings, several critical thinkers have accepted a modified version of Luhmann's (1985; 1992) and Teubner's (1993) 'structural coupling' thesis. We want to: (1) briefly outline this thesis; (2) indicate four worthy beginnings of a further synthesis in Jessop's 'strategic essentialism', Hunt's 'relational sets', Cornell's gender analysis, and chaos theory's 'transformational analysis'; and (3) provide a sketch of our own position of COREL sets which is based on a theory of constitutive dialectics.

The structural coupling thesis

The notion of structural coupling argues that new forms of articulation are developing between co-evolving, autopoietic institutions and structures, all of which share a certain social ecology. The logic of each sphere inter-relates with that of each of the others. A developmental process, involving variation, selection, and retention, assures that more dominant logics prevail. These relatively autonomous 'functional sub-systems' (Luhmann, 1985) may temporarily stabilize around more efficient autopoietic systems, such as those in the economic sphere. But these remain in dynamic flux. As Jessop tells us, 'structures co-evolve in and through the uncoordinated interplay of variations, selections, and restabilizations as structures interact. The final outcome is neither plannable nor forecastable' (1990: 359). Here, each autopoietic structure interconnects with each of the others, has effects within the others, and is simultaneously affected by the others by taking their logics ('inputs') and subjecting them to the unique logic of its own respective autopoietic structure. As Jessop tells us, 'in this sense the devel-opment of one structure affects the evolution of the other: but it neither controls it in a hierarchical relation of command nor subordinates it through a functionalist logic which requires one system to act for and on behalf of the other systems' (1990: 359). The basic structural coupling thesis, however, begs the question of specificity, historicity and the mutuality of their influence. Accordingly, Jessop, Hunt, and Cornell have modified the perspective. Let us briefly examine each.

Jessop's strategic essentialism

Although embracing elements of the 'structural coupling' thesis, Jessop (1990) attempts to go beyond it by indicating that 'strategic coordination' can take place. Strategic intervention can occur with specific outcomes (1990: 359–60). Jessop tells us that certain 'steering mechanisms', such as Habermas' 'steering media' (e.g. money, law, coercion), can influence autopoietic systems. There are two points here. Differential capacities exist concerning the ability to steer, and differential vulnerabilities to being steered exist (consider also Giddens' enabling and constraining properties of structure). But, Jessop points out, there is no necessity thesis at play. Rather, mediating forces capable of action exist in a social formation. These forces may anticipate reactions by other autopoietic systems and orient their own internal logics to them (1990: 360; Scharpf, 1989). In short, shifting capacities to steer and different vulnerabilities to being steered place the given relations among autopoietic systems in an unstable and contingent arrangement. Given this interrelationship, Jessop (influenced by Laclau and Mouffe, 1985: 114) proposes cause in terms of the 'contingent necessity' thesis (1990: 11–13). It is 'the non-necessary interaction of different causal chains to produce a definite outcome whose own necessity originates only in and through the contingent coming together of these causal chains in a definite context' (1990: 11). For Jessop (1990: 12), it is unrealistic to hope to specify any single set of causal relationships that could explain phenomena, because there is always more at play than can ever be articulated. Consider, for example, the multiple competing explanatory frameworks that each claim to explain crime and how at certain historical moments these congeal into what appears as the prevailing theory, only to be displaced later by another group from the set. These 'new criminologies' are never really new, but are new turns on previously dominant ideas.

Hunt's relational sets

A second line of analysis of causality that also draws on the structural coupling thesis is Hunt's (1993) notion of relation sets. In examining the development of hegemonic formations, Hunt (1993: 295) sees Jessop's structural coupling thesis as a useful 'supplement'. Hunt, influenced at times by Foucault and by Fitzpatrick's (1984) concept of 'integral plurality', suggests that law is a mediating factor that comes into play in the co-evolutionary developments among autopoietic structures. (Recall, Jessop already suggested the notion of mediating forces at play.) Hunt suggests that disciplining mechanisms, normalization, and law are linked, and in their linked form act as steering mechanisms. However, law as a steering mechanism is always incomplete in its influence (1993: 300). Thus, both negative and positive coordination can exist, whereby the former leads to the breakdown of structural couplings, and the latter leads to their stabilization and reinforcement (1993: 296).[10] Going beyond Jessop and drawing on Santos' (1987) idea of 'mapping' law, Hunt suggests that since the idea of 'social relations' is a key to Marxist thought, it can be 'mapped' in such a way as to indicate that these relations are always connected with other relations (1993: 251–5). For Hunt, 'each social relation is constituted as a complex of a variety of different types and forms of relations' (1993: 252). This he identifies as a 'relational set'. Each set can be analyzed as to (1) 'the relative predominance of its constituent relations' and (2) 'whether any pattern of dominance exists' (1993: 252). Within this relational set, patterns of interrelation can be specified, and an identification can be made as to whether these patterns conflict or supplement each other.[11] Although Hunt does not develop this line of argument further, it has parallels with our notion of COREL sets and with the thesis of a constitutive dialectics that we expand below.

Henry's analysis of the constitutive interrelations between social formations, their normative orders and state law, provides a good example of this approach. Henry (1983; 1987a; 1987b) analyzed the way in which informal norms and privately constituted rules pertaining to workplace discipline were constituted by varying subunits in formal work organizations. While the broad policy framework of discipline was set by the formal organization, influenced by the structure of capitalist society and its legal order, reliance on the semi-autonomy of the various internal constitutive units resulted in unpredictable and sometimes contradictory reactions to rule-breaking. For example, some acts of employee theft would be accommodated, reinterpreted and redefined in the course of the synoptic projects (Fitzpatrick, 1988; O'Malley, 1991) of new rule formation and by the internal process of applying rules. In these instances, violators might be treated more or less punitively, with the result that the effective prevailing rule of law was modified and in some cases countermanded by the parallel but integral substructures. In so far as this unpredictable divergence and convergence is replicated in a myriad of contexts Henry suggests that a less than linear relationship prevails between constitutive orders, with the result, as Fitzpatrick (1984: 138) observed, that 'law is the unsettled product of relations with a plurality of social forms' and as such 'law's identity is constantly and inherently subject to challenge and change.'[12] Let's briefly move to a third useful elaboration of the structural coupling thesis.

Cornell's Lacanian gender analysis

Cornell (1992), whose work has energized feminist critical theory, has shown how the structural coupling thesis can be integrated with Lacanian psychoanalytic semiotics. In investigating how gender hierarchies are given relatively stabilized forms she indicates that a gender hierarchy operates much like an autopoietic system. Within this autopoietic system (e.g. Oedipal complex, Symbolic Order) a binary code exists. This code is semantically structured and constitutes male and female roles in opposition, with one more privileged (1992: 77). This more dominant autopoietic system interpenetrates other autopoietic systems with its logic. That is, other autopoietic systems subsume this as an operative logic, in the process solidifying the gender hierarchy. For Cornell, and a point we shall return to below, these hierarchies are unstable. Derrida's notion of iteration (feedback or recursivity) is useful for Cornell in indicating how 'the slippage of language' always produces gaps. These 'gaps' offer the potential for reinterpretation, and through iteration assure indeterminate effects. Gender identity, for Cornell, is undermined by these slippages. The possible development of new discursive structures, therefore, is always present given the instability of discourse itself. For Cornell, then, 'structural coupling itself is what continually opens every system to its deconstruction' (1992: 87). Thus for her, it is structural coupling and the effects of iteration that pave the way for the potential of a new 'choreography of sexual difference'.

Here, according to Cornell, 'our singularity, not our gender, would be loved by our Other' (1992: 86).

Chaos and transformational representations

A fourth contribution to the development of our dialectical approach comes from the mathematically oriented topological analysis of chaos theory and cosmological theory. The application of chaos theory to social systems has benefited from recent work that attempts to develop alternatives to linear path analysis (Gregersen and Sailer, 1993; Pickover, 1988). Gregersen and Sailer discuss how chaos theory, which they prefer to call 'transformation theory', can create 'meta-models of social behavior' by drawing on certain analogies to mathematical theorizing that have produced chaos distributions (see Loye and Eisler, 1987). In their suggestive approach, the state of any system is a function of a static snapshot of a dynamic system in process, plus the state of its environment. They indicate an isomorphism between iterative polynomials and social science's specifications of transformational 'causal laws'.[13] By beginning with a deterministic description, however, 'wildly unpredictable behavior' results (1993: 778). Topological portrayals are often used to capture these transformations.[14] Loye and Eisler (1987) have argued that the social chaos approach has already appeared in the literature, such as in dialectical theory (1987: 59), and even some of the noted chaos theorists (e.g. Prigogine) have borrowed from some of the classic sociologists such as Weber, Durkheim, Marx, and Spencer. The authors indicate that all were dealing with the question of an isomorphism.[15]

In our example of a possible application of their work we look at embezzlement, explained by Cressey (1953) as containing three key variables in a causal chain: (1) a non-shareable financial problem, (2) opportunities, knowledge and skills of how to commit embezzlement, and (3) the availability or rationalizations legitimating the commission of embezzlement. The 'causal' flow can be specified in a polynomial. Again this is suggestive. The polynomial represents the laws of transformation, or in other words the 'causal chain' in the occurrence of embezzlement. Applying this to the social sciences we can conceive of the polynomial as representing some 'causal law' (Cressey's stipulated three factors explaining embezzlement), where each factor or variable in a polynomial is a contributing factor to the outcome.[16] It now needs to be iterated (to incorporate feedback influences). These iterated polynomials, although deterministic, produce unpredictable results.[17] These can be represented, not by the path analysis diagrams (Figure 7.1a) offered in the modernist framework, but by such infinitely complex pictures as the Mandelbrot set (Figure 7.2).[18] The Mandelbrot set represents attractor states that chaos theorists call 'outcome basins'. Here, the black areas (areas of 'non-divergence') represent those who engage in embezzlement. White areas represent 'divergence', in this case, those who do not engage in

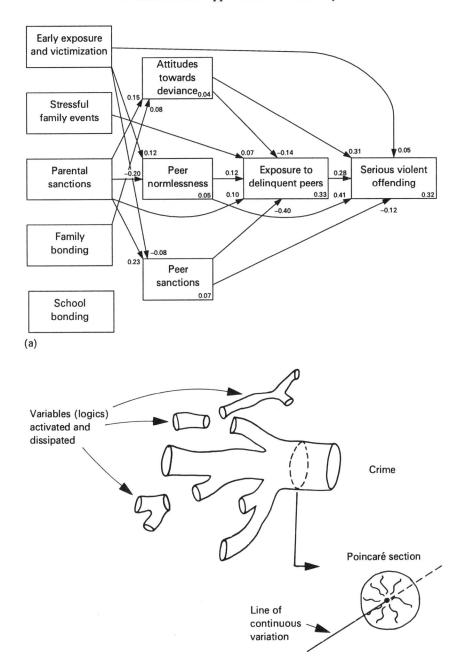

(a)

(b)

Figure 7.1 *Mapping causality: modernist versus postmodernist. (a) Modernist path anlaysis: model of the onset of serious violent offending, New York State (Elliott, 1994: 17). (b) Postmodernist/chaos: trouser diagram*

Figure 7.2 *Outcome basins of the Mandelbrot set (two-dimensional) graphed for the hypothetical embezzler. Area outlined in black represents convergence (those with law-breaking commitment profiles) and the area outside it in white represents divergence (those with law-abiding profiles or other forms of harm) (image of Mandelbrot set created and provided by Neal Kettler)*

embezzlement.[19] This would include law-abiding behavior as well as non-embezzlement law breaking. There are two points to be made here. First, knowing some entity's initial state, its particular environment, and the specific causal 'laws' which account for transformations (e.g. the iterative polynomial) from one time to another, does not of itself produce predictable results. Second, conventional order-based, linear statistical means such as regression analysis (linear or non-linear) cannot predict the discontinuities found in the iterated polynomials (Gregersen and Sailer, 1993: 783; Smith, 1995: 31; Barton, 1994). However, topological portrayals, such as the Mandelbrot set (Figure 7.2), can provide increasingly sophisticated understanding (1993: 783).

The Mandelbrot set as an attractor portrays relatively stable regions (non-chaotic), depicted in black; relatively unstable regions, comprising the areas close to the borders; and diverging points to infinity, represented by the white areas. The critical methodological matters are to select the area of the phase map to sample and then to learn the unique features, such as stability, indeterminacy, and expansion to infinity, of each region (Gregersen and Sailer, 1993: 794–9; Young, 1991a: 10; 1992). As Young tells us, contradictory results exist when looking at the literature on the relationship between jobs and crime. However, 'it turns out that each of several contradictory studies can be valid depending on which region of phase space is sampled' (1991: 10).

It should be noted that perusal of the borders of the Mandelbrot set indicates jagged edges representing discontinuity (which chaos theory calls fractals). By magnification, what appears at a larger level of magnification reappears continuously at finer levels (e.g. recursive symmetries). This means that points which appear near the boundaries have the widest unpredictability. Analysis of variance or regression analysis cannot produce understanding of discontinuities found here (Gregersen and Sailer, 1993: 785). Moreover, Gregersen and Sailer state, 'cross-sectional research on inherently chaotic phenomena may actually produce an *illusion of certainty* (i.e. prediction) for a social phenomenon with underlying unpredictability' (1993: 786, emphasis added).

The boundaries of the Mandelbrot set, then, can be usefully conceptualized as the 'invitational edge' (Matza, 1964); as connected with 'edgework' (Lyng, 1990); as the 'borderland' (Giroux, 1992); the locus of 'pure play' and 'abduction' (Peirce, 1965); 'mimesis' (Irigaray, 1985); or the sphere where alternative myth-making and utopian thinking take form (Cornell, 1992). Space does not allow us at this time to explore this in depth, but we should indicate that useful conceptualizations such as Lorenz's butterfly attractor would seem to 'live' near the boundaries. Matza, as we have seen earlier, has indicated how the juvenile tends to 'drift' between two basins of outcome, law-abiding and law-breaking. At times this butterfly attractor collapses, perhaps when a bifurcation point has been reached during a crisis, whereby a limit attractor becomes the outcome basin (consider also Braithwaite's 1989 'tipping point'). Here, the juvenile crosses the invitational edges and becomes committed in her/his enterprise of crime, or the juvenile 'matures out' of publicly visible forms of crime into convention or into a more stable, less risky invisible form of occupational crime or 'crime by the public' (Gabor, 1994). Consider the corporate manager who may contribute to forming a resistance subculture and a system of rationalizations, or may come to share her/his financial problem with others in some control agency's more reintegrative style of social control.

In order to 'map' these non-linear effects, Gregersen and Sailer (1993), building from others (Pickover, 1988; Sinanoglu, 1981), have provided 'meta-models of social behavior' (see Figures 7.3a, 7.3b). These are suggested as alternative ways of representing complex and dynamic patterns of interaction that are non-linear.[20] In Figure 7.3a, a simple chaotic form composed of one interactive loop indicates we begin at some state (z), with some input (n), which is then iterated (the squiggles represent some transformation, e.g. squaring) and returns for further iteration.[21] This

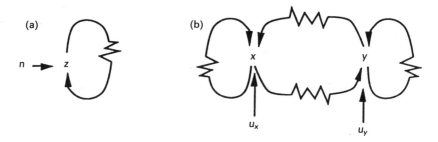

Figure 7.3 *Chaos theory and meta-model of social behavior. (a) One iterative loop. (b) Two iterative loops, mutually interpenetrating (Gregersen and Sailer, 1993: 780, 786)*

iteration is composed of one feedback loop. Consider, for example, self-reflection on the onset of some personal crisis, or labeling theory's explanation of 'biographical reconstruction' or 'retrospective interpretation' leading to the assumption of a secondary deviant identity. Husserl's notion of a 'glancing ray' and 'directed glance of attention' and their iterations can also be seen as an example (1973: 59–126, 175–81). Lacan's extensive use of algorithms as ideograms is also exemplary.[22] Think also of the recollections given by witnesses to crime. Recall also Derrida's analysis of how a word is iterated in different contexts (discussed in Chapter 4). Here, drawing from some notion of 'original intent', for example of some Founding Fathers' written text as embedded in the US Constitution, is pure myth (Fitzpatrick, 1992). But lawyers continue to debate its accuracy and often make use of syllogistic reasoning and deductive logic traced to this 'original intent' as a major premise.

A more complex chaotic form is also represented in Figure 7.3b. Here, x represents commitment (attitudinal, behavioral), y environment (opportunities to embezzle, rationalizations for embezzlement). Note that x and y are each iterative loops, but they are also coupled with u_x and u_y, perhaps some outside environment (e.g. economic conditions). Thus, the outcome of the y iterative loop is coupled with the outcome of the x iterative loop, which in turn is coupled with the y iterative loop, etc. Moreover, these are structurally coupled with u_x and u_y. The squiggly lines, again, represent some iterative operation, some operation done on the variables (e.g. in math, squaring, adding, etc.; in topology theory, some stretching, pulling, twisting, and collapsing operations, and where tearing produces discontinuous change, as in catastrophe theory; in the social sciences, some 'laws' of human interaction). An even more complex diagram, shown in Figure 7.4, could add the number of factors beyond x and y (i.e. formal reward system, worker relationships, etc.) as well as other factors outside of the organizational environment, i.e. the coupling(s) with other autopoietic systems v, w, etc.[23] Here we would have iteration of numerous functions with multiple and intersecting feedback pathways (Pickover, 1988: 136).

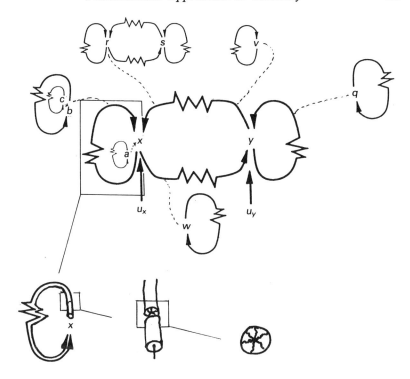

Figure 7.4 *Constitutive interrelational (COREL) sets. Lines should be considered as collapsed tubes; dotted lines represent parallel and coupled iterative loops. Each constitutive iterative loop is composed of numerous interpenetrating others (adapted from Gregersen and Sailer, 1993: 780, 786)*

Chaos theory suggests that in all cases there is a sensitive and non-linear dependency on initial conditions (Gregersen and Sailer, 1993: 790; Barton, 1994). Any slight shift in parameter values will produce unanticipated influences upon iteration. 'Rounding' in mathematics is a basis of disproportional effects upon many iterations. A slight increase in the national inflation rate, a competitive new firm entering the field, a rise in national employment rates, a speed-up with no increase in compensation, etc., could produce disproportional outcomes, such as the onset of new forms of occupational crime, or other harms of reduction or repression, such as spouse and child abuse. But other traditionally assumed minor or insignificant values, such as support groups inside and outside of the organization, or particular outside hobbies and activities, or a dictated move of an office to a less hospitable location, might have disproportional effects. It is the interpenetrating iterative processes that produce such non-linear dynamics.

The four perspectives developed in tandem with the notion of autopoiesis and structural coupling – Jessop's 'contingent necessity', Hunt's mapping of 'relational sets', Cornell's integration of Luhmann, Lacan and Derrida, and chaos theory's suggestive and provocative work on iterative loop relations – contribute to our own notion of cause in constitutive criminology and help in our understanding of the emergence of the excessive investor. Just as Knorr-Cetina and Cicourel and Giddens enlightened us in the discursive interaction that generated macro-social forms, so Jessop's view provides insights to macrosociological developments, Hunt's to more micro-level developments, Cornell's to identity formations (e.g. discursive subject positions), and chaos theory to iterative effects. Jessop identified a major shortcoming with Laclau and Mouffe (1985) in that even though they acknowledge some objects external to thought and that only discourse gives these meaning, they then neglect this connection with the Real. Neither, however, go so far as Cornell, to address the issue of the Imaginary Order and its contributions to imagining an alternative utopia. Cornell, on the other hand, pays less attention to the Symbolic and Real Orders. And Jessop and Hunt maintain a strong commitment to Marxism and hence the modernist (order) paradigm, confining themselves, in the process, to its logic. Cornell, on the other, seems to call for some integration of Derrida, Hegel, Luhmann and Lacan. Our position draws on these developments as applied to the Luhmann-Teubner thesis and replants them in a more macro-micro integrational postmodern metaphysics.

In summary, a reasonable direction in developing a constitutive criminology and a statement as to causality would integrate conceptions from: chaos theory, particularly as to the nature of fractal geometry, the effects of iteration, indeterminate effects, and attractors; discourse analysis, particularly the generation of social forms, ideology and power, from micro-level interaction; Lacan's notion that three orders – Symbolic, Imaginary, Real – in combination are constitutive of subjectivity and reality construction; and a critical dialogical pedagogy rooted in concrete historical developments where the signifier finds its decidability, its grounding in struggle as Freire tells us. A constitutive phenomenology would undertake the task of integrating the micro- with the macro-level of analysis but would not fall within the modernist (order) paradigm metaphysics and would not constitute macro and micro as discrete unitary constructs, abstracted from the infinite range of their continuous possibilities.

Affirmative postmodernism: constitutive dialectics

From our perspective crime is not so much caused as discursively constructed through human processes of which it is one. Crime is the ongoing, recursively produced outcome of numerous different contexts of interrelationship, wherein human subjects progressively lose sight of their productive contribution, and increasingly invest in that which they produce to the point of some becoming excessive investors and others victims of denial, reduction, repression. In Chapter 5 we presented a constitutive typology of victim categories connected with harms of reduction and repression, the flip side of which consisted of offender categories. Our conceptualization of harms of reduction and harms of repression also implicated discursive practices (the 'violence of language') and configurations of COREL sets that cut across these separations. To be clear about the constitution of victim and offender categories we need to connect the foregoing analysis from social theory with causality in explanation of crime.

It is our argument that subjects who are in invested interrelations are sustained in these positions by interrelations among the social forms or COREL sets that they produce. We see these relationships not as deterministic but as dialectical. Unlike the notion of dialectics of Hegel and Marx where some universal logic or law is said to unfold (e.g. Absolute Spirit, dialectical materialism), our constitutive dialectics assumes non-linear developments.

The model of causality that best captures our notion of how crime is constituted is that of constitutive dialectics. We take this to mean co-determination and mutual interrelation without the implications of linear dynamics. According to Lewontin et al., the dialectical notion of co-determination is an

> attempt to provide a coherent, unitary but non-reductionist account of the material universe. For dialectics the universe is unitary but always in change; the phenomena we see at any instant are parts of the process, processes with their histories and futures whose paths are not uniquely determined by their constitutive units. (1984: 11–12)

Co-determination and interrelationship can be represented as several overlapping spheres (as in a Venn diagram) that illustrate how the constitutive social fields or forms are related to each other. The concept of field here might be better characterized in terms of fractal geometry and the discontinuities of moments. We see a complex, dynamic interpenetrating and multi-dimensional space where at best a moment can be specified by a probability statement. The principal constitutive units within the present configuration of social order (offenders, victims, criminal justice, law, society, discursive regions, etc.) exist partly as separate and partly as common social constructions; each is present in the other. The local, then, is always already composed of the global and vice versa; in fact, the hologram is an operative metaphor.[24] We refer to discursive regions in the plural since a number of relatively autonomous and stable regions are continuously reproduced, within which acceptable narrative constructions may take place. As we saw in Chapter 2, each discursive formation is (1) coordinated by the paradigm–syntagm axes, and at the deeper level, by the metaphor–metonymy and condensation–displacement axes (e.g. the semiotic grid: Milovanovic, 1994), and (2) offers discursive subject positions within which a subject may take temporary residence. Also it may be important here to reflect on the differences between the constitutive discourses.[25]

It is apparent that regions of social structure whose agents generate self-referential discourse can be distinguished from the generation of discourse at the interstices which itself merges with and is absorbed by the discursive structure of other regions. At these 'coupling points' (Hayles, 1990: 13, 155, 157) sensitivity to change is maximal. That is, small fluctuations can cause the overall configuration to evolve in indeterminate ways. The generation of such negotiated discourse is both the glue through which human subjects connect different regions and the medium through which their conflicts and compromises are fought out. A third discursive region, a region of alternative discourses, is envisaged, having a quality not dissimilar from the first except that it is constituted in tension with the prevalent discursive regions with a view to providing an alternative for transformation based upon its inevitable interconnectedness, its multiple coupling points, with other regions. We refer to the discourses in this alternative region as 'replacement discourses', as we shall see in the next chapter.

This representation, then, is intended to depict our view that changes in one constitutive order, which may be the product of differences between constitutive orders, necessarily produce changes in the other but that these changes defy temporal prioritizing and linear causal direction. These configurations are provisional, contingent, inherently unstable and shifting coordinates. Given this conceptualization, changes occur not because these various components direct the other, or because they interact with the other, but because some of what constitutes each *is* the other, just as some of the other is constituted by each (see Fitzpatrick, 1984). Nor is the extent of such co-determination fixed: it is an ever-changing, socially constructed dynamic wherein each integral element is constructed sometimes as more corresponding with, and sometimes as more divergent from, other constitutive elements.

Again, we will borrow from chaos theory. It has been demonstrated that strange attractors have many coupling points, each of which may transmit and produce disproportional effects within their orbits (Hayles, 1990: 157).[26] Braithwaite's theory of reintegrating shaming (1989), which proposes to explain crimes of the powerless and powerful, argues that the parameter 'social control' could tip organizational behavior toward law compliance or non-compliance and subcultural adaptations. The oscillation between two possible outcome basins is much like that portrayed in chaos theory's strange attractor. His contribution has to do with the nature of the control parameter. Adversarial forms produce resistance subcultures; regulatory forms that are cooperative and yet firm are more likely to produce law-abiding behavior. Thus shaming could be reintegrative or, if used in excess, contributory to further developments of subcultures of resistance and crime (as in labeling theory). However, Braithwaite seems to overlook the many coupling points existing within organizational as well as street contexts, which interpenetrate the more dominant logics that may be at play. From this perspective, 'minor' linkages may turn out to be more contributory than is otherwise seen through the effects of iteration and disproportional influence (see also Young, 1991a). Indeed, as Young tells us, 'what we find in chaotic social dynamics is a complex basin of outcomes in which three (or more) qualitatively different fates await the same person or firm in a society' (1991a: 4). Braithwaite's call for a 'theory of tipping points' (1989) seems appropriate, and differential shaming is one of the parameters. Chaos theory, however, would also see the middle region between the law-compliance and law-breaking behavior of the powerless and powerful as a region of maximal uncertainty and a space where additional contributory factors (parameters) have their sources in diverse interpenetrating logics that can be understood from the standpoint of our thesis of COREL sets. Even at Braithwaite's 'tipping point' (called a bifurcation point by chaos theorists), one would expect 'ever more complex causal basins' such that 'each region has its own dynamics, hence its own special theory' (Young, 1991a: 10). Given such a vision we cannot proceed in a linear direction, for at each bifurcation point a new outcome basin arises whose complexities are never predictable, and whose indeterminacies through iteration lead to yet more indeterminacies.

Hayles provides a useful metaphor in this context with physicist Berry's example of tennis play in an orchard (1990: 157–8). Two tennis balls could be hit, arguably, in an identical manner in an orchard, but will end up in different locations because each tree that each ball hits will change the trajectory. The more trees hit, the greater indeterminacy in prediction as to where precisely the ball will end up. As Hayles says:

> In this analogy, the trees correspond to coupling points, and the final location of the balls to points along a strange attractor's orbit after several iterations. We may know fairly precisely in what direction a ball is first hit; that is, we know its initial conditions. But unless we know exactly what the direction is – unless, as Feigenbaum pointed out, we know the initial conditions with *infinite precision* – we will not be able to hit a second ball so that it falls even close to the first . . . Thus deterministic systems may also be chaotic. (1990: 158, emphasis in original)

Analogously, human subjects find themselves in a multitude of intersecting logics, conveyed by discourses, and at times in conflicting discursive subject positions within which they take momentary residence to construct reality with others; in the process they both construct reality and are constructed by this very reality. Consider a beat-cop who finds her/himself within the discourse of rights, the subcultural ethics and solidarity of fellow police, the possible liberal education received at a college, the ostensibly developed 'sixth sense' from street work, possible personal prejudices, for many the desire to do good, the always anticipatory constructions of self-justifying discourses (*ex post facto* legal constructions) if things should go wrong, and many more logics.[27] It is, nevertheless, an impossibility to specify with precision the different logics, discourses and assumed discursive subject positions at play at any moment. It may very well be that some 'minor' variable will, with iteration, have disproportional effects.

Given this fluid and dynamic context, crime (as we defined it in Chapter 5) is the ongoing and emergent outcome of such constitutive dialectical chaos, whose reality as an entity grows with each instance of its constructed imagery. Such a process enables some people to sometimes believe it is possible, and often even acceptable, to act on the differences that they create, in such a way as to deny others the freedom to make their own differences. Crime includes symbolic violence, the violence of language, that maintains a culture of silence amongst those denied a stable discourse out of which their pain and suffering can be articulated.[28] In short, an analysis of the cause of crime is not a matter of factors but a matter of the constitutive dialectics of power and control expressed and articulated through structurally coupled COREL sets.

Power implies creation and denial: the ability and the will to force others to comply. The exercise of power over others in a way that causes them pain, loss, deprivation is not adequately depicted as an individual choice or a biological trait, or as a determined outcome of structure and organization. Rather it is a socially and culturally sanctioned and celebrated feature of institutions, economy and polity in Western industrial society (as well as in many other societies) and as these are interrelated in the global political economy. In order to understand how some individuals in whatever context – conventional street crimes, corporate crimes, state crimes, etc. – act out the abstractly internalized constitutive interrelational sets whose logic is one of domination, and in order to comprehend how they conceive of and accumulate the skills necessary to exercise power over others, it is necessary to examine how both the global order and, within that, particular societies are constituted in such a way as to celebrate and sustain inequalities (i.e. differences of power). It is necessary to examine how institutions and governments believe sufficiently in the seriousness of their existence as forces to support ideological practices that result in the delusion that anyone is somehow separate from, different from and unconnected to others in the local, national and global context. It is necessary to explore the state, institutional processes, and constitutive interrelational sets that bolster and legitimate some individuals and groups to accumulate the power to cause pain, whether through cultural hegemony, organizational strategy or personal will. We need to understand how, while exercising their own power that denies others, these institutional processes confirm the power to cause pain and how conceptual and discursive practices enable this process to become pervasive, all-corrupting, undermining of any that seek to counter it.

Illustrations and beginnings of the application of such theory to criminology, albeit implicit, are found in Matza's and Schwendinger and Schwendinger's analysis of the more conventional forms of crime and by others' analysis of occupational and organizational crime.[29] For Matza (1964), various verbalizations that are coupled with legal discourse pave the way to the neutralization of the binds of the law; for Schwendinger and Schwendinger (1985), various rhetorics which derive from and are coupled with market forces interpenetrate the various 'stradoms' in producing juveniles at risk in making the leap at the invitational edge to crime. For those who have investigated corporate crimes, 'neutralizations' found in the occupational and corporate environment have been shown to assuage guilt (Vandivier, 1972; Henry, 1976; 1978). Indeed, Jackall's (1988) insightful analysis of corporate executives indicates that the discourse generated within the vagaries and contradictions found in a corporate context is provisional, fluid, chancy, and allows the manager to always redefine what s/he had said (1988: 134–7). This discourse has as 'its principal purpose . . . to communicate certain meanings within specific contexts with the implicit understanding that should the context change, a new, more appropriate meaning can be attached to the language already used' (1988: 136). But, much like the Schwendingers, Jackall sees a variety of discourses that may be operative: 'various vocabularies of explanation for issues, trends, or events important to an institution get circulated in different organizational circles. Depending on the range of one's social contacts, one adopts different vocabularies to explain the same event' (1988: 147).

Crime then, from our perspective, is 'caused' through institutionally situated and discursively ordered processes, when people lose sight of the humanity and integrity of those with whom they interrelate and whom their actions and interactions affect. It is the outcome of language and thought processes which objectify others as separate, dehumanized entities, mediated through the COREL sets of a particular historical period. Such conception is carried by discourses that pervade and interpenetrate that totality. It is not a quality owned only by those who presently victimize others.

Constitutive criminology differs considerably in its approach. Topological portrayals in two as well as in three or more dimensions become critical. Topology theory is a qualitative math with relevance for our constitutive dialectics. Recent work by cosmologists who attempt to topologically diagram the pathways of the very basic units of 'matter' itself is useful (Peat, 1988). These are often called 'trouser diagrams'. We see them in Figure 7.1b (also called 'world lines', 'closed loops'). Here the outside solid lines of the trousers are porous. These trouser diagrams have been recently proffered by cosmologists and nuclear physicists who have grown disillusioned with the traditional representations of Newtonian physics and Euclidean geometry for portraying the ostensible interactions of 'particles' (Peat, 1988). Quantum mechanics and its indeterminacy principle, for example, necessitated an alternative way of depicting 'probability events'. Here the difference between a particle and a wave is a central problematic. Trouser diagrams indicate that rather than lines we have a plane where a radius of activity is present (a locus). This is evident if we cut a slice (which chaos theorists refer to as a Poincaré section). We can perhaps identify a 'line' at the mythical midpoint, but following Deleuze and Guattari (1987) we have a 'line of continuous variation'.

Trouser diagrams can be particularly helpful in discourse analysis. For example, if we assume that one of the trousers depicts discourse we could investigate certain words or phrases that invoke meaning. Consider the word 'bounce'. It means different things for different people in different contexts: for the child it has to do with a ball or a pogo stick, or what they are not supposed to do on a bed, that is to use it as a trampoline; for a worker, perhaps a check; for a dancer at a disco, the person in charge of the door; for a person doing laundry, a clothes softener; for a computer network user, a delay; for a recently sick person, the moment of recovery; for an employee, the search for a new job; for a skydiver, a person who dies during a skydive. This is not just stating the obvious that words have multiple meanings. Rather, we have a pattern that may emerge in the different nuanced meanings for the word 'bounce', what Volosinov (1986) referred to as its 'multi-accentuality'. This is what gives the appearance of the trouser. Within a slice of this trouser, we cannot specify with exactness the location of an event. We have at best moments in movement. Thus we have local indeterminacy.

Constitutive criminology, in contrast to path analysis, indicates that various 'variables' intersect, interpenetrate, run parallel, combine, interact, etc. and they do this because of their interpenetrating and interrelating discourses, logics, rhetorics.[30] Converging 'trousers' may indicate the confluence of logics producing a higher likelihood of some range of behavior, such as crime. At other times, trousers can dissipate without any manifest effect.

Thus if we look at Figure 7.1b, to the far right of the trouser diagram, we can conceptualize, either a strange attractor or a torus as the best expression of outcome behavior (see Figure 2.4). In each case we have a pattern, which is the distinctive shape of the strange attractor or torus. This indicates the extent or range of global stability. However, when we look within the torus attractor which here reflects periodic motion (again, take a slice) we can identify a range of moments, and consistent with quantum mechanics, we cannot define with precision momentum (velocity) and location simultaneously. In other words, at the local level we have indeterminacy.

However, several qualifications are in order. First, lines that appear in Figures 7.3–7.4 should be replaced by a 'trouser' structure in order to indicate Deleuze and Guattari's (1987) notion of 'lines of continuous variation' which we believe better represents the range of variance of each variable. Thus each simple iterative loop in Figure 7.4 can be blown up to produce a torus attractor with squiggles still representing functions. Second, each variable must be seen as composed of several constitutive iterative loops in dialectical tension. In other words, within each coupled iterative loop are multi-configured iterative loops, producing a source for dis-proportional change (see Figure 7.4). Consider a word (signifier) as an iterative loop or an autopoietic structure. Contained within it are multiple images and symbolic forms (i.e. dictionary meanings). It is the site of a multi-accentuality, a terrain of dispersion (Volosinov, 1986). Lacan (1977) has already told us that sliding under the signifier are the signified, and only at some point is this sliding stabilized as a nodal point (see also Laclau and Mouffe, 1985). In other words, imageries tend toward further iteration as diverse sources of psychic material come to be embodied in visual form.[31] Consider the word 'person' and its multiple iterative loops (i.e. from law, the juridic subject; from positivistic sciences, the determined subject; from the point of view of a system of slavery, the one in bondage; from anti-abortionists, the fetus; from prisoner rights groups, the inmate with rights of the free citizen; from a postmodernist view, a decentered entity; and so on). It is only in a concrete situation that other constitutive iterative loops interact in a particular way producing particular nuanced meanings.

Our third qualification is that two-dimensional pathway diagrams often visually hide parallel and interlocking autopoietic structures that exert their effects laterally. Collins (1933), for example, has argued that race, gender and class harms of reduction and repression are not 'additive' but are parallel and interlocking structures. Chaos theorists refer to these three-dimensional portrayals as 'non-planar networks' (Pickover, 1988: 139). Iterative loops, then, interpenetrate other iterative loops with interactive effects. See Figure 7.4, especially the dotted lines expressing parallel structures. Deleuze and Guattari's notion of the 'rhizome' (1987) is particularly well suited for this type of diagraming.

A fourth qualification recognizes that the appearance of COREL sets in a single plane acknowledges process time as a circular time within the interrelations, but it does not express linear time. This can be incorporated by envisaging each set at any point in time $t+1$ as a development of the constitutive interrelations at time t and as the starting point for the next manifestation at time $t+2$, and so on, with a whole sequence of states of COREL sets to $t+n$ (see Figure 7.4). The progress of a COREL set between any two points in time is continuous, though because of the inner interconnections it may change more rapidly at some points than others. Further, interconnections between COREL sets can be made by inter-connected reference forward or back, more in the random manner of static electricity than in any determined and predictable way. Clearly, there is more than we have fully developed in these ideas, and for the present purposes they should be taken as our contingent position, and one which we shall continue to develop.

Application of COREL set theory to crime

With these qualifications we can now see how our constitutive theory would explain certain criminological phenomena. Its application is appro-priate for considering Matza's notion of 'drift' where human subjects 'vacillate between choice and constraint' (1964: 7) and where juveniles 'flirt now with one, now with the other, but postpone commitment and evade decision' (1964: 59). Cressey's (1953) embezzlers, too, did not devote all their time to embezzlement. Nor did Henry's (1978) hidden economy traders devote all their time to buying and selling stolen goods.

Schwendinger and Schwendinger's (1985) delinquents found themselves articulating at times egoistic, at other times instrumental rhetorics. Lyng's (1990) subjects who were engaged in 'edgework' did not spend all of their time at the 'edge'. Katz's (1988) subjects who committed emotionally charged violent acts also engaged in routine everyday activity without challenge; and so on. Of course, the modernist interpretation is that the legal activity is merely a front to cover the illegal and avoid easy detection. Such a reading, however, misses the genuine interrelatedness between criminal and legal activity, such that each is constitutive of the other. For example, as Henry (1977) says in talking about aspects of property crime, 'it is not the case that one species of actor, "the fence", buys stolen goods, whereas another, "the businessman", buys legitimate ones. Rather . . . businessmen buy cheap goods in order that they may sell at a profit; a greater or lesser proportion of their purchases may be illicit' (1977: 133; see also Klockars, 1974). Similarly, it is not the case that professional fences are just fences, or employee thieves just dishonest. Indeed, as Ditton (1977) has said, employee theft is not opposed to business but is a part of legitimate commerce. Its participants

> do not believe that fiddling [occupational theft] will eventually overthrow the capitalist economy . . . they fully believe themselves to be part of the same commercial army . . . Fiddling, like selling, epitomizes the capitalist 'spirit'. The subculture of fiddling reflects a sort of dutiful anti-hedonism . . . which provides the bedrock of capitalism. (1977: 173–4)

Intervention at any moment, say by police, social workers, psychiatrists, or by an interview, a questionnaire, TV coverage, will arrest this process, providing a static portrayal (a restrictive 'phase space') of an otherwise complex, dynamic event in movement. Given the right contingencies, however, one may, as in Matza, 'mature' out of delinquency or become 'converted' (or 'committed') to her/his enterprise. What constitutive criminology argues is that the dichotomous separation between law-abiding and law-breaking behavior is an artifact of the conventional criminologist (the modernist paradigm).

Moving beyond the descriptive into a humanistic prescriptive analysis guided by constitutive theory, we could draw from more liberating conceptualizations such as in: George Herbert Mead's constituted elements of the self, the 'I' and the 'me', which can be portrayed as attractor states, where the 'me' is the more static (global stability), and the 'I' the more unpredictable (local indeterminacy), and the desirable state would be not role-taking but role-making (personal conversation with T.R. Young, 2/15/ 1995); Unger's 'role defiance' and 'role jumbling', where 'roles can be stretched, pulled apart, combined with other roles, and used incongruously' (1987: 563–81); dialogical pedagogy's notion (Freire, 1985; JanMohamed, 1994) that in order to break away from rigid identifications we should simultaneously engage in disidentification and identification – 'it demands a shift away from the deeply cathected inertia of fixed, sedimented identities and toward an engagement in the process of reidentification' (JanMohamed, 1994: 111); African-American feminist analysis of the multifaceted nature of identities where 'differences are always relational rather than inherent' (Harris, 1991: 250; Collins, 1989; 1993; Matsuda, 1987); or, finally, as in Lacan's Borromean knot construction where three intertwined circles representing the Symbolic, Imaginary, and Real Orders intersect, held together by a repairing mechanism (the symptom) which produces 'consistency' in the subject, but yet indeterminacy at any particular moment (Milovanovic, 1993b). All this goes against the modernist idea of a static subject as in structural functionalism or as in modernist empiricists' imprisoning subjects within demographic grids.

Within the constitutive criminological approach, what are otherwise seen as insignificant 'foreground' factors may be significant, and with the principle of iteration present disproportional and unexpected results. Young gives some examples: 'some white collar professionals caught up in a demanding life style and facing a slight increase in expenses and/or revenue, might begin to exploit their clients; once started, such behavior might become stable' (Young, 1991a: 10; see also Ditton, 1977). He goes on to show that 'some corporations, caught up in small increases in taxes, changing labor costs, and/or profits might well adopt exploitative policy toward their own employees or customers', and further, 'some disemployed or underemployed persons, caught up in growing cycles of desire/demand, having uneven patterns of income, might resort to the forms of street crime that augment income and, thus for a while, reduce uncertainty. Others might not' (1991a: 10). What makes the difference? A compassionate conversation a volunteer has with a 'gang member' might fundamentally produce change; the intervention of a friend with someone who otherwise identifies her/his situation as one where 'a non-shareable financial problem' exists may suddenly move away from a logic that would have culminated in embezzlement; a vote cast which normally would not have been (what would one vote matter?) may lead to other activities that make a difference. In the constitutive view, investigations shift to such moments, to name a few, as 'pacification' (Matza, 1969; Katz, 1988: 8); 'seductions' (Katz, 1988; O'Malley and Mugford, 1994); 'edgework' (Lyng, 1990; O'Malley and Mugford, 1994); the 'invitational edge' (Matza, 1969); hyperreality and its contrived offerings of objects of desire (Baudrillard, 1983a; Lacan, 1977);[32] 'modes of subjectivization' (Salecl, 1993); 'excitement' (O'Malley and Mugford, 1994); and alternative lifestyles of the informal economy (Henry, 1978; 1987c). These are offered in addressing the question, 'Why are people who were not determined to commit a crime one moment determined to do so the next?' (Katz, 1988: 4).

Crime, then, is not caused by things, events, or factors but is an immanent part of discursive processes; subjects, then, construct differences out of the proliferation of dispersion and act toward that which they construct as though it was something other than their own construction. These are dialectical processes that episodically allow people to believe that they are somehow free from their relations with others; these are, as Nietzsche has informed us, 'semiotic fictions' that sustain that which is not.[33] They are processes that allow people to believe that they can be independent individuals in so far as that means insulation from others.[34] They are processes in which others are allowed to be known only through the ultimate denial of their human selves, the stereotypical categories of classification and summary representation.

What 'causes' the crime in any of these cases is the ideology and invocation of discursive practices that divide human relations into categories, that divide responsibility for others and to others into hierarchy and authority relations, and that render some subject positions vulnerable to excessive investment by others. Such a process is the most lethal devised by humanity. At once, it both commands action toward goals, themselves seemingly harmless, and limits the human subject's responsibility to others, now classified as one or other lesser, disposable category, summarized as 'not my business'. The German atrocities against the Jews; the Bosnian Serbs' ethnic cleansing of Bosnian Muslims; the CIA's activities in murdering 'undesirable' members of foreign governments and in organizing clandestine operations directed toward the overthrow of 'undesirable' governments, as in the case of the post-1979 revolutionary Sandinista Nicaraguan regime; the McCarthy attacks on free speech; the governmental attacks against the unionization movement in the early part of this century; the American My Lai massacre; from Watergate to Iran-Contra, from car hijacking to serial murder to the emerging open forms of 'ethnic intimidation crimes', and from drug dealing to domestic violence: all are moments of spontaneous developments in the fabric of the constitutive dialectical discursive process that allows individuals to fuse observations of difference with evaluations of worth, structured by a power hierarchy that manifests the denial of others as human beings and facilitates a policy of investment in social reality. Were this not so, were people imbued with a sense of connectedness to others, were the silence on 'individual freedom' rather than on intersubjectivity, there would be considerably less likelihood of the power play that is crime.

Summary and conclusions

In sum, these suggestions, along with the notion of a revised structural coupling and autopoiesis thesis, provide the basis of our constitutive dialectic approach. Specifically, they are further operationalizations of what we refer to as constitutive interrelational or COREL sets. Harms of reduction and repression are often the outcomes of some of these semi-autonomous developments. Transpraxis, as we will argue in Chapter 8, has much to do with how alternative signifiers can develop that better reflect these complexities and liberate us from the mystification of master discourses which all too often disguise harms of reduction and repression.

Notes

1 Theories that focus on essentialist metaphysics, such as early feminist analyses, are apt to linearly trace the 'causes' of harm to an ostensibly established foundational position.

2 This pattern of action over time is much like that typified by the strange attractor of chaos theory that we discussed in earlier chapters.

3 See also Ferman et al. (1987), Cantor et al. (1992), and Ferman et al. (1993).

4 Henry (1983) found a similar divergence between the discourse of organizational policy on employee discipline and the multiple discourses of informal discipline, which are differently invoked depending upon their relevance for the context and the particular stage of any disciplinary procedure.

5 This might seem little different to the interactionist and ethnomethodological critiques of positivist method (see Phillipson, 1971; Filmer et al., 1972), which claimed that qualitative methods were able to give a more accurate account. However, the postmodernist position is that neither methodology is adequate, since each invests in the idea of an achievable truth based on the researcher getting closer to reality.

6 See Coleman (1985: 195–8), Bromberg (1965), Blum (1972), Box (1983: 37–43), and Frank and Lynch (1992: 101–2, 119).

7 See, for example, Metz (1981), Silverman (1982), and on the news media Surette (1992), and especially Barak's (1988; 1994) 'newsmaking criminology'.

8 This is partly based on abbreviation and partly on the play of allegory to Coral. Although we do not want to extend this allegory too far, coral reefs require a solid foundational environment on which is constituted a growing indeterminate mass from the cast-off skeletal secretions of numerous individual marine animals. It is characterized by an infinite variety of shapes and sizes formed as much by absence as presence, and is populated by the color and vibrancy of the living as well as the dead. However, what is not represented in the analogy is the dynamic interpenetration and mutually constituting process that is the constitutive interrelational set.

9 For Foucault this was the beginning of the normalizing sciences, that theoretical point at which capital logic is concentrated. It is the interpellation point in Althusser and the position of the agent in the discourse of the master as in Lacan.

10 See also Fitzpatrick (1984) and Collins (1993).

11 See also Collins (1993) who shows the parallel and interlocking systems of race gender and class oppression, as does Fitzpatrick (1992) who sees these in the embodied myth that is Western law.

12 See also Harrington (1988). For an application of this dialectical analysis to the relations between formal and informal economies see Henry (1987c; 1988).

13 In more mathematical formulation, the state of the system at any time is a function of state vector z_t, which represents 'a cross-sectional or synchronic profile' at time t, plus environmental vector u_t, which represents the specific constellation or parameters involved. Thus, in order to test the relationship between commitment (x_t, y_t) and environment (u_x, u_y) in investigating corporate crime (embezzlement) we might designate each of the factors: x_t = non-shareable financial problem, behavioral commitment, that is a measurement of an act; y_t = non-shareable financial problem, attitudinal commitment, that is a measurement of belief; u_x = opportunities to commit embezzlement; u_y = availability of rationalizations for embezzlement. Then, by an isomorphism (i.e. analogy, homology: see also Loye and Eisler, 1987: 59; Smith, 1995: 35), we can draw from hypothetical polynomials which are deterministic in that they represent the 'law(s)' of transformation (e.g. 'cause') from one state to another over time. Polynomials are simply expressions containing several variables with one or more raised to some power; they are quadratic equations (e.g. x^2). Consider the polynomial (presented below) by Gregersen and Sailer (1993). Their example is of the relationship between commitment (behavioral, attitudinal) and environment (co-worker relationships, formal reward system). The first is presented in complex numbers, the second as a conversion into real numbers. Complex numbers are increasingly used in quantum theory, in complex statistical analysis, in aircraft

wing design, and in electronic circuits. They come in the form of an imaginary part, the square root of −1, and a real part. Any quadratic equation is also non-linear. See also Lacan's use of the square root of −1 in his discussion of the relationship between a signifier and a signified: it represents a 'lack' (S, a signifier = the square root of −1) (1977: 316–17, 318–20). As he tells it, the square root of −1 symbolizes a 'signifier of the lack' and, as symbol i in complex number theory, 'is obviously justified only because it makes no claim to any automatism in its later use' (1977: 318–19). It represents the 'place of *jouissance*' (1977: 320). In a phallocentric symbolic order, the unifying principle, the law of the father, is the phallus representing not the biological organ, but power, potency, the signifier of ecstasy. As Clement points out, 'Since it is the signifier of a lack, the phallus is analogous in form to the square root of −1, the primordial imaginary number and generator of the whole field of complex numbers . . . [it] is literally indescribable . . . without this generic signifier of negativity, however, no other signifier would exist. It is from this that the phallus derives its generative power' (1983: 180).

The addition, subtraction and multiplication of complex numbers is done as with real numbers. They can also be represented on an x, y coordinate grid, but now it is called a complex plane. Chaos theory has made heavy use of complex numbers in its investigations of phenomena. Gregersen and Sailer's polynomial in the case of embezzlement is represented in complex numbers by $z_{t+1} = z_t^2 - u$, where $t = 0, . . .$, infinity; or in real numbers by $x_{t+1} = x_t^2 - y_t^2 - u_x$; and $y_t + 1 = 2x_t y_t - u_y$, where $t = 0, . . .$, infinity.

Consider Freire's and Lacan's transformational notions of how new master signifiers are generated, respectively through a dialogical pedagogy and by way of the discourse of the analyst – with our qualification, hysteric/analyst – and particularly how they take form with an alternative, more genuine embodiment of desire not in a linear way but in an indeterminable, transcendental way. Gregersen and Sailer point out that this is the 'fanciful part' of their suggested crossover into the social sciences. For example, raising to some power represents some operation or transformation, and when it is used as the basis of further computation it is an iterative function.

14 Many, like Lacan, have used topological constructions, for example to indicate how the twist in a Möbius band represents a distinct operation: an appearing signifier traveling on the band will reappear in inverted form, indicating the signified, but with further movement on the band will be transformed into the signifier (see Milovanovic, 1994c) with a trace (Derrida) of a past impression. This, then, can be perceived as an iterative pathway and operation. Thus the qualitative math of topology perceives transformations and operations as changes in the form, and it can be pictured rather than presented in mathematical form.

15 Consider Whorf's (1956) classic study on linguistic relativity by comparing the Hopi Indian with the standard average European language. He shows that the former was more consistent with quantum mechanics dynamics, but the latter with Newtonian mechanics. See also Capra's (1988) classic study about the parallels between quantum mechanics and Eastern mysticism. See, too, physicist Bohm's (1980) analysis of language and its insufficiency to capture complex, dynamic events, and Peat (1988: 277–80) who tells us that the social/natural science dichotomy is further problematic when one considers isomorphism operates both ways. When Albert Einstein was developing the theory of relativity he was reading philosophers such as Kant, Mach, and Hume (1988: 335). Heisenberg, the developer of the uncertainty principle, was encouraged by Pauli to think more philosophically in developing his theory (1988: 335).

16 See note 13 for an explanation. Also in this context consider other applications: police brutality and neighborhood; juvenile and 'criminogenic environment'; juvenile and 'broken home'; corporate crime and economic environment; Vietnam infantryman and 'free-fire' zone; hysteric and 'invitational edge'; etc.

17 Consider each factor as x, y, z, etc. By computing we could show that two managers, z_1 and z_2, with similar commitments, opportunities and rationalizations for embezzlement, do in fact commit embezzlement, but yet a third, z_3, does not, even though this person is in a similar state and environment ('all else constant').

18 Generally, in path analysis we see a two-dimensional diagram depicting a series of lines (causal arrows) converging on the dependent variable, crime (Figure 7.1a). Each variable is marked by its quantitative contribution (explained variance or R^2), ostensibly leading to the

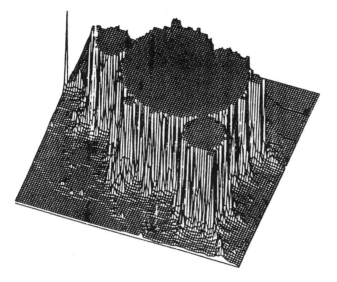

Figure 7.5   *Mandelbrot (three-dimensional) phase map (software provided by Wegner and Tyler, 1993)*

manifestation of the dependent variable. Hence, the goal is to identify the many independent variables and their specific contributions to crime. Empiricists claim that after identifying two or three variables, the contributions of others are somewhat negligible. Positivists often 'hold constant' (stasis) certain variables to see the effects of others. Path analysis, at best, can specify 'limit attractors' which depict static manifestations. For example, limit attractors indicate a circumscribed outcome basin, as in the example of the criminal identity attributed as a master status or role-taking behavior.

19 Computer graphics have been crucial in the development of alternative mapping. Three-dimensional representations could also be provided as portraying stability plots as iteration proceeds (see especially, Pickover, 1988: 147). In these diagrams, the vertical axis represents the number of iterations, and the horizontal represents the complex plane. Thus Figure 7.2 in two dimensions is equivalent to Figure 7.5 in three dimensions.

20 One can progress from a particular iterative polynomial, to a meta-model, to two-dimensional portrayals as in the Mandelbrot set, Figure 7.2, to three-dimensional portrayals as in Figure 7.5.

21 Consider again Lacan's (1977) topological portrayal of the movement of the signifier and its transformation into a signified by the use of the Möbius band. Here the signifier returns in inverted form as an answer posed to a question asked (see also his graphs of desire; Milovanovic, 1992a; 1994c). Here the squiggles could be seen analogously as the twist in the Möbius band. In a more expanded version, Lacan has offered the cross-cap, a projective geometrical figure composed of Möbius bands that come to find their twisting point at a singularity, which for him represents the locus of what holds the psychic apparatus together in a consistent manner (see Milovanovic, 1994c). Topology theory, then, sees each of these operations as having an influence.

22 See, for example, his use of the algorithms for metaphor and metonymy (Lacan, 1977; Milovanovic, 1992a).

23 For example, consider Braithwaite's forms of social control, or the availability of crisis intervention centers.

24 A laser beam shone at a particular part of a photographic plate produces a reflection that reproduces the whole, all at once.

25 For examples applied to adolescent crime see Schwendinger and Schwendinger (1985: 133). For examples of occupational and organizational behavior see Jackall (1988: 6, 134).

26 Recall that the strange attractor is the tendency for complex phenomena to move toward a constituted area, a phase space reflecting global stability and local indeterminacy, pictorially considered as two butterfly wings.

27 In an organizational context consider Jackall's manager's 'dexterity with symbols' (1988: 6, 134–61).

28 See also Freire (1985), Giroux (1992), JanMohamed (1993), McLaren (1994), and Giroux and McLaren (1994).

29 Cressey (1953), Jackall (1988: 134–61), Coleman (1985: 206–12), Poveda (1994: 89–90), and Ermann and Lundman (1992).

30 Again, see Schwendinger and Schwendinger (1985) who indicate that the juvenile finds her/himself at the intersections of various rhetorics. See also Jackall (1988: 134–61).

31 Take for example, Freud's (1965) analysis of 'dream work'; Metz's (1981) work on cinema imageries invoked; or the manipulative practices of the advertisement industries described in Silverman (1983) and Williamson (1987).

32 See also Milovanovic's (1993b) point concerning how the Borromean knot can give tentative stability to sense production in law.

33 Consider some of the discursive obfuscation used in organization contexts (Jackall, 1988: 135), as in Table 7.1.

34 For a lucid examination in the context of juvenile delinquency, where the difference between an 'egoistic' and an 'instrumental' rhetoric is specified as a determinant for delinquent behavior in street contexts, see Schwendinger and Schwendinger (1985).

Table 7.1

Stock phrase	Probable intended meaning
Exceptionally well qualified	Has committed no major blunders to date
Tactful in dealing with superiors	Knows when to keep his mouth shut
Quick thinking	Offers plausible excuses
Meticulous attention to detail	A nitpicker
Slightly below average	Stupid
Unusually loyal	Wanted by no one else
Indifferent to instruction	Knows more than his superior
Strong adherence to principles	Stubborn
Requires work-value attitudinal readjustment	Lazy and hardheaded

8

The Justice Policy of Constitutive Criminology: Reconstruction through Replacement Discourse(s)

In this chapter we engage policy. Several commentators have been highly critical of skeptical postmodernism's abdication of responsibility for what to do about crime. Cohen has vigorously argued that skeptical postmodernism is 'so bizarre and irrelevant to a subject like criminology' because it offers 'no moral, political, practical or policy lines' and is 'little more than an impotent gesture of defiance'. As a result, he says, it becomes 'impossible to defend this version of "skeptical theory"' (1990: 23–4). Similarly, Schwartz and Friedrichs (1994: 227–8) criticize extreme versions of postmodernism for trivializing violence and victim experiences. Skeptical postmodernists, they argue, play irrelevant games with words that result in impenetrable, inaccessible prose – an outcome only possible because of their insulation from the real world in intellectual ghettos. Indeed, they proclaim:

> The more extreme version of postmodernism questions the possibility of changing society; it compels us to consider whether commonplace calls for reform . . . are a self-indulgent fantasy and illusion, and largely meaningless . . . At most it offers a basis for exposing possible pretenses and illusions in the pursuit of a just policy. (1994: 237)

However, as in our direct engagement with the definition of crime and criminals, we shall attempt to be quite explicit about our affirmative postmodernist stance on justice policy. Our position is based on the premises built in the previous chapters of this book.

By now it should be abundantly clear that we endorse the skeptical postmodernist criticism that criminology exaggerates its claims to truth, and is without superior logic. We are especially troubled by modernism's essentialism, its pretentious elitism and, not least, the unforgiving violence of its privileging practices.[1] However, an important issue that distinguishes us from skeptical postmodernism is the relationship between discursive constructions of reality and social action. We are concerned about what people do with what they discursively produce, about how they produce it, how they are shaped in the productive process as well as how they can change it (Freire, 1972; 1973; 1985; Giroux, 1992). We disagree with those skeptical postmodernists who argue that both discursive productions and people's actions toward images of constructed realities are meaningless. We argue, instead, that the human subject's orientation to action, based on a belief in the probability of outcomes concerning constructed realities, is a central problematic. In this regard we are more in agreement with Borgmann's (1992) concept of 'postmodernist realism', than with skeptical postmodernism's nihilism.[2] Borgmann argues that the problems confronting 'hypermodernism' (which includes the expansion and consumption of crime) cannot be met through prohibitions and control 'but through a genuine alternative':

> It is an orientation that accepts the lessons of the postmodernist critique and resolves the ambiguities of the postmodern condition in an attitude of patient vigor for a common order centered on communal celebrations. What can invigorate the attitude and provide a center for celebration is reality . . . A text by itself is helpless; to require help is its virtue . . . Postmodern realism is to comprehend modernism and hypermodernism through a schematic account, thus providing a clearing where reality can come to be present in a narrative recounting. (1992: 116–17, 129)

Thus, we find ourselves desiring to displace harmful discourse and its constructions with replacement discourses and their alternative constructions; in social theory, to stand Durkheim's famous injunction to 'treat social facts as things' on its head. We would replace his methodological stance with a deconstructionist invitation to 'treat social facts as fiction'; but *simultaneously*, to invest energy in diverting those who act toward fictions-as-things from imposing their constructed realities on others, and toward reconstructing more helpful relations with fellow subjects. Therein lies the substance of our policy position. It relates back to Chapter 2 where we established the 'recovering subject' as a contingent, revisable and emergent but never recovered. It relates to Chapter 3, where we entertained this subject in a discursively constituted, mass mediated, 'virtual society'. Our recovering subject has to contend with others who construct gargantuan programs of law, order and control in their empty hope that such bluff will bar the harms of reduction and repression. Meanwhile, others are just as adamantly investing in the reality of crime construction. In our view, this investment, and the harms that are its profit, can only be prevented in the long term by developing replacement discourses that allow a reflexive, recursive reconstruction of less harmful discursive forms.

We categorically reject the nihilistic position of postmodernism that leaves us uncontrollably dangling to the fate of discursive ordering. Our view is that, just because new discursive orders are always in process, and are forever incomplete, does not mean that influence cannot be exerted on their emergent forms. But influence can never be control. To know this is the wisdom of the recovering subject; to imagine there is an end, an arrival, a recovery, is the subject's delusional folly. However, we believe that there is a difference that can be made to the process of producing a more helpful reconstructed subject-social order, one whose emerging product is configured less like the old: that is, more new-new than new-old. We believe that part of arriving at such a new order involves dealing with invested realities, especially those constituting crime as a daily event. Thus we do not endorse a Foucauldian anarchy of resistances as the *only* response. Instead, we believe that the vibrant tone of our policy for replacement discourse is to develop disarming social processes that protect against 'excessive investors' in the reality of crime.[3] Herein lie the practices of 'social judo', a metaphor for law and crime control (Einstadter and Henry, 1995; Henry and Milovanovic, 1993).

In short, constitutive criminology meets policy square on, with a four-part plan: (1) long- and medium-term prevention policy based on the concept of replacement discourse, implemented through local-to-global intervention programs and strategies designed to provide the emerging and recovering subject with an alternative discursive resource base for reflexive, celebrative and expansive transpraxis; (2) short-term refraction, based on the concept of 'social judo', implemented by practice strategies designed to resist and redirect the constitutive energy of the excessive investor; (3) short-term relief for the constituted victim through practical strategies designed to integrate the recovering subject into a relationally oriented community network of fellow subjects; and (4) superliberalism as a synoptic practical political philosophy whose virtuality is recursively generated to maximize diversity and minimize hegemony. Before spelling out these policy implications and accompanying practice strategies we shall take a final brief glance back at modernism, this time at the policy positions implicated by its differing theories of causality. We will first discuss general modernist philosophies of intervention, often referred to as 'philosophies of punishment' or more broadly as 'correctional ideologies'. We will also be concerned with their implied models of justice and preferred strategies of implementation (crime control techniques).[4] Then we turn to postmodernist approaches on penality, specifically Foucault's contribution and Howe's critique. Finally, we present a full consideration of our policy of replacement discourse. In the concluding chapter we shall look at the implementation of this policy through various practice strategies.

Modernist theorizing

Ultimately, modernist criminology is concerned with policies for crime prevention, reduction and control, together with methods and strategies whereby these objectives might be met. In other words, it is based on the modernist belief that people can control each other (Schwartz and Friedrichs, 1994: 223) – precisely the same notion held by those who harm others! Reacting violently to violence, as is the case in the 'criminal justice system', only increases the overall level of violence, and sanctions its use in the name of the state. It might be appropriate to first clarify what we mean by criminal justice policy since this idea is prone to numerous and varied interpretations.

In the modernist vision, policy refers to a course of action deliberately adopted or intended (Harrison, 1964: 509). But there is ambiguity. *Criminal justice policy* may indicate the existence of a considered intention, plan or program but also it may refer to a course of action where a planned program does not exist. Here it describes what practitioners of criminal justice do or did. Further, the concept refers to a series of policies and practices rather than one policy. As a result of this kind of different reading of 'policy', we shall first describe what we believe existing criminal justice policy does in contributing to the constitution of crime, and go on to state what we believe it should do consistent with our constitutive theoretical approach.

Einstadter and Henry define criminal justice policy as

> the overall prescription for addressing law violation that follows logically from a theory's causal analysis of the crime problem. Such policy includes (1) a correctional ideology . . . that incorporates, (a) philosophies that justify the use of state power against offenders . . . and (b) strategies for action to be taken in relation to the offender, which may or may not include the victims, the community, social institutions, and the state itself; (2) an administrative apparatus, the criminal justice system, for processing offenders; and (3) actions, in the form of crime control techniques (e.g. punishment, treatment, reorganization of institutions) to be applied, in conformity with the rules of the administrative system, to satisfy the goals of the philosophies and strategies previously specified. (1995: 18–19)

As with our earlier review of modernism, different modernist positions offer different orientations to policy. This is found particularly in the ideologies used to justify state intervention. A useful analytical starting point for considering the range of these ideologies/policies is Black's (1976) 'styles of social control'. Black identifies the penal, compensatory, therapeutic and conciliatory styles, saying that the first two are accusatory in nature, while the last two are remedial and are designed to help and ameliorate. Einstadter and Henry (1995: 4) use Black's framework as a basis to consider four correctional ideologies (which incorporate philosophies of intervention), to which they add a fifth, 'philosophy of social change'. They also argue that Black fails to address 'the structural level of intervention' (1995: 4). We can see this schema more clearly if, in addition to the distinction between accusatory and remedial (on a vertical plane), we distinguish among three levels of state intervention on a horizontal plane: (1) individual (agent); (2) social-relational (community); and (3) social structure (society).[5] Combining these dimensions gives us six broad ideal-typical categories which, for our present purposes, we shall refer to broadly as 'policies' (see Table 8.1).[6] Let us briefly outline each of these in turn.

First, at the individual level there are *punitive accusatory* policies (Black's penal style) that include punishment, retribution, incapacitation and deterrence. Here 'offenders are harmed or deprived by the state with the aim of preventing them or others from committing future offenses'. We also have *therapeutic remedial* policies (Black's therapeutic style), 'such as treatment, and rehabilitation, where offenders are forced or helped to refrain from future offending' (Einstadter and Henry, 1995: 4). In spite of

Table 8.1 *Types of criminal justice policy*

	Level of intervention		
	Agent (individual)	Social-relational (community)	Structural (society)
Accusatory	Punitive	Compensatory	Radical
Remedial	Therapeutic	Conciliatory	Reformist

their differences, both of these approaches are oriented to the individual level of intervention.

Second, at the social-relational level (community) there are *compensatory accusatory* policies (Black's compensatory style) that include interventions such as 'restitution and reparation, where the offenders are forced to make amends for their past offenses'; and *conciliatory remedial* policies (Black's conciliatory style), where interventions are more facilitative than coercive, and include 'mediation, where offenders and victims are encouraged to resolve their disputes' (1995: 4). Both of these approaches are concerned with the relations between victim and offender, with a view to returning (albeit narrow) interpretations of their standing to its level prior to the offence.

Third, at the structural level (society), we have policies of social change that are based on the idea that 'crime and deviance are . . . indicators of structural, societal or community pathology which requires social and organizational change' (1995: 4). Within this framework there is first the *radical accusatory* policy, where the society as a whole is held at fault for individual subjects' actions. Therefore, the society as a whole is seen as in need of radical transformation. Second, there is *reformist remedial* policy, where the society is seen as pathological but can be engineered by organizational and institutional adjustment aimed at reducing the causes of crime.

As should now be apparent, the various modernist theories we have examined throughout this book have differential affiliations with these policies. Table 8.2 shows broadly how these can be specified. Clearly, we have not the space to examine each of these in depth, and this has been done in reviews of modernist theory (Einstadter and Henry, 1995). Moreover, while for a modernist such meta-classification and its analytical clarity may be helpful, from a postmodernist perspective making distinctions between these different policies is artificial and misleading. For postmodernists, the practice of policy is born both in its proclamation and in the investment of energy to confirm the 'reality' of its belief. But what is done to offenders or social organization *in the name* of policy ranges far wider than that claimed for it at any historical moment.

Suppose we probe incapacitation (or containment) and its preferred intervention practice of prison, as one example of how criminal justice policies are manifested. The penal policy goal of incapacitation is to take

Table 8.2 *Modernist theory, criminal justice policy and control practice*

Theory	Criminal justice policy: Philosophies of intervention
Conservative	**Accusatory punitive** *Incapacitation* Protection of the public by removing the offender's capability of committing further crimes *General deterrence* Symbolic use of public punishment aimed at affecting the future actions of all potential offenders *Retribution* Unlimited punishment in return for harms caused
Classical	**Accusatory punitive** *Just deserts* Punishment deserved for offenses based solely on the harm caused by the act, thus equating the balance of harm *Individual deterrence* Preventing crime specifically by affecting the future behavior of particular individuals who have already offended
Economic, situational and rational choice theories	**Remedial reformist** *Displacement prevention* Encouraging legitimate activity as a preferable choice *Target hardening* Redesigning the environment to increase the cost and perception of rewards from crime targets
Biological theories Personality theories	**Remedial therapeutic** *Treatment* Interventions designed to cure an individual of the cause of their offending *Rehabilitation* Interventions designed to change or correct the offender's future behavior
Social ecology theories Strain theories	**Remedial reformist** *Social justice* Improve the social system and institutional arrangements to minimize injustices and discrimination in society **Remedial conciliatory** *Integration* Improve the adaptation of misfits to society through supportive social programs

Justice model	Features of court	Level of intervention	Preferred intervention practices and control techniques
Crime control	Disregard of legal controls Implicit presumption of guilt High conviction rate Unpleasant experience Support for police, prosecution	Individual Community	Death, prison, fines, corporal punishment, 'short sharp shock' Boot camp, 'scared straight' programs
Due process	Equality before law Rules protecting defendant against error Restraint of arbitrary power Presumption of innocence Celerity Proportional punishment Support for the defence	Individual	Prison, fines
Due process	Equality between parties Rules protecting defendant against error Restraint of arbitrary power Presumption of innocence Support for the community, family, legitimate work	Individual Community Environment	Job creation programs, job training, improved security systems, improved visible law enforcement, environmental design, defensible space, improved effectiveness of criminal justice
Medical	Information collecting Individualization Treatment presumption Discretionary Expert advisers Support for science, expert witness, psychiatrist	Internal biology Family Environment	Neural surgery, drug treatment, genetic counseling, nutrition, hormone balance Family therapy, psychotherapy/analysis, cognitive retraining, individual and group therapy
Social pathology	Information collecting Collective situation Rehabilitation presumption Discretionary Expert advisers Support for social work, probation	Peers or subculture School Work Culture Community Society	Educational opportunity programs such as 'Head Start', 'War on Poverty' programs, employment programs, job training programs, community crime prevention/empowerment such as Chicago Area Project, improved vallues, community involvement programs, probation

Continued overleaf

Table 8.2 *(cont.)*

Theory	Criminal justice policy: Philosophies of intervention
Learning and social control theories	**Remedial conciliatory** *Conciliation* Resolving the conflict or dispute between offender and offended **Remedial reformist** *Displacement prevention* Encouraging legitimate activity as a preferable choice (in this case by developing a relational stake in conformity)
Labeling, social constructionist and conflict theories	**Remedial conciliatory** *Conciliation* Resolving the conflict or dispute between offender and offended *Diversion* Providing alternatives to criminal justice system effects to avoid stigmatizing the offender **Accusatory compensatory** *Restitution* Returning the situation to its pre-offense standing with regard to individual victims *Reparation* Compensation for the offense to be paid to the state or community for the harm caused to collective victims **Remedial reformist** *Decriminalization* Removing offenses from the criminal code
Marxist theories Critical feminist theories (radical, socialist, Marxist)	**Accusatory radical** *Celebration* Using the occasion of crime as an indication of the need for social, institutional or structural change *Revolution* Using the occasion of crime as evidence of the flawed nature of the existing social system and the need for its replacement

Justice model	Features of court	Level of intervention	Preferred intervention practices and control techniques
Bureaucratic	Independence from political considerations Speed and efficiency Acceptance of records Minimization of conflict Minimization of expense Economical division of labor Support for court officials	Family School Community	Improved socialization by family, family therapy, group and individual therapy, behavior modification, reinforcement of community involvement, youth programs, increased involvement in school activities, intensive activity to improve self-control abilities, reduce youth work which conflicts with school/home
Status passage	Public shaming of defendant Priority for community values Agents' control over the process Support for community	Social control agents Criminal justice system	Reduce social reaction to minor offenses, diversion from formal criminal justice system, decriminalization of minor offenses, crimes without victims, status offenses
Power	Reinforces class values Alienation and suppression of defendant Deflection from class conflict Differences between judges and judged Contradictions between rhetoric and performance Support for judge and powerful	Society Inequality Patriarchy	Change structure of society to eliminate inequality, power hierarchies, abandon individualistic treatment and rehabilitation programs

Source: Adapted from Einstadter and Henry, 1995; Empey, 1982; King, 1981; and Young, 1981

offenders 'out of circulation' so that they cannot commit further harms on others. It is based on the assumption that a disproportionate amount of crime is committed by a relatively small number of offenders (Wolfgang et al., 1972).[7] Incapacitation policy asserts that by putting these people 'in prison' they are stopped from practicing criminal behaviors, with the result that the 'outside world' is correspondingly safer, albeit temporarily. From a postmodernist perspective this policy is both misleading and reifying. It falsely separates what goes on internally, within prison, from what goes on externally, in the 'real world'. It further implies a separation of prison from what goes on 'on the outside', in society. Indeed, we argue that being in prison is also being in society, since prison is physically, socio-structurally and symbolically integral to our experience. There are no impermeable 'walls of imprisonment', rather there is continuity between 'in' and 'out'. There are several ways that this can be demonstrated.

First, the incarcerated are not incapacitated since they can commit more and worse harms in their new architectural spaces.[8] These new architectural spaces are a reifying medium for the generation of reactive behavior and for the amplification of previously constituted articulations of excessive investors' street or suite power. Second, those kept in prison are not just doing worse harm to each other, but they are doing it to those 'in corrections', who as human subjects come to construct themselves in self- and species-deprecating ways.[9] Prison officers are corrupted in their stressed lives to escape *their* imprisonment through a conspiratorial dance with the inmate which both mocks us and oppresses themselves. Third, incapacitation means that material costs have to be shifted from other areas of government expenditure to corrections (prisons instead of, for example, education). We pay the economical cost of prison programs instead of the economical cost of property crime. Fourth, the prison expansion is accompanied not by increased feelings of security but by increased fear of crime, with the irony that the 'outside society' is increasingly appearing like an imprisoned society, as it arms itself against crime through such means as increased surveillance, bars, alarms, personal protection devices, guns, and video cameras in the stores and in the streets, in homes and in schools, offices and factories (Marx, 1988; Einstadter, 1992; Einstadter and Henry, 1991). Fifth, the incapacitation notion has its dialectical enabling in the false security of social order and the 'safer with them behind bars' perception. But the paradox is that, for each constitutive brick of incapacitation, we release another swirl of freedom for those 'accident makers' (Bhopal), 'liberators' (Iran–Contra), 'job creators' (GM's Jeffery Smith) and 'risk takers' (Boesky, Milken, Leeson). How then does incapacitation make for a safer society? All it does is make for the illusion, the Great Fiction, of a safer society. It gathers and concentrates the site for the production of harm, but does little to reduce harm; rather, it adds its own harm.

A similar analysis can be applied to each of the other criminal justice policies. Let us take two other much debated examples: just deserts and treatment or rehabilitation. Just deserts is the philosophy claiming that harms of reduction or deprivation, committed by an offender on another, justify the state exacting similar harms on the offender based upon the seriousness of their crime. For example, violence is responded to with violence, murder with death: 'To say someone "deserves" to be rewarded or punished is to refer to his [her] past conduct and assert that its merit or demerit is the reason for according him [her] pleasant or unpleasant treatment' (Von Hirsch, 1976: 15–16). From a postmodernist position, this age-old retributive concept uses one harm as the legitimate grounds for committing further harm. It is not about reducing harm, but about increasing it. The issue is typically presented as: 'If someone has killed others, they deserve to forfeit their life.' Arguments about who started the harm, and who is responding to whose harm, submit to an endless cycle of resentment and outrage as each discursively constituted subject or social agent seeks to reduce, repress or destroy the other for the harm that has been done to them. Put simply, just deserts is a policy of counter-harm (crime), that recursively reproduces and invigorates harms of reduction and repression rather than replacing them with less harmful forms. Instead of reconstituting the discursive construction of harm production, individual renditions are excised (capital punishment) in the mistaken belief that somehow this makes a difference. The difference it makes is to who is harmed next (displacement effect), not whether people are harmed at all. If we also consider recidivism rates, just deserts adds to the overall amount of harm inflicted in society.

On the surface it would appear that a rehabilitation/treatment philosophy fares better. It justifies interventions designed to change or 'cure' an individual of the cause or circumstances that lead them to commit harm, on the assumption that future harms will be prevented. While the prevention of harm implied by this policy seems preferable to inflicting further harm (in that it claims to reduce harm), several commentators have pointed out that the treatment can be more punitive and more unjust than the punishment.[10] More importantly, failure to recognize the discursive production of harmful acts results in an individual focus that neglects the social construction of humans as subjects. The process is similar to drug or alcohol detoxification, which provides temporary relief from intoxification, but which fails to deal with the relational and contextual issues surrounding the abusing subject. Unless the discursive context is reconfigured, the probability exists that the same processes producing alcohol abusing behavior, and its accompanying perceptions of reality (questions of self-esteem and so on), will be reproduced in the wider culture, as will the same abusing behavior. Similarly, with the production of harm to others. Unless discursive constructions of harm and their accompanying social-relational matrixes are replaced with discourses committed to producing less harm, there are no grounds for imagining that rehabilitation will be anything more than a temporary displacement.

A similar analysis can be made of each of the other modernist policy approaches, since what each contributes in its isolation from the others is a relatively insignificant impact on total discursive production. Moreover, imagining that each policy is somehow not only different but separate from the society from which it is distilled, is part of the problem: i.e. modernism's non-relational approach to criminal justice policy that fragments human subjects into human objects. As Harris has said:

> We need to struggle against the tendency toward objectification, of talking and thinking about crime and criminals as if they were distinct entities . . . We also need to reject the idea that those who cause injury or harm to others should suffer severance of the common bonds of respect and concern that bind members of a community. We should relinquish the notion that it is acceptable to try to 'get rid of' another person, whether through execution, banishment, or caging away people about whom we do not care. We should no longer pretend that conflicts can be resolved by the pounding of a gavel or the locking of a cell door. (1991: 93)

However, it is not just criminal justice policy makers and practitioners in conjunction with the offending subject that impart significant energy to this process. The analytical discourse of criminologists and penologists makes a contribution through the kind of ideal-typical classification and abstraction presented above, and in tables and charts like Table 8.2.

Criminologists and the constitution of crime

Modernist criminologists' order-making discursive work invites us to make sense of a disarray of correctional practices and to 'explain' why disorder occurs. Adopting such schemas, one inadvertently connives at the constitutive work done by policy makers and penologists of a particular historical era. Conventional criminology fails to recognize that earlier models were themselves abstractions. It fails to analyze the process whereby invoking certain discourses constitutes the medium of debate and, through it, policy as a practice. Criminal justice policy makers and criminologists (critical and conventional) who research this literature can readily find themselves imprisoned within a particular discourse. They are disciplined by the pervasive nature of the dominating mode of discursive construction, inadvertently contributing to the grand production: the signification of crime. Part of the constitutive process, whereby criminologists and penologists confirm established realities, not only invokes existing forms of response, but also innovates discourse and constructs 'new' categories by making distinctions and drawing contrasts. Acting toward their constructions as though they were realities, criminologists research the effects of these categories on aspects of social organization. The 'scientific results' of these studies concretize and affirm the original reality. For example, one empirical debate within the discursive models mentioned above is founded on a distinction between 'what works' and, by implication, 'what does not'.[11] Neglected in these debates, however, is any consideration of the way that, for example, prison as an entity is being reconstituted by its liberal and radical critics. These commentators, instead of deconstructing the form, take its reality for granted and reassert its presence through their claims about different approaches to corrections.

Even the identification of distinctive styles of social control, or the separation of criminal justice policies based on the prevalence of a unique vocabulary, is suspect. This is because such typological distinctions portend an alternative truth claim without analyzing the constitution of reality that is its product. Further, they do not reintegrate the analyzed parts back to the whole.[12] In short, we argue that the conceptual and institutional apparatus of society appears to continuously stand above us, disciplining us in accord with political economy (Foucault, 1977), because of our elevation of it. This occurs through a continual process of active engagement and disengagement of our own subjectively constituted agency in a given historical era. These structural and institutional forms appear independent and real because of our submission to what we produce. This reificatory process is part of the constitutive work engaged in when human subjects objectify their social relations through discursive practices. Criminology and criminal justice policy provide some of the constitutive work that gives form, sustenance, and permanence to the subordination of human agency to its product. For example, debates over being in and out of prison, building more or fewer prisons, prison overcrowding and prison over-spending, alternatives to prison and challenges to defenders of prison, all essentialize *prison*. They neglect the continuous and reconstitutive nature of historically structured disciplinary discourse, whose building blocks we construct around our selves. Theorists, critical or otherwise, criminal justice policy makers and practitioners, as well as those harming others, co-produce a discourse that gives form and permanence to the very entity that they, and we, collectively despise. Therein we are all imprisoned. This is not linguistic determinism. We do not give priority to discourse. Rather, we argue that meaning is *both* pre-constituted by historically situated structural processes and shaped by human subjects in their recursive use of discourse in everyday interaction. It is our contention that the verbalized goals and policies at the manifest level of criminal justice policy are sustained by contradictory discursive practices which may support, oppose, and attempt to replace them.

Consider penal policy and the case of corrections, where the discursively structured routine of prison life and the meaning of being in prison must be understood in relation to various and frequently contradictory discursive practices. In turn, these discursive practices constitute the framework that shapes and conveys structures of meaning. But as concentrations of discursively structured meaning, prisons can only be adequately discussed in the context of other developments in a political economy. As Box (1987) has shown, being in prison is related not so much to the vagaries of the business cycle, or to unemployment *per se*, but to judges' *perceptions* of the threat of political and economic instability from the 'dangerous classes'. As others have demonstrated, being in prison also results from the direct effects of ideological politics such as the 'war on drugs' (Johns, 1992;

Tonry, 1995), or in the case of women and crime, from discontinuing the 'chivalry factor' (Simon, 1975). We argue, therefore, that the discursive practices whose invocation constitutes both penology and the reality of prison life are far from separate but are integrally related to our 'protected' lives. We are our own jailers, sentenced by our sentences, imprisoned by our words.

Omitted in most modernist analyses of criminal justice policy and practice is the way in which policy makers, practitioners, targeted agents, and theorists de-emphasize some aspects of constructed reality, as aberrant, unofficial, informal or untypical, in order to make claims about its formal operational identity.[13] For example, by distinguishing between formally espoused criminal justice policy goals and informal practices such as plea bargaining, discretion, prison discipline and oppositional cultural adaptations, criminologists add to the edifice that constitutes the crime business. Instead of showing how the recursive definition of these practices, as aberrations, sustains the reality that is criminal justice policy, and instead of showing how this, in turn, contributes to the reality of crime, modernists elaborate and intellectualize the discourse of harm. Omitted in modernist theorizing about criminal justice policy is the use made of a constitutive refining of diversity into patterns. This phenomenological twist leaves us making order out of disorder, which can even seduce us into beginning to construct models of these models of policy. As Baudrillard (1983a) might argue, to do so reifies the process to the extent that the hyperreality of criminal justice policy contained in such analytical schema feigns a reality in the actual operation of its institutions that is no more than a mirage of itself.[14]

Therefore, we see criminal justice policy as one among a number of reality-claiming discursive practices whose use forms part of the constitutive work that sustains the system as a reality. In order to examine constitutive work we rely on a theory of discursive production that focuses on the recursive development of relatively stable meaning constructions. In these are acknowledged the self-referential character of particular discourses and the existence of linguistic mechanisms that order disorder. So as to avoid engaging in such constitutive policy work while analyzing the manifestation of policy, we use a semiotic approach. This allows us to outline what an alternative direction might look like, one providing an opportunity for the development of new 'replacement discourses'. Our approach draws from poststructuralism, feminist postmodernism, semiotic analysis and some versions of modernism.

Transitions: semiotic analysis and criminal justice policy

From the perspective of semiotics, criminal justice policy can be conceptualized in terms of particular discourses. These discourses are meta-theories reflecting patterns of action that are seen as constitutive of a particular ideological orientation. Particular words, as signifiers, therefore, have denotative as well as connotative value. They do not reside in a neutral state awaiting instrumental use; rather, their use calls out a particular rendition of 'reality' (Whorf, 1956). Words also have a performative dimension. Once constructed they call out certain effects in the other while also being the basis of action by the producing subject (Milovanovic, 1994c: 106).[15] Deleuze and Guattari (1987), for example, see the function of words more in terms of their command quality, in the idea of 'order words' ('*mots d'ordre*') (1987: 79, 81, 107); Lacan, of course, has indicated to us that the 'discourse of the master' conveys certain meanings, an ideology embedded in signifiers. Human subjects, therefore, are located within certain bounded spheres of discursive practices, wherein can be found appropriate terminology, rationalizations, and justifications. Human subjects are not passive to this process. They invoke and recreate pre-existing discourse and they innovate, inventing new forms and new applications (Freire, 1972; 1973; 1985).

Modernist criminology discusses the importance of respective models of criminal justice policy, and draws distinctions between them. In contrast, a constitutive perspective suggests that we begin by suspending belief in the reality of those social constructions that are taken to underlie each model. It further suggests that the distinctions between them are no more than discursive devices. We start by suspending those claims that make distinctions between types of structure and their various discourses. Instead, we analyze the discursive practices as they are employed in debates that continue construction of the phenomenon subject to analysis.

By segmenting this process, criminologists have merely sustained a view that neglects the active work of agents-as-theorists in the production of criminality and corrections (Gilsinan, 1982). From a semiotics perspective, speech production invariably uncovers gaps – anomalies, contradictions, unexplainables – which generate a search for those objects that may overcome or explain them, be it in an illusory way (*objet petit* (a)). Here signifiers 'suture', or stitch over, the gaps to produce a coherent, complete picture of 'what happened'. Situating oneself within a particular discourse also places the speaker (interlocutor) within the purview of these readily available objects of desire. Therefore, one temporarily claims ownership of available (pre-constituted, 'filled-in') signifiers. It follows from this analysis that, by situating oneself within one linguistic coordinate system rather than another, one can produce different collages of 'what happened' as one is circumscribed in the selection process both paradigmatically and syntagmatically.[16] In our contribution, we present a view that situates agents as active and discursive contributors to their reality, who carry through their actions without regard to contradictory background relevancies.

In each area of institutional criminal justice, from law enforcement through corrections, images of reality are constructed to stand for 'what happened'. For example, Mastrofski and Parks have argued that in the police context, 'there is a well-established desire for people to construct empirical and moral meaning about their actions *ex post facto* to reduce disparity among cognition, action, and longstanding beliefs' (1990: 499). Moreover, they argue that police officers 'consider their actions beforehand and rationalize them afterward in ways that affect future actions' (1990: 477). Gilsinan's (1982) examination of police behavior describes how police attempt to constitutionally 'dress up' otherwise illegally obtained evidence or illegal practices for prosecutory purposes. A similar process has been recognized by legal realists and critical legal studies theorists in their examination of the *ex post facto* legal narrative constructions by judges. On a formal level, judges articulate their decisions in deductive logic, syllogistic reasoning, and coherent narrative form, belied, however, by an underlying decision based more on hunch, feel, temperament, or fleeting and transitory thoughts and stereotypes of the moment (Jackson, 1985; 1988; Milovanovic, 1994a). In the case of prisoner litigation, as Thomas (1988: 169) aptly states, 'the law often becomes a motive to justify a decision at least as much as it determines the decision.' While public as well as private rhetoric (discourse) used in constructing 'reality' may often be contradictory, we shall seek to expose the process whereby the distinction is used to sustain a sense of the orderliness of disorder.[17] Perhaps nowhere is this as well illustrated than in the postmodernist analysis of penality. It is here that the whole self-evident truth of penal policy was deconstructed by Foucault's 'historical' analysis which highlighted the role of discursive production in the constitution and control of human subjects.

From penology to penality: Foucault's contribution

Foucault's (1977) conception of the tripartite relationship among power, knowledge and the body, as interrelated facets of the totality of subjugation and domination (Garland, 1990; Howe, 1994), presents a major contrast to modernist conceptions of penology. Instead of accepting penal policy at face value as a shift from punishment to humanism, Foucault develops a conception of 'penality'. He sees this as the displacement of one form of domination, one punitive of the physical body, with another, corrective of the mind/soul. The new form of penality involved a political technology of the body. This change resulted not from a new sensibility to the humanistic benefits of reduced punishment, but from a desire to improve the effectiveness of strategies of power and the formulas for domination and control in rendering the population a mass of docile bodies (Howe, 1994: 91). Moreover, for Foucault, the central technology for rendering docility is discipline of the human subject. Thus penality refers to a certain type of discursive production of the human subject, one in which a discourse of surveillance displaced the exemplary penalty.

Discipline, for Foucault, is not repressive constraint so much as it is productive and constitutive of human subjects through its training and normalizing processes aimed at their transformation. As such it represents the very use of power that we earlier argued defined crime. Nor is discipline the property of particular institutions, though it may be more concentrated and visible in some than others. Rather, it is dispersed throughout the social body forming the 'disciplinary society'. Here it is 'capillary' in that it operates at the lowest extremities of the social body, and 'touches people's lives more fundamentally through their social practices than their beliefs' (Fraser, 1989: 18). Thus for Foucault, 'Discipline may be identified neither with an institution nor with an apparatus; it is a type of power, a modality for its exercise, comprising a whole set of instruments, techniques, procedures, levels of application, targets; it is a "physics" or an "anatomy" of power, a technology' (1977: 215). Moreover, it is through social sciences and its cluster of knowledges that the power of discipline is formalized and generalized toward intrusive invasions of the political and social body, as well as toward its constituted subjects, in the forms of correction, therapy, treatment, rehabilitation and cure. This particular form of logic can be pervasive through society. It is similar to the notion of 'recursive symmetries'; it is transmitted at 'coupling points'. In our notion of COREL sets it can be seen as one of the interpenetrating and constitutive influences, but cannot be seen as having linear effects.

Thus prison here is an epitome of the disciplinary society, the model for the synoptic gaze, and a way whereby the law-breaking of the powerful can be symbolically separated from the political opposition of the powerless whose protests are emasculated into pathologies of delinquency: prison is productive of the pathologized subject. Moreover, its reach extends beyond the justice system, the institutional site of discipline, through what has been called 'net widening' (Cohen, 1979) to discipline the whole society through a regime of unknowing surveillance which results in human subjects disciplining themselves. Prison then, for Foucault, is just one end of a disciplinary continuum which legitimizes the power to punish, to order, and to normalize the production of difference as knowledge by experts in the production of undecipherable discourse, whose purpose is the intrusive gaze on individual 'cases' enabling their continuous self-discipline (Fraser, 1989: 22–3), and through this, the continuous 'self-formation of the subject' through relationships of power (Foucault, 1988: 3; Howe, 1994: 103).

Although Foucault's thesis has become subject to an industry of critical commentary regarding its historical and empirical accuracy (see Garland, 1990; Howe, 1994), the central message of the use of discourse as power to configure the human subject, as discourse is itself in the process of self-constitution as a self-evident knowledge of truth, is one that resonates with the position that we take here. The self-admittedly 'fictional' nature of Foucault's own *dis*claim to truth, simultaneously recognizing the possibility 'for a fictional discourse to induce effects of truth' (Foucault, 1980: 193), is consistent with our analysis of the 'reality' of social structures and the investment of energy into control forms that define and defend them. The ultimate contingency of his position, that is recursively rewritten in further attempts to restart his breaching of self-evident truths, to us is less an attempt to escape criticism than it is the subject of Foucault's attempt to remain critically engaged, whose evidence of success is the Foucault effect. However, we agree with those critics who question Foucault's lack of attention to human agency (Merquior, 1985). Moreover, we also accept Howe's (1994) criticism that Foucault's work, in discursively constituting social forms as generic (albeit contingent), without recognizing their particular ordering, misses a considerable dimension of his subject. His view cannot account for the wherewithal of the revolutionary subject. Indeed, it is not that human subjects are constituted, but that gendered subjects are constituted. Failure to recognize this makes his work 'profoundly masculinist' (Howe, 1994: 114).

Foucauldian penality and the challenge of feminist postmodernism

Howe argues that the silence on gender in Foucault's penality resulted in a failure to acknowledge the discursive discipline that constitutes the female subject, and that has done so prior to, and without relation to, debates about shifting penality, in the civil society best captured in 'the family'. Thus is suggested a 'properly-constituted "social" analysis of penality' of the kind offered by Howe (1994: 116), in which not only is the constitution of the gendered subject at the forefront, but attention is paid to the emotive cultural sensibilities, passion, and 'urge to punish' (Garland, 1983; 1990). In contrast to Garland's legalistic confining of punishment, Howe (1994) insists this must also include the range of non-legal, implicit disciplinary controls that have so significantly harmed women the most. Indeed, she argues that in spite of Foucault's attempts at disrupting self-evident truths of the familiar, his work represents an abject 'failing to problematize the most familiar relationship of all, that of gender, thereby failing, from beginning to end, to breach the self evidence of the thoroughly masculinist paradigms which have imprisoned the theorisation of penality all along' (Howe, 1994: 120–1). Howe favorably cites Lees' (1989) study of the discourse of moral censure through sexual reputation, and Sumner's (1983; 1990) attempt to establish a sociology of social censure and regulation involving 'master censures of deviance', as illustrations of what a gendered postmodernist approach to penality might look like. She celebrates this transcendence over the androcentric Foucauldian perspective, while also appropriating Foucault.

For Howe the overlooked discursive formation of gendered subjects, such as the corrective socialization of resistant adolescent girls into femininity, and the concomitant gendering of boys into masculinity, is a central issue in understanding the broader concept of penality.[18] In Lees' (1986) work, Howe sees the power of the language of sexuality contained in the derogatory labels used by young males in their moral censure and confinement of the female subject. Not only does this censure of girls to certain gender subject positions preclude an alternative language by which these subjects can describe themselves, but, in ordering their own moral subject positions, the language operates as a self-disciplining regime of domination, self-censure and pain. Howe argues that a thoroughly 'social' analysis of penality 'will have to be appraised of the differential effects of sexed discourses' in justifying the imposition of pain and penal practices and 'their role in constituting the gendered subjectivities of girls' (1994: 190).

Drawing on Sumner (1983; 1990), Howe shows how the very concept of discipline in Foucault cannot fail to produce gendered rather than gender-neutral subjects because it is a gendered discourse born of military discipline which is profoundly masculine and which censors both men's and women's bodies and speech if they deviate from the masculine and feminine subject expectations. But by drawing on Bartky's (1988) study of the docile female body, Howe takes the postmodernist penality argument beyond Sumner, suggesting that women have distinct bodily experiences of an unbound and dispersed disciplinary power from the surveilling gaze of a 'generalized male witness', which must be accounted for in so far as women are constituted as self-policing subjects of their bodies' visible form and movement (1994: 195–9).[19] Howe sees Bordo's (1989) study as indicating how the female body can become a site for resistance against practical cultural control, though one which may further entrap, enmesh and contain her with her pain. And she see's Young's (1990) study of hystericization of protesting women through the moral and physical control of the 'fleshy body', via associational media images of disgust and revulsion equated with dirt, filth and disease, as a traversing of the discursive and non-discursive censure. Herein the discursively produced feminine subject position necessarily entails censure. It is a position where women are locked in as woman, whether in or out of prison (1994: 205). Howe's ultimate aim is to provide both the theoretical grounding and the practice techniques whereby the female subject is liberated from these discursive productions of control. Clearly any reformulation of justice policy must take account of this feminist postmodernist position on the gendered subject as well as Lacan.

Constitutive criminology and justice policy: replacement discourse

We are now in a position to clearly state the justice policy that derives from our affirmative postmodernist constitutive criminology. As stated at the outset, our policy comprises an integrated approach ranging from dealing with the totality to focusing on the practice specifics, including restructuring our socio-political organization. Recall that our overall policy deals with the long and medium term and is based on the concept of replacement discourse. As we shall see in the next chapter, this is to be implemented through local-to-global intervention programs and strategies designed to provide the emerging and recovering subject with an alternative discursive resource base for reflexive, celebrative and expansive transpraxis. Let us begin in this chapter by first outlining the theory of this policy.[20]

Replacement discourse, as we conceive it, is not merely another package of ways to talk and make sense of the world, but a language of 'trans-praxis' (Henry and Milovanovic, 1991). It is a non-reificatory connecting of the way we speak with our social relations and institutions. By its use we are made continuously aware of the interrelatedness of our agency and the structures it reproduces through constitutive productive work such as talking, perceiving, conceptualizing and theorizing.

Replacement discourse is not the same as oppositional discourse, even though both may result in public challenges to prevailing crime truths. In our view oppositional discourse is as constitutive of existing reality as is supportive discourse. Each addresses, and therein reproduces, the prevailing conceptions and distinctions while disputing their content. For example, Selva and Bohm (1987) have emphasized that, in many respects, an oppositional legal discourse, which utilizes the existing structure of legal discourse, may prove productive and liberating. But, this downplays the significance of the constitutive effects of 'liberating' practices in law. A no more graphic example of this is oppositional adolescent reaction to school by working class kids. While they 'resist' and reject the system that rejects them, it is this discursively organized reaction formation (Cohen, 1955) that subsequently consigns them to the bottom of the very hierarchy they despise (Willis, 1977).

Replacement discourse, in contrast, is directed toward the dual process of deconstructing prevailing structures of meanings and displacing them with new conceptions, distinctions, words and phrases, which convey alternative meanings.[21] The critical component of replacement discourse resides in the criminologist's ability to deconstruct that which is established truth, while at the same time to provide the replacement aspect to claim any newly created space with its own internally generated alternatives. Perhaps the classic example of a criminologist successfully interjecting replacement discourse into the popular culture is Sutherland's call through his writing (1940; 1941), and public addresses as president of the American Society of Criminology, for an expansion of the definition of 'crime' to include the concept of 'white collar crime'. Drawing attention to 'a large area of criminal behavior that had been neglected by criminologists' he insisted that 'white collar crime is "really" crime' because, like offenses against criminal laws, violations of regulatory laws have both the key elements: 'legal definition of an act as socially injurious and legal provision of a penalty for the act' (1949: 511; 1945).[22]

Other more recent examples of replacement discourse offering alternative visions can be found in Foucault's (1977) replacement of penology by 'penality'; the work of Christie (1977), with his notion of 'conflict as property'; the sociology of deviance reconceived as a 'sociology of accept-ance' (Bogdan and Taylor, 1987); Katz's subjects' (1988) formulation of murder as 'righteous slaughter'; and Pepinsky (1991), with his expansive reconstruction of crime and violence as the antithesis of democratic human interaction via his ideas of 'peacemaking criminology' (Pepinsky and Quinney, 1991).

Replacement discourse, then, is not simply critical and oppositional, but provides both a critique and an alternative vision. A direct consequence of its activist approach is that criminologists deconstruct crime as a separate entity by withdrawing their energy. They cease to invest in the unitary concept of crime and deny crime's status as an independent reality. Simultaneously, a policy of replacement discourse requires that we write new scripts to show the intertwined connections among: (1) human subjects, (2) activities that harm, and (3) the whole of which we are a part. Replacement discourse, therefore, involves substituting for 'control talk' (Cohen, 1985), 'organizational talk' (Manning, 1988), and 'law talk' (Milovanovic, 1986; Thomas, 1988), reflexive discourses which allow for the nuances of being human. Such discourses should retain a vision of society as a recurrent and emergent outcome of human activity (as developed in Chapter 3), but privileging neither individual nor social forces. However, such alternative constructions of the harms that are crimes are unlikely to impact the public domain if they remain wedded to the dormitories of academic discourse. Replacement discourses should intercede in the public debate primarily, though by no means exclusively, through the news media and popular culture. Thus while alternative discourses must be developed outside of traditional criminological contexts in order to minimize the inadvertent contamination (or recursive reconstruction) that comes through incorporation of existing constructions, they must also be reinserted into public debate. Primarily this demands an activist approach whereby criminologists transfuse their alternative research informed conceptions into the popular culture. Before exploring the practical interventionist strategies whereby this may be accomplished (see Chapter 9), we want to address the theoretical question of how replacement discourses develop.

First, some human subjects must invest the energy of their agency into making a difference, by taking the initiative to develop and shape new discursive forms. Although, from our perspective, these are always spontaneously generated (systemically and recursively) constructive forms require a deliberate effort and awareness. We might use Unger's (1987) and Giroux's (1992) term, 'cultural revolutionary' to describe those who take up this challenge. The cultural revolutionary finds her/himself both assuming a dialogical discursive subject position and taking a more activist and interventionist stance, based on provisional and contingent universalities established through ongoing struggles (Butler, 1992).

Replacement discourses, as we previously have said, can be understood as derived from several perspectives: Lacanian, Freireian, feminist, social constructivist, etc. In each case, ongoing dominant discursive structures are said to silence voices of the disempowered, alienated, repressed, and marginalized. Additionally, disempowered subjects often reconstitute dominant symbolic arrangements (hegemony). Since these arrangements are co-productive of harms, in order to break this cycle we need alternative discourses grounded in political economy: one version of this is a narrative therapy (we will address this practice strategy in the final chapter). We want to first actively address these discursive perspectives and then suggest an integrative, constitutive redirection.

From a Lacanian perspective, we are addressing the question of the Symbolic Order. We are also confronting the question of Lacan's Imaginary Order. In the concluding chapter, we will confront his Real Order as we turn our attention to structural transformations. These three orders are necessarily co-implicated in the development of replacement discourses, as they are in the production of existing hegemonic order.

Previously we presented Lacan's notion of the four discourses. We would like, now, to briefly come to terms with Lacan's fourth discourse, that of the analyst. The discourse of the analyst has been claimed to offer a way of constructing new master signifiers that better embody the desire of alienated, distressed, despairing, resisting (oppositional), and hysteric subjects (Lacan, 1991; Bracher, 1988; 1993). Recall that the 'hysteric' finds her/himself in a reconstituting (recursive) discourse that reinforces dominant signifiers and linguistic coordinate systems:[23]

$$\frac{\$}{a} \begin{matrix} \rightarrow \\ \leftarrow \end{matrix} \frac{S1}{S2}$$

Here the sender of the message, $\$$, the despairing, resisting or protesting subject, attempts to communicate her/his suffering to the other. The other, even in spite of good intentions, struggles to provide anything more than master (dominant) signifiers (S1) (i.e. stereotypes, clinical descriptions, common-sense notions, conventional wisdom, dominant conceptualizations and categories, etc.). This produces and reproduces conventional knowledge (S2), which in turn becomes the sphere within which the alienated and resisting subject finds her/himself as lacking, left out, not-all (*pas-toute*), symbolized as 'a'. In other words, existing signifiers and the linguistic coordinate system in use, with its attendant discursive subject positions, fail to provide an adequate medium within which to embody desire. Much remains unsaid. This maintains the despairing status of the hysteric ($\$$). In a Freireian analysis it might explain how colonial or conquering powers impose a regime of truth on indigenous populations and how reality construction becomes increasingly circumscribed to reflect dominant understandings. However, something is always left out, an indigenous ethos (a). In criminology we see how those who are often caught within the machinery of criminal justice are dispossessed of a language that reflects their internecine existence. Lawyers, in defending their client, resituate their 'stories' into the acceptable framework of law. The actual behavior, beliefs and accounts of subjects are 'wrenched out of their original contexts and pressed into a procrustean bed of acceptable action and morality. The language of law – like a magical incantation – creates the illusion of consistency and coherence' (Scott and Lyman, 1970: 108).[24] Similarly, guards, police, counselors, probation officers and others situate these accounts in the framework of blaming the victim. Criminologists situate them within conventional paradigms. Reporters situate them in dominant understandings of popular culture. The advertising industry situates them in desirable roles that ostensibly provide access to objects of desire. In short, political economic regimes often find the subject vulnerable to the imposition ('territorialization') of its mapping of desire, i.e. the docile subject (Foucault, 1977).

Oppositional groups, too, often find themselves too quickly offering a master discourse as an answer. This is very evident in dogma, and truth claims based on wishful thinking and grandiose political theory, that have characterized activism on the political right and left. Indeed, recall Marx's lament that:

> The tradition of countless dead generations is an incubus to the mind of the living. At the very times when they seem to be engaged in revolutionizing themselves and their circumstances, in creating something previously non-existent, at just such epochs of revolutionary crisis they anxiously summon up the spirits of the past to their aid, *borrowing from them names, rallying cries, costumes, in order to stage the new world historical drama in this time-honored disguise and borrowed speech.* (Marx, 1852: 115, our emphasis)

For Marx, the crucial issue for the revolutionary was whether the concepts and discourse of the past could be used selectively (or even not used at all), to enable the liberation of the future. Until the spirit of revolutionary change could be captured and used without reference to the past, automatically and spontaneously, it was but a bourgeois revolution, short lived, soon reaching its climax.

Lacan, however, offers the discourse of the analyst (therapist) as the antidote:

$$\frac{a \;\rightarrow\; \$}{S2 \;\leftarrow\; S1}$$

Here, the analyst (a), not knowing all, reflects a truth to the hysteric ($\$$) gained from the hysteric's generated discourse. The analyst offers the hysteric, then, the left out, the not-all (*pas-toute*), and the hysteric is encouraged to find an alternative embodiment of desire in master signifiers (S1) which better embody it. The previous master alienating signifiers are encouraged to be dropped as inefficient and part of the problem: not reflective, too restrictive, too stereotyped and too clinically imposed. In other words, the resisting subject first undergoes alienation and separation, a non-identification with her/his previous master signifiers, and then a reconstruction, a re-identification with alternative master signifiers that more appropriately reflect her/his being in the world. According to Bracher (1993: 71), 'the analyst reflects or refracts the analysand's demand in such a way as to reveal the a, cause of the analysand's desire, and thus to expose the underlying fantasy . . . which functions as a bedrock meaning for the analysand.' The goal of revolutionary work in this schema, according to Bracher, is thus to be not anarchists but analysts, which means positioning oneself in such a way as to interrogate how culture participates in the position of mastery . . . that is, exposing, and thus allowing subjects to work through the knowledge/ belief (S2), ideals (S1), want-of-being ($), and forbidden *jouissance* (a) that the various cultural discourses establish as dominant. (1993: 73–4)

Much of this could also be reconceptualized in terms of Lacan's work on the Borromean knots (Milovanovic, 1993b). Here it was shown that three interlocking circles (representing the interpenetrating effects of the Imaginary, Symbolic and Real Orders) indicate how the subject finds a degree of stability in her/his psychic functioning and in sense production, but nevertheless is vulnerable to knot-breaking and reconfigurations. The knot, in other words, provides the nodal point (Laclau and Mouffe, 1985) which anchors signifiers to signifieds in more permanent states. It is at the center of the intersecting circles (orders) that the *objet petit* (a) is situated, and it is at the intersection of the Symbolic and Imaginary Orders that sense production takes place.

This is a start. Certainly subjects in revolt or in protest need to disengage from identification with master signifiers that maintain their bondage and subservience, and Lacan provides some important insights to this end. But unlike Lacan, or Bracher, we see the sign as 'decidable' in the concrete sphere of social conflict.[25] It is within discursive historical struggles that the sign finds embodiment. And here lies the importance of Freire's work in grounding theory in practical struggles.

Lacan's thesis on the discourse of the analyst as the savior is inadequate for another reason. It assumes that the analyst is somehow above the inherent demands of various struggles. Lacan himself suggested that the discourse of the analyst could slip back into a discourse of the master, where a dominant discourse is offered and subjects are interpellated into subject positions. What is to get us beyond this? We offer several thoughts.

First, *cultural revolutionaries* should resist situating themselves in the analyst's discursive subject position. Rather, a combined discourse of the analyst and hysteric, one in which the sender and receiver of the message find themselves alternatively within each's discursive subject position, together constructing reality (the active learning model in education where the 'teacher' is also 'student' and the student is also teacher, or the self-help model where the problem sufferer is also the problem solver), gives us some assurance that both find better master signifiers. This is a 'dialogical encounter', a symmetrical relationship.

Second, for this to take place, we are persuaded by the work of Freire who shows, ultimately, it is in a dialogical pedagogy that 'speaking true words' can take place (1972: 57–67).[26] It is here that action and reflection are combined. In speaking 'true words' persons change the world; they become active agents in the process of becoming (1972: 76, 167).[27] Pertinent here are Freire's chapters, 'Education and Conscientizacao' (1973) and 'Cultural Action and Conscientization', (1985) where he explains how codifications take place and especially how 'generative words' are established reflective of socio-economic conditions ('generative themes').[28] The predominant mode of being in dominant structures is 'semi-intransitive' (1985: 75), whereby the subject is immersed in socio-economic conditions without substantial reflexivity. The goal of *conscientization* is for the disenfranchised to 'exercise the right to participate consciously in the socio-historical transformation of their society' (1985: 50). To this end, Freire spells out a process by which the cultural revolutionary, in dialogue with the oppressed, decodifies key signifiers. Key signifiers are broken down into their constitutive elements and are presented in their connectedness with a socio-political reality (e.g. signifieds). This process allows the disenfranchised 'to penetrate the whole in terms of the relationships among its parts, which until then the [disenfranchised] did not perceive' (1985: 92). It encourages distancing from what was, followed by 'an authentic process of abstraction', and the development of visions of what could be. Alternative signifiers are connected with alternative realities. This has some similarity with Lacan's discourse of the analyst, but roots practice in concrete historical struggles. The key, of course, is to determine how to avoid this being confined to the discursive ghettos of liberation. Freire provides a beginning in the creation of replacement discourses, the 'language of possibility' (Giroux, 1992). As Giroux tell us, 'this suggests a politics and pedagogy developed around new languages capable of acknowledging the multiple, contradictory, and complex subject positions people occupy within different social, cultural, and economic relations' (1992: 21).

Third, as suggested by Giroux (1992), cultural workers and revolutionaries should encourage 'border crossings', and embrace a 'border pedagogy' (1992: 19–36, 133–41, 170–6).[29] Here, traditional boundaries of knowledge are transgressed: 'As part of a radical pedagogical practice, border pedagogy points to the need for conditions that allow students to write, speak, and listen in a language in which meaning becomes multi-accentual and dispersed and resists permanent closure' (1992: 29). It is within these borderlands that students, indigenous populations and the disenfranchised regain their histories and possibilities. According to Giroux, these borderlands are

> criss-crossed within a variety of languages, experiences, and voices . . . There are no unified subjects here, only students whose multilayered and often contradictory voices and experiences intermingle with the weight of particular histories that will not fit easily into the master narrative of a monolithic culture. Such borderlands should be seen as sites for both critical analysis and as a potential source of experimentation, creativity, and possibility. (1992: 34)

Fourth, we need not see the postmodern subject disappear into oblivion, as in the 'death of the subject'. The subject is not negated as in some forms of skeptical postmodernism or as in some critiques of postmodernist theory. Rather, subjects are constituted within multiple sites of struggle. No essences define the subject; rather, the postmodern subject, the recovering subject, is one who is polyvocal, multiple, decentered, but an inter-penetrated subject constituted by differences and struggle (1992: 60–1). This subject is capable of dialogically developing 'contingent universalities' (Butler, 1992) which become the grounds for social movements (Mouffe, 1992; JanMohamed, 1994). Especially recognized by African-American feminist critique are the interlocking and interpenetrating forms of dominations, not merely their 'additive' or their essentialist forms (Hooks and West, 1991; hooks, 1989; Collins, 1989; 1990; 1993; Giroux, 1992: 125–41). Constitutive criminology, then, is concerned with how co-production of signifiers takes place, but also with how interpenetrating logics have often been cloaked with master signifiers. These need to be decoded and recoded in alternative more reflective signifiers that resist closure, somewhat akin to dissipative structures.

Fifth, chaos theory offers a way of mapping the subject without imposing rigid, positivistic assumptions or ordering structures, and offers insights concerning the type of environment where the postmodern recovering subject may flourish. As to the mapping of the subject, we can conceptualize the recovering subject finding him/herself within two loci of activities, much like the two wings of the butterfly attractor: one wing representing a 'disidentification', the other an identification with discursive subject positions (JanMohamed, 1994). As JanMohamed says, 'it is therefore . . . a process of forming affiliations with other positions, of defining equivalences and constructing alliances' (1994: 111). These are the border crossers. We could also conceptualize each of the wings of the butterfly attractor as representing, respectively, the discourses of the hysteric and the analyst. Here each position is assumed in turn, which quickly turns into the other; the 'I' and the 'thou' are intricately connected in being (see also Buber, 1958; Freire, 1972: 167–8). One begins to codify alternative realities, even as the other, through the first, codifies hers.

As to chaos' second contribution on insights concerning an alternative 'order', we shall have more to say in the final chapter. Here, we merely wish to argue that chaos' conception of the dynamics of far-from-equilibrium conditions offers a vibrant notion of environmental conditions within which maximal variability, order and disorder, and transcendence are possible. Here the recovering subject finds her/himself within an environment where desire is offered creative forms for expression.

Sixth, and finally, discussions of Lacan's Symbolic Order must be connected with those analyzing his Imaginary Order. To this end, the works of feminist postmodernists[30] and African-American feminist theory,[31] as well as early critical legal theorists,[32] have contributed useful insights as to the potential for utopian thinking. Here, not only a version of standpoint(s) epistemology(ies) must be invoked, but also the wherewithal of utopian thinking. Cornell, for example, borrowing from Irigaray's notion of 'mimesis', shows how various forms of domination can be disrupted and transformed into an affirmation. She also builds on Cixous' notion of 'retelling of the myth' by which traditional stories are retold by excavating silenced voices (see Cornell, 1991: 147–52, 169–78). Cornell, building on Lacan, shows how the imaginary, constituted by metaphor and metonymy, always witnesses slippages, excesses (Lacan's *le plus de jouir*), which appear in myths. It is within this 'space' that an alternative Imaginary Order can be constructed. Consider Arrigo's observation on experiential feminism:

> Precisely because the myth is a story, its beginnings are born in the imagination's capacity to conceive of and describe on-going, lived experience in intimately meaningful ways ... The work of experiential feminism through myth is to render the telling of narratives that more authentically depict the experience of women and the situations in which they find themselves. (1992: 26)

Thus, necessary for a transpraxis is the poetic. As Cornell says: 'Without the aesthetic evocation of utopian possibility of feminine difference, we are left with the politics of revenge ... the politics of feminism needs its poetry' (1991: 185). In *re*creating myths, we create an 'elsewhere':

> consciousness-raising must involve creation, not just discovery. We need our poetry, our fantasies and our fables; we need the poetic evocation of the feminine body in Irigaray and in Cixous if we are to finally find a way beyond the muteness imposed by a gender hierarchy in which our desire is 'unspeakable'. (1991: 201)

This notion of the free play of the imaginary has also been identified by Charles S. Peirce in his notion of 'pure play' (1965: 313), where moments of unrestrained, free-floating imaginary play provide the source for novel insights. It is closely connected with 'abduction' as a counter to deductive or inductive logic, by which he means that the development of ideas entails both (1956: 152). We shall have more to say about abduction in the final chapter.

Suggestive already in the criminology literature are several proposals, some old, some new, which indicate a worthy direction for further inquiry. De Haan (1990) has offered the notion of 'redress' whereby problematic behavior is given semiotic form reflective of the complexities involved. Morris (1973) has provided the controversial idea of a 'pre-trial hearing' where victims face the victimizer directly. Gilsinan (1981) has suggested the idea of forms of conflict regulation whereby alternative narratives are constructed. Black (1989) has proposed the notion of a 'sociology of the case' whereby legal constructions of reality are understood as being constituted by extra-legal factors, not by formal rationality alone: and so on. All these suggestions chart the waters for inquiry, whereby the Symbolic and Imaginary Orders are expanded to consider denied voices and visions.

Summary and conclusions

In sum, in this chapter we have indicated some theoretical foundation for our policy of replacement discourse. This entails change in the Symbolic Order as well as in the Imaginary Order. Decidability is contingent, but yet grounded in historical struggles. In the next chapter and by way of a contingent conclusion, we want to indicate how replacement discourses could develop with power to transform those who frame the social realities of crime. We will also show that it is within far-from-equilibrium conditions, a situation sharing an ecological space with Unger's proposal for a superliberalism, that alternative replacement discourses are able to more freely develop.

Notes

1 As Cohen (1990) has pointed out, these criticisms are very similar to ones offered by sociological phenomenology and ethnomethodology against positivism in social sciences, over twenty years earlier. See especially Phillipson (1971) and Filmer et al. (1972), and more generally, Feyerabend (1975).

2 However, we do not endorse his ultimately romantic and essentialist 'community of celebration' or its focus on common religious values.

3 For the offender as excessive investor, see Chapter 6.

4 See Shover and Einstadter (1988), Einstadter and Henry (1995).

5 As in the earlier analyses we have avoided the micro-meso-macro delineation since it obscures too much from the continuum.

6 Moreover, instead of implying that these exist in reality, we are concerned here with their appearance in the modernist criminological literature associated with particular criminologies (as were Einstadter and Henry, 1995).

7 The empirical data that support this position are contingent upon narrow and particular assumptions about what counts as crime, or even serious crime. If the activities of corporate or state violence were included the conclusion would change, as it would were occupational crimes and crimes within relationships to be included. For a dramatic example, consider how the small number of those who commit murder would change if data included state crimes of genocide. See especially Barak (forthcoming).

8 Aside from publicly documented violence, there is trade in weapons, drugs, alcohol, prostitution, gambling that Kalinich (1980) found pervasive in prison and which requires necessary connections to the 'outside'. See also Kalinich and Stojkovic (1985).

9 See Zimbardo's (1972) classic study of prison guards (see also Haney et al., 1973).

10 Indeed, this was the basis of rehabilitation's criticism by neo-classicist justice model theorists such as American Friends Service Committee (1971), Fogel (1975), and Von Hirsch (1976).

11 See Martinson (1974), Palmer (1975), Whitehead and Lab (1989), Lab and Whitehead (1990), and Andrews et al. (1990).

12 This point was fundamental to marxist dialectical analysis of the relationship between parts and wholes, where 'the part . . . cannot be abstracted from the whole and sociologically examined apart from it and then mechanically inserted again after the analysis.' Rather the parts, in this case the 'different' correctional ideologies, philosophies of punishment, strategies and technologies of social control, 'must be integrated into a whole or they remain abstract and theoretically misleading' (Swingewood, 1975: 44–5).

13 For examples of attempts to counter this trend from within modernist criminology see Kalinich (1980; 1986) and Kalinich and Stojkovic (1985).

14 This hyperreality often appears to be relatively autonomous, with a generated sign system that is self-referential. In the process we forget that it is we who give energy to the system and to the meanings invoked and constructed.

15 See also Lee (1990: 76, 148–54), Lacan (1981: 273; 1977: 314), and Granon-Lafont (1985: 88).

16 Bannister and Milovanovic (1990), Milovanovic (1988; 1989b), and Manning (1988).

17 Chaos theory is helpful here as it was earlier for, as we have seen, it moves away from

deterministic examination. Chaos theorists argue, instead, for a science of orderly disorder as a fundamental meta-theory. In other words, a 'soft determinism' (Matza, 1964) is created within chaotic situations. Here, determinism, captured by the notion of attractors, opposes any formulation of conceptually static, orderly, predictable, precisely definable, linear notions of phenomena. See Hayles (1990), Milovanovic (1995), Stewart (1989), and in literature, Serres (1982a; 1982b).

18 Howe draws on the empirical work of Hudson (1984), Cain (1989), Ferreri-Bravo and Arcidiacono (1989), Lees (1986), Bartky (1988), Bordo (1989), Young (1990), and Carlen (1990) to inform her feminist postmodern position on penality.

19 See also Lacan's (1985) discussion of woman being *pas-toute*, in a phallic Symbolic Order, but nevertheless having access to an alternative basis of *jouissance*.

20 It should again be emphasized that, to be transformational, each of the practice components must necessarily occur together as part of an overall policy of harm reduction.

21 See also Freire (1972; 1973; 1985), Giroux (1992), McLaren (1994), and JanMohamed (1994).

22 In spite of its controversial birth, 'white collar crime' has become an accepted dimension of public consciousness, with surveys reporting between 80% and 90% of the public believing that white collar offenders deserve prison for their crimes (Newman, 1968; Gibbons, 1969; Braithwaite, 1982; Cullen et al., 1983).

23 We expand the meaning of the hysteric here to include those who do not have adequate symbolic representation with which to embody desire.

24 A similar process occurs with jailhouse lawyers: see Thomas (1988), Milovanovic (1988), and Milovanovic and Thomas (1989).

25 Consider Bracher's suggestion that 'at the present time it is in the literature classroom that such analyses [discourse of the analyst] have the best chance of producing positive results' (1993: 191). In contrast, see McLaren (1994: 206), Ebert (1991a: 293; 1991b), Zavarzadeh and Morton (1990: 156), and Volosinov (1986).

26 Freire's approach reflects much of Husserl's phenomenology. More recently, Laclau (1991) finds his work a key for transformative practices. See also Peters and Lankshear (1994) showing compatibilities between hermeneutics, as developed by Heidegger and Gadamer, and Freire. Feminist analysis has also benefited from his insights (Weiler, 1994; Brady, 1994). Although Freire's work would not be considered postmodernist, it probably rests on the borders of postmodern and modernist intellectual inquiry.

27 See also Peters and Lankshear (1994: 178), McLaren (1994: 200), and Giroux (1992).

28 We see these generative words as master signifiers. See also Volosinov's (1986) view that the nature of the sign is multi-accentual: it reflects diverse perspectives in struggle.

29 See also McLaren (1994), JanMohamed (1994), and Aronowitz and Giroux (1991).

30 Consider especially Cornell (1991; 1993), Cixous (1976; 1986; 1990), Irigaray (1985; 1993), and Kristeva (1986).

31 Collins (1989; 1990; 1993), Cains (1990), Smith (1987; 1992), Harding (1991), Giroux (1992: 125–41), and Arrigo (1992).

32 Consider Peirce (1956; 1965) and also Unger (1987: 579–80).

9

The Justice Practice of Constitutive Criminology: Replacing Technologies of Discipline with Languages of Possibility

In the previous chapter we made plain our policy position on replacement discourse. In this concluding chapter we stipulate what we think should be done in practice. As should be clear, there is considerable overlap between policy and practice. However, here we are concerned less with theory. The focus is on specific strategies for bringing off our stated overall policy of harm reduction through replacement discourse. As we earlier argued, several interlocking strategies are necessary. To make enough of a difference, these need to be implemented simultaneously.

First, are strategies designed to provide an alternative, discursive, resource base for reflexive, celebrative and expansive transpraxis. These strategies require intervention into the generative sites of discursive production which, on a mass scale, must involve intervention into popular culture. This will occur principally through the media, and particularly by means of newsmaking criminology (Barak, 1988).

Second, are strategies that we call refractory. These are based on the concept of 'social judo' (Einstadter and Henry, 1995) which implies intervention designed to resist and redirect the constitutive energy of excessive investors. Such investors in the reality of power are turned away from harm production, and toward reinvesting in positive connections with a relationally oriented community of fellow human subjects. We see this being accomplished in several ways, but especially through peacemaking conflict reduction (Pepinsky and Quinney, 1991) and narrative re-visions (Parry and Doan, 1994).

Third, are strategies designed to assist the constituted victim to become a recovering subject within their local community. Here we rely on what are referred to conventionally as support groups. More specifically, these are ways whereby problem sufferers (in this case victims of harm) can share strength from their common situation, and draw on empowering solutions from their own experiential knowledge (Robinson and Henry, 1977; Pfuhl and Henry, 1993: 209–35).

Finally, it is necessary to transcend these micro-technologies of the local, in order to set a facilitative, formative structural context that will undergird the specific interventions. Put simply, programs, strategies and practices, that were for Foucault (1977) the technologies of discipline, are here presented as the technologies, more accurately the languages, of possibility. As such, they alone are insufficient; they can be undermined by contradictory macro-structural contexts. This implies that the most critical transformation must deal with the political economy. Without its reorganization, the other possibilities remain just that. They are no more than romantic melodies in someone else's grand performance. As such they are unlikely to sustain sufficient difference before being absorbed by the wider context – the existent totality of capitalist hierarchies of order and control. Our social judo metaphor suggests that discernible instances of harms and the prevalence of energized excessive investors are not merely occasions for local actions, but opportunities for understanding the harmful structural configurations of COREL sets. These should then form the basis of an interventionist social justice practice. Thus, we see structural transformation as a crucial co-partner of constructive social change. Moreover, we see the best promise for this societal-level transformation in Unger's (1987) superliberalism. This is envisioned as a practical, political philosophy whose synoptic virtuality is recursively generated to maximize diversity and minimize hegemony. Likewise, however, superliberalism on its own is unlikely to be sustainable without the micro-technologies of possibility that invigorate the cultural body. Thus let us return then to the first of these strategies: newsmaking criminology as replacement discourse.

Newsmaking criminology as replacement discourse

Journalists are professional account makers, skilled at purposive elimination, tuned to resonant enhancement.[1] As regularizers of the irregular, they are fiction writers *par excellence*. They reflect what they describe, therein constituting that described as 'real'. Through their media, journalists' accumulated constitutive work permeates the very relationships they purport to describe, giving it sustenance, form and shape. They selectively and systematically omit in order to sharpen and differentiate. To focus on a topic is to enhance by elimination. Journalists, more than any other, are the constructors of the 'readerly text' (Barthes, 1974; Silverman, 1983: 237–83). Their business is the presentation of linear portrayals of reality that readers (viewers) are encouraged to accept, along with its master signifiers and discursive subject positions, in constructing both 'the what happened' and the 'what's happening'.

Nor are criminologists inactive in this process. Our assent to communicated truths is emergent through our silences. These, too, are accumulated and constitutive of the real. As Foucault (1979) has reminded us, silences are strong tools in the construction of reality. So in considering crime, itself a socially constructed category, journalists form alliances with agents of social control, vocal public commentators, interest groups, offenders and victims, to co-produce crime events, crime patterns and crime trends. Ultimately, they co-produce the substance that is criminological phenomena.[2]

To transcend our passive contribution to such socially constructed and publicly consumed crime truths, and thereby to cease investing in the continuity of harm, it is necessary for criminologists to actively intercede in the constitutive process. Newsmaking criminology consists of criminologists actively challenging silences, identifying omissions, and resurrecting the eliminated through participating in the making of news stories about crime. Here, then, we are concerned with newsmaking criminology as replacement discourse, as textual production in its written or visual forms.

The activist criminologist assumes a 'writerly *visée*' whereby encouraged is 'an infinite play of signification; in it there can be no transcendental signified, only provisional ones which function in turn as signifiers' (Silverman, 1983: 246). Closure is denied, displacements are encouraged, and the reader or viewer is encouraged to assume multiple, discursive subject positions. As Silverman says, 'the writerly project "dis-places" the reader or viewer, alienates her or him from the all-too-familiar subject-positions of the existing cultural regime' (1983: 248–9; see also Milovanovic, 1992a). The latter leaves room only for negative narrative – criticism, rejection, outrage (in marginalized lesser spaces such as 'letters to the editor') – a resource for bar room politics.

One of the few criminological scholars to recognize the importance of developing an activist agenda of replacement discourse is Gregg Barak (1988; 1994) with his call for a 'newsmaking criminology'. Barak says that 'in the post-modern era, social problems such as homelessness, sexual assault, or drug abuse are politically constructed, ideologically articulated, and media produced events' (Barak, 1991a: 5). He advocates that criminologists should become credible spokespeople, make criminological news and participate in the popular construction of images of crime and crime control. They should produce crime themes, 'as a means of bringing about social change and social justice' (Barak, 1988: 585).[3] Before criminologists embark on this quest for the possible, it is necessary to examine the limits to strategies designed to replace discourse.

Styles of newsmaking criminology

In so far as several constitutive agents comprise the newsmaking enterprise, each offers opportunities for intercession. Four styles have been identified (Henry, 1994): (1) disputing data; (2) challenging journalism; (3) self-reporting; and (4) confronting media. These are by no means exhaustive and have been chosen here for the purpose of illustration. Each relies on expressed journalistic interest in a particular facet of crime and its reportage. Each is not, however, evenly or equally classifiable as replacement discourse. In the following sections, we briefly outline the approach taken in each style, point out some of its advantages and disadvantages and explain what would be necessary to elevate it to a more active form of replacement discourse.

Disputing data: the criminologist as expert This is the classic form of reactive involvement by criminologists challenging published news reports and crime stories, disputing the truth of their content. Typically, the dispute is over claimed distortions in the image presented of offenders, victims, policy or crime. It may involve charges of omission but importantly, from the replacement discourse perspective, it also involves new or alternative data to correct the original image. The typical forms taken by data disputing are letters to the editor, open forums, or being available as a criminological expert to be called on by journalists.[4]

A problem with most forms of data disputing is that journalists retain control over the story. As a result, criminological input, especially because it is challenging other content, becomes 'one side' of what may be a two- or many-sided account. In such a scenario, control of the overall image or media impression is lost to the notion that 'experts disagree' (see Henry, 1994 for an illustration). This is not to deny that data disputing is unimportant as a contributor to informing popular culture about crime, but it does little more than reinforce existing conceptions of crime. Its ability to generate alternative discourse is limited by journalistic (rather than deconstructive/reconstructive) agendas and by the criminologist's pre-cast role, as one who necessarily employs the concepts contained in the initial statements, in order to 'challenge' them. In the second type of newsmaking criminology, challenging journalism, the same type of data dispute is handled differently.

Challenging journalism: the criminologist as journalist One way to make 'disputing data' into an exercise of replacement discourse is for criminologists to write crime news articles, rather than allowing themselves to be used as subjects or side-shows within them. Here the criminologist either becomes a freelance journalist, writing commentary or feature articles, or becomes a freelance reporter. Some have similarly placed themselves in the public domain by anchoring or hosting a regular radio or television slot. Such strategies have the advantage of shaping the total image of crime but the disadvantages of being subject to editorial reconstruction and being limited in their scope to the immediate listening or viewing audience (unlike, for example, educating crime reporting journalists). (See Henry, 1994.)

In order to bring about both deconstruction and reconstruction at the level of media, it seems necessary for criminologists not simply to passively respond to journalists' desires to write crime news stories but to claim control of the crime news space themselves. Such innovation requires more energy than simply responding to journalists' questions. Nor is it immune from the reproductive effects of journalistic agendas by which prevailing stereotypes and pre-existing conceptions (dominant signifiers) are purveyed. This is because the news media retain control over the title, the nature and placing of any accompanying photographic or illustrative material, and often the opening and closing paragraphs, as well as any extracted highlights. Such journalistic 'packaging practices' can compromise, if not completely undermine, any critical reconstructive attempt.

Self-reporting: the criminologist as subject   Here criminologists overcome some of the limitations inherent in disputing data since they are the primary initiators of the story or its sole subject. Typically, they are involved in a research study, program evaluation, or program implementation and either actively publicize the results or provide the words for local journalists to describe their work, with a view that the story may become syndicated regionally or preferably nationally. In this approach the criminologist relies on the journalists' general interest in covering crime stories, but also appeals to their concern for the new, the tantalizing and even the human interest story.

An excellent example of this approach can be found with criminologist Mimi Silbert's influential attempt to replace prevalent notions of rehabilitation, to go 'beyond rehabilitation' (see Henry, 1994 for an elaborated illustration). Transformation or personal change is shown not as the result of external forces or treatments – indeed, the word 'treatment' is not mentioned – but as the outcome of an ongoing process of taking personal responsibility in the context of an extended family, based upon the principle that 'people change by "doing" for somebody else' (Whittmore, 1992: 5). This form of newsmaking criminology is powerful in its ability to transform crime concepts held in the current popular culture. It is powerful because the criminologist being interviewed is immersed in his/her own discourse rather than the dominant one. In this case, it is clear that an alternative meaning is given to rehabilitation, in which it is transformed into a process of struggle for personal and social change. The advantage of this form of intercession is that the criminologists' newsmaking is the prime, if not exclusive, source for the story, which allows considerable depth of discourse and the opportunity to establish various connections between human agency and social structure. It is a form of 'border crossing', and a development of a 'border pedagogy'. As such, considerable strides can be made in creating and claiming news space about crime. A disadvantage of the criminologist-as-subject style of replacement discourse is that, as with disputing data and challenging journalism, the journalist and editors, as well as the historically established style of the media outlet, can again result in packaging that kills. Another disadvantage of this approach is that, unless there is an extended communication of the criminologist's own discourse and an empathetic journalist, the approach risks trivialization or marginalization from the crime mainstream, even by well-intended sympathetic journalists. Moreover, it may be perceived by the public as 'just another study' or 'just another program' or 'just another case of bleeding-heart liberalism'. Again, this can be pre-empted by criminologists reporting their own research or programs, while striving to deconstruct an existing conception of crime and replace it with a more enlightened one.

Confronting media: the criminologist as educative provocateur   Here the media are both the direct target and the medium of the newsmaking criminologist. The media are both the subject of the study and the object of criticism. The aim is to get the media to engage in reassessment through self-analysis, prompted by the criminologist as critical catalyst. It is an encouragement for the co-production of a 'writerly text', co-border crossings. There are several approaches to this style of newsmaking criminology (see Henry, 1994). The advantage of this style of newsmaking is that the initial statement is developed outside of the media and is thereby controlled by the criminologists. The content drives the media interest and reasonably assures subsequent stages of coverage. In this approach to newsmaking, criminologists directly address journalists. The disadvantage is that, unless the attempt is repeated, the weight of standard approaches will outweigh the educative attempt. Further, the very critical nature of the approach may alienate the very journalists one is seeking to court. Moreover, successive stages progressively wrest control from the criminologist until the content is reduced to a form of 'the experts disagree'. One way of pre-empting the progressive deterioration of the replacement component of a newsmaking piece is for the criminologist to retain control over the content by becoming the journalist, as we saw above. However, unless this is done competently, it is likely that the issue will be relegated to a one-time opinion type commentary. This can be overcome by attempting to critically address journalists themselves, either through their conferences or through journalists' in-house journals and professional magazines. Perhaps in this context, newsmaking criminology that attempts to directly engage journalists through their own professional associations and journals has the advantage of permeating a wide variety of media as well as influencing the constitutive process whereby future crime news is deconstructed and replaced by a discourse of possibilities.

Replacement discourses in the prevention and reduction of harm

Replacement discourses, then, provide not just another package of ways to talk and make sense of the world, but a language of 'transpraxis' (Henry and Milovanovic, 1991). A replacement discourse is a non-reificatory connecting of the way we speak with our social relations and institutions. Through its use, we are continuously aware of the interrelatedness of our agency and the structures it reproduces through our talking, perceiving, conceptualizing and theorizing. A genuinely alternative replacement discourse envelops not just crimes as popularly understood but harms that cause pain, regardless of whether these have been defined as criminal by the political process. It includes all the players in the construction of harm: the victims, the offenders and the agencies of the criminal justice system. Here it captures not only the declarations of policy but the ways its practitioners and policy makers distinguish their reality from the totality that is the social order. Replacement discourse requires a 'bringing back in' of the under-emphasized, informal, unofficial, marginalized practices (the unspoken) that are part of the totality of the criminological enterprise. It speaks for providing various (repressed, marginalized) discursive practices with a forum for genuine consideration. Only with such a comprehension of the totality and the contribution of these excluded parts to the reality making process is it possible to provide an alternative understanding of the phenomena of crime and crime control in our society. Only from such an understanding of the total constitutive process is it possible to generate a replacement discourse that completes the cycle from deconstruction to reconstruction. While it is impossible for replacement discourse to be fully autonomous, it is possible for those generating it to be reflexively aware of the importance of the dialectics of control whereby their alternative structuring and conceptualization can be coopted, weakened and contaminated. At the same time, replacement discourse is capable of having transformational power over established orders. Each of the approaches to transformative newsmaking criminology illustrated above recognizes the need to generate alternative concepts and cosmologies, while realizing that there is minimal room for such activity owing to the common discourse that pervades the totality and that provides the initial medium for any alternative form.

Having established a cultural-level interventionist strategy to modulate the mediated harms that are crime, let us now turn to the short-term control strategy of our policy. We shall look first at how constitutive criminology deals with the 'excessive investor' in harm and then at the reintegration of the constituted victim.

Social judo, radical refraction and the excessive investor

Here we examine short-term control, based on the concept of 'social judo', implemented by strategies designed to resist the constitutive energy of excessive investors. In so far as we have defined crime as an excessive investment of energy in the power to control others, an obvious question that arises is how concrete cases of harm get reduced, or prevented, without using counter-power/force. Indeed, to simply respond by the use of counter-force is no less a use of power even under the title 'resistance', and leads us to very slippery arguments about 'justifiable' violence, wars, homicides. Even on the critical left, once this logic is in place, the initial trickle can lead to an overwhelming self-justified avalanche of 'humanistically inspired terror' (e.g. political correctness, 'schmarxism'). In our view, use of the power to deny others, whoever uses it, is not justified. It is crime. Here 'peacemaking criminology' (Pepinsky and Quinney, 1991) has much to offer, with its rejection of the idea that violence can be overcome by the use of state violence. A postmodernist version of 'peace studies' offers some useful suggestions for more peaceful ways of dealing with conflict.[5] European abolitionists are also beginning to have their voices heard on the

American continent.[6] Instead of reaction, peacemaking criminologists propose to pre-empt crime through societal transformations whereby people are reconnected with others, while remaining globally aware that societies 'not obsessed with crime' are those with considerably greater occasions of face-to-face interaction than those who are obsessed with both crime and control (Adler, 1983; see Faith's 1993 interview with Adler).

Earlier we had presented some possible long- and medium-term prevention directions for the development of replacement discourses and the recovering subject. The problem is not only how to get from here to there, and whether anyone other than postmodern romantics would want to, but how to deal with instances of power as crime, now, today, in the violence of domestic, urban and corporate America, and in the closets of rural torment and its public denial. The response for the short term we call 'radical refraction', the notion of bending or channeling others' exercise of power over us into their exercise of that power over themselves or toward constructive outcomes. It is, as Einstadter and Henry (1995) have insightfully described it, the 'judo metaphor of crime control' or what we might refer to as *social judo*, where people act together to defensively employ the strength and power of oppressors toward their self-limitation:

> By the Judo Metaphor we refer to the philosophy behind judo and other martial arts. Judo means 'gentle way' and is based on the seeming paradox that the best defense is non-fighting and that one gains victory over an opponent by yielding – gentle turns away the sturdy opponent (Kim and Shin, 1983). It is a method whereby the energy of the violent is redirected against the opponent to diffuse the violence. In a metaphorical sense this is a model stance that might release us from the punitive trap. (1995: 315)

Social judo, then, requires a minimal use of energy toward redirecting the considerable power of those seeking to exercise power over us. The object is that they are made abundantly aware that the more energy they expend in harming us the more that energy converts into constraining them, limiting their further ability to harm us. This is a challenge to a transformative political agenda.

A transformative agenda incorporates the philosophy of radical refraction. The possibility for this turning back of power is exemplified, even in its most overt expressions. Foucault's (1977) 'panopticon' of asymmetrical power, for example, has overlooked the potential for symmetry re-established in its operation. This is becoming apparent at Stateville Prison in Illinois, where the 'round-house', which is constructed in the image of Bentham's panopticon, provides a spectacle of instances of excessive abuse of power by prison authorities. Not only are prisoners entirely visible to controlling authority (as in Foucault), but the actions of prison guards are subject to the gaze of all inmates and make visible what, in the privacy of the individual cell, has often been invisible. In short, asymmetrical forms of power can become more symmetrical.

In its most fundamental sense, social judo is an undermining of the power to deny others and the attempt to develop strategies that re-enforce the integration of people with their social context – which means with each other. Let us take three illustrative strategies, consistent with this alternative policy of criminal justice intervention, that demonstrate its difference from much current practice. The first case illustrates how to deal with excessive investors whose past actions render them a present physical danger to others and whom current criminal justice dispositions sentence to prison or jail time. Here our model is the 'just community'. Second, we look at the philosophy of Delancey Street's 'beyond rehabilitation' as a way of dealing with non-violent offenders. Finally, we raise the possibility of using 'narrative therapy' as an alternative treatment model.

Beyond imprisonment: the just community

This approach developed out of Lawrence Kohlberg's research on moral communities. Here participants develop a community of shared responsibility in which members treat each other with mutual respect. Peter Scharf, a colleague of Kohlberg, describes such an experimental 'just community' that began in a Connecticut women's prison in 1971 in response to a crisis of control and near riot. During 1971, inmates, guards, and prison administrators met in a 'constitutional convention' and rules were proposed for a model democratic framework in which 'inmates would control internal discipline and define objectives and activities. All prison offenses, apart from the major felonies, would be referred to a "cottage community meeting"' (Scharf, 1977: 104).[7] Thus, instead of the traditional approach of coercive power and control, that simply reproduces and reaffirms the reality of the excessive investor, inmates and guards had their conventional roles reconstructed toward a shared and democratic relationship. This is consistent with JanMohamed's (1994) call for a 'de-identification' and 're-identification', and with Lacan's and Freire's suggestions for the development of alternative master signifiers and a potentially new knowledge base. Here too we have the basis for the development of new discursive subject positions.

Members of 'the just community' were able to call a meeting at any time. When a 'cottage rule offense' was discovered the meeting acted as a jury to determine guilt or innocence. If discipline was considered necessary, the issue was referred to a board comprising two inmates and one staff member chosen at random:

> Routine issues, involving matters like work assignments, love triangles, or personal conflict are dealt with through open discussion. The committee occasionally deals with issues of contraband, assault and attempted escape. Cottage rules are redefined every twelve weeks in a marathon meeting. Here there are often further negotiations with administrators as to the kind of issues that cottage democracy may deal with. (Scharf, 1977: 104)

Inmates in the just community are not diagnosed or treated and no assumptions are made about character or personality traits. The absence of professionals, says Scharf, 'makes it more difficult for program staff members to exempt themselves from the judgements of the group or to deny the moral claims of inmates by means of psychotic roles, labels, or terminology' (1977: 105).

In a similar experiment in prison democracy, Barlinnie prison in Scotland also developed a just community after the failure of conventional control systems, and a violent riot. A community was established in which each prisoner and staff member at the meetings had an equal vote on discipline and other issues, and as a result: 'A startling sense of comradeship evolved in the unit. Instead of the "them" and "us" attitude between prisoners and warders, "them" and "us" came to denote the unit and the rest of the prison system' (Hilton, 1977: 12). Here we see an excellent example of replacement discourse as new meanings become signified by old signifiers.

The just community, then, provides a way of making what is nearly always a finite confinement of the excessive investor into a constructive learning experience which deconstructs existing power relations and provides a forum for the development of shared responsibility built on relational respect for others. As such, the just community is a crucial component of the overall policy of replacement discourse since it provides the presently imprisoned and sometime-to-be-released offender with humanitarian alternatives in relating to others that are redirected toward shared cooperation and away from individual competitive survival.

Beyond rehabilitation: reconstruction and recovery

The model for this approach to dealing with ex-offenders and especially those released from existing confinement is Mimi Silbert's self-supporting Delancey Street Project that, as we saw earlier, attempts to deconstruct both the stereotypical and limited public beliefs about offenders and those similar beliefs that offenders hold about themselves. Through 'dissipation' sessions Delancey residents 'get rid of the tremendous guilt over what they did in the past' (Whittmore, 1992: 6). At the same time, their lives are reconstructed to become 'recovering subjects'. By giving ex-offenders democratic participation and shared responsibility, members of Delancey Street learn to become self-reliant, self-confident and mutually respectful, stressing each member's responsibility for their own actions and their capacity to make a difference to their own and others' lives. Through these means the Delancey operation has built a multi-million dollar commercial center on San Francisco's Embarcadero, runs an upscale bistro, operates a moving company and several other businesses, all self-run by the former offenders. The approach is beyond rehabilitation. Thus Silbert rejects causal theories of crime that assume a passive human subject, replacing these with an active human subject who acknowledges individual responsi-bility and capacity to make a difference. Also, new master signifiers and a new relatively stable linguistic coordinate system are generated through this process. Within this new discursive framework alternative embodiments of desire and constructions of reality can take place. It also provides a form of 'knot-breaking' and reconfiguration in which a new basis of psychic stability is being constructed.

Central to Delancey Street's success, then, is its policy of deconstruction and reconstruction using the strategy of replacement discourse. Both projects and personal activities are organized to reflect this deconstructive and reconstructive approach, the de-emphasis of what was negative and destructive and the emphasis of what is positive: 'We ask them to act as if they were upstanding citizens or successful executives, even though they feel the opposite. Through external imitation, something gets internalized' (Whittmore, 1992: 5). This use of replacement discourse is illustrated in Silbert's response to those inmates who felt like quitting during the building of the foundation's waterfront complex:

> I know you're hammering away and thinking that this isn't worth it, but you're hammering away on your *lives* . . . You're building your *own* foundation. If you make a mistake with that wall, tear it down and rebuild it! That's what we're doing at Delancey Street, for *ourselves* – tearing down bad things and making good things to replace 'em. And if you're too guilty and angry and hopeless to fight for yourself, then do it for the next guy. Because he's counting on you. Meanwhile you're learning new skills. You're getting something that nobody can take away from you. You're building your lives. (Whittmore, 1992: 5, quoting Mimi Silbert)

Thus, instead of resurrecting the idea of born to crime, Delancey emphasizes how previously excessive investors in power over others 'can be taught to help themselves to be responsible and self-reliant' and points out that helping them becomes 'a critical part of turning around the rest of society' (Whittemore, 1992: 5).

Beyond treatment: narrative therapy

Where excessive investors do not respond in the group settings or continue to harm others around them, preparation for their own reconstruction as recovering subjects might benefit from closely supervised narrative therapy. Our suggestions here are predicated on the assumption that a sizable group of excessive investors, many of whom can be better framed within conflict dynamic situations (e.g. Black's 'conciliatory' style of social control), may be provided with narrative therapy as an alternative to more punitive reactions rooted in violence. However, we acknowledge that not all will benefit. Since we are only providing some directions, we see our suggestion here as one of many possible directions that need to be developed using postmodernist conceptualizations.

Narrative therapy developed as part of family therapy, and recently a number of postmodernist-oriented 'narrative therapies' have emerged. Unlike conventional therapy, which privileges therapists' stories over those of the client, this approach reconfigures the therapist–client relationship. Instead of being the arbiter of truth, the therapist becomes a skilled and compassionate editor helping clients regain a sense of personal authority and enabling them to construct more liberating life narratives.[8] The postmodernist assumption is made that life narratives are inextricably linked to self-concept; they are constitutive of selves. Thus the aim is not to discover the true life narrative, since none is uniquely 'true'. Rather, the aim is 'the replacement of an inchoate life narrative by a congruent one, and the transformation of meanings that previously blocked the person's story with new ones' (Omer and Strenger, 1992: 253). Narrative therapies privilege pluralistic discursive production.[9] They provide a redirection of the constitutive energy of the excessive investor and an affirmative medium for her/his recovering authorship (a de-reification), particularly in interpersonal relations.

Although a relatively new concept, narrative therapy is an approach to individualized treatment that takes seriously the importance of the postmodernist 'narrative turn' and imports it into clinical practice (Parry and Doan, 1994). A number of recent narrative therapists advocate deconstruction, re-visioning, and narrative reconstruction. Narrative therapy then is a discovery of untold stories and a reconstruction of the unspeakable, the unsaid. Rather than a family therapy engaged in normalizing the problem, whereby the suffering subject's experiences are placed in grand narratives with their attendant diagnostic categories (which serve as a master discourse), postmodernist narrative therapists 'invite their clients to become their own authors' and to become poets (1994: 47, 27).

A starting point in doing narrative therapy is the assumption that many conflicts stem from 'negative misreadings' of the intentions of others, our own, or both (1994: 29). To respond to the other by a further negative misreading is to perpetuate the cycle. This process needs to be interrupted. Interruption can occur not by providing a 'more accurate' reading, a normalizing technique, as in a master discourse, but by taking an intentional stance of 'compassionate misreading'. This is a 'decision to interpret the actions of the other as, in Rorty's term, a "fellow sufferer"' (1994: 29).[10] As Parry and Doan suggest,

> we can conclude that an offending other is likely to be acting more out of anxiety, hurt, or confusion than out of meanness, perversity, or dislike of us. There is always the chance that such an interpretation will be wrong, but the *performative* consequences are still more likely to be beneficial than those proceeding from a negative misreading. (1994: 29)

There are two major steps involved in a postmodern narrative therapy. First, an 'externalization' is required (similar to deconstruction) whereby the client is encouraged to separate her/himself from the dominant narratives that constrain her/him.[11] Second, it is necessary to actively search and construct alternative narratives (reconstruction), 'revisionings', narratives of differences that give symbolic form (e.g. the embodiment of desire) to the 'unspeakable', the unsaid, *pas-toute*. The excessive investor, in becoming transformed into the recovering subject, is encouraged to be a recovering author. The newly constructed narratives and texts are more of the 'writerly form' than of the 'readerly form' of Barthes (1974).

In other words, these are texts that defy closure and maintain internal tensions.[12]

Other postmodern approaches to narrative replacement have been derived from chaos theory.[13] Butz's (1992c) theory is an advance because he identifies the symbolic nature of the change that takes place through narrative re-visions. He argues that people periodically find themselves in a 'stress–anxiety causal loop' such that: order $\rightarrow$ stress $\rightarrow$ untamed instinctual energy $\rightarrow$ tension $\rightarrow$ anxiety $\rightarrow$ symbolic genesis $\rightarrow$ full symbolic expression (1992b: 212).[14] At the end of this process, Butz locates a Mandelbrot set. He also indicates that this has some similarity with the notion of 'mandala' that Jung had developed that periodically appears in the Imaginary as a symbol of wholeness. Here it functions as an attractor, generated during the onset of chaos (Butz, 1992a: 1059–60). He then diagrams a loop that surrounds this inner loop and shows a parallel with chaos developments. He begins with a 'transitory self' and moves on to: bifurcation $\rightarrow$ second bifurcation $\rightarrow$ third bifurcation $\rightarrow$ fourth bifurcation $\rightarrow$ chaos $\rightarrow$ struggle or preparation $\rightarrow$ acceptance of chaos $\rightarrow$ psychic death $\rightarrow$ transcendence $\rightarrow$ transitory self. His transitory self has similarities to our notion of the recovering subject. Butz tells us there is an 'interdependent relationship with the environment'. His approach is concerned with the coupling of the development of the transitory self with transcendent cycles (1992b: 214; see also Grotstein, 1990). This construction has a parallel structure with the coupled constitutive iterative loops that we developed in Chapter 7. However, although indicating the importance of the symbol, Butz does not sufficiently develop the connectedness of symbolic systems to chaos processes.

Several other works could augment Butz's analysis. Parry and Doan (1994), for example, indicate that at bifurcation points alternative, often competing narratives, are being constructed. A re-visioning takes place in the dialogical encounter between therapist and client. This occurs both in producing a death of previous less useful narratives, and in preparation for transcendence. Lacan, too, indicates that previous master signifiers are discarded and new more appropriate master signifiers are developed. Thus an alienation/separation occurs within the Imaginary, Symbolic and Real Orders, by way of the discourse of the analyst, and in our appropriation, the discourse of the hysteric/analyst (1991; Bracher, 1993: 54, 63–80). We use the combination hysteric/analyst, for it implies that the analyst/therapist must also be engaged in self-discovery. S/he must become transparent to those s/he works with (Parry and Doan, 1994: 132, 136, 191–3).[15] Cornell's (1991) development of Irigaray's work on 'mimesis', whereby subordination is turned into an affirmation, due to the excesses produced in the metaphoric displacements of images in the phallocentric Symbolic Order, is also noteworthy here (1991: 147–52, 162–3, 182, 199).

In relation to our earlier conceptualization, narrative reconstructions are constitutive iterative loops (see Chapter 7). They provide additional 'squiggles' that transform otherwise more linear developments. The recovering subject-as-author is encouraged to develop narratives and constitutive master signifiers that better embody desire (i.e. Lacan's ethical principle of 'avowing one's desire', 1992: 309), that provide a language of possibility (Giroux, 1992).

Thus new challenging postmodernist forms of narrative therapy provide one entrance for the Trojan horse. But this approach cannot be disconnected from the existing historically situated socio-economic conditions. Indeed, it is just such conditions that are the formative context of the conflicts that divide human subjects from themselves. Yet it seems that narrative therapies can also be helpful in this wider struggle against oppressive conditions, since they dovetail into recent attempts to develop a peacemaking criminology. Postmodernist narrative therapies can be usefully developed in dispute management/mitigation forms of social control and in peace pedagogues (Harris, 1990).[16] This framework allows disputants to: (1) move away from zero-sum conflicts; (2) see alternative and more expansive possibilities of resource use; (3) recognize the interests in the other; (4) see opportunities to de-escalate otherwise spiraling conflict (Kriesberg, 1991: 404–6); (5) engage in a mutual accommodation; and (6) develop alternative narratives and master signifiers that better reflect their reconstructed notions of the 'what happened'. The process is a continuous one.

A recent experiment in a conciliatory style of intervention has begun in a maximum security prison at the Augusta Correctional Center in Virginia (Deans, 1994). The program, 'Peace Studies/Alternatives to Violence', was started by two prisoners in 1992 and initially involved a dozen of the prison's violent inmates. The program has three phases. In the initial phase the prisoners, who are not promised any form of credit toward parole, participate in a twelve-week program (classes for three days a week) where they are introduced to such peacemaking theorists and activists as Gandhi, Martin Luther King Jr, Tolstoy, and Merton in order to enable them to rethink their use of violence. Phase two consists of further classes, victim/offender workshops, and outreach projects. This includes participation with various non-prisoner educational groups. The third phase includes job training. They boast a recent graduating class of 60 in 1994, and a waiting list of 250. The selection committee for participation includes four members; priority is given to those who have been convicted of violent crimes, have substantial records of violence in prison, and indicate a willingness to change. Participants' disciplinary records are tracked. One recent report by Deans (1994), writing for the newsletter of Murder Victims' Families for Reconciliation (MVFR), states that in the nearly two years since inception no graduates of the program have been charged with a prison violation even though most had extensive histories of prison violations up to the time of their induction into the program. The program participants also publish a newsletter, *The Mediator*, and various pamphlets.

This program is consistent with the ideals of narrative therapy as well as a conciliatory method of intervention. The recovering subject is offered an alternative discourse and discursive subject position within which to take up residence in the construction of how violence develops and how alternatives may be applied. It is clear that in such programs alternative master signifiers can be developed, especially so when a holistic program attempts to reconnect the word with action as Freire instructs. In so much as the prisoners' program interfaces with one of the largest national victims' rights organizations (Deans, 1994) the interpenetration of otherwise diametrically opposed discourses should prove beneficial in creating social realities that better explain the various onsets of harms of reduction and repression and hence a knowledge base for better interventionist policies that reduce the infliction of harm by the excessive investor.

Our suggestions are particularly appropriate to what Black (1976; see also Scimecca, 1991) called the conciliatory style of social control (see Chapter 8). We see the conciliatory style of law providing a context wherein alternative constructions can take place, a 'borderland' (Giroux, 1992) where a language of possibility can take form. Sites of struggle, and the spheres of potential social transformations, therefore, are multiple. A number of authors have suggested this conflict regulation approach to social control that may focus on various institutional forms: (1) in the international sphere;[17] (2) in the sphere of management–labor conflicts;[18] (3) in environmental conflict;[19] (4) in the sphere of community conflict;[20] and (5) in the sphere of family conflict.[21] Moreover, there are several views as to the meaning of this approach: conflict resolution (the desirable end is a resolution of the problem and stability is sought), conflict settlement (some third party imposes a solution), conflict mitigation (whereby 'one seeks to control the adverse consequences of the way a conflict is waged') (Kriesberg, 1991: 404), and conflict management (conflict is seen as stemming from organizational configurations) (Scimecca, 1991: 264–5; Burton, 1987; 1990; Kriesberg, 1991: 404–6). At times, in the literature, the adjective 'conflict' is replaced by 'dispute' (e.g. dispute management, etc.). Conflict management implies that 'For the most part . . . no real structural changes in the conditions that produced the conflict are altered. It is their conflict that is managed, not the conflict that is produced by the workplace' (Scimecca, 1991: 265; Burton, 1987). In so much as our constitutive criminological approach sees much of the harms of reduction and repression stemming from COREL sets, we see a desirable emphasis on conflict regulation/ mitigation, in so much as after identifying some of the COREL sets as energizing harm and the excessive investor, an initiated radical pluralism would indicate that the spheres of conflict may increase at all levels (Unger, 1987) with the emphasis on giving legitimacy in dispersion in far-from-equilibrium conditions. But the psychological stance toward change and diversity and the mechanism for dealing with conflict would be altered as our thesis suggests (in the last main section in this chapter, concerning an 'empowered democracy', we follow Unger's 1987 lead in developing some suggested protective rights). In our view, too, since COREL sets are implicated in much of the harms of reduction and repression and in the energizing of the excessive investor, an equal emphasis should be placed on a new social justice policy that addresses the configurations that consistently produce harm. We are suggesting, then, some interventionist strategies that would break the normally developed limit attractors found in equilibrium states; or to put it in the language we developed in Chapter 7, we are suggesting ways of adding transformational factors, the squiggles in the constitutive iterative loops, which would assure continuous change, an orderly disorder. Since all is 'coupled', that is since our notion of constitutive iterative loops has it that parallel and interpenetrating structures abound, then change in one sphere will have an effect in others. And since there is a sensitive dependence on initial conditions, these changes cannot be predicted with precision as to their eventual outcome. Thus change, spontaneity, irony, chance, indeterminacy, non-linear developments, etc. are expected phenomena in far-from-equilibrium conditions.

Since our thesis of constitutive interrelational sets indicates dispersion in discursive production, the development of a plurality of master signifiers and narrative constructions cannot find a universality, as Lyotard (1984: 65–6) quite appropriately criticizes Habermas' goal of an 'ideal speech situation' as doing. Our social judo metaphor provides the idea that the heightened powers of the excessive investor must be the basis of a refraction in the development of alternative narratives.

Of course, as several critics have argued (Harrington and Merry, 1988; Cain, 1985; Abel, 1982), many of the current approaches to social change and conflict resolution still rest on the order framework and the desire for a form of consensual justice. For example, many in peace studies, family therapy, and conflict resolution still maintain a desirable end as homeostasis or the re-establishment of equilibrium or consensus. Given our constitutive position on the proliferation of differences and ongoing dispersion, the instances of conflict will continue to be ubiquitous. What is most important is developing some contingent notion of desirable societal dynamics: in our view, a far-from-equilibrium dynamic in an empowered democracy, which does not see consensus as an inherently desirable stable state (see also Lyotard, 1984) but yet safeguards against oppressive practices and liberates human potentialities. Accordingly, in our main concluding section we will see whether alternative narrative constructions can find a proliferation of forms of expression in far-from-equilibrium conditions.

Thus it is inappropriate, from a constitutive view, to idealize 'resolution' or the disappearance of conflict. As Unger points out (1987: 562), there is indeed a 'zone of heightened mutual vulnerability' in the revised notion of community. But here conflict can be more fully aired. This can be the basis of 'moments of ardor and empowerment, and the quality that life attains at these privileged moments can under favorable circumstances be perpetuated in lasting personal commitments and diffused through a broader social experience' (1987: 582). Here there will be an ongoing dialectic: the new community, 'although jeopardized by conflict, also thrives on it' (1987:

582). Before examining the nature of this new community in more detail we need to consider one more aspect of the local: the constituted victim.

A note on the administration of justice

At this point, we acknowledge that we have been silent on the administration of justice. What do we suggest should happen to the courts? In our view, law, and in particular its perpetuation as a constituted reality through the courts, is part of what sustains a modernist, hierarchically divided society. On this, modernists might agree ('that is law's function!'). Unlike most critics of capitalist legality, we do not think the system of administering justice should be reformed or replaced. Rather, like great debates of a former era, we believe it should fall into relative disuse. This is not so much a replay of Marxist arguments concerning the withering of the state. Instead, we believe that with the realization of empowered recovering subjects in a fully democratic society, the proliferation of decentralized non-state alternative, informal or private forms of justice and conflict resolution will diminish the relevance of the centralized state system of justice. In other words, when everyone is his/her own musician, going to see a concert loses much of its superordinate importance – though it will still have a place. So too will the formal administration of justice, for in the end it is necessary to preserve sufficient capability to protect the superliberal democratic order from those with ambitions to undermine its momentum. Consider Knopp's radical feminist position on abolition in which she argues that any necessary restraint of excessive investors should be qualified by two principles: '(1) that public safety and constitutional rights of victims and offenders be the overriding guiding principle, and (2) that the least restrictive and most human option for the shortest period of time in the most remedial and restorative environment be applied' (1993: 59). Thus we are not so naive as to embrace the anarchist's faith in mutualism. We are only too well aware that should all the laws and all the police be swept away, there would be nowhere to run from the tyranny of the would-be excessive investor. The point is to minimize the role of this formal system to be fitting with the minimal social needs, not to abolish it entirely. Such is our reinvention of justice.

Reintegrating the victim: reconstructing the recovering subject

This third component of the overall policy takes seriously the realist criminologist's concern for the victim, tempered by the postmodernist analysis of victimage (see Chapter 3). Here we examine short-term relief for the constituted victim through strategies designed to integrate the recovering subject into a relationally oriented community network of fellow subjects.

Much of the concern about victims fails to empower them directly;

whether this is from the recent left realist celebration of working class victims at the feet of the conspiring forces of capitalism, patriarchy and racism, mediated through a state social control apparatus,[22] or the more traditional concerns of victimology toward the victim as an active agent in the criminal process.[23] It either uses them, as in realism, to buttress failing arguments for the rehabilitation of offenders, or else blames them for conspiring at their own fate and offers liberation through self-defense and restricted domains of action and movement, as in much victimology.

More recently, these ideas have merged into the concept of the victim's charter. This goes beyond traditional victimology which advocates restitution (as opposed to mere compensation) from the offender for the harm they caused.[24] Instead, it advocates state financial compensation (on the basis that the state did not sufficiently protect the victim), sympathetic treatment by the criminal justice system, and the need for victim support services (Morgan and Zedner, 1992). Additionally, there has been recognition of a therapeutic need for victims to become an active part of the justice process through victim–offender mediation programs, and not by simply being a passive recipient of compensation or restitution (Hughes and Schneider, 1989).

From our constitutive perspective it is necessary to recognize that any empowerment of victims of harm must begin by recognizing the constituted nature of the victim. At its simplest, this was Schafer's (1976: 147) insight when he recognized that the victim–offender relationship was a pre-connected one, and that these categories were not discrete but were overlapping and interrelated through a 'mutuality of doing and suffering between the participants in crime'. A critical modernist reading of this traditional position fuels suspicion that victimology is all about blaming the victim. However, from a constitutive postmodern perspective it is a recognition of the interrelated nature of the human subject as both potential excessive investor and constituted victim. As such, this has clear implications for post-crime (harm) relationships.

The constituted victim's experience of harm comprises the emotional stress, conflict, tension and pain resulting from the sudden difference between the ideal or anticipated social position in which the offense has redefined them, together with the loss of familiar and anticipated social roles and demands to behave differently in relation to their new situation. The critical question from a victim-oriented position is how to best deal with the pain and associated anger of being 'so harmed'. Conventional victimology, with a few exceptions, seeks restoration of the victim to their former standing: a reversion to past roles and a resurrection of the familiar.

A constitutive victimology, in contrast, takes the view that crimes of harm are occasions of severe disturbance of the constituted order for those victimized. Rather than restore the human subject to their pre-victim status (i.e. render them whole as a renewed potential victim), with the added confirmation of their now interrelated potential for harming others, we see victimization as an opportunity for reconfiguration as recovering subjects.

In dealing with this problem, mutual aid (self-help) groups can be a significant catalyst in turning the constituted victim of crime into a recovering subject, since they operate primarily through a form of narrative reconstruction.[25] Let's briefly explore the discursive dynamics of these groups.

The dynamics of mutual aid for the constituted victim

Studies of self-help and mutual aid groups demonstrate that human subjects who seek to solve traumatic and life-threatening problems with fellow sufferers start out by sharing their problems in groups that lead to a desire for change.[26] Several common characteristics have been identified that operate to deconstruct the pain of the status occupied by the problem sufferer.[27] First, is the belief that the other members of the group have experienced the same problems; that no one is separate, superior or professional. They are equal problem sufferers. This is important for empowerment because, unlike in professional–client relationships, members of mutual aid groups have an empathetic understanding of their members' problems from first-hand experience. Moreover, by excluding those with claims to expert knowledge, the separation of problem sufferers from each other is dissolved.

Second, this shared situation and empathetic understanding, which is exemplified by descriptive instances of one's own experience through which another can identify, provides a sense of relief by lifting the burden of self-imposed failure, resentment, guilt and helplessness that Levine (1988: 40) refers to as 'self-ostracization'. A person might feel isolated in their loss, but sharing this in a context with many similarly situated others allows feelings of normality to predominate over those of deviance. Related to this, the public moral meaning of the victim status is likely to be suspended, with the result that interactive stress is reduced: 'interactions with others are likely to be less strained, more rewarding, and more intimate than relations with non-stigmatized people' (Gibbons, 1986: 141).

Third, mutual aid and support from regular group meetings form a basis for developing an informal network of contacts. Because all members are also helpers, the feeling that support is ever ready is bolstered and this matches the nature of the problem which is enduring and isolating (see Deans, 1994).

Fourth, the 'helper-therapy principle' (Riessman, 1965) operates such that in a situation in which people help others with a common problem, it is the helper that benefits most from the exchange. As Levine (1988: 42) says, 'The role of helper alleviates the degraded social identity experienced when the member is enmeshed in a deviant role.' The negative experiences associated with the original loss are converted to positive ones as the victim is able to assist fellow victims. As a result their whole self-system is slowly questioned and reconstructed. Moreover, the ability of victims to help others and thereby demonstrate their ability to cope, serves as a role model to newcomers, and as with other mutual aid groups, shows that 'someone not too different has overcome a seemingly insurmountable problem' (Levine, 1988: 42). The emphasis on reinforcement of self-concepts hastens the person's separation from their investment in being a powerless sufferer. This is facilitated by collective will-power and belief.

Perhaps most important, when considering the postmodernist perspective on mutual aid groups as transformatory for socially constructed victim categories, is the observation that such groups are 'not merely a forum for deconstructing members' problems by coping with practicalities and coping with stigma', but also a 'positive process, enabling members to reconstruct a new way of living through project work' (Robinson and Henry, 1977: 94). Crucial to the interrelated processes of deconstruction and reconstruction is the emphasis given by many groups to a factual understanding of their problem. Members share not only problem experiences but diverse collections of data gathered from their own experiences of 'what works'. This reliance on experiential knowledge as a priority over objective or expert knowledge is part of the empowering process of replacement discourse. It is particularly relevant to the first stage of a three-stage process that constitutes 'project work'.[28]

Project work

In the first stage of project work, central difficulties are defined simply and practical information is shared about how to manage day-to-day problems (e.g. information on agencies who provide services, on legal rights, etc.). Members have been found to have superior coping skills in crisis situations (Rychtarik, 1986). Central to communicating practical coping skills is building up a body of expertise about the problem. This information elevates each member into their own authority and simultaneously provides them with the resources to combat the ignorance of others in everyday encounters. Coping with the transformed, reduced or repressed status involves continuous support, a re-education of the member and of the outside world. However, in order to be successful, project work must involve selecting, from among all the problems confronted, those that are simple, clear and manageable. These are then used to demonstrate to the member that they can control aspects of their everyday life and ultimately their own destiny. This also entails a form of 'narrative therapy', by which new master signifiers and discourses begin to take form which help empower the person in conflict mitigation. Hence, the empowering nature of focused, technical project work.

The second stage of project work involves constructive action towards shared goals based upon the philosophy that members are changed by active participation in projects. Projects involve working jointly with others toward a goal that enhances the group for the members. The most significant projects are those relating to helping other fellow problem sufferers. A project may be anything from typing letters about a future activity, photocopying or mailing, to organizing a campaign or conference. It is through such projects that the third stage of the reconstruction process takes place, beyond the group to a network of friends.

The purpose of the third stage of project work is to help the person give up relying on the all-embracing support of the group and to enable them to form new friendship networks in the community. This 'ends social isolation and replaces it with a social network, which enhances the individual's opportunities for receiving coping assistance' (Levine, 1988: 42; Thoits, 1986). Thus project work at this level is crucial to rewriting the human subject from victim to recovering subject. The transformational aspect of mutual aid groups is what makes their members coming together a different response than can be accomplished alone or through the assistance of formal agencies. In reconstructing life to replace that devalued by victimization, the painful experiences are flooded with positive experiences whereby their negative impact is minimized and absorbed into the wider context of everyday living (Pfhul and Henry, 1993).

For many groups, reconstruction of the subject through project work is the end in itself, leading to a new way of life. For others, however, reconstruction involves a more public form of project work: transformation of the public definition of the problem, in our case crime and victimization. As Levine argues,

> This can lead to a redefinition of one's problem as a matter of social oppression as it becomes clear to members that forms of legal or institutional discrimination or powerlessness are related to the problems members experience. The new consciousness can provide a basis for social and political action to relieve oppression, either by seeking an increase in the allocation of resources to the group's cause, by working for a change in the public's definition of the problem, or by seeking relief through litigation and legislation. (1988: 41)

For the victim this marks their metamorphosis into a recovering subject. The aim here is to alter the public meaning of the victim's situation. It also means engaging in replacement discourse. As Levine says,

> Each group tends to develop its own language and conceptual tags for common experiences . . . As members discuss their experiences, they are interpreted within the group in terms of the group's ideology, language and slogans . . . The concept, as represented by the language or the slogan, enters a member's consciousness. The concept is used to interpret new situations, to reinterpret continuing ones, to guide choices and actions, and in consequence to affect feelings. (1988: 41)

Thus, what we have here, in Lacan's terms, is nothing less than the generation of new master signifiers: words that reflect Freire's notion of a connectedness between action and reflection. Here desire can be empowering. It may also lead to a better understanding of COREL sets and their contribution to harms of reduction and repression and hence possible change. Recognizing that redefining and controlling the knowledge about being a victim requires investment in mutual aid by those victimized does not blind us to the forces of dissension and the power of dominant groups to undermine movements for change.

The limits of mutual aid

The fact that marginalized subjects come together around their mutual interests does not necessarily mean that they constitute a movement, are democratic, or that they form a counter-culture. There are several reasons for this. First, groups of deviants who come together for the purposes of transforming their stigma focus on *their* problems and those of their members, but rarely do they focus on the wider social context in which their problem is framed, and they may even exacerbate the underlying problems.

Second, such groups exist in dependent relationships with professionals who are relied upon to solve their technical problems and to obtain legitimacy. This allows professionals to reciprocally rely on them as 'support groups' which coopts them to a subordinate role within the structure of existing power relationships. In such circumstances some of the more vociferous advocates for political change may be palliated, if for no other reason than having their energies diverted to self-serving rather than transforming work. A similar problem arises as a result of groups' ambivalent relationship with the media (see Pfuhl and Henry, 1993).

Third, these groups can readily be undermined and controlled through their relationships to the outside world.

Finally, the very attempt by some groups to bring about change in their members is one that often discourages critical questioning. Newcomers are discouraged from questioning basic principles and those who are disruptive are dismissed as 'sick'. A form of master discourse is invoked. Members who stray are frowned upon and the groups exert extreme pressure to inner loyalty through shaming and ostracism, compounding the problems of transparency and secrecy.

In summary then, the politics of mutual aid groups shows the dialectical nature of transformation. Transformation is a complex interwoven process in which attempts to change others result in changes to selves and as a result the outcome of any deliberate strategy is, as chaos theorists have told us, unpredictable at the very least. However, this is all the more reason why it is important to deal with the wider structure of society which provides the formative context for the recovering subject's ongoing recovery. It is to this structural level of transformation that we now turn.

Structural transformation toward superliberalism: not by words alone

The final set of broad strategies for the practice implications of our overall justice policy recognizes the modernist social critic's view that local action alone is inadequate to transform structural, state and institutional systems that are discursively entrenched. Solely focusing on the Symbolic Order and/or the Imaginary Order will not suffice. We need to also consider the Real Order, the sphere of generation of primordial sense data reflective of COREL sets. To assist in devising a broad structural framework that is facilitative of, and receptive to, emerging and recovering subjects, it is necessary that humans have a genuine power of self-determination in the wider political economy. A useful starting point here is Unger's notion of superliberalism. Unger's vision is of 'a society in which people are more fully empowered through the development of institutional arrangements that both diminish the gap between framework-preserving routine and framework-transforming conflict and weaken the established forms of social division and hierarchy' (1987: 362). As in chaos theory, this logic can be recurring at different levels as self-similarity ('recursive symmetries').

Unger's call for a dynamic, non-ossifying social structure shares common ecological space with chaos theory. Chaos theory, as we have seen, privileges far-from-equilibrium conditions and the dissipative structures that arise as bifurcation points are negotiated. In equilibrium conditions (e.g. as envisioned by structural functionalists and assumed in the order framework), the formal bureaucratic apparatus tends towards functional rigidity (ossification), becoming insensitive to human input. In this model, organizational change is seen as linear; deterministic assumptions rule (Leifer, 1989; Jantsch, 1980).[29] For chaos theorists, it is within far-from-equilibrium conditions that structural instabilities produce periodic crises which necessitate change.

Change in organizational structures occurs in various ways, and we shall not review the exhaustive literature on this here but focus on just two models. In one of these, change entails recoding the many environmental factors for organizational preserving purposes.[30] Another way change occurs involves dissipative structures undergoing fundamental reorganization, whereby they gain additional energy in the process (autopoietic structures are instances of this form). It is this second model of change that has similarities to Unger's vision. The bureaucratic structure, on the other hand, attempts to maintain equilibrium conditions within the organization, leading to a disconnection from its environment and eventual stagnation.

Dissipative structures, however, are structures that are especially sensitive to their environments. At a critical point, the previously existing coping capabilities of the organization are exceeded, necessitating change (a bifurcation point is reached). The dissipative structures existing in far-from-equilibrium conditions handle increasing complexity in more efficient ways, as a result of their ability to import energy and skills from the environment. Thus, more usable energy remains (Leifer, 1989: 905) and entropy (the measure of energy used) is actively and creatively overcome (Leifer, 1989; Jantsch, 1980: 27, 31). Here, disorder leads to order. Put another way, symmetry breaking or structural decoupling leads to the establishment of a new structural arrangement that is more efficient in dealing with its environment. This also involves 'cultivating enthusiasm for improvisation and minimal constraints, which prepare and indoctrinate people for easy, low resistance response to trigger events' (Leifer, 1989: 907; see our discussion on narrative therapy earlier in this chapter).

Within far-from-equilibrium conditions, change is ubiquitous. Dissipative structures maintain an interdependent and sensitive relationship with their environment (Gemmill and Smith, 1985; Baker, 1993: 133–41). As Unger says:

> The kernel of this revised ideal of community is the notion of a zone of heightened mutual vulnerability, within which people gain a chance to resolve more fully the conflict between the enabling conditions of self-assertion: between their need for attachment and for participation in group life and their fear of the subjugation and depersonalization with which such engagement may threaten them. (1987: 562)

Accordingly, consistent with Unger, and our theory of COREL sets, change can originate from multiple sites. Forces are mobilized in order to maintain far-from-equilibrium conditions, but in a way that safeguards the basic security of recovering subjects and assures them necessary welfare rights. Thus, these proposals attempt to protect against (1) 'instruments of subjugation' and (2) limits being placed on 'effective challenge and revision' (1987: 516).

In establishing a radically democratic, alternative political economy, 'the first and basic constructive principle is that the security of the individuals should be established in ways that minimize both the immunity of institutional arrangements to challenge and conflict and the ease with which some individuals can reduce others to dependence' (1987: 513). The development of this empowered democracy entails: expanding the scope of 'context-revising conflict' by maintaining a disequilibrium state between it and 'context-preserving routine' (1987: 514, 516);[31] and protecting humans from retaliatory efforts by providing certain rights. These include: (1) market rights, which offer capital to teams of workers; (2) destabilization rights, that assure a person's uninhibited criticism of existing social structures; (3) immunity rights, which include the freedom from governmental or private oppression, and assure welfare entitlements to material and other resources for well-being such as housing, health care, education, nourishment, etc.; and (4) solidarity rights, which include rights that assure mutual, cooperative development, such as the assurance of trust and good faith dealings (1987: 520–39). To these we add Abel's (1982b) concept of the right to define your own risk, perhaps measured in terms of 'contingent valuation'.[32] Only in totality do these rights protect against subjugation.

In Unger's schema of social structure, the new image of community will add 'a zone of heightened mutual vulnerability' (1987: 562), but within this environment, 'people gain a chance to resolve more fully the conflict between the enabling conditions of self-assertion: between their need for attachment and for participation in group life and their fear of the subjugation and depersonalization with which such engagement may threaten them' (1987: 562). These experiments in states of heightened vulnerability would provide the context of empowerment, leading to an overall increase in quality of life that would carry over into future social encounters. For Unger,

> The citizen of the empowered democracy is the empowered individual. He [she] is able to accept an expanded range of conflict and revision without feeling that it threatens intolerably his [her] most vital material and spiritual interests . . . The constitutional basis for this willingness to accept the risks of expanded conflict lies in the guarantee of immunity afforded by a system that precludes entrenched dependence or domination and keeps every issue open for another day. (1987: 579)

An empowered democracy produces three psychological tendencies: (1) 'attenuation of desire, of its scope and intensity'; (2) an enlargement of imagination; and (3) 'broadening of the actual opportunities to realize in practice the transformed desires produced by the first two tendencies' (1987: 580). Hence, fantasy, enactment and empowerment go hand in hand. Especially important are factors that would encourage 'role-jumbling' or 'role defiance'. Here the 'cultural revolutionary wants to show how roles can be stretched, pulled apart, combined with other roles, and used incongruously' (Unger, 1987: 538, 563–6). In short, rather than role-taking, role-making is at a premium. Only in this way can we engage in alternative textual production of others, ourselves and our mutually constituted social realities. The call is for reconstituting given discursive subject positions.

One practice strategy whereby this may be achieved within the present structure of criminal justice is for different functionaries (officials), such as judges, lawyers, probation officers, guards, police, counselors, to rotate their positions. This will avoid their present tendency to get caught up in narrowly drawn discursive subject positions. By spending periods in such roles (job enrichment) they will be able to draw on and contribute to the production of alternative signifiers and a more diverse linguistic coordinate system. The usual objection to this practice is that the incumbent does not have adequate training to do the tasks that the position requires. However, it is clear that this training could be part of criminal justice professional education, and examples of the English lay magistrate system and socialist workers' courts or people's courts have demonstrated that non-specialists, with some minimal training, can undertake even some of the more complex tasks of administering justice.

We find others in support of this position. Giroux tells us about the desirability of being 'border crossers' and of the development of a 'border pedagogy' where humans are encouraged 'to develop a relationship of non-identity with their own subject positions and with the multiple cultural, political, and social codes that constitute established boundaries of power, dependency, and possibility' (Aronowitz and Giroux, 1991: 199–200; Giroux, 1992: 133–41, 170–6).[33] Through such de-identification and re-identification, the person will be able to better understand the interlocking nature of many forms of oppression. In doing so, COREL sets that contribute to an increase in harms can be identified and actively confronted. In the process, the recovering subject moves away from being a passive subject, one constituted by a 'semi-intransitive consciousness' (Freire, 1985) to one where s/he becomes an active agent of social transformation. The recovering subject must actively resist and reject the internalized subject of dominant groups.[34] This calls for a liberation politics which can articulate 'contingent universalities' concerning struggles against diverse, interpenetrating, and interlocking forms of race, class, and gender domination.[35]

The superliberal agenda of Unger might also benefit from contingently and provisionally based distributive principles as articulated in Reiman's (1990) 'labor theory of moral values'. Although we would disagree with many of Reiman's overly modernistic concepts, which arguably retrench and reconstitute investment in existing forms of wage-labor relations, we would embrace his transitional redistributive principle where *both* the well-off and the disenfranchised are benefited. However, this would merely be a contingent position, to be ultimately replaced by fully participative structures in which employees increasingly share equity in their work organizations, based on the longevity of their service and current levels of profitability.[36]

A materialistically based change in socio-economic and political conditions would be coupled with cultural and discursive changes. We draw from a variety of critical scholars and persuasions to argue that with the movement toward an empowered democracy, both the dominant form of existing discursive formations, and those more unique to particular auto-poietic systems, will undergo modification.[37] From Freire's dialogical pedagogy (1972; 1973; 1985) we can see that new, more responsive signifiers (S1), that are more reflective of existing socio-political and economic arrangements, will be created in dialogical encounters (a joint production connecting the dialectical play of reflection and action).[38] In more equilibrium conditions or in conditions where hierarchical structures are dominant, the sign tends toward 'uniaccentuality', an accenting that privileges dominant groups in a unilateral way. Under these new conditions, the sign would return to a state of 'multiaccentuality': embedded within the sign is the tension and struggle among various polycentered groups striving for acceptance of their particular accenting of 'reality' (Volosinov, 1986; Bakhtin, 1981). Emergent discursive regions and their signifiers would come to be more constituted as dissipative structures, as the referent (signified) begins to be more reflective of existing conditions of existence. But newly developing master signifiers are always in process, never attaining rigidity.

From Lacan we have two insights. With his four discourses we can see that the discourses of the hysteric and the analyst, in conjunction with Freire's dialogical pedagogy, produce new signifiers that defy closure. Such a process again summons dialogical encounters where denied voices now find embodiment in newly created signifiers (Lacan, 1991; Milovanovic, 1993a). From Lacan's work on the Borromean knots we can see the bases of knot-breaking and its replacement by a different configuration which becomes the source of sense production (Milovanovic, 1993b). These knots would no longer be based on the inherent Law-of-the-Father, but rather on a principle of difference and sameness, the 'I' and the 'thou' as inseparably constitutive of social beings, more reflective of the butterfly attractor.

From feminist postmodernist analysis, we see that a polemic with Lacan and with his descriptive analysis of the wherewithal of the phallocentric Symbolic Order (which denies the medium for women of the embodiment of desire) can be extended to other disenfranchised, disempowered, and marginalized groups and becomes the basis of strategizing new signifier production (Cornell, 1992; Brennan, 1994). What results, in short, is the development of new discursive formations which offer a medium (signifiers that are polyvocally centered), a 'contingent universality', by which desire may be embodied in more reflective forms, i.e. Lacan's (1991) 'avowal of desire', producing a 'language of possibility' (Giroux, 1992) rather than a discourse of despair.

This language of possibility, we emphasize, is not offered as a universality. Rather, it is a contingent form that is subject to further clarification, critique, revision and ongoing substitution, by other revisable forms. What seems appropriate for further progress is a system, not of deductive or inductive logic, but of 'abduction' as offered by Peirce (1965) whereby explanatory hypotheses are constituted loosely by both logics.[39] Here, the direction in which logic runs is problematic. In other words, logic (and major premises) never attain a permanent, stable state but act much like a dissipative structure. Although Pierce's abduction seems to go beyond deduction and induction, it insufficiently incorporates the provisional and contingent influences of COREL sets. What is needed is a creative abduction that transcends conventional knowledge and paradigms in inventing provisional and contingent rules and premises that are accommodative of revisable explanations or solutions. Consider Lyotard's summoning of the postmodern subject:

> A postmodern artist or writer is in the position of a philosopher: the text he [she] writes, the work he [she] produces are not in principle governed by preestablished rules, and they cannot be judged according to a determining judgment, by applying familiar categories to the text or to the work. Those rules and categories are what the work of art itself is looking for. The artist and the writer, then, are working without rules in order to formulate the rules of what *will have been done* . . . it must be clear that it is our business not to supply reality but to invent allusions to the conceivable which cannot be presented. (1984: 81; see also Uusitalo, 1991: 180)

In this direction, de Haan has offered a worthy notion of 'redress' (1990: 158). With this concept, problematic events (those calling forth intervention by the control apparatus) are not automatically subsumed under universalistic categories, but are established in the discovery process of understanding and creative response.

In short, our analysis leads to the view that far-from-equilibrium conditions inevitably lead to bifurcation moments where abduction is the process by which new contingent orders (dissipative structures) take form; the latter further contribute to existing far-from-equilibrium conditions. Unger's suggestions, then, point to a direction in which these conditions may be maintained without being a further source of oppression. Failure to recognize this marks the ultimate flaw of all hitherto revolutions, as anarchists have long pointed out. Unfortunately, the anarchist proselytizing for an absence of structure fails even to provide the myth of security.

Thus, contrary to the nihilism of skeptical postmodernism – its fatalism, and its anarchy of knowledge leading to the undecidability of anything – constitutive criminology 'locates the sign in the materiality of social struggle'; it 'does not float in some pan-historical space ... but is "decidable" in the concrete arena of social struggle' (McLaren, 1994: 206; Zavarzadeh and Morton, 1990: 156).

Summary and conclusions

It is abundantly clear to us that any one of the justice practice components discussed in this chapter, taken in isolation, is in danger of being coopted, subverted, or used to reaffirm the existing realities rather than to liberate humans to a new order. Our earlier analysis found the concept of a recovering subject to be the more viable position for humans found in a virtual and infinitely revisable society and global order. In reconceiving crime as power – the power to harm others by denying them their own creative possibilities to make a difference – we came upon the postmodern conception of the criminal. This is not necessarily an evil individual or the passive product of social forces. Rather, the criminal and potential purveyor of harm is found to be a believer in the omnipotence of reality, truth and certainty – an excessive investor in representations of reality, and an investor in the power to frame others' realities in ways that mangle their creative souls. Such is investment in propagation and defense that excessive investors grow with their discursive organizational products, resulting in co-determining, mutually reinforcing orders of oppression and liberation. Our analysis of structure, as constitutive interrelational (COREL) sets, presented both the problem and possibility of liberating discursive formations, the language and technology of possibility. Existing criminal justice policy was found deficient in its conception of the problem of crime and co-constitutive of its ongoing vitality. Instead of a criminal justice policy we suggested a justice policy of replacement discourse. This showed how the liberating forces of COREL sets can be harnessed, albeit contingently, through radical refraction, social judo and radical pluralism. By recognizing the potential of infinitely revisable recovering subjects in conjunction with a dynamic, fluid and ever-emergent structure, we believe it is possible to steer a course through our presently dangerous waters, toward a relatively harm-free world. This is the challenge of our optimism, the nemesis to postmodernism's nihilism.

Notes

1 This section draws heavily from Henry (1994).

2 Chibnall (1977), Cohen and Young (1980), Surette (1984), and Barak (1994).

3 See also Barak and Bohm (1989) and Barak (1991b; 1994).

4 National examples are the contributions of criminologists James Alan Fox of Northeastern University with his numerous media incursions on such issues as profiles of serial killers, children as murderers, and employees who kill (Fox and Levin, 1993); Robert Sampson of the University of Chicago on his response to criminal career paths; Larry Sherman, formerly with the Police Foundation, on the effects of more formal responses by the police to 'disturbance calls'; and James Fyfe of American University in response to police brutality and the Rodney King trial and verdict.

5 See Pepinsky and Quinney (1991), Pepinsky (1991); see also Volpe (1991), Scimecca (1991); and see also Kriesberg (1991) and Harris (1990).

6 See Knopp et al. (1976), Knopp (1991; 1993), MacLean and Pepinsky (1993), Mathiesen (1986), Steinert (1986), and Scheerer (1986).

7 See also Murton's (1976) 'participatory management model' for prisons.

8 Yochelson and Samenow's (1977) criminal personality theory presents a modernist approach which has some parallels to the kind of therapy discussed here. It ultimately fails because it considers excessive investors not as capable human subjects but as programmed personalities with dysfunctional thought processes. However, their intervention techniques are designed to identify and destroy current destructive criminal patterns of thought and decision-making, by confronting offenders directly. They create new thought processes through manipulation of rewards and by confronting offenders with their behavior as victimizers of society in an attempt to increase feelings of guilt and self-disgust. But they also claim to teach how to suppress criminal thoughts and to substitute non-criminal ones in their place. Thus their analysis of crime as power and human subjects as active, if misguided and in need of replacement thought processes, offers some insight toward appropriate therapy, but one that is lost by their narrow behaviorist view of the subject.

9 See, for example, White (1983; 1986; 1988a; 1988b; 1991), White and Epston (1989), Epston and White (1992), de Shazer (1985; 1988), Parry (1990; 1991a; 1991b); Parry and Doan (1994), and Doan (1991).

10 See Foucault (1977), Parry and Doan (1994: 53), Zimmerman and Zimmerman and Dickerson (cited in Parry and Doan, 1994: 53).

11 Recall the discussion of Silbert in the examples above. See also White (1986; 1991), White and Epston (1989), Parry and Doan (1994: 17, 42–3, 52–4). Note that Freire (1972) and Lacan (1991) advocate a similar first step in separating from previously oppressive master signifiers.

12 See Silverman's (1983) idea of 'segmentation', and also Deleuze and Guattari's (1986: 16–23, 28) notion of a 'minor literature'.

13 See Gibney (1987), McLeod (1988), Stevens (1991), Elkaim (1981), Elkaim et al. (1987), Grotstein (1990), and Butz (1992c).

14 By untamed instinctual energy, Butz draws from Jung's work in indicating an undifferentiated source of psychic energy (1992a: 832).

15 See also Parry and Doan (1994) and Freire's (1985) critical dialogical pedagogy. Freire's work is useful in indicating how the subject now recovers the word in its necessary action–reflection dialectical state. See also Lacan's work on the Borromean knots (Milovanovic, 1993b).

16 For an application to criminal justice, see Volpe (1991). In the Dutch context see Slump and Emmen (1993) and their alternative to penal/criminal processing based on experimental civil law.

17 See Burton (1969; 1988; 1990; 1991), Doob and Fotz (1987), Kelman (1987), Kriesberg (1991), and Wedge (1971).

18 See Colosi (1987) and Colosi and Berkely (1986).

19 See Richman (1987), Susskind and Cruikshank (1987), and Bingham (1985).

20 See Scimecca (1988), Pompa (1987), Hofrichter (1987), Tomasic and Feeley (1982), and Kriesberg (1991).

21 See Koopman (1987) and Saposnek (1983).

22 On left or radical realism, see Kinsey and Young (1982), Lea and Young (1984), Matthews and Young (1986), Kinsey et al. (1986), MacLean (1991), Young (1979; 1987), Matthews (1987), Matthews and Young (1992), and Young and Matthews (1992).

23 See von Hentig (1948) and Schafer (1968).

24 Compensation is victim initiated requests for payment for loss from offenders; restitution is court ordered reparation to a victim to restore their position and the rights that were damaged or destroyed by an offender, with the dual purpose of both compensation and penal correction of the offender (Schafer, 1976: 163).

25 For illustrations of this in the case of those suffering from alcohol abuse, see Henry and Robinson (1978a; 1978b; Robinson, 1979; Robinson and Henry, 1977).

26 The remainder of this section draws heavily from Pfuhl and Henry (1993: 215–36).

27 Killilea (1976), Gibbons (1986), Levine and Perkins (1987), and Levine (1988).

28 Robinson and Henry (1977), Henry and Robinson (1978a; 1978b), Pfuhl and Henry (1993).

29 For the influence of rationality in organizational change, see Thompson's (1967) influential work.

30 Consider Luhmann (1985) for a case in point. See also Manning's (1988) semiotic study on how police emergency 911 calls were handled, and Yngvesson's (1993) analysis of how the court clerk acted to screen certain citizen complaints as worthy of processing.

31 This lends itself to a mapping portraying the strange attractor, a state of orderly disorder.

32 Contingent valuation involves economists' surveys of costs as perceived by the individual and their willingness to pay a certain price for a certain amount of risk.

33 See also JanMohamed (1994: 246–51), Foucault (1986), Ebert (1991), and Mouffe (1988: 42).

34 Freire (1972; 1985), JanMohamed (1994: 246–7), Laclau (1990: 17). See also Foucault (1986: 22) and Giroux (1992: 21).

35 See Butler (1992), McLaren (1994: 211), Mouffe (1992); and on interlocking forms of domination see Collins (1993), Giroux (1992: 21), and McLaren (1994: 211).

36 As yet undeveloped, this position presents a challenge for humanistic scholars who need to be mindful of *cul-de-sac* reforms that reconstitute existing power relations, or those that are so extremely radical that they neglect the force of existing totalities. Thus, we envisage an ongoing development of the profit-bonus schemes whereby, instead of receiving cash, employees receive company stock, to build up equity and ultimately co-ownership/partnership of their corporations. On the varieties and promise of such operations as well as their limits, see Flanagan and Rayner (1988).

37 To help facilitate this process it might be necessary to make some fundamental changes to the accessibility that powerful agencies (excessive investors), such as corporations, have to freely buy media time to advertise the images of their products. Such invasions and intrusions into public space might require a limit on media advertising time to single-line announcements, as is typical of public radio and television's one-liners.

38 See McLaren (1994), Aronowitz and Giroux (1991), Giroux (1992), JanMohamed (1992; 1994), and Volosinov (1986).

39 See also Eco (1984); for an application to law, see Uusitalo (1991) and Brion (1995).

References

Abbott, J.H. (1982) *In the Belly of the Beast*. London: Hutchinson.

Abel, R. (1981) 'Conservative conflict and the reproduction of capitalism: the role of informal justice', *International Journal of the Sociology of Law*, 9: 245–67.

Abel, R. (1982a) *The Politics of Informal Justice*. 2 vols. New York: Academic Press.

Abel, R. (1982b) 'A socialist approach to risk', *Maryland Law Review*, 41: 695–754.

Abrahamsen, D. (1944) *Crime and the Human Mind*. New York: Columbia University Press.

Abrahamsen, D. (1960) *The Psychology of Crime*. New York: Columbia University Press.

Adler, F. (1983) *Nations not Obsessed with Crime*. Littleton, CO: Rothman.

Agnew, R.S. (1985) 'A revised strain theory of delinquency', *Social Forces*, 64: 151–67.

Agnew, R.S. (1991a) 'The interactive effect of peer variables on delinquency', *Criminology*, 29: 47–72.

Agnew, R.S. (1991b) 'Strain and subcultural crime theories', in J.F. Sheley (ed.), *Criminology: A Contemporary Handbook*. Belmont, CA: Wadsworth. pp. 273–94.

Agnew, R.S. (1992a) 'Foundation for a general strain theory of crime and delinquency', *Criminology*, 30: 47–87.

Agnew, R.S. (1992b) 'An empirical test of general strain theory', *Criminology*, 30(4): 475–99.

Agnew, R.S. (1995) 'Determinism, indeterminism and crime: an empirical exploration', *Criminology*, 33(1): 83–109.

Ahluwalia, S. (1991) 'Currents in British feminist thought: the study of male violence', *Critical Criminologist*, 3(1): 5–6, 12–14.

Aichhorn, A. (1935) *Wayward Youth*. New York: Viking Press.

Akers, R.L. (1967) 'Problems in the sociology of deviance: social definitions and behavior', *Social Forces*, 46: 455–65.

Akers, R.L. (1985) *Deviant Behavior: A Social Learning Approach*. Belmont, CA: Sage.

Akers, R.L. (1993) *Criminological Theories: Introduction and Evaluation*. Los Angeles: Roxbury.

Alger, C.F. (1984–85) 'Bridging the micro and the macro in international relations research', *Alternatives: a Journal of World Policy*, 10: 319–44.

Althusser, L. (1971) *Lenin and Philosophy*. New York: Monthly Review Press.

American Friends Service Committee (1971) *Struggle for Justice*. New York: Hill and Wang.

Andrews, D.A. et al. (1990) 'A human science approach or more punishment and pessimism: a rejoinder to Lab and Whitehead', *Criminology*, 28(3): 419–26.

Archard, D. (1984) *Consciousness and the Unconscious*. La Salle, IL: Open Court.

Armstrong, G. and Wilson, M. (1973) 'City politics and deviancy amplification', in I. Taylor and L. Taylor (eds), *Politics and Deviance*. Harmondsworth: Penguin. pp. 61–89.

Aronowitz, S. and Giroux, H.A. (1991) *Postmodern Education*. Minneapolis: University of Minnesota Press.

Arrigo, B. (1992) 'An experientially-informed feminist jurisprudence: rape and the move toward praxis', *Humanity and Society*, 17(1): 28–47.

Arrigo, B. (1993) *Madness, Language and the Law*. Albany, NY: Harrow and Heston.

Arrigo, B. (1994a) 'Legal discourse and the disordered criminal defendant: contributions from psychoanalytic semiotics and chaos theory', *Legal Studies Forum*, 18(1): 93–112.

Arrigo, B. (1994b) 'The insanity defense: a study in psychoanalytic semiotics and chaos theory', in R. Kevelson (ed.), *The Eyes of Justice*. New York: Peter Lang. pp. 57–83.

Arrigo, B. (1995) 'Postmodern criminology on race, class, and gender', in M. Schwartz and D.

Milovanovic (eds), *The Intersections of Class, Gender, Race in Criminology*. New York: Garland.

Ashley, D. (1990) 'Marx and the excess of the signifier: domination as production and as simulation', *Sociological Perspectives*, 33(1): 129–46.

Baack, D. and Cullen, J.B. (1992) 'A catastrophe theory model of technological and structural change', *Journal of High Technology Management Research*, 3: 125–45.

Baack, D. and Cullen, J.B. (1994) 'Decentralization in growth and decline: a catastrophe theory approach', *Behavioral Science*, 39: 213–28.

Baker, P. (1993) 'Chaos, order, and sociological theory', *Sociological Inquiry*, 63(2): 123–49.

Bakhtin, M. (1981) *The Dialogical Imagination*. Austin, TX: University of Texas Press.

Balbus, I. (1977a) 'Commodity form and legal form: an essay on the relative autonomy of law', *Law and Society Review*, 11: 571–87.

Balbus, I. (1977b) *The Dialectics of Legal Repression*. New York: Russell Sage.

Balkan, S., Berger, R. and Schmidt, J. (1980) *Crime and Deviance in America: A Critical Approach*. Belmont, CA: Wadsworth.

Balkin, J.M. (1987) 'Deconstructive practice and legal theory', *Yale Law Journal*, 96(4): 743–86.

Bandura, A. (1973) *Aggression: A Social Learning Analysis*. Englewood Cliffs, NJ: Prentice-Hall.

Bandura, A. (1977) *Social Learning Theory*. Englewood Cliffs, NJ: Prentice-Hall.

Bandura, A. (1979) 'The social learning perspective: mechanisms of aggression', in H. Toch (ed.), *Psychology of Crime and Criminal Justice*. New York: Holt, Rinehart and Winston.

Bannister, S. and Milovanovic, D. (1990) 'The necessity defense, substantive justice, and oppositional linguistic praxis', *International Journal of the Sociology of Law*, 18(2): 179–98.

Barak, G. (1988) 'Newsmaking criminology: reflections on the media, intellectuals, and crime', *Justice Quarterly*, 5: 565–87.

Barak, G. (1991a) 'Homelessness and the case for community-based initiatives: the emergence of a model shelter as a short-term response to the deepening crisis in housing', in H. Pepinsky and R. Quinney (eds), *Criminology as Peacemaking*. Bloomington: Indiana University Press. pp. 47–68.

Barak, G. (1991b) *Crimes by the Capitalist State: An Introduction to State Criminality*. Albany, NY: State University of New York Press.

Barak, G. (ed.) (1994) *Media, Process and the Social Construction of Crime: Studies in Newsmaking Criminology*. New York: Garland Press.

Barak, G. (forthcoming) *Integrating Criminologies*. Boston: Allyn and Bacon.

Barak, G. and Bohm, B. (1989) 'The crimes of the homeless or the crimes of homelessness? On the dialectics of criminalization, decriminalization and victimization', *Contemporary Crisis*, 13: 275–88.

Barkum, M. (1968) *Law Without Sanctions*. New Haven, CT: Yale University Press.

Barnett, H. (1981) 'Corporate capitalism, corporate crime', *Crime and Delinquency*, 27: 4–23.

Barthes, R. (1974) *S/Z*. Trans. R. Miller. New York: Hill and Wang.

Bartky, S. (1988) 'Foucault, femininity, and the modernization of patriarchal power', in I. Diamond and L. Quinby (eds), *Feminism and Foucault: Reflections on Resistance*. Boston: Northeastern University Press.

Bartlett, K. (1991) 'Feminist legal methods', in K. Bartlett and R. Kennedy (eds) *Feminist Legal Theory*. Oxford: Westview Press.

Bartol, C.R. (1991) *Criminal Behavior: A Psychological Approach*. 3rd edn. Englewood Cliffs, NJ: Prentice-Hall.

Barton, S. (1994) 'Chaos, self-organization, and psychology', *American Psychologist*, 49(1): 5–14.

Baudrillard, J. (1975) *The Mirror of Production*. Trans. M. Poster. St Louis: Telos Press.

Baudrillard, J. (1981) *For a Critique of the Political Economy of the Sign*. St Louis: Telos Press.

Baudrillard, J. (1983a) *Simulacra and Simulations*. Trans. P. Foss, P. Patton, and P. Beitchman. New York: Semiotext(e).

Baudrillard, J. (1983b) *Les Stratégies Fatales*. Paris: Bernard Grasset.

Baudrillard, J. (1985) 'The masses: implosion of the social in the media', trans. M. Maclean, *New Literary History*, 16(3): 577–89.

Baudrillard, J. (1991) 'La Guerre du Golfe n'a pas eu lieu', *Liberation*, 29 March.

Beccaria, C. (1764) *On Crimes and Punishments*. Trans. Henry Paolucci. Indianapolis: Bobbs-Merrill.

Beck, U. (1992) *Risk Society*. Trans. M. Ritter. London: Sage.

Becker, G.S. (1968) 'Crime and punishment: an economic approach', *Journal of Political Economy*, 76(2): 169–217.

Becker, H.S. (1963) *Outsiders: Studies in the Sociology of Deviance*. New York: Free Press, 1966.

Beirne, P. (1979) 'Empiricism and the critique of Marxism on law and crime', *Social Problems*, 26: 373–85.

Beirne, P. (1991) 'Inventing criminology: the "science of man" in Cesare Beccaria's Dei delitti e delle pene (1764)', *Criminology*, 29(4): 777–820.

Beirne, P. and Sharlet, R. (eds) (1980) *Pashukanis: Selected Writings on Marxism and Law*. New York: Academic Press.

Bennet, L. and Feldman, M. (1981) *Reconstructing Reality in the Courtroom*. New Brunswick, NJ: Rutgers University Press.

Benson, M.L. (1989) 'The influence of class position on the formal and informal sanctioning of white-collar offenders', *The Sociological Quarterly*, 30: 465–79.

Bentham, J. (1765) *An Introduction to the Principles of Morals and Legislation*. Ed. J.H. Burns and H. L. A. Hart. London: Athlone Press, University of London.

Benveniste, E. (1971) *Problems in General Linguistics*. Coral Gables, FL: University of Miami Press.

Berger, P. and Luckmann, T. (1966) *The Social Construction of Reality*. New York: Doubleday.

Berger, P. and Pullberg, S. (1966) 'Reification and social critique of consciousness', *History and Theory*, 4: 196–211

Bergesen, A. (1993) 'The rise of semiotic Marxisms', *Sociological Perspectives*, 36(1): 1–22.

Berry, M.V. (1977) 'Quantum mechanics', in A. Bullock and O. Stallybrass (eds), *The Fontana Dictionary of Modern Thought*. London: Fontana. pp. 517–18.

Best, S. and Kellner, D. (1991) *Postmodern Theory: Critical Interrogations*. New York: Macmillan.

Bingham, G. (1985) *Resolving Environmental Disputes: A Decade of Experience*. Washington, DC: The Conservation Foundation.

Black, D.J. (1976) *The Behavior of Law*. New York: Academic Press.

Black, D.J. (1989) *Sociological Justice*. New York: Oxford University Press.

Blum, R. (1972) *Deceivors and Deceived*. Springfield, IL: Charles Thomas.

Blumer, H. (1969) *Symbolic Interactionism: Perspective and Method*. Englewood Cliffs, NJ: Prentice-Hall.

Bogdan, R. and Taylor S. (1987) 'Toward a sociology of acceptance: the other side of the study of deviance', *Social Policy*, 18: 34–9.

Bohm, D. (1980) *Wholeness and The Implicate Order*. New York: ARK.

Bohrnstedt, G.W. (1974) 'Path analysis', in *Encyclopedia of Sociology*. Guilford, CT: Dushkin.

Bonger, W. (1916) *Criminality and Economic Conditions*. Boston: Little, Brown.

Borch-Jacobsen, M. (1991) *Lacan: The Absolute Master*. Stanford, CA: Stanford University Press.

Bordo, S. (1989) 'The body and the reproduction of femininity: a feminist appropriation of Foucault', in A. Jaggar and S. Bordo (eds), *Gender/Body/Knowledge: Feminist Reconstructions of Being and Knowing*. New Brunswick, NJ: Rutgers University Press.

Borgmann, A. (1992) *Crossing the Postmodern Divide*. Chicago: University of Chicago Press.

Bourdieu, P. (1977) *Outline of a Theory of Practice*. Cambridge: Cambridge University Press.

Bourdieu, P. (1984) *Distinction: A Social Critique of the Judgement of Taste*. Cambridge, MA: Harvard University Press.

Bourdieu, P. (1985) 'The genesis of the concepts of "Habitus" and "Field"', *Sociocriticism*, 2(2): 11–24.

Bourdieu, P. (1987) 'The force of law: toward a sociology of the juridical field', *The Hastings Law Journal*, 38: 814–53.

Bourdieu, P. (1990) *In Other Words: Essays Toward a Reflexive Sociology*. Cambridge: Polity Press.

Bourdieu, P. and Wacquant, L.J.D. (1992) *An Invitation to Reflexive Sociology*. Chicago: University of Chicago Press.

Box, S. (1971) *Deviance, Reality and Society*. New York: Holt, Rinehart and Winston.

Box, S. (1983) *Power, Crime, and Mystification*. London: Tavistock.

Box, S. (1987) *Recession, Crime and Punishment*. London: Macmillan.

Bracher, M. (1988) 'Lacan's theory of the four discourses', *Prose Studies*, 11: 32–49.

Bracher, M. (1993) *Lacan, Discourse, and Social Change*. Ithaca: Cornell University Press.

Brady, J. (1981) 'Sorting out the exile's confusion: or a dialogue on popular justice', *Contemporary Crisis*, 5: 31–8.

Brady, J. (1994) 'Critical literacy, feminism, and a politics of representation', in P. McLaren and C. Lankshear (eds), *Politics of Liberation*. New York: Routledge. pp. 142–53.

Braithwaite, J. (1982) 'Challenging just deserts: punishing white collar criminals', *Journal of Criminal Law and Criminology*, 73: 723–64.

Braithwaite, J. (1984) *Corporate Crime in the Pharmaceutical Industry*. London: Routledge and Kegan Paul.

Braithwaite, J. (1985) 'White collar crime', in R.H. Turner and J.F. Short (eds), *Annual Review of Sociology*, vol. 11. Palo Alto, CA: Annual Reviews.

Braithwaite, J. (1989) *Crime, Shame and Reintegration*. Cambridge: Cambridge University Press.

Braithwaite, J. (1993) 'Shame and modernity', *The British Journal of Criminology*, 33: 1–18.

Brantingham, P.J. and Brantingham, P.L. (1981) 'Introduction: the dimension of crime', in P.J. Brantingham and P.L. Brantingham (eds), *Environmental Criminology*. Beverly Hills: Sage. pp. 7–26.

Brantingham, P.J. and Brantingham, P.L. (1984) *Patterns of Crime*. New York: Macmillan.

Brennan, T. (1993) *History after Lacan*. New York: Routledge.

Briggs, J. and Peat, F.D. (1989) *Turbulent Mirror*. New York: Harper and Row.

Brigham, J. (1987) 'Right, rage, and remedy: forms of law in political discourse', *Studies in American Political Development*, 2: 303–16.

Brigham, J. and Harrington, C. (1989) 'Realism and its consequences: an inquiry into contemporary socio-legal research', *International Journal of the Sociology of Law*, 17: 41–62.

Brion, D. (1991) 'The chaotic law of tort: legal formalism and the problem of indeterminacy', in R. Kevelson (ed.), *Peirce and Law*. New York: Peter Lang.

Brion, D. (1995) 'The chaotic indeterminacy of tort law: between formalism and nihilism', in D. Caudill and S. Gold (eds), *Radical Philosophy of Law*. New Jersey: Humanities Press. pp. 179–99.

Bromberg, W. (1965) *Crime and Mind: A Psychiatric Analysis of Crime and Punishment*. New York: Macmillan.

Buber, M. (1958) *I and Thou*. New York: Charles Scribner's Sons.

Burgess, E.W. (1925) 'The growth of the city', in R.E. Park, E.W. Burgess and R.D. McKenzie (eds), *The City*. Chicago: University of Chicago Press.

Burgess, E.W. (1950) 'Comment to Hartung', *American Journal of Sociology*, 56: 25–34.

Burgess, R. and Akers, R.L. (1966) 'A differential association-reinforcement theory of criminal behavior', *Social Problems*, 14: 128–47.

Bursik, R.J. Jr (1986) 'Ecological stability and the dynamics of delinquency', in A.J. Reiss and M. Tonry (eds), *Communities and Crime*, Series in Crime and Justice: An Annual Review of Research, vol 8. Chicago: University of Chicago Press. pp. 35–66.

Bursik, R.J. Jr (1988) 'Social disorganization and theories of crime and delinquency: problems and prospects', *Criminology*, 26: 519–51.

Bursik, R.J. Jr and Grasmick, H.G. (1993) *Neighborhoods and Crime: The Dimensions of Effective Community Control*. New York: Lexington Books.

Burton, J.W. (1969) *Conflict and Communication: The Use of Controlled Communication in International Relations*. London: Macmillan.

Burton, J.W. (1988) 'Conflict resolution as a political system', Working Papers, Center of Conflict Analysis and Resolution, George Mason University, Fairfax, Virgina.

Burton, J.W. (1990) *Conflict and Prevention*. London: Macmillan.

Burton, J.W. (1991) 'The need for human needs theory', in J.W. Burton (ed.), *Human Needs and Conflict Resolution*. London: Macmillan.

Butler, J. (1992) 'Contingent foundations: feminism and the question of "postmodernism"', in J. Butler and J.W. Scott (eds), *Feminists Theorize the Political*. London: Routledge.

Butler, J. (1993) *Fundamental Feminism*. New York: Routledge.

Butz, M.R. (1992a) 'The fractal nature of the development of the self', *Psychological Reports*, 71: 1043–63.

Butz, M.R. (1992b) 'Systematic family therapy and symbolic chaos', *Humanity and Society*, 17(2): 200–22.

Butz, M.R. (1992c) 'Chaos, an omen of transcendence in the psychotherapeutic process', *Psychological Reports*, 71: 827–43.

Cain, M. (1985) 'Beyond informal justice', *Contemporary Crisis*, 9: 4–11.

Cain, M. (1989) *Growing up Good: Policing the Behaviour of Girls in Europe*. London: Sage.

Cain, M. (1990) 'Realist philosophy and standpoint epistemologies or feminist criminology as a successor science', in L. Gelsthrope and A. Morris (eds), *Feminist Perspectives in Criminology*. Milton Keynes: Open University Press.

Callinicos, A. (1990) *Against Postmodernism: A Marxist Critique*. New York: St Martin's Press.

Cantor, R., Henry, S. and Rayner, S. (1993) *Making Markets: An Interdisciplinary Perspective on Economic Exchange*. New York: Greenwood Press.

Capra, F. (1988) *The Tao of Physics*. New York: Bantam Books.

Carlen, P. (1990) *Alternatives to Women's Imprisonment*. Milton Keynes: Open University Press.

Carlen, P. and Worrall, A. (eds) (1987) *Gender, Crime and Justice*. Milton Keynes: Open University Press.

Carson, W.G. (1971) 'White-collar crime and the enforcement of factory legislation', in W.G. Carson and P. Wiles (eds), *The Sociology of Crime and Delinquency in Britain. Vol. 1: The British Tradition*. London: Martin Robertson. pp. 220–36.

Caudill, D. (1991) 'Freud and critical legal studies: contours of a radical-legal psychoanalysis', *Indiana Law Journal*, 66(3): 651–97.

Caudill, D. (1992) '"Name-of-the-father" and the logic of psychosis: Lacan's law and ours', *Legal Studies Forum*, 16(4): 23–46.

Caudill, D. (1993) 'Coming to terms with Lacan', *International Journal for the Semiotics of Law*, 17: 203–20.

Caudill, D. and Gold, S. (eds) (1995) *Radical Philosophy of Law: Contemporary Challenges to Mainstream Legal Theory and Practice*. Atlantic Highlands, NJ: Humanities Press International.

Chambliss, W. (1975) 'Toward a political economy of crime', *Theory and Society*, 2: 149–70.

Chambliss, W. (1988) *On the Take: From Petty Crooks to Presidents*. 2nd edn. Bloomington, IN: Indiana University Press.

Chambliss, W. and Seidman. R.B. (1971) *Law, Order and Power*. Reading, MA: Addison-Wesley.

Chambliss, W. and Seidman, R.B. (1982) *Law, Order and Power*. 2nd edn. Reading MA: Addison-Wesley.

Chesney-Lind, M. (1989) 'Girl's crime and woman's place: toward a feminist model of female delinquency', *Crime and Delinquency*, 35(1): 5–29.

Chibnall, S. (1977) *Law and Order News*. London: Tavistock.

Christie, N. (1977) 'Conflicts as property', *British Journal of Criminology*, 17: 1–19.

Cicourel, A.V. (1968) *The Social Organization of Juvenile Justice*. New York: Wiley.

Cicourel, A.V. (1981) 'Notes on the integration of micro- and macro-levels of analysis', in K. Knorr-Cetina and A.V. Cicourel (eds), *Advances in Social Theory: Towards an Integration of Micro- and Macro- Sociologies*. London: Routledge and Kegan Paul. pp. 51–80.

Cixous, H. (1976) 'The laugh of the Medusa', *Signs*, 7(1).

Cixous, H. (1986) *The Newly Born Woman*. Minneapolis, MN: University of Minnesota Press.

Cixous, H. (1990) *Reading with Clarice Lispector*. Minneapolis: University of Minnesota Press.

Clarke, R.V. (1983) 'Situational crime prevention: its theoretical basis and practical scope', in M. Tonry and N. Morris (eds), *Crime and Justice: An Annual Review of Research*, vol 4. Chicago: University of Chicago Press. pp. 225–56.

Clarke, R.V. and Cornish, D.B. (eds) (1983) *Crime Control in Britain: A Review of Policy and Research*. Albany: State University of New York Press.

Clement, C. (1983) *The Lives and Legends of Jacques Lacan*. New York: Columbia University Press.

Clinard, M.B. and Quinney, R. (1973) *Criminal Behavior Systems*. New York: Holt, Rinehart and Winston.

Clinard, M.B. and Yeager, P. (1980) *Corporate Crime*. New York: Free Press.

Clinard, M.B., Yeager, P.C., Brissette, J.M., Petrashek, D. and Harris, E. (1979) *Illegal Corporate Behavior*. Washington, DC: US Government Printing Office.

Cloud, D.L. (1994) 'Socialism of the mind: the new age of post-Marxism', in H.W. Simons and M. Billig (eds), *After Postmodernism: Reconstructing Ideology Critique*. London: Sage.

Cloward, R.A. (1959) 'Illegitimate means, anomie and deviant behavior', *American Sociological Review*, 24: 164–76.

Cloward, R.A. and Ohlin, L.E. (1960) *Delinquency and Opportunity: A Theory of Delinquent Gangs*. New York: Free Press.

Cohen, A.K. (1955) *Delinquent Boys: The Culture of the Gang*. Glencoe, IL: Free Press.

Cohen, L.E. and Felson, M. (1979) 'Social change and crime rate trends: a routine activities approach', *American Sociological Review*, 44: 588–608.

Cohen, L.E. and Machalek, R. (1988) 'A general theory of expropriative crime: an evolutionary ecological approach', *American Journal of Sociology*, 94: 465–501.

Cohen, S. (1979) 'The punitive city: notes on the dispersal of social control', *Contemporary Crisis*, 3: 339–63.

Cohen, S. (1985) *Visions of Social Control*. Cambridge: Polity Press.

Cohen, S. (1990) 'Intellectual scepticism and political commitment: the case of radical criminology', paper presented at the Inaugural Willem Bonger Memorial Lecture, University of Amsterdam, Holland.

Cohen, S. (1993) 'Human rights and crimes of the state: the culture of denial', *Australian and New Zealand Journal of Criminology*, 26: 97–115.

Cohen, S. and Young, J. (1980) *The Manufacture of News*. London: Constable.

Cole, W.E. (1949) 'Causation of crime', in V.C. Branham and S.B. Kutash, (eds), *Encyclopedia of Criminology*. New York: Philosophical Library. pp. 45–6.

Coleman, J.S. (1978) 'Power and the structure of society', in M.D. Ermann and R.J. Lundman (eds), *Corporate and Governmental Deviance*. New York: Oxford University Press. pp. 21–7.

Coleman, J.S. (1982) 'The asymmetric society', M.D. Ermann and R.J. Lundman (eds), *Corporate and Governmental Deviance*. New York: Oxford University Press. pp. 95–104.

Coleman, J.W. (1985) *The Criminal Elite*. New York: St Martin's Press.

Coleman, J.W. (1987) 'Toward an integrated theory of white-collar crime', *American Journal of Sociology*, 93: 406–39.

Coleman, J.W. (1994) *The Criminal Elite*. New York: St Martin's Press.

Collins, H. (1987) 'Roberto Unger and the critical legal studies movement', *Journal of Law and Society*, 14: 387–410.

Collins, P.H. (1989) 'The social construction of black feminist thought', *Signs*, 14(4): 745–73.

Collins, P.H. (1990) *Black Feminist Thought: Knowledge, Consciousness and the Politics of Empowerment*. New York: Routledge.

Collins, P.H. (1993) 'Toward a new vision: race, class, and gender as categories of analysis and connection', *Race, Sex and Class*, 1(1): 25–45.

Colosi, T.R. (1987) 'A model for negotiation and mediation', in D.J.D. Sandole and I. Sandole-Staroste (eds), *Conflict Management and Problem Solving: Interpersonal to International Applications*. New York: New York University Press.

Colosi, T.R. and Berkely, A.E. (1986) *Collective Bargaining: How it Works and Why*. New York: American Arbitration Association.

Colvin, M. and Pauly, J. (1983) 'A critique of criminology: toward an integrated structural-Marxist theory of delinquency production, *American Journal of Sociology*, 89: 513–51.

Conklin, J.E. (1977) *Illegal But Not Criminal: Business Crime in America*. Englewood Cliffs, NJ: Prentice-Hall.

Cook, A. (1990) 'Beyond critical legal studies: the reconstructive theology of Dr. Martin Luther King Jr', *Harvard Law Review*, 103: 985.

Cooley, C.H. (1902) *Human Nature and the Social Order*. New York: Charles Scribner.

Cooley, C.H. (1909) *Social Organization: a Study of the Larger Mind*. New York: Charles Scribner.

Cornell, D. (1991) *Beyond Accommodation: Ethical Feminism, Deconstruction and the Law*. New York: Routledge.

Cornell, D. (1992) 'The philosophy of the limit: system theory and feminist legal reform', in D. Cornell, M. Rosenfeld and D. Carleson (eds), *Deconstruction and the Possibility of Justice*. New York: Routledge.

Cornell, D. (1993) *Transformations: Recollective Imagination and Sexual Difference*. New York: Routledge.

Cornish, D.B. and Clarke R.V. (eds) (1986) *The Reasoning Criminal*. New York: Springer.

Cornish, D.B. and Clarke R.V. (1987) 'Understanding crime displacement: an application of rational choice theory', *Criminology*, 25(4): 933–47.

Cortes, J.B. and Gatti, F.M. (1972) *Delinquency and Crime: a Biopsychosocial Approach*. New York: Seminar Press.

Coser, L. (1956) *The Functions of Social Conflict*. New York: Macmillan.

Coughlin, E. (1993) 'Miami a unique sociological laboratory, researchers on immigration find', *Chronicle of Higher Education*, September 1: 6–7, 10–11.

Crenshaw, K. (1988) 'Race, reform and retrenchment: transformation and legitimation in antidiscrimination', *Harvard Law Review*, 101: 1356–87.

Cressey, D.R. (1953) *Other People's Money*. Glencoe, IL: Free Press.

Cressey, D.R. (1960) 'The theory of differential association: an introduction', *Social Problems*, 8: 2–6.

Cressey, D.R. (1970) 'The respectable criminal', in J. Short (ed.), *Modern Criminals*. New York: Transaction-Aldine. pp. 105–16.

Cullen, F., Mathers, R., Clark, G., and Cullen, J. (1983) 'Public support for punishing white-collar crime: blaming the victim revisited?', *Journal of Criminal Justice*, 11: 481–93.

Currie, D.H. (1989) 'Women and the state: a statement on feminist theory', *The Critical Criminologist*, 1(2): 4–5.

Currie, D.H. (1990) 'Battered women and the state: from the failure of theory to a theory of failure', *Journal of Human Justice*, 1(2): 77–96.

Currie, D.H. (1991) 'Challenging privilege: feminist struggles in the Canadian context', *The Critical Criminologist*, 3(1): 1–2, 10–13.

Currie, D.H. (1992) 'Feminist encounters with postmodernism: exploring the impasse of the debates on patriarchy and law', *Canadian Journal of Women and the Law*, 5(1): 63–86.

Curtis, L.A. (1975) *Violence, Race and Culture*. Lexington, MA: D.C. Heath.

Dahrendorf, R. (1959) *Class and Class Conflict in an Industrial Society*. London: Routledge and Kegan Paul.

Dalton, K. (1961) 'Menstruation and crime', *British Medical Journal*, 3: 1752–3.

Daly, K. (1989) 'Gender and varieties of white-collar crime', *Criminology*, 27(4): 769–93.

Daly, K. (1990) 'Reflections on feminist legal thought', *Social Justice*, 17(3): 7–24.

Daly, K. and Chesney-Lind, M. (1988) 'Feminism and criminology', *Justice Quarterly*, 5(4): 497–538.

de Shazer, S. (1985) *Keys to Solutions in Brief Therapy*. New York: Norton.

de Shazer, S. (1988) *Clues: Investigating Solutions in Brief Therapy*. New York: Norton.

de Haan, W. (1990) *The Politics of Redress*. Boston: Unwin Hyman.

Deans, M. (1994) 'Non-violence program sponsored by MVFR', *The Voice*, no. 3, Fall.

DeKeseredy, W. and Hinch, R. (1991) *Woman Abuse: Sociological Perspectives*. Toronto: Thompson.

Deleuze, G. (1983) *Nietzsche and Philosophy*. New York: Columbia University Press.

Deleuze, G. (1988) *Foucault*. Minneapolis: University of Minnesota Press.

Deleuze, G. and Guattari, F. (1986) *Kafka: Toward a Minor Literature*. Minneapolis, MN: University of Minnesota Press.

Deleuze, G. and Guattari, F. (1987) *A Thousand Plateaus*. Minneapolis, MN: University of Minnesota Press.

Derrida, J. (1973a) *Speech and Phenomena*. Evanston, IL: Northwestern University Press.

Derrida, J. (1973b) *Of Grammatology*. Baltimore: Johns Hopkins University Press.

Derrida, J. (1978) *Writing and Difference*. London: Routledge and Kegan Paul.

Derrida, J. (1981) *Positions*. Chicago: University of Chicago Press.

Dews, P. (1987) *Logics of Disintegration: Post-Structuralist Thought and the Claims of Critical Theory*. New York: Verso.

Di Tullio, B. (1969) 'The causes of criminality', *Monographs of the Criminal Law Education and Research Center*, 3: 53–79.

Diamond, S. (1973) 'The rule of law versus the order of custom', in D. Black and M. Milesky (eds), *The Social Organization of Law*. New York: Seminar Press.

Dickens, D. (1990) 'Deconstruction and Marxist inquiry', *Sociological Perspectives*, 33(1): 147–58.

DiCristina, B. (1995) *Method in Criminology*. New York: Harrow and Heston.

Ditton, J. (1977) *Part-Time Crime: An Ethnography of Fiddling and Pilferage*. London: Macmillan.

Doan, R. (1991) 'Investigating specifications for personhood: escaping the influence of role rigidity', *The Calgary Participator*, 1(2): 18–20.

Doob, L.W. and Fotz, W. (1987) 'Conflicts', *International Journal of Group Tensions*, 1–4: 15–27.

Dorfman, A. (1984) 'The criminal mind: body chemistry and nutrition may lie at the root of crime', *Science Digest*, 92 (October): 44–7.

Douglas, J.D. (ed.) (1972) *Research on Deviance*. New York: Random House.

Douzinas, C., Warrington, W. and McVeigh, S. (1991) *Postmodern Jurisprudence: The Law of Text in the Texts of Law*. London: Routledge.

Dugdale, R.L. (1877) *The Jukes: A Study in Crime, Pauperism, Disease and Heredity*. New York: Putnam.

Durkheim, E. (1893) *The Division of Labor in Society*. New York: Free Press.

Durkheim, E. (1951) *Suicide: A Study in Sociology* (1898). New York: Free Press.

Durkheim, E. (1982) *The Rules of Sociological Method and Selected Texts on Sociology and its Method*. Ed. S. Lukes, trans. W.D. Halls. London: Macmillan.

Dworkin, R. (1968) *Taking Rights Seriously*. London: Duckworth.

Dworkin, R. (1986) *Law's Empire*. London: Fontana.

Eagleton, T. (1983) 'Jacques Lacan', in A. Bullock and R.B. Woodings (eds), *The Fontana Biographical Companion to Modern Thought*. London: Fontana. pp. 417–18.

Eagleton, T. (1991) *Ideology: An Introduction*. London: Verso.

Ebert, T. (1991a) 'Writing in the political: resistance (post)modernism', *Legal Studies Forum*, 15(4): 291–303.

Ebert, T. (1991b) 'Political semiosis in/of American cultural studies', *The American Journal of Semiotics*, 8: 113–35.

Eco, U. (1984) *Semiotics and the Philosophy of Language*. London: Macmillan.

Edelhertz, H. (1970) *The Nature, Impact and Prosecution of White-Collar Crime*. Washington, DC: US Government Printing Office.

Edelman, M. (1964) *The Symbolic Uses of Politics*. Urbana, IL: University of Illinois Press.

Edelman, M. (1988) *Constructing the Political Spectacle*. Chicago: University of Chicago Press.

Edwards, S. (1990) 'Violence against women: feminism and the law', in L. Gelsthorpe and A. Morris (eds), *Feminist Perspectives in Criminology*. Milton Keynes: Open University Press. pp. 144–59.

Ehrlich, E. (1913) *Fundamental Principles of the Sociology of Law*. Cambridge, MA: Harvard University Press.

Ehrlich, I. (1973) 'Participation in illegitimate activities: an economic analysis', *Journal of Political Economy*, 81: 521–67.

Ehrlich, I. (1982) 'The market for offences and the public enforcement of laws: an equilibrium analysis', *British Journal of Social Psychology*, 21(2): 107–20.

Einstadter, W. (1992) 'Asymmetries of control: surveillance, intrusion, and corporate theft of privacy', *Justice Quarterly*, 9(2): 285–98.

Einstadter, W. and Henry, S. (1991) 'The inversion of the invasion of privacy', *The Critical Criminologist*, 3(4): 5–6.

Einstadter, W. and Henry, S. (1995) *Criminological Theory: An Analysis of its Underlying Assumptions*. Fort Worth, TX: Harcourt, Brace.

Eisenstein, Z. (1979) *Capitalist Patriarchy and the Case for Socialist Feminism*. New York: Monthly Review Press.

Elkaim, M. (1981) 'Non-equilibrium, chance and change in family therapy', *Journal of Marital and Family Therapy*, 7: 291–7.

Elkaim, M., Goldbeter, A. and Goldbeter-Merinfeld, E. (1987) 'Analysis of the dynamics of a family system in terms of bifurcation', *Journal of Social and Biological Structures*, 10: 21–36.

Elliott, D.S., (1994) '1993 Presidential Address: Serious violent offenders: onset, developmental course and termination', *Criminology*, 32(1): 1–21.

Elliott, D.S., Agerton, S. and Canter, R. (1979) 'An integrated theoretical perspective on delinquent behavior', *Journal of Research on Crime and Delinquency*, 16: 3–27.

Elliott, D.S., Huizinga, D. and Ageton, S. (1985) *Explaining Delinquency and Drug Use*. Beverly Hills, CA: Sage.

Ellis, L. (1988) 'Neurohormonal bases of varying tendencies to learn delinquent and criminal behavior', in E. Morris and C. Braukmann (eds), *Behavioral Approaches to Crime and Delinquency*. New York: Plenum.

Empey, L. (1982) *American Delinquency: Its Meaning and Construction*. 2nd edn. Homewood: Dorsey Press.

Empey, L. and Stafford, M.C. (1991) *American Delinquency: Its Meaning and Construction*. 3rd edn. Belmont, CA: Wadsworth.

Engels, F. (1845) *The Condition of the Working Class in England*. New York: International Publishers.

Epston, D. and White, M. (1992) *Experience, Contradiction, Narrative, and Imagination*. Adelaide, Australia: Dulwich Centre Publications.

Ericson, R. and Carriere, K. (1994) 'The fragmentation of criminology', in D. Nelken (ed.), *The Futures of Criminology*. London: Sage.

Ermann, D. and Lundman, R. (1978) 'Deviant acts by complex organizations: deviance and social control at the organizational level of analysis', *Sociological Quarterly*, 19: 55–67.

Ermann, D. and Lundman, R. (1992) *Corporate and Governmental Deviance*. (1982) New York: Oxford University Press.

Estabrook, A.H. (1916) *The Jukes in 1915*, New York: Washington, DC: Carnegie Institute.

Eysenck, H.J. (1977) *Crime and Personality* (1964). London: Routledge and Kegan Paul.

Eysenck, H.J. (1983) 'Personality, conditioning and anti-social behavior', in S. Laufer and J.M. Day (eds), *Personality Theory, Moral Development and Criminal Behavior*. Lexington, MA: Lexington Books.

Eysenck, H.J. and Gudjonsson, G.H. (1989) *The Causes and Cures of Criminality*. New York: Plenum.

Faith, K. (1993) 'An Interview with Freda Adler', *The Critical Criminologist*, 5(1): 3–4, 6–10.

Faris, E. (1944) 'Robert E. Park: 1864–1944', *American Sociological Review*, 9: 322–5.

Feeley, M. and Simon, J. (1992) 'The new penology: notes on the emerging strategy of corrections and its implications', *Criminology*, 30: 449–74.

Feeley, M. and Simon, J. (1994) 'Actuarial justice: the emerging new criminal law', in D. Nelken (ed), *The Futures of Criminology*. London: Sage. pp. 173–201.

Feldstein, R., Fink, B. and Jaanus, M. (eds) (1995) *Reading Seminar XI*. Albany, NY: State University of New York Press.

Felson, M. (1986) 'Routine activities and crime prevention in the developing metropolis', in D.B. Cornish and R.V. Clarke (eds), *The Reasoning Criminal*. New York: Springer.

Felson, M. (1987) 'Routine activities, social controls, rational decisions and criminal outcome', *Criminology*, 25: 911–31.

Ferman, L.A., Berndt, L.E. and Henry, S. (eds) (1993) *Work Beyond Employment in Advanced Capitalist Countries: Classic and Contemporary Perspectives on the Informal Economy, vol I: Concepts, Evidence and Measurement; Volume II: Revisions and Criticism*. Lewiston: The Edwin Mellen Press.

Ferman, L.A., Henry, S. and Hoyman, M. (eds) (1987) 'The Informal Economy', *The Annals of the American Academy of Political and Social Science*, vol. 493. Newbury Park: Sage.

Ferrell, J. (1993) *Crimes of Style: Urban Graffiti and the Politics of Criminality*. New York: Garland.

Ferrell, J. (1994) 'Confronting the agenda of authority: critical criminology, anarchism', in G. Barak (ed.), *Varieties of Criminology: Readings from a Dynamic Discipline*. Westport, CT: Praeger. pp. 161–78.

Ferri, E. (1886). *Criminal Sociology*. Boston: Little, Brown.

Ferrrari-Bravo, G. and Arcidiacono, C. (1989) 'Relations between staff and girls in an Italian juvenile prison', in M. Cain (ed), *Growing up Good: Policing the Behavior of Girls in Europe*. London: Sage.

Feyerbend, P. (1975) *Against Method*. London: New Left Books.

Filmer, P., Phillipson, M., Silverman, D. and Walsh, D. (1972) *New Directions in Sociological Theory*. London: Collier-Macmillan.

Firby, P.A. and Gardiner, C.F. (1982) *Surface Topology*. New York: Ellis Horwood.

Fish, S. (1980) *Is There a Text in This Class? The Authority of Interpretive Communities*. Cambridge, MA: Harvard University Press.

Fish, S. (1984) 'Fish v. Fiss', *Stanford Law Review*, 36(6): 1325–47.

Fish, S. (1989) *Doing What Comes Naturally: Change, Rhetoric, and the Practice of Theory, in Literary and Legal Studies*. Durham, NC: Duke University Press.

Fitzpatrick, P. (1983) 'Law, plurality and underdevelopment', in D. Sugerman (ed.), *Legality, Ideology and the State*, London: Academic Press.

Fitzpatrick, P. (1984) 'Law and societies', *Osgoode Hall Law Journal*, 22: 115–38.

Fitzpatrick, P. (1988) 'The rise and rise of informalism', in R. Matthews (ed.), *Informal Justice?* London: Sage.

Fitzpatrick, P. (1992) *The Mythology of Modern Law*. London: Routledge.

Flanagan, J.G. and Rayner, S. (eds) (1988) *Rules, Decisions, and Inequality in Egalitarian Societies*. Aldershot: Avebury.

Flax, J. (1990) 'Postmodernism and gender relations in feminist theory', in L.J. Nicholson (ed.), *Feminism/Postmodernism*. New York: Routledge, Chapman and Hall.

Fletcher, R. (1977) 'Social structure', in A. Bullock and O. Stallybrass (eds), *The Fontana Dictionary of Modern Thought*, London: Fontana.

Fogel, D. (1975) *We are the Living Proof: The Justice Model for Corrections*. Cincinnati: Anderson.

Foucault, M. (1972) *The Archaeology of Knowledge*. Trans. A. Sheridan. New York: Pantheon.

Foucault, M. (1973) *The Order of Things* (1970). New York: Vintage Books.

Foucault, M. (1977) *Discipline and Punish*. New York: Pantheon.

Foucault, M. (1979) *The History of Sexuality. Vol. 1: An Introduction*. London: Allen Lane.

Foucault, M. (1980) *Power/Knowledge: Selected Interviews and Other Writings 1972–1977*. Ed. C. Gordon. Brighton: Harvester Press.

Foucault, M. (1986) 'Of other spaces', *Diacritics*, 16(1): 22–7.

Foucault, M. (1988) 'The ethic of care for the self as a practice of freedom', in J. Bernauer and D. Rasmussen (eds), *The Final Foucault*. Cambridge: MIT Press.

Fowler, R. (1985) 'Power', *Handbook of Discourse Analysis*, 4: 61–82.

Fox, J.A. and Levin, J. (1993) *How to Work with the Media*. Newbury Park, CA: Sage.

Frank, N. and Lynch, M. (1992) *Corporate Crime, Corporate Violence*. Albany, New York: Harrow and Heston.

Fraser, N. (1989) 'Foucault on modern power: empirical insights and normative confusions', in N. Fraser (ed.), *Unruly Practices*, Minnesota: University of Minnesota Press. pp. 17–34.

Freeman, A.D. (1982) 'Antidiscrimination law: a critical review', in D. Kairys (ed.), *The Politics of Law: A Progressive Critique*. New York: Pantheon Books. pp. 96–116.

Freire, P. (1972) *Pedagogy of the Oppressed*. New York: Herder and Her.

Freire, P. (1973) *Education for Critical Consciousness*. New York: Seabury Press.

Freire, P. (1985) *The Politics of Education*. South Hadley, MA: Bergin and Garvey.

Freud, S. (1923) *The Ego and the Id*. Trans. J. Riviere. London: Hogarth Press.

Freud, S. (1927) *Civilization and Its Discontents*. Garden City, NY: Doubleday.

Freud, S. (1950) 'Criminals from a sense of guilt', in *Gesammelte Werke*, vol 14. London: Imago. pp. 332–3.

Freud, S. (1965) *The Interpretation of Dreams*. New York: Avon Books.

Friedlander, K. (1947) *The Psychoanalytical Approach to Juvenile Delinquency*. London: International Universities Press.

Friedrichs, D. (1992) 'White collar crime and the definitional quagmire: a provisional solution', *The Journal of Human Justice*, 3: 5–21.

Friedrichs, D. (1995a) 'White collar crime and the class-race-gender construct', in M. Schwartz and D. Milovanovic (eds), *Intersections of Race, Gender, and Class in Criminology*. New York: Garland Press.

Friedrichs, D. (1995b) *Trusted Criminals: White Collar Crime in Contemporary Society*. Belmont, CA: Wadsworth.

Gabor, T. (1994) *Everybody Does it! Crimes by the Public*. Toronto: University of Toronto Press.

Galliher, J.F. (1989) *Criminology: Human Rights, Criminal Law and Crime*. Englewood Cliffs, NJ: Prentice-Hall.

Gane, M. (1991) *Baudrillard: Critical and Fatal Theory*. New York: Routledge.

Garafalo, R. (1914) *Criminology*. Boston: Little, Brown.

Garcia, L. (1991) *The Fractal Explorer*. Santa Cruz: Dynamic Press.

Garfinkel, H. (1956) 'Conditions of successful degradation ceremonies', *American Journal of Sociology*, 61: 420–4.

Garland, D. (1983) 'Durkheim's theory of punishment: a critique', in D. Garland and P. Young (eds), *The Power to Punish*. London: Heinemann.

Garland, D. (1990) *Punishment and Modern Society*. Oxford: Clarendon Press.

Garza, C. (1992) 'Postmodern paradigms and Chicana feminist thought: creating a space and language', *The Critical Criminologist*, 4(3/4): 1–2, 11–13.

Geertz, C. (1973) *The Interpretation of Cultures*. New York: Basic Books.

Geertz, C. (1983) *Local Knowledge: Further Essays in Interpretive Anthropology*. New York: Basic Books.

Geis, G. (1992) 'White-collar crime: what is it?', in K. Schlegel and D. Weisburd (eds), *White-Collar Crime Reconsidered*. Boston: Northeastern University Press.

Gemmill, G. and Smith, C. (1985) 'A dissipative structure model of organization transformation', *Human Relations*, 38(8): 751–66.

Georges-Abeyie, D. (1984) *The Criminal Justice System and Blacks*. New York: Clark Boardman.

Georges-Abeyie, D. (1990) 'Criminal justice processing of non-white minorities', in B.

MacLean and D. Milovanovic (eds), *Racism, Empiricism and Criminal Justice*. Vancouver, BC: Collective Press. pp. 25–34.

Geras, N. (1987) 'Post-Marxism?', *New Left Review*, 163: 40–82.

Gibbons, D.C. (1969) 'Crime and punishment: a study of social attitudes', *Social Forces*, 47: 391–7.

Gibbons, D.C. (1994) *Talking about Crime and Criminals: Problems and Issues in Theory Development in Criminology*. Englewood Cliffs, NJ: Prentice-Hall.

Gibbons, D.C. and Krohn, M.D. (1991) *Delinquent Behavior*, 5th edn. Englewood Cliffs, NJ: Prentice-Hall.

Gibbons, F.X. (1986) 'Stigma and interpersonal relations', in S.C. Ainley, G. Becker and L.M. Coleman (eds), *The Dilemma of Difference*. New York: Plenum.

Gibney, P. (1987) 'Co-evolving with anorectic families, difference is a singular moment', *Australian and New Zealand Journal of Family Therapy*, 8(2): 71–80.

Giddens, A. (1984) *The Constitution of Society: Outline of the Theory of Structuration*. Oxford: Polity Press.

Gierke, O. (1900) *Political Theories of the Middle Age*, Cambridge: Cambridge University Press.

Gill, O. (1977) *Luke Street: Housing Policy, Conflict and the Creation of the Delinquency Area*. London: Macmillan.

Gilsinan, J. (1982) *Doing Justice: How the System Works – As Seen by the Participants*. Englewood Cliffs, NJ: Prentice-Hall.

Giroux, H. (1992) *Border Crossings*. New York: Routledge.

Giroux, H. and McLaren, P. (1994) *Between Borders: Pedagogy and the Politics of Cultural Studies*. New York: Routledge.

Glazer, D. (1978) *Crime in Our Changing Society*. New York: Holt, Rinehart and Winston.

Gleick, J. (1987) *Chaos: Making a New Science*. New York: Viking.

Glueck, S. and Glueck, E. (1950) *Unraveling Juvenile Delinquency*. New York: Commonwealth Fund.

Goddard, H.H. (1912) *The Kallikak Family: A Study in the Heredity of Feeblemindedness*. London: Macmillan.

Godel, K. (1962) *On Formally Undecidable Propositions in 'Principia Mathematica' and Related Systems*. Ed. R.B. Braithewaite. New York: Basic Books.

Goff, C. and Reasons, C. (1986) 'Organizational crimes against employees, consumers and the public', in B. MacLean (ed.), *The Political Economy of Crime*. Scarborough, Ontario: Prentice-Hall Canada.

Goffman, E. (1959) *The Presentation of Self in Everyday Life*. Harmondsworth: Penguin.

Goffman, E. (1963) *Stigma: Notes on the Management of Spoiled Identity*. Englewood Cliffs, NJ: Prentice Hall.

Goffman, E. (1971) *Relations in Public*. Harmondsworth: Penguin.

Goffman, E. (1974) *Frame Analysis*. New York: Harper and Row.

Goffman, E. (1981) *Forms of Talk*. Oxford: Basil Blackwell.

Goldfarb, P. (1992) 'From the worlds of "others": minority and feminist responses to critical legal studies', *New England Law Review*, 26: 683–710.

Goodrich, P. (1987) *Legal Discourse: Studies in Linguistics, Rhetoric and Legal Analysis*. London: Macmillan.

Goodrich, P. (1990) *Languages of Law: From Logics of Memory to Nomadic Masks*. London: Weidenfeld and Nicolson.

Goodrich, P. (1992) 'Poor illiterate reason: history, nationalism and common law', *Social and Legal Studies*, 1(1): 7–28.

Gordon, D. (1971) 'Class and the economics of crime', *Review of Radical Political Economy*, 3: 51–75.

Gordon, D. (1973) 'Capitalism, class and crime in America', *Crime and Delinquency*, 19: 163–86.

Gordon, L. (1988) *Heroes of Their Own Lives*. New York: Viking Penguin.

Goring, C. (1913) *The English Convict: A Statistical Study*. London: HMSO.

Gottfredson, M.R. and Hirschi, T. (1990) *A General Theory of Crime*. Stanford: Stanford University Press.

Granon-Lafont, J. (1985) *La Topologie Ordinaire de Jacques Lacan*. Paris: Point Hors Ligne.

Grant, J. (1993) *Fundamental Feminism: Contesting the Core Concepts of Feminist Theory*. New York: Routledge.

Green, G. (1990) *Occupational Crime*. Chicago: Nelson-Hall.

Greenberg, D.F. (ed.) (1981) *Crime and Capitalism: Readings in Marxist Criminology*. Palo Alto, CA: Mayfield.

Gregersen, H. and Sailer, L. (1993) 'Chaos theory and its implications for social science research', *Human Relations*, 46(7): 777–802.

Greimas, A. (1990) *The Social Sciences: A Semiotic View*. Minneapolis: University of Minnesota Press.

Griffiths, J. (1979) 'Is law important?', *New York University Law Review*, 54: 339–74.

Gross, E. (1978) 'Organizational sources of crime: a theoretical perspective', in N.K. Denzin (ed), *Studies in Symbolic Interaction*. Greenwich, CT: JAI Press.

Grosz, E. (1990) *Jacques Lacan: A Feminist Introduction*. New York: Routledge.

Grotstein, J. (1990) 'Nothingness, meaningless, chaos and the "black hole" 1', *Contemporary Psychoanalysis*, 26(2): 257–90.

Groves, W.B. and Sampson, R.J. (1987) 'Traditional contributions to radical criminology', *Journal of Research in Crime and Delinquency*, 24: 181–214.

Groves, B. and Frank, N. (1987) 'Punishment, privilege and the sociology of structured choice', in B. Groves and G. Newman (eds), *Punishment and Privilege*. Albany, NY: Harrow and Heston.

Gurvitch, G. (1947) *The Sociology of Law*. London: Routledge and Kegan Paul.

Gusfield, J.R. (1967) 'Moral passage: the symbolic process in public designations of deviance', *Social Problems*, 15: 175–88.

Hagan, F.E. (1986) *Introduction to Criminology*. Chicago: Nelson-Hall.

Hagan, J. (1985) *Modern Criminology*. New York: McGraw-Hill.

Hagan, J. (1989) *Structural Criminology*. New Brunswick, NJ: Rutgers University Press.

Hagan, J., Gillis, A.R. and Simpson, J. (1985) 'The class structure and delinquency: toward a power-control theory of common delinquent behavior', *American Journal of Sociology*, 90: 1151–78.

Hagan, J., Simpson, J. and Gillis, A.R. (1987) 'Class in the household: a power-control theory of gender and delinquency', *American Journal of Sociology*, 92: 788–816.

Hall-Williams, J.E. (1964) 'Crime', in J. Gould and W. Kolb (eds), *A Dictionary of the Social Sciences*. London: Tavistock. pp. 147–8.

Halleck, S. (1971) *Psychiatry and the Dilemmas of Crime*. (1967) Berkeley: University of California Press.

Haney, C., Banks, C. and Zimbardo, P. (1973) 'Interpersonal dynamics in a simulated prison', *International Journal of Criminology and Penology*, 1: 69–97.

Harding, D. (1991) *Whose Science? Whose Knowledge? Thinking From Women's Lives*. Ithaca. NY: Cornell University Press.

Harding, S. (1986) *The Science Question in Feminism*. Ithaca, NY: Cornell University Press.

Harding, S. (1991) *Whose Science? Whose Knowledge? Thinking From Women's Lives*. New York: Cornell University Press.

Hare, R.D. (1970) *Psychopathy: Theory and Research*. New York: Wiley.

Hare, R.D. and Connolly, J.F. (1987) 'Perceptual asymmetries and information processing in psychopaths', in S. Mednick, T. Moffitt, and S. Stack (eds), *The Causes of Crime: New Biological Approaches*. Cambridge: Cambridge University Press.

Harrington, C. (1985) *Shadow Justice: The Ideology and Institutionalization of Alternatives to Court*. Westport, CT: Greenwood Press.

Harrington, C. (1988) 'Moving from integrative to constitutive theories of law: comments on Itzkowitz', *Law and Society Review*, 22(5): 963–7.

Harrington, C. and Merry, S. (1988) 'Ideological production: the making of community mediation', *Law and Society Review*, 22(5): 709–35.

Harrington, C. and Yngvesson, B. (1990) 'Interpretive sociolegal research', *Law and Social Inquiry*, 15: 135–48.

Harris, A. (1991) 'Race and essentialism in feminist legal theory', in K. Bartlett and R. Kennedy (eds), *Feminist Legal Theory*. Boulder, CO: Westview Press. pp. 235–62.

Harris, I. (1990) 'Principles of peace pedagogy', *Peace and Change*, 15(3): 254–71.

Harris, K.M. (1991) 'Moving into the new millennium - toward a feminist view of justice', in H.E. Pepinsky and R. Quinney (eds), *Criminology as Peacemaking*. Bloomington, IN: Indiana University Press. pp. 83–97.

Harrison, W. (1964) 'Policy', in J. Gould and W.L. Kolb (eds), *A Dictionary of the Social Sciences*. London: Tavistock. pp. 509–10.

Hart, H.L.A. (1961) *The Concept of Law*. London: Oxford University Press.

Hawkins, J.D. and Weis, J.G. (1985) 'The social development model: an integrated approach to delinquency prevention', *Journal of Primary Prevention*, 6(2): 73–97.

Hawkins, R. (1984) 'Employee theft in the restaurant trade: forms of ripping off by waiters at work', *Deviant Behavior*, 5: 1–15.

Hawley, A.H. (1950) *Human Ecology: A Theory of Community Structure*. New York: Ronald Press.

Hayles, K. (1990) *Chaos Bound*. New York: Cornell University Press.

Healy, W. and Bronner, A. (1926) *Delinquents and Criminals: Their Making and Unmaking*. New York: Macmillan.

Healy, W. and Bronner, A. (1936) *New Light on Delinquency and its Treatment*. New Haven, CT: Yale University Press.

Heineke, J.M. (ed.) (1978) *Economic Models of Criminal Behavior*. New York: North-Holland.

Heineke, J.M. (1988) 'Crime, deterrence and choice: testing the rational behavior hypothesis', *American Sociological Review*, 53: 303–5.

Heisenberg, W. (1958) *Physics and Philosophy*. New York: Harper Torchbooks.

Henderson, C.R. (1893) *An Introduction to the Dependent Defective Delinquent Classes*. Boston: D.C. Heath.

Henry, S. (1976) 'Fencing with accounts: the language of moral bridging', *The British Journal of Law and Society*, 3: 91–100.

Henry, S. (1977) 'On the fence', *The British Journal of Law and Society*, 4(1): 124–33.

Henry, S. (1978) *The Hidden Economy: The Context and Control of Borderline Crime*. Oxford: Martin Robertson. Port Townsend, WA: Loompanics Unlimited, 1988.

Henry, S. (1983) *Private Justice*. London: Routledge and Kegan Paul.

Henry, S. (1985) 'Community justice, capitalist society and human agency: the dialectics of collective law in the co-operative', *Law and Society Review*, 19: 303–27.

Henry, S. (1987a) 'The construction and deconstruction of social control: thoughts on the discursive production of state law and private justice', in J. Lowman, R. Menzies and T. Palys (eds), *Transcarceration: Essays in the Sociology of Social Control*. Aldershot: Gower Press.

Henry, S. (1987b) 'Private justice and the policing of labor', in C. Shearing and P. Stenning (eds), *Private Policing*, Beverly Hills: Sage. pp. 45–71.

Henry, S. (1987c) 'The political economy of informal economies', in L. Ferman, S. Henry and M. Hoyman (eds), *The Informal Economy*. Special Issue of *The Annals of the American Academy of Social and Political Sciences*, vol. 493 (September): 137–53.

Henry, S. (1988) 'Can the hidden economy be revolutionary?', in C. Robinson and B. Bishop (eds), *Dynamics of the Informal Economy*. Special issue of *Social Justice*, 15(3–4): 29–60.

Henry, S. (1989a) 'Justice on the margin', *The Howard Journal of Criminal Justice*, 28: 255–71.

Henry, S. (1989b) 'Constitutive criminology: the missing paradigm', *The Critical Criminologist*, 1(3): 9, 12.

Henry, S. (1994) 'Newsmaking criminology as replacement discourse', in G. Barak (ed.), *Media, Process and the Social Construction of Crime: Studies in Newsmaking Criminology*. New York: Garland Press.

Henry, S. and Mars, G. (1978) 'Crime at work: the social construction of amateur property theft', *Sociology*, 12: 245–63.

Henry, S. and Milovanovic, D. (1991) 'Constitutive criminology', *Criminology*, 29(2): 293–316.

Henry, S. and Milovanovic, D. (1993) 'Back to basics: a postmodern redefinition of crime', *The Critical Criminologist*, 5(2/3): 1–2, 6, 12.

Henry, S. and Milovanovic, D. (1994) 'The constitution of constitutive criminology: a postmodern approach to criminological theory', in D. Nelken (ed.), *The Futures of Criminology*. London: Sage.

Henry, S. and Robinson, D. (1978a) 'Talking out of alcoholism: results from a survey in England and Wales', *The Journal of the Royal College of General Practitioners*, 28: 414–19.

Henry, S. and Robinson, D. (1978b) 'Understanding Alcoholics Anonymous: results from a survey in England and Wales', *The Lancet*, 18 February: 372–5.

Hills, S.L. (1971) *Crime, Power and Morality*. Scranton, PA: Chandler.

Hilton, I. (1977) 'Out of the tiger cages', *The Sunday Times*, 7 August: 12.

Hindess, B. and Hirst, P.Q. (1977) *Pre-Capitalist Modes of Production*. London: Routledge and Kegan Paul.

Hippchen, L.J. (ed.) (1978) *Ecologic-Biochemical Approaches to the Treatment of Delinquents and Criminals*. New York: Van Nostrand Reinhold.

Hirschi, T. (1969) *The Causes of Delinquency*. Berkeley, CA: University of California Press.

Hirschi, T. (1983) 'Crime and family policy', *Journal of Contemporary Studies*, 4: 3–16.

Hirschi, T. and Gottfredson, M. (1987) 'Causes of white-collar crime', *Criminology*, 25: 949–74.

Hirschi, T. and Gottfredson, M. (1989) 'The significance of white-collar crime for a general theory of crime', *Criminology*, 27: 359–71.

Hirst, P.Q. (1975) 'Marx and Engels on law crime, and morality', in I. Taylor, P. Walton and J. Young (eds), *Critical Criminology*. London: Routledge and Kegan Paul. pp. 203–32.

Hofrichter, R. (1987) *Neighborhood Justice in Capitalist Society: The Expansion of the Informal State*, Westport, CT: Greenwood Press.

Hollinger, R.C. (1991) 'Neutralizing in the workplace: an empirical analysis of property theft and production deviance', *Deviant Behavior*, 12: 169–202.

Hooker, M. (1975) *Legal Pluralism: An Introduction to Colonial and Neo-Colonial Laws*. Oxford: Clarendon Press.

hooks, b. (1989) *Talking Back: Thinking Feminist, Thinking Black*. Boston: South End Press.

hooks, b. and West, C. (1991) *Breaking Bread: Insurgent Black Intellectual Life*. Boston: South End Press.

Hooton, E.A. (1939) *The American Criminal: An Anthropological Study*. Cambridge, MA: Harvard University Press.

Horning, D.M. (1970) 'Blue collar theft: conceptions of property and attitudes towards pilfering and work group norms in a modern plant', in E. Smigel and H.L. Ross (eds), *Crimes Against Bureaucracy*. New York: Van Nostrand Reinhold. pp. 46–64.

Howe, A. (1994) *Punish and Critique: Towards a Feminist Analysis of Penality*. London: Routledge.

Hudson, B. (1984) 'Femininity and adolescence', in A. McRobbie and M. Nava (eds), *Gender and Generation*. London: Macmillan.

Hughes, S.P. and Schneider, A.L. (1989) 'Victim-offender mediation: a survey of program characteristics and perceptions of effectiveness', *Crime and Delinquency*, 35(2): 217–33.

Hunt, A. (1987) 'The critique of law: what is "critical" about critical theory?', *Journal of Law and Society*, 14: 5–19.

Hunt, A. (1990) 'The big fear: law confronts postmodernism', *McGill Law Journal*, 35: 507–40.

Hunt, A. (1993) *Explorations in Law and Society: Toward a Constitutive Theory of Law*. New York: Routledge.

Hurwitz, S. and Christiansen, K.O. (1983) *Criminology*. London: George Allen and Urwin.

Husserl, E. (1973) *The Phenomenology of Internal Time-Consciousness*. Bloomington, IN: Indiana University Press.

Huyssen, A. (1986) *After the Great Divide: Modernism, Mass Culture, Postmodernism.* Bloomington, IN: Indiana University Press.

Irigaray, L. (1985) *This Sex Which is Not One.* Ithaca, NY: Cornell University Press.

Irigaray, L. (1993) *Je, Tu, Nous: Toward a Culture of Difference.* New York: Routledge.

Itzkowitz, G. (1988) 'Social theory and law: the significance of Stuart Henry', *Law and Society Review*, 22: 949–61

Jackall, R. (1988) *Moral Mazes: The World of Corporate Managers.* New York: Oxford University Press.

Jackson, B. (1985) *Semiotics and Legal Theory.* New York: Routledge and Kegan Paul.

Jackson, B. (1988) *Law, Fact and Narrative Coherence.* Merseyside: Deborah Charles.

Jacobs, P.A. et al. (1965) 'Aggressive behavior, mental subnormality and the XYY male', *Nature*, 208: 1351–2.

Jaggar, A. (1983) *Feminist Politics and Human Nature*, Totowa: NJ: Rowman and Allenheld.

Jakobson, R. (1971) 'Two aspects of language and two types of aphasic disorders', in R. Jakobson and M. Halle (eds), *Fundamentals of Language.* Paris: Mouton.

Janikowski, R. and Milovanovic, D. (eds) (1995) *Legality and Illegality: A Semiotic View.* Peter Lange.

JanMohamed, A.R. (1992) 'Worldliness-without-world, homelessness-as-home: toward a definition of the specular border intellectual', M. Sprinker (ed.), *Edward Said: A Critical Reader.* Boston: Blackwell. pp. 96–120.

JanMohamed, A.R. (1994) 'Some implications of Paulo Freire's border pedagogy', in H. Giroux and P. McLaren (eds), *Between Borders.* New York: Routledge.

Jantsch, E. (1980) *The Self-Organizing Universe.* New York: George Braziller.

Jeffery, C.R. (1965) 'Criminal behavior and learning theory', *Journal of Criminal Law, Criminology and Police Science*, 56: 294–300.

Jeffery, C.R. (1971) *Crime Prevention through Environmental Design.* Beverly Hills: Sage.

Jeffery, C.R. (1978) 'Criminology as an interdisciplinary behavioral science', *Criminology*, 16(2): 149–69.

Jeffery, C.R. (1990) *Criminology: An Interdisciplinary Approach.* Englewood Cliffs, NJ: Prentice-Hall.

Jeffery, C.R. (1993) 'Genetics, crime and the canceled conference', *The Criminologist*, 18(1): 1, 6–8.

Jeffery, C.R. (1994) 'Biological and neuropsychiatric approaches to criminal behavior', in G. Barak (ed.), *Varieties of Criminology: Readings from a Dynamic Discipline.* Westport, CT: Praeger. pp. 15–28.

Jessop, B. (1982) *The Capitalist State.* New York: New York University Press.

Jessop, B. (1990) *State Theory: Putting the Capitalist State in its Place.* Cambridge: Polity Press.

Johns, C.J. (1992) *Power, Ideology, and the War on Drugs: Nothing Succeeds Like Failure.* Westport, CT: Greenwood Press.

Johnson, R.E. (1979) *Juvenile Delinquency and its Origins.* Cambridge: Cambridge University Press.

Kairys, D. (ed.) (1982) *The Politics of Law: A Progressive Critique.* New York: Pantheon Books.

Kalinch, D.B. (1980) *The Inmate Economy.* Lexington, MA: D.C. Heath.

Kalinch, D.B. and Stojkovic, S. (1985) 'Contraband: The basis for legitimate power in a prison social system', *Criminal Justice and Behavior*, 12(4): 435–51.

Kane, T.E. (1990) 'Here there be dragons: some elements of Stuart Henry's constitutive criminology'. Master's paper, Saint Paul's College, Winnipeg, Manitoba.

Kaplan, M. and Kaplan, N. (1991) 'The self-organization of human psychological functioning', *Behavioral Sciences*, 36: 161–78.

Katz, J. (1988) *Seductions of Crime: Moral and Sensual Attractions of Doing Evil.* New York: Basic Books.

Kelman, H.C. (1987) 'The political psychology of the Israel–Palestinian negotiations: how can we overcome the barriers to a negotiated solution?', *Political Psychology*, 3: 347–63.

Kerruish, V. (1991) *Jurisprudence as Ideology*. New York: Routledge.

Killilea, M. (1976) 'Mutual help organizations: interpretations in the literature', in G. Kaplan and M. Killilea (eds), *Support Systems and Mutual Help: Multidisciplinary Explorations*. New York: Grune and Stratton.

Kim, D. and Shin, K.S. (1983) *Judo*. Dubuque, IA: Wm. C. Brown.

Kitsuse, J.I. (1964) 'Societal reaction to deviant behavior: problems of theory and method', in H. Becker (ed), *The Other Side*. New York: Free Press. pp. 87–102.

Klare, K. (1979) 'Law-making as praxis', *Telos* 40: 123–35.

Klein, D. (1980) 'The etiology of female crime: a review of the literature', in S.K. Datesman and F.R. Scarpitti (eds), *Women, Crime and Justice*. New York: Oxford University Press. pp. 70–105.

Klockars, C.B. (1974) *The Professional Fence*. New York: Free Press.

Knopp, F.H. (1991) 'Community solutions to sexual violence: feminist/abolitionist perspectives', in H. Pepinsky and R. Quinney (eds), *Criminology as Peacemaking*. Bloomington, IN: Indiana University Press.

Knopp, F. H.(1993) 'On radical feminism and abolition', in B. MacLean and H. Pepinsky (eds), *We Who Would Take No Prisoners*. Vancouver, BC: Collective Press.

Knopp, F.H., Boward, B., Morris, M., Schnapper, M.B. (1976) *Instead of Prisons: A Handbook for Abolitionists*. Syracuse, NY: Prison Research Education Action Project.

Knorr-Cetina, K. (1981) 'Introduction: the micro-sociological challenge of macro-sociology: towards a reconstruction of social theory and methodology', in K. Knorr-Cetina and A. Cicourel (eds), *Advances in Social Theory and Methodology: Toward an Integration of Macro- and Micro-Sociologies*. London: Routledge and Kegan Paul.

Knorr-Cetina, K. and Cicourel, A. (eds) (1981) *Advances in Social Theory and Methodology: Toward an Integration of Macro- and Micro-Sociologies*. London: Routledge and Kegan Paul.

Koopman, E.J. (1987) 'Family mediation: a developmental perspective on the field', in D.J.D. Sandole and I. Sandole-Staroste (eds), *Conflict Management and Problem Solving: Interpersonal to International Applications*. New York: New York University Press.

Kretschmer, E. (1925) *Physique and Character*. New York: Harcourt, Brace.

Kriesberg, L. (1991) 'Conflict resolution applications to peace studies', *Peace and Change*, 16(4): 400–17.

Krisberg, B. (1975) *Crime and Privilege: Towards a New Criminology*. Englewood Cliffs, NJ: Prentice-Hall.

Kristeva, J. (1980) *Desire in Language*. New York: Columbia University Press.

Kristeva, J. (1986) *Revolution in Poetic Language*. New York: Columbia University Press.

Krohn, M. (1991) 'Control and deterrence theories', in J.F. Sheley (ed.), *Criminology: a Contemporary Handbook*. Belmont, CA: Wadsworth. pp. 295–313.

Kropotkin, P. (1912) *The Conquest of Bread*. New York: Benjamin Blom.

Lab, S.P. and J.T. Whitehead (1990) 'From "nothing works" to "the appropriate works": the latest stop on the search for the secular grail', *Criminology*, 28(3): 405–17.

Lacan, J. (1977) *Écrits*. Trans. A. Sheridan. New York: Norton.

Lacan, J. (1981) *The Four Fundamental Concepts of Psycho-Analysis*. New York: W.W. Norton.

Lacan, J. (1985) *Feminine Sexuality*. New York: Norton and Pantheon Books.

Lacan, J. (1991) *L'Envers de la Psychanalyse*. Paris, France: Editions du Seuil.

Lacan, J. (1992) *The Ethics of Psychoanalysis*. New York: Norton.

Laclau, E. (1988) 'Metaphor and social antagonism', in C. Nelson and L. Grossberg (eds), *Marxism and the Interpretation of Culture*. Urbana, IL: University of Illinois Press.

Laclau, E. (1987) 'Psycho-analysis and Marxism', *Critical Inquiry*, 13: 330–3.

Laclau, E. (1991) *New Reflections on the Revolutions of Our Time*. London: Verso.

Laclau, E. and Mouffe, C. (1985) *Hegemony and Socialist Strategy*. New York: Verso.

Laclau, E. and Mouffe, C. (1987) 'Post Marxism without apologies', *New Left Review*, 166: 79–106.

Landowski, E. (1988) 'Towards a semiotic and narrative approach to law', *International Journal for the Semiotics of Law*, 1(1): 101–5.

Lash, S. (1990) *Sociology of Postmodernism*. London: Routledge.

Lauretis, T. (1989) 'The violence of rhetoric: considerations on representation and gender', in N. Armstrong and L. Tennenhouse (eds), *The Violence of Representation: Literature and the History of Violence*. London: Routledge.

Lea, J. and Young, J. (1984) *What is to be Done About Law and Order?* Harmondsworth: Penguin.

Lecercle, J.J. (1985) *Philosophy through the Looking Glass: Language, Nonsense, Desire*. London: Hutchinson.

Lecercle, J.J. (1990) *The Violence of Language*. New York: Routledge.

Lecercle, J.J. (1991) *The Violence of Language*. New York: Routledge.

Lee, S.L. (1990) *Jacques Lacan*. Amherst, MA: University of Massachusetts Press.

Lees, S. (1986) *Losing Out: Sexuality and Adolescent Girls*. London: Hutchinson,

Lees, S. (1989) 'Learning to love: sexual reputation, morality and the social control of girls', in M. Cain (ed.), *Growing up Good: Policing the Behavior of Girls in Europe*. London: Sage.

Leifer, R. (1989) 'Understanding organizational transformation using a dissipative structure model', *Human Relations*, 42: 899–916.

Lem, S. (1981) 'Metafantasia: the possibilities of science fiction', *Science-Fiction Studies*, 8: 54–71.

Lemert, E.M. (1951) *Social Pathology*. New York: McGraw-Hill.

Lemert, E.M. (1967) *Human Deviance, Social Problems and Social Control*. Englewood Cliffs, NJ: Prentice-Hall.

Lenin, V. (1949) *The State and Revolution*. Moscow: Foreign Languages Publishing House.

Levine, M. (1988) 'How self-help works', *Social Policy*, 18 (Summer): 39–43.

Levine, M. and Perkins, D.V. (1987) *Principles of Community Psychiatry*. New York: Oxford University Press.

Lewontin, R.C., Rose, S. and Kamin, L.J. (1984) *Not in Our Genes*. New York: Pantheon Books.

Lichtman, R. (1982) *The Production of Desire: The Integration of Psychoanalysis into Marxist Theory*. New York: Free Press.

Lofland, J.H. (1969) *Deviance and Identity*. Englewood Cliffs, NJ: Prentice Hall.

Lombroso, C. (1876) *L'Uomo Delinquente*. Torino: Fratelli Boca.

Love, N. (1986) *Marx, Nietzsche, and Modernity*. New York: Columbia University Press.

Lovibond, S. (1989) 'Feminism and postmodernism', *New Left Review*, 178: 5–28.

Lowman, J. and MacLean, B.D. (eds) (1992) *Realist Criminology*. Toronto: University of Toronto Press.

Loye, D. and Eisler, R. (1987) 'Chaos and transformation: implications of nonequilibrium theory for social science and society', *Behavioral Science*, 32: 53–65.

Luhmann, N.A. (1985) *Sociological Theory of Law*. Boston: Routledge and Kegan Paul.

Luhmann, N.A. (1988) 'The third question of a legal system in law and legal history', *Journal of Law and Society*, 15: 153.

Luhmann, N.A. (1990) 'The coding of a legal system', in A. Febbrajo and G. Teubner (eds), *State, Law, Economy as Autopoietic Systems*. Milano: Giuffre.

Luhmann, N.A. (1992) 'Operational closure and structural coupling: the differentiation of the legal system', *Cardozo Law Review*, 13(5): 1419–41.

Lynch, M. and Patterson, E.B. (1990) 'Racial discrimination in the criminal justice system: evidence from four jurisdictions', in B. MacLean and D. Milovanovic (eds), *Racism, Empiricism and Criminal Justice*. Vancouver, BC: Collective Press. pp. 51–9.

Lyng, S. (1990) 'Edgework: a social psychological analysis of voluntary risk taking', *American Journal of Sociology*, 95(4): 851–86.

Lyotard, J. (1984) *The Postmodern Condition: A Report on Knowledge*. Trans. G. Bennington and B. Massouri. Minneapolis, MN: University of Minnesota Press.

MacCannell, J.F. (1986) *Figuring Lacan*. Lincoln, NB: University of Nebraska Press.

MacKinnon, C. (1982) 'Feminism, Marxism, method, and the state: an agenda for theory', *Signs*, 7(2): 515–44.

MacKinnon, C. (1983) 'Feminism, Marxism, method, and the state: toward feminist jurisprudence', *Signs*, 8(4): 635–58.

MacKinnon, C. (1987) *Feminism Unmodified: Discourses on Life and Law*. Cambridge, MA: Harvard University Press.

MacKinnon, C. (1989) *Toward a Feminist Theory of the State*. Cambridge, MA: Harvard University Press.

MacLean, B.D. and Pepinsky, H. (1993) *We Who Would Take no Prisoners: Selections from the Fifth International Conference on Penal Abolition*. Vancouver, BC: Collective Press.

MacLean, B.D. (1991) 'The origins of left realism', in B.D. MacLean and D. Milovanovic (eds), *New Directions in Critical Criminology*. Vancouver: Collective Press. pp. 9–14.

Mair, L. (1969) *Witchcraft*. New York: McGraw-Hill, World University Library.

Mama, A. (1989) 'Violence against black women: gender, race and state responses', *Feminist Review*, 32: 30–48.

Mandelbrot, B. (1983) *The Fractal Geometry of Nature*. New York: W.H. Freeman.

Mankoff, M. (1971) 'Societal reaction and career deviance: a critical analysis', *The Sociological Quarterly*, 12: 204–18.

Manning, P.K. (1988) *Symbolic Communication: Signifying Calls and the Police Response*. Cambridge: MIT Press.

Manning, P.K. (1990) 'Semiotics and postmodernism', in D. Dickens and A. Fontana (eds), *Post Modernism and Sociology*. Chicago: University of Chicago Press.

Marini, M. (1992) *Jacques Lacan*. New Brunswick, NJ: Rutgers University Press.

Mars, G. (1974) 'Dock pilferage', in P. Rock and M. McIntosh (eds), *Deviance and Social Control*. London: Tavistock. pp. 205–28.

Mars, G. (1982) *Cheats at Work: An Anthropology of Workplace Crime*. London: George Allen and Unwin.

Martinson, R. (1974) 'What works? Questions and answers about prison reform', *Public Interest*, 35: 22–54.

Marx, G. (1988) *Undercover: Police Surveillance in America*. Berkeley: University of California Press.

Marx, K. (1852) 'The eighteenth Brumaire of Louis Bonaparte', in E. Kamenka (ed.), *The Portable Marx*. Harmondsworth: Penguin, 1984.

Marx, K. (1859) 'Preface to a contribution to the critique of political economy', in K. Marx and F. Engels (eds), *Selected Works*, vol. 1. Moscow: Progress Publishers. pp. 502–6.

Marx, K. (1868) *Capital*. 3 vols. New York: International Publishers.

Marx, K. (1968) 'Thesis on Feurbach, no. 6', in K. Marx and F. Engels (eds), *Collected Works*. New York: International Publishers.

Mastrofski, S. and Parks, R. (1990) 'Improving observational studies of police', *Criminology*, 28(3): 475–96.

Mathiesen, T. (1986) 'The politics of abolition', *Contemporary Crises*, 10(1): 81–94.

Matsuda, M.J. (1987) 'Looking to the bottom: critical legal studies and reparations', *Harvard Civil Rights-Civil Liberties Law Review*, 22(2): 323–99.

Matthews, R. and Young, J. (eds) (1986) *Confronting Crime*. Beverly Hills, CA: Sage.

Matthews, R. and Young, J. (eds) (1992) *Issues in Realist Criminology*. Beverly Hills, CA: Sage.

Matthews, R. (ed.) (1988) *Informal Justice?* London: Sage.

Matthews, R. (1987) 'Taking realist criminology seriously', *Contemporary Crisis*, 11: 371–401.

Maturana, H. and Varela, F. (1980) *Autopoiesis and Cognition*. Boston: D. Reidel.

Maturana, H. and Varela, F. (1987) *The Tree of Knowledge*, Boston: New Science Library.

Matza, D. (1964) *Delinquency and Drift*. New York: Wiley.

Matza, D. (1969) *Becoming Deviant*. Englewood Cliffs, NJ: Prentice-Hall.

Matza, D. and Sykes, G. (1961) 'Juvenile delinquency and subterranean values', *American Sociological Review*, 26: 712–19.

McCabe, S. (1983) 'Crime', in D. Walsh and A. Poole (eds), A *Dictionary of Criminology*. London: Routledge and Kegan Paul. pp. 49–52.

McCaghy, C.H. and Cernkovich, S.A. (1987) *Crime in American Society*. New York: MacMillan Publishing Company.

McCahery, J. (1993) 'Modernist and postmodernist perspectives on public law in British critical legal studies', *Social and Legal Studies*, 2(4): 397–421.

McLaren, P., and Lankshear, C. (1994) *Politics of Liberation*. London: Routledge.

McLaren, P. (1994) 'Multiculturalism and the postmodern critique: toward a pedagogy of resistance and transformation', in H. Giroux and P. McLaren (eds), *Between Borders: Pedagogy and the Politics of Cultural Studies*. New York: Routledge. pp. 192–222.

McLaren, P. (1994) 'Postmodernism and the death of politics: a Brazilian reprieve', in P. McLaren and C. Lankshear (eds), *Politics of Liberation: Paths from Freire*. New York: Routledge.

McLeod, W.R. (1988) 'Epistemology and constructivism, some implications for therapy', *Australian and New Zealand Journal of Family Therapy*, 9(1): 9–16.

McRobie, A. and Thompson, M. (1994) 'Chaos, catastrophes and engineering', in N. Hall (ed.), *Exploring Chaos*. New York: Norton.

Mead, G.H. (1934) *Mind, Self and Society*. Ed. C.W. Morris. Chicago: University of Chicago Press.

Mednick, S.A. (1974) *Genetics, Environment and Psychopathology*.

Mednick, S.A. (1979) 'Biosocial factors and primary prevention of anti-social behavior', in S.A. Mednick and Shoham, S.G. (eds), *New Paths in Criminology: Interdisciplinary and Intercultural Explanations*. Lexington, MA: D.C. Heath.

Mednick, S.A. and Christiansen, K.O. (1977) *Biosocial Bases of Criminal Behavior*. New York: Gardiner Press.

Mednick, S.A., Gabrielle, W. and Hutchings, B. (1987) 'Genetic factors in the etiology of criminal behavior', in S. Mednick, T. Moffitt and S. Stack (eds), *The Causes of Crime: New Biological Approaches*. Cambridge: Cambridge University Press. pp. 74–91.

Mednick, S.A., Moffitt, T. and Stack, S. (eds) (1987) *The Causes of Crime: New Biological Approaches*. Cambridge: Cambridge University Press.

Merquior, J.G. (1985) *Foucault*. London: Fontana.

Merry, S.E. (1985) 'Concepts of law and justice among working-class Americans: ideology as culture', *Legal Studies Forum*, 9(1): 59–69.

Merry, S.E. (1988) 'Legal pluralism', *Law and Society Review*, 22: 869–96.

Merry, S. E. and Milner, N. (1993). *The Possibility of Popular Justice*. Ann Arbor, MI: The University of Michigan Press.

Merton, R.K. (1938) 'Social structure and anomie', *American Sociological Review*, 3: 672–82.

Merton, R.K. (1968) *Social Theory and Social Structure* (1957). New York: Free Press.

Messerschmidt, J.W. (1983) *The Trial of Leonard Peltier*. Boston: South End Press.

Messerschmidt, J.W. (1986) *Capitalism, Patriarchy, and Crime: Toward a Socialist Feminist Criminology*. Totowa, NJ: Rowman and Littlefield.

Messerschmidt, J.W. (1993) *Masculinities and Crime: Critique and Reconceptualization of Theory*. Boston: Rowman and Littlefield.

Messner, S., Krohn, M.D. and Liska, A.E., (eds), (1989) *Theoretical Integration in the Study of Deviance and Crime: Problems and Prospects*. Albany, NY: State University of New York Press.

Metz, C. (1981) *The Imaginary Signifier*. Bloomington, IN: Indiana University Press.

Michael, J. and Adler, M.J. (1933) *Crime, Law and Social Science*. New York: Harcourt Brace Jovanovich.

Michalowski, R. (1985) *Order, Law, and Crime*. New York: Random House.

Michalowski, R. and Kramer, R. (1987) 'The space between the laws: the problem of corporate crime in transnational context', *Social Problems*, 34: 34–53.

Mills, C.W. (1940) 'Situated actions and vocabularies of motive', *American Sociological Review*, 5: 904–13.

Mills, C.W. (1956) *The Power Elite*. New York: Oxford University Press.

Mills, C.W. (1969) *Power, Politics and People*. New York: Oxford University Press.

Milovanovic, D. (1981) 'The commodity exchange theory of law: in search of a perspective', *Crime and Social Justice*, 15: 41–9.

Milovanovic, D. (1983) 'Weber and Marx on law: demystifying ideology and law – toward an emancipatory political practice', *Contemporary Crises*, 7: 353–70.

Milovanovic, D. (1986) 'Juridico-linguistic communicative markets: towards a semiotic analysis', *Contemporary Crisis*, 10: 281–304.

Milovanovic, D. (1987) 'The political economy of "liberty" and "property" interests', *Legal Studies Forum*, 11: 267–93.

Milovanovic, D. (1988) 'Jailhouse lawyers and jailhouse lawyering', *International Journal of the Sociology of Law*, 16: 455–75.

Milovanovic, D. (1989a) *Weberian and Marxian Analysis of Law: Structure and Function of Law in a Capitalist Mode of Production*. Aldershot, England: Gower Publishers.

Milovanovic, D. (1989b) 'Critical criminology and the challenge of post-modernism', *Critical Criminologist*, 1(4): 9–10, 17.

Milovanovic, D. (1991a) 'Schmarxism, exorcism and transpraxis', *The Critical Criminologist*, 3(4): 5–6, 11–12.

Milovanovic, D. (1991b) 'Images of unity and disunity in the juridic subject and the movement toward the peacemaking community', in H. Pepinsky and R. Quinney (eds), *Criminology as Peacemaking*. Bloomington, IN: Indiana University Press. pp. 209–27.

Milovanovic, D. (1992a) *Postmodern Law and Disorder: Psychoanalytic Semiotics, Chaos and Juridic Exegeses*. Liverpool, UK: Deborah Charles.

Milovanovic, D. (1992b) 'Re-thinking subjectivity in law and ideology: a semiotic perspective', *Journal of Human Justice*, 4(1): 31–54.

Milovanovic, D. (1993a) 'Lacan's four discourses', *Studies in Psychoanalytic Theory*, 2(1): 3–23.

Milovanovic, D. (1993b) 'Borromean knots and the constitution of sense in juridico-discursive production', *Legal Studies Forum*, 17(2): 171–92.

Milovanovic, D. (1994a) *Sociology of Law*. 2nd edn. Albany, New York: Harrow and Heston.

Milovanovic, D. (1994b) 'The postmodern turn: Lacan, psychoanalytic semiotics, and the construction of subjectivity in law', *Emory International Law Review*, 8(1): 67–98.

Milovanovic, D. (1994c) 'The decentered subject in law: contributions of topology, psychoanalytic semiotics and chaos theory', *Studies in Psychoanalytic Theory*, 3(1): 93–127.

Milovanovic, D. (1995) 'Dueling paradigms: modernist versus postmodernist', *Humanity and Society*, 19(1): 1–22.

Milovanovic, D. and Henry, S. (1991) 'Constitutive penology', *Social Justice*, 18: 204–24.

Milovanovic, D. and Thomas, J. (1989) 'Overcoming the absurd: legal struggle as primitive rebellion', *Social Problems*, 36(1): 48–60.

Minow, M. (1990) *Making All the Difference: Inclusion, Exclusion and American Law*. Ithaca, NY: Cornell University Press.

Moi, T. (1985) *Sexual/Textual Politics*. London: Methuen.

Moi, T. (1987) *French Feminist Thought: A Reader*. New York: Blackwell.

Moi, T. (ed.) (1990) *The Kristeva Reader*. Oxford: Blackwell.

Moore, S.F. (1973) 'Law and social change: the semi-autonomous field as an appropriate subject of study', *Law and Society Review*, 7: 719–46.

Morgan, J. and Zedner, L. (1992) 'The victim's charter: a new deal for child victims?', *Howard Journal of Criminal Justice*, 31(4): 294–307.

Morgan, L.H. (1877) *Ancient Society*. New York: Meridian.

Morris, N. (1973) *The Future of Imprisonment*. Chicago: University of Chicago Press.

Morris, T.P. (1957) *The Criminal Area: A Study in Social Ecology*. London: Routledge and Kegan Paul.

Mouffe, C. (1979) *Gramsci and Marxist Theory*. London: Routledge and Kegan Paul.

Mouffe, C. (1988) 'Hegemony and new political subjects: toward a new concept of democracy', in C. Nelson and L. Grossberg (eds), *Marxism and the Interpretation of Culture*. Urbana, IL: University of Illinois Press. pp. 89–104.

Mouffe, C. (1992) 'Feminism, citizenship and radical democratic politics', in J. Butler and J.W. Scott (eds), *Feminists Theorize the Political*. London: Routledge.

Moyer, K.E. (1976) *The Psychobiology of Aggression*. New York: Harper and Row.

Mueller, J. and Richardson, W. (1982). *Lacan and Language: A Reader's Guide to Écrits*. New York: International Universities Press.

Muraskin, R. and Alleman, T. (eds) (1993) *It's a Crime: Women and Justice*. Englewood Cliffs, NJ: Prentice-Hall.

Murton, T. (1976) *The Dilemma of Prison Reform*. New York: Praeger.

Naffine, N. (1987) *Female Crime: The Construction of Women in Criminology*. London: George Allen and Unwin.

Nelken, D. (1986) 'Beyond the study of "law and society"?: Henry's Private Justice and O'Hagan's The End of Law', *American Bar Association Research Journal*, 2: 323–38.

Nelken, D. (ed.) (1994) *The Futures of Criminology*. London: Sage.

Nelkin, D. (1993) 'The grandiose claims of geneticists', *The Chronicle of Higher Education*, 3 March: B1–B3.

Newman, O. (1972) *Defensible Space*. New York: Macmillan.

Newman, O. (1973) *Architectural Design for Crime Prevention*. Washington, DC: National Institute of Law Enforcement and Justice, US Department of Justice.

Newman, D.J. (1968) 'Public attitudes toward a form of white-collar crime', in G. Geis (ed), *White-Collar Criminal*. New York: Atherton Press.

Nielsen, J. (1968) 'The XYY syndrome in a mental hospital', *British Journal of Criminology*, 8(2): 186–203.

Nye, I.F. (1958) *Family Relationships and Delinquent Behavior*. New York: Wiley.

O'Malley, P. (1991) 'Legal networks and domestic security', *Law Politics and Society*, 111: 171–90.

O'Malley, P. (1992) 'Risk, power and crime prevention', *Economy and Society*, 21: 252–75.

O'Malley, P. and Mugford, S. (1994) 'Crime, excitement, and modernity', in G. Barak (ed.), *Varieties of Criminology: Readings from a Dynamic Discipline*. Westport, CT: Praeger. pp. 189–211.

Omer, H. and Strenger, C. (1992) 'The pluralist revolution: from one true meaning to an infinity of constructed ones', *Psychotherapy*, 29(2): 253–61.

Palmer, T. (1975) 'Martinson revisited', *Journal of Research in Crime and Delinquency*, 12: 133–52.

Park, R.E. and Burgess, E. (1924) *Introduction to the Science of Sociology*. 2nd edn. Chicago: University of Chicago Press.

Park, R.E. and Burgess, E. (1925) *The City*. Chicago: University of Chicago Press.

Parry, A. (1991a) 'A universe of stories', *Family Process*, 30: 37–54.

Parry, A. (1991b) 'Shared stories: the tie that binds', *The Calgary Participator*, 1(3): 17–21.

Parry, A. and Doan, R. (1994) *Story Re-Visions: Narrative Therapy in the Postmodern World*. New York: Guilford Press.

Parsons, T. (1951) *The Social System*. Glencoe, IL: The Free Press.

Parsons, T. and Shils, E.A. (1951) *Toward a General Theory of Social Action*. Cambridge, MA: Harvard University Press.

Parsons, T. (1962) 'The law and social control', in W.M. Evan (ed.), *Law and Sociology*. Chicago: Free Press. pp. 64–69.

Pashukanis, E. (1978) *Law and Marxism: A General Theory*. Ed. C.J. Arthur. London: Ink Links.

Pashukanis, E. (1980) 'The general theory of law and Marxism', in P. Beirne and R. Sharlet (eds), *Pashukanis: Selected Writings on Marxism and Law*. New York: Academic Press.

Passas, N. (1990) 'Anomie and corporate deviance', *Contemporary Crises*, 14: 157–78.

Pavarini, M. (1994) 'Is criminology worth saving?', in D. Nelken (ed.), *The Futures of Criminology*. London: Sage.

Pearce, F. and Snider, L. (1992) 'Crimes of the powerful', special issues editors, *Journal of Human Justice*, 3.

Pearce, F. (1976) *Crimes of the Powerful*. London: Pluto Press.

Pearson, F.S. and Weiner, N.A. (1985) 'Toward an integration of criminological theories', *Journal of Criminal Law and Criminology*, 76(1): 116–50.

Peat, D. (1988) *Superstrings and the Search for the Theory of Everything*. Chicago: Contemporary Books.

Pecheux, M. (1982) *Language, Semantics and Ideology*. New York: St Martin's Press.

Peirce, C.S. (1956) *The Philosophy of Peirce: Selected Writings*. Ed. J. Buchler. London: Routledge and Kegan Paul.

Peirce, C.S. (1965) *The Collected Papers of Charles Sanders Peirce*. Ed. C. Hartshorne and P. Weiss. Cambridge, MA: Harvard University Press.

Penrose, R. (1989) *The Emperor's New Mind*. New York: Oxford University Press.

Pepinsky, H. (1976) *Crime and Conflict: A Study of Law and Society*. Oxford: Martin Robertson.

Pepinsky, H. (1978) 'Communist anarchism as an alternative to the rule of criminal law', *Contemporary Crisis*, 2: 315–27.

Pepinsky, H. (1991) *The Geometry of Violence and Democracy*. Bloomington, IN: Indiana University Press.

Pepinsky, H. and Quinney, R. (eds) (1991) *Criminology as Peacemaking*. Bloomington, IN: Indiana University Press.

Peters, M. and Lankshear, C. (1994) 'Education and hermeneutics: a Freirean interpretation', in P. McLaren and C. Lankshear (eds), *Politics of Liberation*. London: Routledge.

Petersillia, J. (1983) *Racial Disparities in the Criminal Justice System*. Santa Monica, CA: Rand Corporation.

Pfohl, S.J. (1985) *Images of Deviance and Social Control: A Sociological History*. New York: McGraw-Hill.

Pfuhl, E.H. and Henry, S. (1993) *The Deviance Process*. 3rd edn. New York: Aldine De Gruyter.

Phillipson, M. (1971) *Sociological Aspects of Crime and Delinquency*. London: Routledge and Kegan Paul.

Pickover, C. (1988) 'Pattern formation and chaos in networks', *Communications of the ACM*, 31(2): 136–51.

Platt, T. (1974) 'Prospects for a radical criminology in the United States', *Crime and Social Justice*, 1: 2–10.

Pompa, G.G. (1987) 'The community relations service', in D.J.D. Sandole and I. Sandole-Staroste (eds), *Conflict Management and Problem Solving: Interpersonal to International Applications*. New York: New York University Press.

Pospisil, L. (1971) *Anthropology of Law*, New York: Harper and Row.

Poster, M. (ed.) (1988) *Jean Baudrillard: Selected Writings*. Stanford: Stanford University Press.

Poston, T. and Stewart, I. (1978) *Catastrophe Theory and its Applications*. London: Pitman.

Poulantzas, N. (1973) *Political Power and Social Class*. Atlantic Fields, NJ: Humanities Press.

Poulantzas, N. (1978) *State, Power and Socialism*. London: New Left Books.

Pound, R. (1959) *Jurisprudence*. St Paul, MN: West Publishing.

Poveda, T.G. (1994) *Rethinking White-Collar Crime*. Westport, CT: Praeger.

Prigogine, I. (1977) 'Physics and metaphysics', *Advances in Biological and Medical Physics*, 76: 241–65.

Prigogine, I. (1978) 'Time, structure, and fluctuations', *Science,* 201: 777–85.

Prigogine, I. and Stengers, I. (1984) *Order out of Chaos*. New York: Bantam.

Quinney, R. (1970) *The Social Reality of Crime*. Boston: Little, Brown.

Quinney, R. (1974) *Critique of the Legal Order* (1973). Boston: Little, Brown.

Quinney, R. (1975) 'Crime control in a capitalist society', in I. Taylor, P. Walton and J. Young (eds), *Critical Criminology*. London: Routledge and Kegan Paul.

Quinney, R. (1977) *Class, State, and Crime*. New York: David McKay.

Quinney, R. and Wildeman, J. (1991) *The Problem of Crime: A Peace and Social Justice Perspective*. 3rd edn. London: Mayfield.

Quinton, A. (1977) 'Causality', in Alan Bullock and Oliver Stallybrass (eds), *The Fontana Dictionary of Modern Thought*. London: Fontana. pp. 91–2.

Raab, S. (1993) 'Ex-rogue officer tells panel of police graft in New York', *New York Times*, 28 September: A1, B3.

Ragland-Sullivan, E. (1986) *Jacques Lacan and the Philosophy of Psychoanalysis*. Chicago: University of Illinois Press.

Rajchman, J. (1991) *Truth and Eros: Foucault, Lacan, and the Question of Ethics*. New York: Routledge.

Reckless, W.C. (1961) 'A new theory of delinquency and crime', *Federal Probation*, 25: 42–6.

Reckless, W.C. (1970) 'Causes of crime', in H.P. Fairchild (ed.), *Dictionary of Sociology and Related Sciences*. Totowa, NJ: Littlefield, Adams. pp. 73–4.

Reckless, W.C. (1973) *The Crime Problem* (1950). Englewood Cliffs, NJ: Prentice-Hall.

Redl, F. and Wineman, D. (1951) *Children Who Hate*. New York: Free Press.

Redl, F. and Wineman, D. (1952) *Controls from Within*. New York Free Press.

Reichman, N. (1986) 'Managing crime risks: toward an insurance based model of social control', *Research in Law and Social Control*, 8: 151–72.

Reiman, J. (1979) *The Rich Get Richer and the Poor Get Prison*. New York: Wiley.

Reiman, J. (1990) *Justice and Modern Moral Philosophy*. New Haven: Yale University Press.

Reiss, A.J. (1951) 'Delinquency as the failure of personal and social controls', *American Sociological Review*, 16: 196–207.

Rice, M. (1990) 'Challenging orthodoxies in feminist theory: a black feminist critique', in L. Gelsthorpe and A. Morris (eds), *Feminist Perspectives in Criminology*. Milton Keynes: Open University Press. pp. 57–69.

Richman, R. (1987) 'Environmental mediation: an alternative dispute settlement system', in D.J.D. Sandole and I. Sandole-Staroste (eds), *Conflict Management and Problem Solving: Interpersonal to International Applications*. New York: New York University Press.

Riessman, F. (1965) 'The "helper-therapy" principle', *Social Work*, 10: 27–32.

Roberts, S. (1979) *Order and Dispute: An Introduction to Legal Anthropology*. Harmondsworth: Penguin.

Robinson, D. (1979) *Talking Out of Alcoholism*. London: Croom Helm.

Robinson, D. and Henry, S. (1977) *Self-help and Health: Mutual Aid for Modern Problems*. Oxford: Martin Robertson.

Rosenau, P.M. (1992) *Postmodernism and the Social Sciences: Insights, Inroads, and Intrusions*. Princeton, NJ: Princeton University Press.

Roshier, B. (1989) *Controlling Crime: The Classical Perspective in Criminology*. Philadelphia: Open University Press.

Ross, E. (1901) *Social Control: A Study of the Foundations of Social Order*, New York: Macmillan.

Rychtarik, R.G. (1986) 'Behavioral assessment of coping skills in spouses of alcoholics', presented at 94th Annual Meeting of the American Psychological Association, Washington, DC, cited in Levine (1988).

Salecl, R. (1993) 'Crime as a mode of subjectivization: Lacan and the law', *Law and Critique*, 4(1): 2–20.

Salyers, L. (1989) 'Captives of law: judicial enforcement of the Chinese exclusion law', *Journal of American History*, 76: 91–117.

Salyers, L. (1991) 'The constitutive nature of law in American history', *Legal Studies Forum*, 15(1): 61–4.

Samenow, S.E. (1984) *Inside the Criminal Mind*. New York: Times Books.

Sampson, R.J. (1987) 'Communities and crime', in M.R. Gottfredson and T. Hirschi, *Positive Criminology*. Newbury Park, CA: Sage Publications. pp. 91–114.

Sampson, R.J. and Wilson, W.J. (1993) 'Toward a theory of race, crime and urban inequality', in J. Hagan and R. Peterson (eds), *Crime and Inequality*. Stanford, CA: Stanford University Press.

Samuels, R. (1993) *Between Philosophy and Psychoanalysis*. New York: Routledge.

Santos, B.S. (1985) 'On modes of production of law and social power', *International Journal of the Sociology of Law*, 13: 299–336.

Santos, B.S. (1987) 'Law: a map of misreading. Toward a postmodern conception of law', *Journal of Law and Society*, 14: 279–302.

Saposnek, J.A. (1983) *Mediating Child Custody Disputes: A Systematic Guide for Family Therapists, Court Counselors, Attorneys, and Judges*. San Francisco: Jossey-Bass.

Sarup, M. (1989) *Post-Structuralism and Postmodernism*. Athens, GA: University of Georgia Press.

Sarup, M. (1992) *Jacques Lacan*. Toronto: University of Toronto Press.

Schafer, S. (1968) *The Victim and His Criminal: A Study in Functional Responsibility*. New York: Random House.

Schafer, S. (1976) *Introduction to Criminology*. Reston, VA: Reston Publishing.

Scharf, P. (1977) 'The just community', *New Society*, 21 April: 104–5.

Scharpf, F. W. (1989) 'Politische steuerung und politische institutionen', *Politische Vierteljahresschrift*, 30(1): 10–21.

Scheerer, S. (1986) 'Toward abolitionism', *Contemporary Crises*, 10(1): 5–20.

Schlapp, M.G. and Smith, E.H. (1928) *The New Criminology*. New York: Boni and Liveright.

Schmidt, P. and Witte, A.D. (1984) *An Economic Analysis of Crime and Justice: Theory, Methods, and Applications*. Orlando, FL: Academic Press.

Schrager, L. and Short, J. (1978) 'Toward a sociology of organizational crime', *Social Problems*, 25: 407–19.

Schur, E.M. (1971) *Labeling Deviant Behavior: Its Sociological Implications*. New York: Harper and Row.

Schur, E.M. (1973) *Radical Non-Intervention: Rethinking the Delinquency Problem*. Englewood Cliffs: Prentice-Hall.

Schur, E.M. (1980) *The Politics of Deviance: Stigma Contests and the Uses of Power*. Englewood Cliffs, NJ: Prentice-Hall.

Schutz, A. (1967) *The Phenomenology of the Social World* (1932). Evanston, IL: Northwestern University Press.

Schwartz, M.D. (1991) 'The future of criminology', in B. MacLean and D. Milovanovic (eds), *New Directions in Critical Criminology*. Vancouver: Collective Press. pp. 119–24.

Schwartz, M.D. and Friedrichs, D.O. (1994) 'Postmodern thought and criminological discontent: new metaphors for understanding violence', *Criminology*, 32(2): 221–46.

Schwartz, M.D. and Milovanovic, D. (eds) (1995) *The Intersections of Class, Gender and Race in Criminology*. New York: Garland.

Schwendinger, H. and Schwendinger, J. (1970) 'Defenders of order or guardians of human rights?', *Issues in Criminology*, 5: 123–57.

Schwendinger, H. and Schwendinger, J. (1985) *Adolescent Subcultures and Delinquency*. New York: Praeger.

Schwendinger, J. and Schwendinger, H. (1983) *Rape and Inequality*. Beverly Hills: Sage.

Scimecca, J.A. (1988) 'Conflict resolution: not just for children', *Peace in Action*, 1: 20–3.

Scimmeca, J.A. (1991) 'Conflict resolution and a critique of "alternative dispute resolution"', in H. Pepinsky and R. Quinney (eds), *Criminology as Peacemaking*. Bloomington, IN: Indiana University Press. pp. 263–79.

Scott, M. and Lyman, S. (1970) 'Accounts, deviance and the social order', in J. Douglas (ed.), *Deviance and Respectability*. New York: Basic Books. pp. 89–119.

Scraton, P. (1981) *Class, Marginality and State Control*. London: Macmillan.

Scraton, P. and South, N. (1984) 'The ideological construction of the hidden economy: private justice and work-related crime', *Contemporary Crisis*, 8: 1–18.

Sellers, S. (1991) *Language and Sexual Difference: Feminist Writings in France*. New York: St Martin's Press.

Sellin, T. (1938) *Culture Conflict and Crime*. New York: Social Science Research Council.

Selva, L. and Bohm, B. (1987) 'Law and liberation: toward an oppositional legal discourse', *Legal Studies Forum*, 113: 255–76.

Serres, M. (1982a) *Hermes: Literature, Science, Philosophy*. Baltimore: Johns Hopkins University Press.

Serres, M. (1982b) *The Parasite*. Baltimore: Johns Hopkins University Press.

Shah, S.A. and Roth, L.H. (1974) 'Biological and psychophysical factors in criminality', in D. Glaser, *Handbook of Criminology*. Chicago: Rand McNally. pp. 101–73.

Shaw, C.R. and McKay, H.D. (1931) *Social Factors in Juvenile Delinquency*. Report of the Causes of Crime. National Commission on Law Observance and Enforcement, Report no. 13. Washington, DC: US Government Printing Office.

Shaw, C.R. and McKay, H.D. (1942) *Juvenile Delinquency and Urban Areas: A Study of Delinquents in Relation to Differential Characteristics of Local Communities in American Cities*. Chicago: University of Chicago Press.

Sheldon, W.H., Hartl, E.M. and McDermott, E. (1949) *Varieties of Delinquent Youth*. New York: Harper and Brothers.

Sheldon, W.H., Stevens, S.S. and Tucker, W.B. (1940) *The Varieties of Human Physique*. New York: Harper and Row.

Shover, N. and Einstadter, W.J. (1988) *Analyzing American Corrections*. Belmont CA: Wadsworth.

Silverman, K. (1982) *The Subject of Semiotics*. New York: Oxford University Press.

Simmel, G. (1955). *The Sociology of Conflict*. Trans. K.H. Wolff and *The Web of Group Affiliations*. Trans. R. Bendix. Glencoe, IL. Free Press.

Simon, J. (1987) 'The emergence of a risk society: insurance, law and the state', *Socialist Review*, 95: 93–108.

Simon, J. (1988) 'The ideological effects of actuarial practices', *Law and Society Review*, 22: 771–800.

Simon, D.R. and Eitzen, D.S. (1982) *Elite Deviance*. Boston: Allyn and Bacon.

Simon, R. (1975) *Women and Crime*. Lexington, MA: D.C. Heath.

Simon, J. (1987) 'The emergence of a risk society: insurance, law, and the state', *Socialist Review*, 95: 93–108.

Simon, J. (1988) 'The ideological effects of actuarial practices', *Law and Society Review*, 22: 772.

Simpson, S.S. (1989) 'Feminist theory, crime, and justice', *Criminology*, 27(4): 605–31.

Sinanoglu, O. (1981) '1- and 2-topology of reaction networks', *Journal of Mathematical Physics*, 22(7): 1504–12.

Slump, G.J. and Emmen, M. (1993) 'Dading: a civil law alternative to the Dutch system', in B. MacLean and H. Pepinsky (eds), *We Who Would Take no Prisoners*. Vancouver, BC: Collective Press.

Smart, B. (1983) *Foucault, Marxism and Critique*. London: Routledge and Kegan Paul.

Smart, C. (1984) *The Ties that Bind: Law, Marriage and the Reproduction of Patriarchal Relations*. London: Routledge and Kegan Paul.

Smart, C. (1989) *Feminism and the Power of Law*. London: Routledge.

Smart, C. (1990) 'Feminist approaches to criminology, or postmodern woman meets atavistic man', in L. Gelsthorpe and A. Morris (eds), *Feminist Perspectives in Criminology*. Milton Keynes: Open University Press. pp. 70–84.

Smart, C. (1992) 'The women of legal discourse', *Social and Legal Studies: An International Journal*, 1: 29–44.

Smigel, E. and Ross, H.L. (eds) (1970), *Crimes Against Bureaucracy*. New York: Van Nostrand Reinhold.

Smith, C. and Comer, D. (1994) 'Self-organization in small groups: a study of group effectiveness within non-equilibrium conditions', *Human Relations*, 47(5): 553–81.

Smith, C. and Gemmill, G. (1991) 'Change in the small group: a dissipative structure perspective', *Human Relations*, 44(7): 697–716.

Smith, D. (1987) *The Everyday World as Problematic: A Feminist Sociology*. Toronto: University of Toronto Press.

Smith, D. (1992) 'Sociology from women's experience: a reaffirmation', *Sociological Theory*, 10(1): 60–87.

Smith, D. (1995) 'The inapplicability principle: what chaos means for social science', *Behavioral Science*, 40: 22–40.

Spelman, E. (1982) 'Theories of race and gender: the erasure of black women', *Quest*, 5: 26–32.

Spencer, H. (1858) 'Prospectus of a system of philosophy', in J. Rumney (ed.), *Herbert Spencer's Sociology: A Study in the History of Social Theory*. New York: Atherton.

Spitzer, S. (1975) 'Towards a marxian theory of deviance', *Social Problems*, 22: 638–51.

Spitzer, S. (1980) 'Left-wing criminology: an infantile disorder', in J. Inciardi (ed.), *Radical Criminology: The Coming Crisis*. Beverly Hills, CA: Sage. pp. 169–90.

Stark, R. (1987) 'Deviant places: a theory of the ecology of crime', *Criminology*, 25(4): 893–909.

Steffensmeier, D. (1989) 'On the causes of "white-collar" crime: an assessment of Hirschi and Gottfredson's claims', *Criminology*, 27: 345–58.

Steinert, H. (1986) 'Beyond crime and punishment', *Contemporary Crises*, 10(1): 21–38.

Stevens, B.A. (1991) 'Chaos: a challenge to refine systems theory', *Australian and New Zealand Journal of Family Therapy*, 12(1): 23–6.

Stewart, I. (1989) *Does God Play Dice?* New York: Blackwell.

Sudnow, D. (1965) 'Normal crimes: sociological features of the penal code in a public defender office', *Social Problems*, 12(3): 255–70.

Sullivan, R.F. (1973) 'The economics of crime: an introduction to the literature', *Crime and Delinquency*, 19(2): 138–49.

Sumner, C. (1983) 'Rethinking deviance', in S. Spitzer (ed.), *Research on Law, Deviance and Social Control*, vol. 5. Greenwich: JAI Press.

Sumner, C. (1990) 'Foucault, gender and the censure of deviance', in L. Gelsthorpe and A. Morris (eds), *Feminist Perspectives in Criminology*. Milton Keynes: Open University Press.

Surette, R. (ed.) (1984) *Justice and the Media*. Springfield, IL: Charles C. Thomas Publisher.

Surette, R. (ed.) (1992) *Media, Crime and Criminal Justice: Images and Realities*. Pacific Grove, CA: Brooks/Cole.

Susskind, L.E. and Cruikshank, J. (1987) *Breaking the Impasse: Consensual Approaches to Resolving Public Disputes*. New York: Basic Books.

Sutherland, E.H. (1939) *Principles of Criminology*. (1924) Philadelphia: J.B. Lippincott and Co.

Sutherland, E.H. (1940) 'White collar criminality', *American Sociological Review*, 5: 1–12.

Sutherland, E.H. (1941) 'Crime and business', *Annals of the American Academy of Political and Social Science*, 217 (September): 112–18.

Sutherland, E.H. (1945) 'Is white collar crime, crime?', *American Sociological Review*, 10: 132–9.

Sutherland, E.H. (1949) 'The white collar criminal', in V.C. Branham and S.B. Kutash (eds), *Encyclopedia of Criminology*. New York: Philosophical Library. pp. 511–15.

Sutherland, E.H. and Cressey D.R. (1966) *Principles of Criminology*. (1961) Philadelphia: J.B. Lippincott.

Suttles, G. (1968) *The Social Order and the Slum*. Chicago: University of Chicago Press.

Suttles, G. (1972) *The Social Construction of Communities*. Chicago: University of Chicago Press.

Swingewood, A. (1975) *Marx and Modern Social Theory*. London: Macmillan Press.

Sykes, G.M. and Matza, D. (1957) 'Techniques of neutralization: a theory of delinquency', *American Sociological Review*, 22: 664–70.

Tannenbaum, F. (1938) *Crime and the Community*. Boston: Ginn.

Tappan, P.W. (1947) 'Who is the criminal?', *American Sociological Review* 12: 96–102.

Tarde, G. (1890) *G. Tarde's Laws of Imitation*. Trans. E. Parsons. New York: Henry Holt, 1903.

Taylor, I., Walton, P. and Young, J. (1973) *The New Criminology: For a Social Theory of Deviance*. London: Routledge and Kegan Paul.

Telfer, M., Baker, D. and Clark, G.R. (1968) 'Incidence of gross chromosomal errors among tall criminal American males', *Science*, 159: 1249–50.

Teubner, G. (1988) *Autopoietic Law: A New Approach to Law and Society*. New York: Walter de Gruyter.

Teubner, G. (1989) 'How the law thinks: toward a constructivist epistemology of law', *Law and Society Review*, 23(5): 727–57.

Teubner, G. (1992) 'The two faces of Janus: rethinking legal pluralism', *Cardozo Law Review*, 13(5): 1443–62.

Teubner, G. (1993) *Law as an Autopoietic System*. Oxford: Blackwell.

Teubner, G. (1994) 'Company interest: the public interest of the enterprise "in itself"', in R. Rogowski and T. Wilthagen (eds), *Reflexive Labour Law*. Amsterdam: Kluwer.

Teubner, G., Farmer, L. and Murphy, D. (eds), (1994) *Environmental Law and Ecological Responsibility: The Concept and Practice of Ecological Self-Organization*. New York: Wiley.

Thoits, P. (1986) 'Social support as coping assistance', *Journal of Consulting and Clinical Psychology*, 54: 416–23.

Thom, R. (1975) *Structural Stability and Morphogenesis: An Outline of a General Theory of Models*. Reading, MA: W.A. Benjamin.

Thomas, J. (1988) *Prisoner Litigation: The Paradox of the Jailhouse Lawyer*. Totowa, NJ: Rowman and Littlefield.

Thomas, W.I. (1923) *The Unadjusted Girl*. Boston: Little, Brown.

Thompson, J. (1967) *Organizations in Action*. New York: McGraw-Hill.

Thrasher, F.M. (1927) *The Gang*. Chicago: University of Chicago Press.

Tifft, L.L. and Sullivan, D. (1980) *The Struggle to be Human: Crime, Criminology and Anarchism*. Sanday, Orkney, UK: Cienfuegos Press.

Toby, J. (1957) 'Social disorganization and stake in conformity: complementary factors in the predatory behavior of hoodlums', *Journal of Criminal Law, Criminology and Police Science*, 48: 12–17.

Tomasic, R. and Feeley, N.M. (eds) (1982) *Neighborhood Justice: Assessment of an Emerging Idea*. New York: Longman.

Tonry, M (1995) *Malign Neglect: Race, Crime and Punishment in America*. New York: Oxford University Press.

Trasler, G. (1962) *The Explanation of Criminality*. London: Routledge and Kegan Paul.

Turk, A.T. (1966) 'Conflict and criminality', *American Sociological Review*, 31: 338–52.

Turk, A.T. (1969) *Criminality and the Legal Order*. Chicago: Rand McNally.

Turk, A.T. (1976) 'Law as a weapon in social conflict', *Social Problems*, 23: 276–91.

Unger, R.M. (1976) *Law in Modern Society*. New York: Free Press.

Unger, R.M. (1987) *False Necessity*. New York: Cambridge University Press.

Ursel, J. (1986) 'The state and the maintenance of patriarchy: a case study of family, labour and welfare legislation in Canada', in J. Dickinson and B. Russell (eds), *Family Economy and State: The Social Reproduction Process under Capitalism*. Toronto: Garamond Press.

Uusitalo, J. (1991) 'Abduction, legal reasoning, and reflexive law', in R. Kevelons (ed.), *Peirce and Law*. New York: Peter Lang.

Vandivier, K. (1972) 'Why should my conscience bother me?', in *In the Name of Profit*. New York: Doubleday. pp. 11–33.

Vaughan, D. (1980) 'Crime between organizations: implications for victimology', in G. Geis and E. Stotland (eds), *White Collar Crime: Theory and Research*. Beverly Hills, CA: Sage.

Vaughan, D. (1983) *Controlling Unlawful Organizational Behavior: Social Structure and Corporate Misconduct*. Chicago: University of Chicago Press.

Vold, G.B. (1958) *Theoretical Criminology*, 2nd edn. with Thomas Bernard, London: Oxford University Press, 1979.

Vold, G.B. and Bernard, T.J. (1986) *Theoretical Criminology*. 3rd edn. New York: Oxford University Press.

Volosinov, V. (1986) *Marxism and the Philosophy of Language*. Cambridge, MA: Harvard University Press.

Volpe, M. (1991) 'Mediation in the criminal justice system: process, promises, problems', in H. Pepinsky and R. Quinney (eds), *Criminology as Peacemaking*. Bloomington, IN: Indiana University Press.

von Hentig, H. (1948) *The Criminal and His Victim*. New Haven, CT: Yale University Press.

Von Hirsch, A. and Jareborg, N. (1991) 'Gauging criminal harm: a living standard analysis', *Oxford Journal of Legal Studies*, II(1): 1–38.

Von Hirsch, A. (1976) *Doing Justice: The Choice of Punishments*. New York: Hill and Wang.

Walker, J.T. (1994) 'Human ecology and social disorganization revisit delinquency in Little Rock', in G. Barak (ed.), *Varieties of Criminology: Readings from a Dynamic Discipline*. Westport, CT: Praeger. pp. 47–78.

Walsh, D.P. (1983) 'Causes, causation', in D. Walsh and A. Poole (eds), *A Dictionary of Criminology*. London: Routledge and Kegan Paul. pp. 30–1.

Warming, E. (1909) *Oecology of Plants: An Introduction to the Study of Plant Communities*. Oxford: Oxford University Press.

Weber, M. (1954) *On Law, Economy and Society*. Ed. M. Rheinstein. New York: Simon and Schuster.

Weber, M. (1978) *Economy and Society*, vols. 1 and 2. Ed. G. Roth and C. Wittich. Los Angeles: University of California Press.

Wedge, B. (1970) 'Communication analysis and comprehensive diplomacy', *Social Education*, 1: 19–27.

Wedge, B. (1971) 'A psychiatric model for intercession in intergroup conflict', *Journal of Applied Behavioral Science*, 7: 733–61.

Weeks, J. (1985) *The Shape of Space*. New York: Marcel Dekker.

Wegner, T. and Tyler, B. (1993) *Fractal Creations*. Corte Madera, CA: Waite Group Press.

Weiler, K. (1994) 'Freire and a feminist pedagogy of difference', in P. McLaren and C. Lankshear (eds), *Politics of Liberation*. New York: Routledge. pp. 12–40.

Weinrib, E. (1989) 'Understanding tort law', *Valparaiso University Law Review*, 23(3): 485–526.

Weinstein, D. and Weinstein, A. (1993) 'Postmodernizing (macro)sociology', *Sociological Inquiry*, 63(2): 224–37.

Weisburd, D., Wheeler, S., Waring, E. and Bode, N. (1991) *Crimes of the Middle Classes*. New Haven, CT: Yale University Press.

Wheeler, S., Weisburd, D., Bode, N. and Waring, E. (1988) 'White-collar crimes and criminals', *American Criminal Law Review*, 25: 331–57.

White, M. (1983) 'Anorexia nervosa: a trans-generational perspective', *Family Process*, 22(3): 255–73.

White, M. (1986) 'Negative explanation, restraint, and double description: a template for family therapy', *Family Process*, 25: 169–84.

White, M. (1988) 'Assumptions and therapy', *Dulwich Centre Newsletter*, Autumn: 5–7.

White, M. (1989) 'The externalization of the problem and the re-authoring of lives and relationships', *Dulwich Centre Newsletter*, Summer: 3–30.

White, M. (1991) 'Deconstruction and therapy', *Dulwich Centre Newsletter*, Autumn: 21–40.

White, M. and Epston, D. (1989) *Literate Means to Therapeutic Ends*. Adelaide, Australia: Dulwich Centre Publications.

Whitehead, J.T. and Lab, S.P. (1989) 'A meta-analysis of juvenile correctional treatment', *Journal of Research in Crime and Delinquency*, 26: 276–95.

Whittmore, H. (1992) 'Hitting bottom can be the beginning', *Parade Magazine*, 15 March: 4–6.

Whorf, B. (1956) *Language, Thought, and Reality*. Ed. J. Carrol. New York: John Wiley.

Wilkins, L.T. (1964) *Social Policy, Action and Research*. London: Tavistock.

Wilkins, L.T. (1968) 'Offense patterns', *International Encyclopedia of the Social Sciences*, 3: 476–83.

Williams, J. (1991) 'Deconstructing gender', in K. Barlett and R. Kennedy (eds), *Feminist Legal Theory*. Boulder, CO: Westview Press.

Williamson, J. (1987) *Decoding Advertisement: Ideology and Meaning in Advertising*. New York: Marion Boyars.

Willis, P. (1977) *Learning to Labor*. Aldershot: Gower Press.

Wilson, J. and Herrnstein, R. (1985) *Crime and Human Nature*. New York: Simon and Schuster.

Wilson, W.J. (1987) *The Truly Disadvantaged: The Inner City, the Underclass and Public Policy*. Chicago: University of Chicago Press.

Wolfgang, M., Figlio, R. and Sellin, T. (1972) *Delinquency in a Birth Cohort*. Chicago: Chicago University Press.

Yngvesson, B. (1993) *Virtuous Citizens: Disruptive Subjects*. New York: Routledge.

Yochelson, S. and Samenow, S.E. (1976) *The Criminal Personality*. Vol. 1. New York: Jason Aronson.

Yochelson, S. and Samenow, S.E. (1977) *The Criminal Personality*. Vol.2. New York: Jason Aronson.

Young, A. (1990) *Femininity in Dissent*. London: Routledge.

Young, A. (1996) *Imagining Crime*. London: Sage.

Young, A. and Rush, P. (1994) 'The law of victimage in urban realism: thinking through inscription of violence', in D. Nelken (ed.), *The Futures of Criminology*. London: Sage. pp. 154–72.

Young, J. (1971) 'The role of police as amplifiers of deviancy, negotiators of reality and translators of fantasy', in S. Cohen (ed.), *Images of Deviance*. Harmondsworth: Penguin.

Young, J. (1979) 'Left idealism, reformism and beyond', in B. Fine, et al. (eds), *Capitalism and the Rule of Law*. London: Hutchinson. pp. 13–28.

Young, J. (1981) 'Thinking seriously about crime: some models of criminology', in M. Fitzgerald, G. McLennan, and J. Pawson (eds), *Crime and Society: Readings in History and Society*. London: Routledge and Kegan Paul. pp. 248–309.

Young, J. (1986) 'The failure of criminology: the need for a radical realism', in R. Matthews and J. Young (eds), *Confronting Crime*, London: Sage. pp. 4–30.

Young, J. (1987) 'The tasks facing a realist criminology', *Contemporary Crisis*, 11: 337–56.

Young, J. and Matthews, R. (eds) (1992) *Rethinking Criminology: The Realist Debate*. Newbury Park, CA: Sage.

Young, T.R. (1991a) 'Chaos and crime: nonlinear and fractal forms of crime', *Critical Criminologist*, 3(4): 3–4, 10–11, 13–14.

Young, T.R. (1991b) 'Change and chaos theory', *Social Science*, 28(3).

Young, T.R. (1992) 'Chaos theory and human agency: humanist sociology in a postmodern era', *Humanity and Society*, 16(4): 441–60.

Zavarzadeh, M. and D. Morton (1990) 'Signs of knowledge in the contemporary academy', *American Journal of Semiotics*, 7(4): 149–60.

Zeeman, D. (1976) 'Catastrophe theory', *Scientific America*, 234: 65–83.

Zeleny, M. (1980) *Autopoiesis, Dissipative Structures and Spontaneous Social Orders*. Boulder, CO: Westview Press.

Zimbardo, P.G. (1972) 'Pathology of imprisonment', *Society*, 9(April): 4–8.

Zizek, S. (1989) *The Sublime Object of Ideology*. New York: Verso.

Name Index

Subject Index